1926. Disturbances & Agitations

SUBJECT

Naval & Military guards for Vulnerable ...
" " aid – Requisitions for. Memo re procedure
Emergency Cable Companies. Mr Broome reports.
H.O. Warrants on Trade Union Congress & Overseas telegrams. Cancellation

...ount of Swiss Syndicalist Union for British Strikers. Copy desp. from H.M. Rep. Berne
... 13A & 27.
...sistance for H.M. Govt. during the strike. Copy telegram to H.M. Rep. Buenos Aires

THE GENERAL STRIKE, 1926

THE GENERAL STRIKE
1926

edited by

JEFFREY SKELLEY

1976
LAWRENCE AND WISHART
LONDON

SBN 0 85315 337 X (harback)
SBN 0 85315 338 8 (paperback)

Printed in Great Britain by
The Camelot Press Ltd., Southampton

CONTENTS

THE EDITOR AND AUTHORS

JEFFREY SKELLEY joined Lawrence & Wishart Ltd. in 1973 and was appointed managing director in 1975. Joining the Communist Party in 1939, he was in the Army throughout the war and after demobilisation worked in engineering and at the BBC. From 1948–73 he was a full-time worker for the Communist Party in the London District, where he had a great diversity of political experience—including Stepney organiser and, later, organiser of the part of East London which includes the Docks, Ship Repair and the boroughs of Poplar and Newham. Here he was active with a group that produced *The Lansbury Story* at the Poplar Civic Theatre, and various pamphlets on Labour history, including the Gasworkers Union at Beckton, Bethnal Green's Joe Vaughan and on Lansbury himself. For some time he was in charge of Marxist education in the London District, and in that capacity helped to launch the first Communist University of London, in 1969.

JOHN FOSTER is a lecturer in the Politics Department at Strathclyde University. He is also in charge of Marxist education in Scotland for the Scottish Committee of the Communist Party, and is editor of *Our History*, the journal of the Party's History Group. Born in 1940, he was educated at Guildford Grammar School and St. Catharine's College, Cambridge, where he studied history. He was awarded a Ph.D. for a thesis on working-class consciousness in the early nineteenth century, and subsequently published *Class Struggle and the Industrial Revolution: early industrial capitalism in three English towns*, as well as articles on class consciousness and the national question. He was a Research Fellow at St. Catharine's College in 1965–8.

JAMES KLUGMANN, chairman of the Board of Directors of Lawrence & Wishart Ltd., is editor of the Communist Party's theoretical journal *Marxism Today*, author of two volumes of the *History of the Communist Party of Great Britain*, and editor of two books on "Christian-Marxist Dialogue". He was educated at Gresham School,

Holt, studied modern languages at Trinity College, Cambridge, with a period of research from 1931–5, and joined the Communist Party in 1933. From 1935–9 he was Secretary of the World Student Association for Peace and Freedom, travelling extensively in Eastern Europe, the Arab countries, India and China. Called up as a private in 1940, he finished the war as a major attached to the British Military Mission to the Yugoslav Partisans, and then in 1945–6 Personal Assistant to the Chief of the UNNRA Yugoslav Mission. From 1947 he has worked full-time for the Communist Party—as editor of *World News and Views*, 1947–50, head of the Education Department, 1950–61, and member of the Executive Committee and the Political Committee, 1952–62.

PAUL CARTER works as a geologist with a firm of consulting engineers. He is a member of the Scottish Labour History Society and is Political Education Officer for the West Stirlingshire Constituency of the Labour Party. Co-author of "The Miners of Kilsyth in the 1926 General Strike and Lockout" (*Our History*, No. 58), he has contributed several articles on industrial history to the local press and to the *Morning Star*. He is thirty-two years of age and lives near Kilsyth in the new region of Strathclyde in Scotland.

IAN MACDOUGALL has been honorary secretary of the Scottish Labour History Society since it was formed in 1961. He left school at fifteen to become a newspaper reporter, and joined the Labour Party at seventeen. After National Service he gave up journalism and studied History at Edinburgh University. He became a teacher, at present employed at Newbattle Abbey Adult College near Edinburgh. From 1967–9 he was a Research Fellow at Strathclyde University, engaged on research into the records of working-class movements in Scotland, a catalogue of which he is preparing. He edited the *Minutes of Edinburgh Trades Council, 1859–1873*, published in 1969 by the Scottish Labour History Society.

EDMUND FROW is a retired toolmaker and Secretary of the Manchester District of the Amalgamated Union of Engineering Workers. He is Treasurer of the Society for the Study of Labour History and an active local historian in Manchester. RUTH FROW is Deputy Head Teacher at a Manchester comprehensive school.

PETER WYNCOLL, who was born and brought up in Nottingham, is now living at Coalville in the Leicestershire coalfield and for the past six years has been a full-time trade union official for the National Union of Public Employees. He left Secondary Modern school at fifteen and, after completing National Service, worked as a shop assistant before winning a scholarship at Ruskin College when twenty-five years of age. He was subsequently awarded a Mature State Scholarship to take a degree course at the University of Hull.

GEORGE BARNSBY is a teacher of economics at Dudley Technical College. He was born in London in 1919, his father a railway porter, who died in 1922 as a result of being gassed in the 1914–18 war—leaving a widow to bring up two children on a war pension. George Barnsby left school at fifteen, having failed in the 11-plus examination. After six years' war service he spent his Army gratuity taking university entrance examinations and then took a first-class degree at the London School of Economics. After ten years' teaching at primary and secondary schools he gave up his job to write on the history of the working-class movement in the Black Country, 1815–67, for an M.A. degree, and later gained a Ph.D. for work on social conditions in the Black Country in the nineteenth century.

PAUL HASTINGS is Principal Lecturer in History at Middleton St. George College of Education, County Durham, and is currently researching into poverty and the Poor Laws in the North Riding of Yorkshire. He was born in Birmingham in 1933 and read History at Birmingham University where he later gained an M.A. degree for research into the Birmingham Labour Movement between the wars. From 1956–66 he taught history at two Birmingham comprehensive schools and was then appointed Lecturer in History at Hereford College of Education. He has also worked extensively in Adult Education with various University Extramural Departments and the WEA, and is the author of four books and a number of articles. His essay in the present volume is an extended version of his article "The General Strike in Birmingham, 1926" in *Midland History*, Vol. II, No. 4, 1974, and is published here by kind permission of Phillimore & Co., Chichester.

HYWEL FRANCIS is staff tutor in History at the Department of Extramural Studies, University College, Swansea, where he is also responsible for the development of the South Wales Miners' Library as a centre for research and trade union and adult education. The son of Dai Francis, until 1975 President of the South Wales Area of the National Union of Mineworkers, he was born in the mining village of Onllwyn in the Dulais Valley. He graduated in History at University College, Swansea, in 1968, and was then a research worker for the TUC before returning to South Wales in 1972 to become a senior research officer on the Coalfield History Project. He is at present completing a Ph.D. thesis on "Welsh Politics and the Spanish Civil War" and is writing a book with David Smith entitled *The South Wales Miners—from Defeat to Vindication.*

JOHN ATTFIELD has been secretary of the Communist Party's History Group since 1973, and is currently employed as a research worker in the field of industrial marketing. Born in 1949, he has lived in Lewisham all his life. He studied economic history at the London School of Economics from 1967–73, finishing with a M.Sc. (Econ.) degree. JOHN LEE is a history student at Birkbeck College, University of London, where he serves on the Student Union Council and the Library Committee.

ANGELA TUCKET, who now lives in Swindon, was from 1948–62 Manager and Assistant Editor of *The Labour Monthly*. Born in the West Country, she earned the distinction of being the first woman solicitor in Bristol, specialising in maintaining rights of way. Joining the Communist Party in 1931, she was actively engaged through the 'thirties in the unemployed, anti-war and anti-fascist movements, and is at present equally active in Swindon. She was formerly a delegate to the London and Holborn Trades Councils, and full-time legal adviser to the National Council of Civil Liberties. From 1942 to 1948 she worked with the *Daily Worker*. Her publications include *Civil Liberties and the Industrial Worker*, and official histories of the Scottish Commercial Motormen's Union, the Blacksmiths' Union and the Swindon Trades Council.

PETER KERRIGAN was at the time of the General Strike Vice-chairman of the Glasgow Trades and Labour Council and was Chairman of the Glasgow Central Strike Committee. Born in the Gorbals in 1899, he served his apprenticeship as a turner, joined the Communist Party in 1921, and was a member of its Executive Committee from 1927–9 and from 1931 to his retirement in 1965. He was leader of the two Hunger

Marches of the unemployed from Glasgow to London in 1934 and 1936, served as a Political Commissar in the Spanish War, and has been successively Scottish Secretary, National Organiser and Industrial Organiser of the Communist Party. A lifelong member of the Amalgamated Engineering Union, he served in Glasgow as shop steward, shop stewards' convenor and chairman of shop stewards' committee, and was awarded by the Union the Award of Merit and the Special Award of Merit for forty years' service. He has been a union delegate to the Scottish TUC, the Scottish Labour Party Conference and, in 1927, the National Labour Party Conference. A sportsman in earlier years, he was Scottish welterweight champion in 1919, and was awarded the Scottish Cup-winners' Medal in 1924.

BOB DAVIES was born in St. Helens in 1901. A foundation member of the Communist Party, he left Council school at fourteen and started work as a blacksmith's striker at Pilkington's Glass Works. He was elected a shop steward at the age of seventeen. A member of the Smiths' and Strikers' Union, which in 1920 became part of the Amalgamated Engineering Union, he served on the union District Committee for five years and subsequently as full-time organiser for the Communist Party in the Lancashire coalfield.

BILL CARR was born in 1908 and, starting at the age of fourteen, was for 42 years a coal miner. He has held many positions in the National Union of Mineworkers, including six years on the Yorkshire NUM Executive. He joined the Communist Party in 1946, and in 1946–7 studied at Ruskin College. He was for 14 years a member of the Yorkshire District Committee of the Communist Party, and was a Communist Councillor on the Thorne Rural District Council from 1958–74.

D. A. WILSON, a native of Bradford, was secretary of the Bradford Branch of the Railway Clerks' Association at the time of the General Strike, and a member of the National Minority Movement.

JULIUS ("JULIE") JACOBS, born in Hackney in 1906, was secretary of the London Trades Council from 1945 to its de-registration by the TUC in 1952. As a boy he attended the Hackney Socialist Sunday School, and later he became a member of the Young Socialist League and transferred to the Young Communist League on its formation. He joined the Shop Assistants' Union in 1922 and the National Amalgamated Furnishing Trades Association in 1928, serving as shop steward in various factories. Active in the unemployed movement in the 'thirties, he was organising secretary of the Hackney Branch of the National Unemployed Workers' Movement and leader of the Kent contingent of the 1932 Hunger March. He became National Secretary of the National Association of Tenants and Residents and then took up full-time work in the Industrial Department of the Communist Party.

HARRY WATSON was a senior apprentice lighterman in 1926, and a member of the Lightermen's Union. After working all his life in the London Docks he retired in 1972 and was awarded the Union's Gold Badge for outstanding service. He joined the Communist Party in 1941, and in 1959 was elected President of the Union—holding this position until 1971 when the Lightermen amalgamated with the Docks and Waterways Section of the Transport and General Workers' Union.

MARTIN JACQUES is lecturer in Economic and Social History at Bristol University, and author of articles on "The Intellectuals", "Youth Culture", "The Universities and Capitalism", and the contemporary political situation. He is currently working on a study of TUC policy, 1926–35. Born in Coventry, and now twenty-nine years of age, he was an undergraduate at Manchester University and a research scholar at Cambridge, and is currently a member of the Executive Committee of the Communist Party.

FOREWORD

This book is published as a contribution towards the better understanding of the General Strike of 1926, at the time of its fiftieth anniversary. Fifty years after, what has seemed most important to its authors is, first, to undertake some rethinking on the background, causes and consequences of the General Strike and, second, to gather together fruits of research in the localities into its day-to-day conduct.

The General Strike is now, indeed, "history". But its lessons remain alive enough today. Then, the demand was made that all workers' wages must come down. Now, and this time to curb inflation, it is that at least their real earnings must. In this book it is attempted to look once more at the economic policies which led to a confrontation of government and trade unions, and at the social bases and consequences of divisions within the Labour movement itself.

Neither government nor "official" Labour, the one in its preparations, the other in its lack of preparations, anticipated the scope and intensity of mass response which the strike call evoked. The turmoil throughout the length and breadth of the land and the actions and initiatives of the unnamed masses of workers make up the most essential part of the historical record. The whole power of the State, with battleships threatening the ports and tanks in action at the docks, could not quell them—only the betrayal by its official leaders could break the strike.

We have also sought to arrive at some assessment of the role of the Communist Party of Great Britain in the General Strike. The fact is that at that time its few thousand members played a part and exerted an influence altogether out of proportion to their numbers. Wherever the Councils of Action were most effective, wherever the local strike was most solid, there a knot of Communist Party members was usually to be found in the thick of it. The Communist Party was then, as it has since proved to be, a political party with considerable influence among the industrial workers. But on this aspect most of the many books on the General Strike have been markedly reticent.

The book is divided into four parts. The first begins with a study of the background of the Strike in the post-war crisis of British capitalism, the policies of the bankers and financiers who dominated the Baldwin Government, and the changing composition and organisation of the working class. This is followed by an examination in detail of how, in the year preceding the Strike and in the Strike itself, the opposition of militancy against reformism developed in the ranks of Labour—an opposition of which the best organised and most articulate expression was found in the policies of the Communist Party.

The second part contains a number of regional studies (arranged in order from North to South); and the third, personal reminiscences of the Strike from several regions. The fourth and concluding part deals with the aftermath of the Strike, its consequences in the organisation and policies of the trade union and Labour movement, including the adoption of "Mondism" as official policy. Thus the book begins and ends with general analysis of the economic and political causes and consequences of the General Strike, while the central part shows what the masses of workers were doing and how they organised to do it—and what it felt like to be involved in such a struggle.

Brief details of the contributors have been recorded following the list of Contents. And a chronological table of the events of the Nine Days and of the immediately preceding and following periods is given at the end.

JEFFREY SKELLEY
London, 1976

PART ONE

HISTORICAL BACKGROUND

BRITISH IMPERIALISM AND THE LABOUR ARISTOCRACY

by JOHN FOSTER

The general strike of 1926 lasted only nine days and directly involved less than two million workers. It was called by a reluctant, apprehensive TUC to defend the living standards of one single section of the trade union movement, the miners. And it failed to do so. Yet despite this and despite the other setbacks that followed, it is one of those few episodes in British history that have refused to lie buried in the history books. First of all, perhaps, because its lessons still remain—fifty years later—of irreplaceable importance for the working-class movement. At no time since has the capitalist nature of the British State been so thoroughly exposed. For a few days in 1926 working people saw every organ of local and central government, the police and army, radio and press, scabs, employers and fascists united as one instrument against the labour movement. And because *this* was exposed, so equally was the character of those labour leaders who chose to work within the limits of the constitution and so became its captives. Such moments of truth are rare in British history. Rarer still, however, was the feeling of power and self-confidence which the strike gave working people. Locally, on hundreds of strike committees up and down the country, trade unionists became the temporary masters of towns and villages. While this experience directly involved only a small minority, for them the memory was indelible, totally transforming their political perspectives and in the subsequent struggles giving the conviction of real life to the idea of working-class power.

In addition, however, the strike was also—like war—history in which everyone took part, a time when individual lives interlocked with a larger struggle which was seen to have been of determining importance on an international scale. For apart from what it taught (and still has to teach), the general strike of 1926 also *made* history. Like the capitalist wars of intervention against the young Soviet Union or the 1923 uprising in Silesia, it represented one of those crucial tests by which the balance of class forces in the inter-war years was established. In what was still the biggest imperial power a final attempt was being made to turn the clock back, to re-establish the pre-1914 conditions of capitalist stability, and whatever the short-term victories, this was not achieved. The trade union movement was weakened but not destroyed. Wages were not driven down. The memory of mass class solidarity remained.

As history, therefore, the general strike was a key moment in the development of British imperialism, and as such poses crucial questions about the nature and social base of British imperialism. Indeed, the strike's very character and timing pose questions: Why 1926—five years *after* the apparent peak of the post-war working-class offensive? Why was it the government itself that invited confrontation—exposing in so uncharacteristic a way the class nature of its rule? More fundamentally there is the whole problem of working-class consciousness in Britain: of how the British people remained for so long acquiescent accomplices in their rulers' imperialism.

For the years before 1914 Engels, and later Lenin, attributed this to a 'labour aristocracy'—to the use of imperial profits to bribe trade union leaders and an upper stratum of the workforce. There is good evidence to support this—particularly in view of the subsequent growth of a new working class militancy when this easy bribery ended during the war years and after. But how, then, is one to explain the movement's ultimate containment and the reassertion of establishment control in the course of the 1920s? Was a labour aristocracy revived in some modified form—or were altogether new types of social control introduced? How in particular does one account for the strange contrast between the unprecedented explosion of creative, innovating class solidarity generated by the general strike and the apparently unresisting acceptance of right-wing leadership in the years that followed? Was this just another example of the 'British phenomenon' of militancy without socialist consciousness? Or was it something more than this, a real contradiction revealing the social fragility of post-war capitalism, no longer basing its control of the situation on real social divisions within the working population, on their lack of cohesion and organisation, but now entirely on an ability—by no means guaranteed—to manipulate and control key parts of labour's newly extended class organisations?

These are some of the questions posed by the general strike. The job of this essay is to set both them and the strike itself in a wider historical context. It will start by looking at the characteristics of British imperialism and the problems it faced in the 1920s, then examine the special role of the labour aristocracy in Britain and finally outline the government's strategies for renewed control that culminated in 1926.

1. IMPERIALISTS AND BANKERS

In 1914 Britain was the imperial state par excellence. The figures are still staggering. A colonial population of 400 million—seven times that of its nearest rival, France. Overseas investment of £4,000 million—almost half the world's total. A volume of capital export that by 1914 exceeded current home investment and at times neared 10 per cent of total national income.

But while Britain's empire was big, it was also old-fashioned and vulnerable—a tempting prize in the conditions of 1914 for allies and enemies alike. And if we are to understand the crisis brought on by the first world war, we must start with those characteristics that made it so different from most other imperial powers, so exceptional in terms of the overall development of modern imperialism.

Generally speaking, modern imperialism develops out of monopoly. A few firms become big enough to dominate markets and control prices. They secure superprofits at the expense of non-monopoly producers and non-monopoly sectors. They therefore need outlets where these superprofits can be invested at an equally high rate but without diluting the home monopoly situation. Hence the drive for overseas investment. Generally, too, this process involves the industrial monopolies in close relationship with the big banks, producing what is called 'finance capital', and finance capital in turn seeks closer association with the state in order to maintain the *political* conditions for monopoly. Increasingly, therefore, the state becomes subordinated to the interests of just one section of the capitalist class, monopoly capital. Capitalism pure and simple becomes state monopoly capitalism—committed by its very nature to maintain the maximum profit conditions for 'its own' capital overseas against that of other states. Such at any rate is the general pattern, and by 1914 it could already be seen emerging in Germany, America and Japan.

Britain's development was quite different. It exported more capital than anybody else—but had very few monopolies. It annexed more territory—but over half its investment was outside the empire. Its big banks were closely involved with the state machine and capital export—but had no close links with industry.

To get at the reasons why, one has to go back to Britain's special position as the first capitalist state and the head start which this gave it over its competitors. As a result the country was able to dominate world trade throughout the earlier nineteenth century—making sterling the strongest world currency, 'as safe as the Bank of England', and enabling the City of London to attract deposits at the lowest rates. From the beginning, therefore (and long before the growth of monopoly), Britain possessed a strong and increasingly influential banking sector—not just because so much of world trade passed through Britain (up to 40 per cent in the mid-nineteenth century) but also because British bankers quickly saw the relationship between what they lent overseas and the foreign demand for British goods (and thus the amount of money to be made off bill broking and short-term trading credit which always remained the banks' bread and butter). However, it was only in the middle and later years of the nineteenth century that the banking sector became really predominant and this coincided with a transformation in the character and volume of capital export.

It is not easy to say what exactly caused this. In certain industries (textiles, farming after the lifting of the corn laws) foreign competition was at last making itself felt and persuading the generally small employers to reinvest their profits elsewhere. In industries where Britain still held its lead (railway construction, civil engineering, shipbuilding) continued expansion came to depend more and more on the pace of industrialisation outside Britain in continental Europe and America. And in all industries the intense class struggles of the 1840s had forced concessions (including higher wage differentials for the labour aristocracy) that made it far more difficult to maintain the old profit rates. But whatever the reasons, the results are not in doubt. By the end of the century the scale of capital export had already set in motion an accelerating process of economic degeneration. As successive industries lost their competitive edge, so the scale of disinvestment increased. As home investment declined (particularly in basic industries like steel), so the profit rate fell for the economy as a whole. Yet as the economy became less competitive in overseas markets it also became more dependent on them to finance the rising tide of capital export. By the 1900s a third of all goods produced were going into the export market—and increasingly these came from low technology industries (like the textiles going to India or China) or were simply raw materials (particularly coal).

Naturally, to the bankers these long-term consequences were not particularly worrying. Much of the money involved was itself derived from existing foreign investment and London's position as a centre of world trade and fiance still seemed absolutely unshakeable. For, of course, the cash pay-off was immense. The profits to be made abroad were higher than at home and the profits accruing to the banks that controlled and manipulated the investment higher still. Moreover, the banks were by now also politically dominant. It may be too much to speak of a firm interpenetration of the banks and the state, but clearly the process of linkage had begun. Already there was a degree of overlap between the Treasury and the Bank of England—whose governing committee was elected by the tightly organised inner ring of merchant banks. The growing cabinet committee system and the new professional élite of administrative civil servants (developed after 1870 under Treasury surveillance) provided ready channels for City influence which by-passed parliament and buttressed the growing power of the cabinet. Quite how dominant the banks were is difficult to tell. But certainly on the question of protective tariffs they were victorious despite very strong industrial opposition. From the bankers' standpoint such tariffs posed a dangerous threat to London's international position as a trading and finance centre, to the free movement of goods and investment. For the manufacturers the lack of such tariffs did much to prevent the development of monopoly conditions.

So, in brief, Britain's pre-1914 imperialism was of a rather special type, not really 'modern imperialism' at all. Unlike Germany or America there was little or no interpenetration between the banks and the comparatively small group of monopolies. Most of the capital came from the rentier petty bourgeoisie, from the *weakest*, least competitive sectors of industry. The very scale of Britain's original industrial dominance had produced its own gravedigger: a banking sector which siphoned away funds for reinvestment, distorted the pattern of industrial demand and by its opposition to tariffs created conditions which meant that only industries with the highest degree of concentration could make monopoly profits. The whole economy was held in a state of suspended animation, unable to move forward to the higher monopoly stage, and increasingly out of place in a world now dominated by the 'modern imperialism' of rival powers.[1]

These, then were the features of British imperialism on the eve of the first world war—features which did much to determine its response to the crisis that resulted.

On the surface, Britain bore the economic burdens of war surprisingly well. Strict government control of industrial capacity plus the repatriation of overseas dividends made it possible to plug almost all the gaps in the balance of trade. The one big drain was the loans that became necessary to keep Britain's allies in the war (£1,700 million in all), which had to be raised by borrowing £1,400 million abroad—the great bulk from America—and selling off £250 million of the country's £4,000 overseas holdings. None the less at the end of the war the pound remained relatively strong against other currencies and the bulk of overseas assets were still intact.[2]

Structually, however, fundamental economic changes had taken place. First of all, the war had created conditions for a rapid (but precariously based and artificial) monopolisation. Foreign imports were restricted. The government became the major buyer in many industries and set up its own regulating boards usually manned by businessmen from the biggest firms. Competition virtually ceased, and profits accumulated rapidly. Secondly, there were the inflationary effects of war finance. Throughout the war the government preferred borrowing to taxing (to the tune of £7,000 to £2,500 million) and its favourite method of short-term borrowing had the effect of fictitiously expanding the cash reserves of the Joint Stock Banks and thus their ability to lend still more to the government. Combined with the spread of monopoly practices in industry, the result was a massive rate of inflation that successfully passed on much of the cost of the war to the less well-organised sections of the working class—particularly (and ironically) the families or widows of soldiers. By the end of the war the pound had fallen to one half its 1914 value. Finally, there were big changes in the relative international position of British capitalism. Two powers, America and Japan, had rapidly increased their industrial capacity so that by 1919 the USA was producing two-thirds of the world's steel. Germany also had emerged with its enlarged industrial base still intact. In the colonial world, too, Britain's position had weakened. Before the war India and China had bought the great bulk of British textiles (to the total value of almost one-fifth of all exports). Now, having profited by the disappearance of British products, they had set up their own competing industries. Even in Europe economic collapse or socialist revolution had removed a number of traditional British markets. Moreover, as a final blow, the embargo on gold transfers imposed in

1914 had effectively taken the pound off the gold standard and New York was now rapidly replacing London as the international banking centre.

It was, it hardly needs adding, this last development that was the most distressing—and not only to the bankers. Just because the structure of British industry had previously been so strongly geared to particular export markets and these in turn had been so dependent on credit supplied through London, sizeable sections of industry also saw any disruption of London's financial role as an immediate threat. This was especially so now that they had to compete on still more unfavourable terms with foreign industry.

It is not surprising, therefore, that the question of the gold standard—and the restoration of the international role of the City of London—dominated the post-war period. However, and this is a vital point, it was no longer an automatic dominance. There were now powerful forces willing to pose an alternative strategy for British imperialism: that its world banking role should be abandoned and instead there should be a rapid development of modern (monopoly) imperialism inside the protective limits of Britain's still vast formal empire. As yet historians have hardly begun to identify the economic base of these forces (or even how far the alternative strategies had different bases at all). The sheer rapidity of change in the immediate post-war years—inflation and then deflation, monopolisation followed by its partial breakdown—make it very difficult to isolate continuing alignments. However, there can be no doubt that intense struggles were going on, struggles which underline the seriousness of the crisis for the ruling class, and which in detail do much to illuminate the interior contradictions that led up to the general strike.

Take, for instance, the speculative boom of 1919–20. Had the City of London been in exactly the same relationship to industry and the government as it was before 1914 this boom could never have occurred. Starting a few months after the war there was a positive orgy of banking credit creation—involving both government and industry—that drove prices up to three times their 1914 level by April 1920. It was this post-war burst of inflation that finally pushed sterling out of line with the dollar (the exchange rate fell from 4·76 in March 1919 to 3·50 in autumn 1920) and so made impossible any return to the gold standard at the 1914 level without a massive attack on domestic wage rates. Why, therefore, was it allowed to happen—particularly, when the Cunliffe committee on post-war financial policy (representing both the Treasury and the Bank of England) had strongly recommended a speedy return to gold?

We know that the Cabinet itself was split. Austen Chamberlain, on behalf of the Treasury, urged restraint while Lloyd George, Milner and Bonar Law were quite content to let the inflationary boom ride. The main arguments put forward for not deflating were political. Cheap finance was needed for reconstruction—'our insurance against Bolshevism'—and there was concern about what might happen if demobilised servicemen could not find jobs. Quite probably these reasons were genuine (and underline the vigour of the post-war working class challenge which will be examined later). But at least in the case of Milner and Bonar Law one suspects that their opposition to deflation was also linked to their advocacy of an alternative empire-based economic policy.

More fundamentally, there would seem to have been a temporary breakdown of the authority of the Bank of England over the banks as a whole. With the rapid wartime development of monopoly conditions in industry (and a financial policy that penalised non-productive investment) the banking sector seems for the first time to have become seriously interested in domestic industrial investment. Conversely the high-profit areas of industry urgently wanted investment outlets of their own. Very quickly, therefore, conditions matured for the merger of monopoly and banking capital. The era of finance capital had finally arrived. The classic example would be the transformation of the immensely profitable explosives firm Nobel Industries (the future ICI) into a conglomerate holding company with at least some City links and investments in a dozen different industries, notably motors. But as well as being sudden, these conditions were in most cases also *temporary*. For large parts of industry, as a number of bankers were wise enough to see, monopoly was unlikely to survive the outbreak of peace. Import controls and tariffs would be relaxed, while the structures of most industries remained too fragmented to permit easy rationalisation. Consequently the post-war boom represented a final opportunity for these investors to pull out while the going was good—floating of companies on the stock exchange or at least watering the capital. In these very fluid conditions it seems that at least certain banks were more concerned with the immediate job of getting in and out of the market at the right moment than any long-term strategic vision of restoring Britain's world role.[3]

Eventually, of course, the Bank of England did regain control. The boom itself started to run out of steam. The Bank was able to use its links with the Treaury to restrict money supply and so compel the government to raise the Bank rate. By April 1920 it had reached 7 per cent and coincided with savage cuts in government expenditure. By December 1920 unemployment had risen to over a million. In this situation the combined results of overcapitalisation and the collapse of pricing arrangements forced many firms into financial difficulties and the Bank of England was finally able to use its control of credit to discipline errant banks. This done, the banking establishment could once again set its sights on the return to gold.

But, though shortlived, the episode is also very instructive. It demonstrates the degree of questioning within the banking community itself: a feeling that the future might well lie more with monopoly production than international banking pure and simple. Already the penal costs of maintaining sterling were becoming apparent. Exports were in trouble and the earning power of overseas investments not enough to make up the difference. Moreover, although the American central bankers were encouraging a return to gold (and ready to provide the vitally necessary bridging loans), it was quite plain these offers were made on American terms. There were demands for a sterling-dollar exchange rate so high that London would remain permanently dependent on New York for support. What is more, the very fact that Britain kept its commitment to free trade—did not adopt the alternative strategy of building up empire tariff walls on the French model—would mean that the world's biggest market would remain an easy target for American competition. So merely on a theoretical level there were grounds for caution (and it is perhaps significant that the main proponents of the gold standard were found in the central banking institutions developed during the period of Britain's banking hegemony). But in addition, real changes had occurred inside the economy. At least certain finance capital groupings had consolidated themselves. In alliance with the now much larger section of industry demanding protection they could pose a serious threat to old-style banking dominance.

It is not surprising, therefore, that the gold standard strategists moved slowly and carefully, where possible buying off potential opponents. The transition to gold was to be *slow*, a matter of years. Wartime tariffs were to be maintained for certain industries not vital for export earnings (particularly those producing highly profitable domestic luxury goods like motors and electricals, where banking capital was still invested heavily). There was to be Bank of England help in organising cartels to keep empire minerals in British hands. In 1923 Baldwin himself, the politician who seems to have been most closely committed to the gold standard, found it necessary to make still further moves towards protection to stop Lloyd George grabbing the issue and using it to win away the Tory base in industry.[4]

But if all this shows the banking sector's weakness compared with pre-war, the fact remains that it kept its state power dominance. It was the gold standard strategy that was eventually (and at great cost) adopted. To understand why, one has to take into account the still weaker state of industry. Traditional leading sectors like steel, shipping and shipbuilding—the corner stones of finance capital complexes abroad—were in a state of advanced disintegration. Textiles and the exporting areas of the coal industry were even worse hit. Repeatedly in the years that followed the Bank of England had to come to the rescue in a way that would have been unthinkable before the war. Acting as a virtual government agency it supplied a mixture of short-term credit and eventual compulsory cartellisation to restore viability. Indeed, it is probably precisely this fact—that many of the key institutions of state monopoly capitalism were forged during two decades of *industrial* depression—which accounts for the special and dominating position which banking capital enjoyed for so long in Britain.

That, then, seems to have been the state power background to the return to gold. It is unnecessary to go into the actual stages by which it was eventually achieved: the savage assault on wages in 1921–2, the debt settlement in 1923, the final negotiations with the American bankers (which seem to have ensured that the return took place at the quite unrealistic rate of 4·86 dollars to the pound).[5] The crucial point is the effect it had on industry.

Added to the existing difficulties, it meant that two virtually distinct economies came into being. On the one side there were the industries mainly concerned with the home market: services trades and manufacturing protected by tariffs. Here real wages *rose* between 1920 and 1926 and unemployment was, if anything, lower than before the war. On the other hand, the reverse was true for the industries working for export markets and which had to maintain the gold backing for sterling. These experienced a serious fall in real wages and much higher unemployment ([footnotes 6–8] Figures 1 to 3). So where before the war it had been the docks, gasworks and transport that had been at the bottom of the pile, the situation was now reversed and heavy industry,

Figure 1 Real wages 1924: percent increase or decrease on 1914[6]

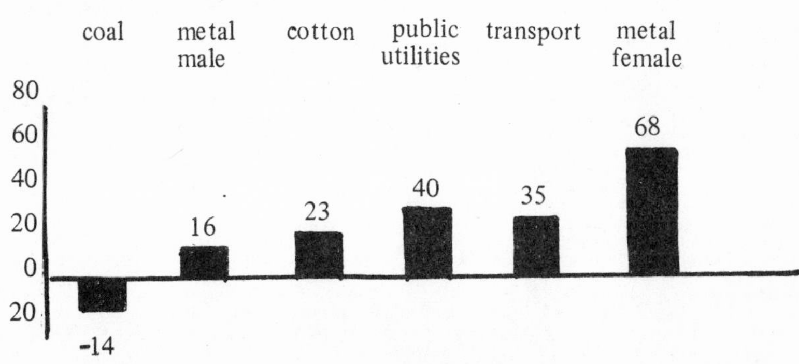

Figure 2 Real wages 1924: percent increase or decrease on 1920[7]

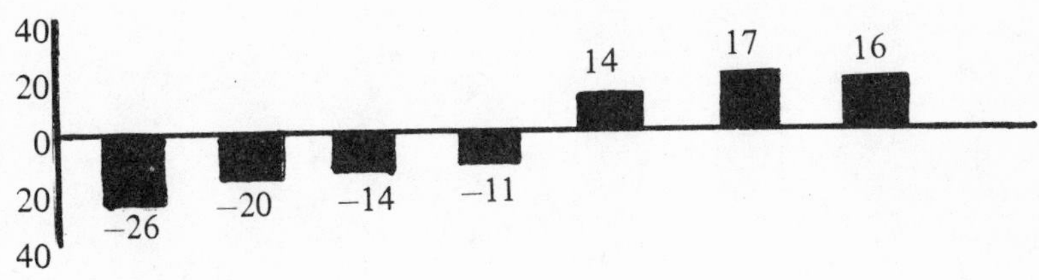

Figure 3 Unemployment 1926: percent of insured workers unemployed[8]

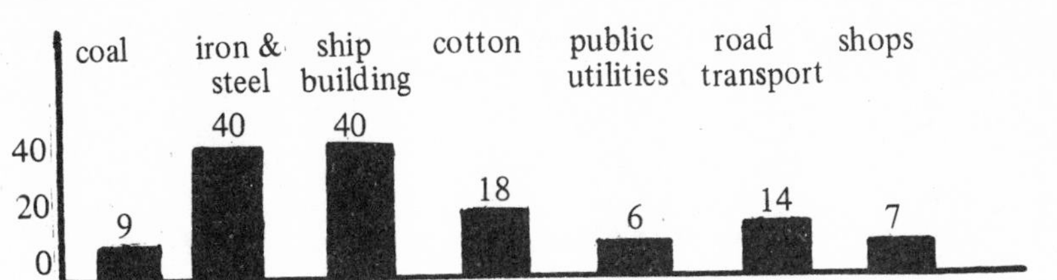

Figure 4 Coal & Metal Workers 1931[9]

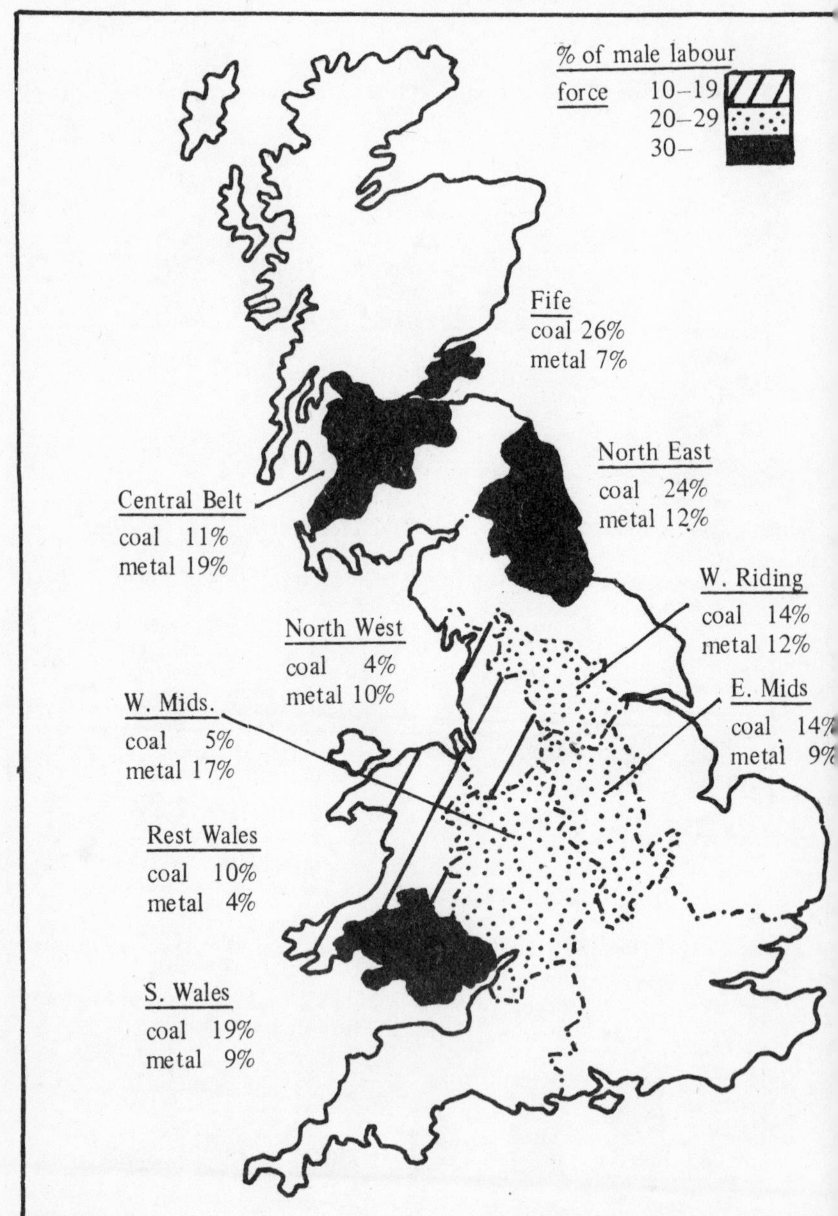

Figure 5 Unemployed Spring 1926[10]

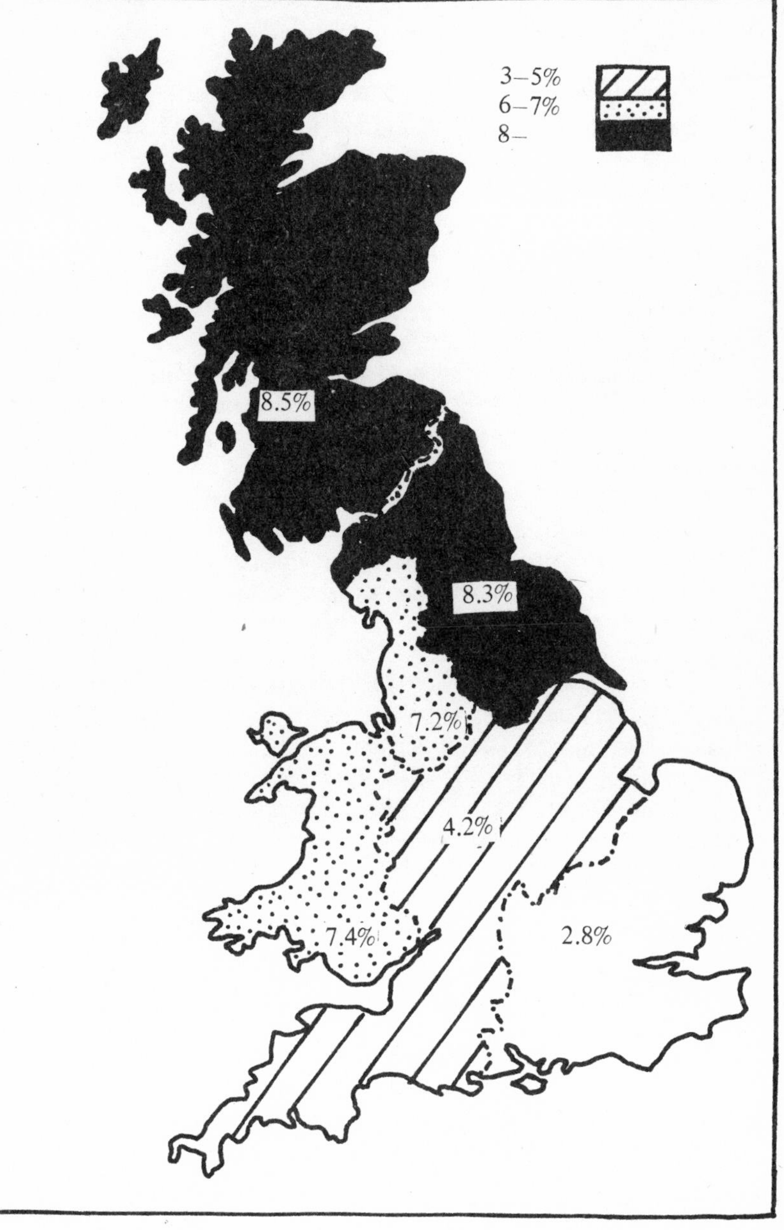

coal and engineering suffered the sharpest blows. Geographically this new situation is reflected by the continued depression of the old high-wage areas of the north and west ([notes 9–10] Figures 4 & 5). Moreover, by 1925 to maintain sterling at 4·86, even greater cuts were demanded—which brings us to the eve of the general strike and Labour's fight back.

Finally, therefore, to sum up the findings so far. There was British imperialism on the eve of war: old fashioned, still in a premonopoly stage, dominated by banking capital, its economy distorted by the vast scale of capital and commodity export and increasingly dependent on the markets and raw materials of its immense colonial empire. Then there was war—transforming the balance of world forces, creating hothouse conditions for domestic monopoly. But without the outcome that one might have expected. Unlike France, previously somewhat similar to Britain with dominant banks and weak industry, there was no fundamental reconstruction, no decisive move into the era of monopoly capital. So tightly was the banking sector bound into the British state, so dependent was the structure of its economy on the old system (and perhaps so deceptive was the helping hand from the rival American imperialism) that an attempt was made to continue the already outdated rule of banking capital. True, it was not done in altogether the old way. Finance capital groupings were germinating within it. The great companies controlling colonial raw materials (oil, copper, gold, rubber, vegetable fats) were closely linked with the City and saw the re-establishment of sterling as of vital importance in maintaining their hold against overseas rivals. At home industrial concentration was moving ahead (the hundred largest companies were controlling 24 per cent of manufacturing output by 1935 as against 15 per cent in 1909).[11] In sheltered, home market industries a merger of banking and monopoly capital was certainly taking place. Yet throughout the 1920s the basic strategy remained that of revival rather than fundamental change—a revival of which the tremendous costs were to be borne by the working class. It was this, as we shall see, that doomed it to failure.

2. SOCIAL CHANGE AND THE LABOUR ARISTOCRACY

"The British labour movement, for a long time yet, unfortunately promises to serve as a deplorable example of how the isolation of the labour movement from socialism inevitably leads to degeneration and bourgeois ideas."[12] This was how Lenin described the labour movement in Britain before the first world war. It was one of the biggest, oldest and best organised in Europe, with four million members in 1914. In parliament it had over forty trade union MPs. But politically there can be no doubt that Lenin was right. Almost without exception its leaders were content to act as the left-wing of the Liberal Party and in doing so maintained a position that had existed more or less since the collapse of Chartism sixty years before. During all those years the bulk of organised labour—as well as the much bigger mass of unorganised—remained sealed off from any effective political challenge to the capitalist system, and the result was inevitably "degeneration and bourgeois ideas".

The question why has dominated Marxist debate ever since. The usual explanation is the existence of a labour aristocracy: the use of a small portion of empire profits to split and bribe the upper strata of the labour force. Yet, as Lenin himself demonstrated, to be useful this explanation has to be taken a good deal further. In particular it has to take into account the active historical *development* which the labour aristocracy underwent, as a social factor assisting the ruling class to preserve its control without effective challenge, in the half-century to 1914. So accordingly, if we want to understand how the movement eventually broke free, the first thing to grasp is how much change did occur inside the movement, how volatile the situation often was and the way in which the original form of labour aristocracy had to be successively modified in order to contain it.

Only for the middle years of the century does it seem possible to talk about a labour aristocracy pure and simple. At this period one does find emerging in the major industries distinct grades of skilled workers exercising authority over the rest, winning increasing wage differentials and enjoying virtually exclusive rights of organisation. In many instances these grades were directly descended from the old craft unions, but now operating in a quite different form, abandoning any serious attempt at workshop control and collaborating with the management in training and disciplining a new semi-skilled labour force. To some extent this transformation fitted in with current technological developments. The new outflow of capital export demanded the rapid growth (indeed virtual industrialisation) of heavy steel, heavy engineering and machine goods. But the real driving force seems to have been the intense and detailed local efforts by which the industrial bourgeoisie sought to head off the rising working-class challenge of the 1830s and '40s. Two tactics were used. Combined with an uncompromising legal and military offensive against committed anti-establishment forces, substantial concessions were made to effectively organised skilled workers: better wages, the promise of the vote and the legalisation of purely economic trade union activity (this last a good generation before it was done elsewhere in Europe). Culturally, too, there was a decisive change of line. A whole battery of local institutions was created to win such workers for bourgeois ideas (mechanics' institutes, adult education, temperance societies, Sunday schools), while among the residuum of semi-skilled and labourers there was covert encouragement for loyalism and anti-Irish prejudice. But the linchpin was the labour aristocracy—successful precisely because it incorporated, recognised and *used* the bargaining force which the unions had developed over the previous generation. At this stage the bribe was, in a sense, distributed locally *through the market* in response to union bargaining and in doing so transformed a power previously used more generally, on behalf of all workers, into a sectional weapon that maintained (and often increased) differentials and tended to be concretely expressed in an increasingly distinct, alien and petty bourgeois culture.[13]

It would seem to be this that explains the strange ambivalence of the trade union movement in this period: its combination of ideological retreat with a degree of organisational advance. For the working class as a whole the 1850s were of disastrous defeat. There was the loss of almost every previous institutional expression of class unity—of the whole organisational heritage developed during that extraordinarily rich period of working-class creativity which marked the earlier nineteenth century. Even now it is sobering to remember how much was first won and then lost. There were the rudiments of a disciplined and nationally organised working-class party: the National Charter Association. There was a thriving radical press—very near to becoming the practical organiser and educator of working-class struggle. There were local and sometimes near national general strikes (with all that this represented in terms of heightened class solidarity). There was a developing body of specifically anti-capitalist theory. Most important of all, there were the *local* institutions of class unity: the political unions, open to all workers, in some districts tracing their origins back to the revolutionary mass actions of the 1800s, and carrying within them the tested experience of working-class combativeness (arming and drilling) and detailed local opposition to capitalist state power. It was within this framework that trade union activity had previously taken place, and it was the resulting political *class* relevance of apparently purely economic struggle which was probably the most serious victim of Chartism's collapse.

Nonetheless, as so often in history, the loss was not total. When one turns to what happened in the two decades that followed, to the real and indeed pioneering organisational advances then achieved by the British trade union movement, one is continually struck by echoes of these earlier forms. The trades councils set up in the 1860s, despite being restricted to skilled workers—"trades" councils—and at first being politically little more than adjuncts to the Liberal Party, did grow in the same soil as the political unions and reflected the need for some replacement form of local labour unity. The same could be said at national level of the centralised amalgamated unions and the Trades Union Congress formed in 1868. Once experienced, the memory of united national action remained—however sectional the new use.

So although representing only the 5 to 10 per cent minority of organised workers and sometimes turned against the rest, the institutions of the labour aristocracy did incorporate some aspects of class power. It was this, of course, that made them so effective as means through which the ruling class could keep control. But it was also this that rendered them potentially double-edged when market conditions changed in the 1870s and '80s and hence demanded repeated ruling-class intervention. The unionisation of significant sections of non-skilled workers during the temporary peaks of full employment in the early 1870s and again in 1889–90 did much to challenge the practice of sectional, aristocratic unionism and at least posed the *possibility* of trade unions acting as general instruments of class unity. Such a possibility was not lost on the ruling class—especially since it was accompanied by a steady chipping away of the old assumptions inside the skilled unions themselves. As Britain's world monopoly started to crumble (and the revolutionary threat of the 1840s became a distant memory), local employers became far more concerned with maintaining profit levels than with the wider issues of social control. Tough countrywide employers' associations developed in shipbuilding and the iron trades. In light engineering the proportion of semi-skilled workers increased sharply, while cyclical unemployment in the heavy industry trades—the flow of capital export went alternately in great booms and bursts—did much to break down the commitment of individual skilled workers to the culture and authority of their employers. Although it is important not to overstate this, the resulting slow erosion does seem to have done much to produce a nucleus of recruits for directly oppositional working-class politics. By the late 1870s London's radical clubs were again becoming quite effective centres for socialist agitation and in 1881 combined with other anti-imperialist and pro-Irish forces to form the Democratic Federation (becoming the Social Democratic Federation in 1884).[14] This organisation had its faults, probably the worst being its leader, H. M. Hyndman, and never came near to developing a mass movement. But it did provide many of the militants who helped organise the unemployment campaigns in the 1880s, the new general unions in 1889–90 and again the unemployed in 1893–5. Certainly by that date the potential mass appeal of socialism was gravely worrying the establishment, and Rhodes' stark alternative of empire or revolution was fairly typical of contemporary establishment debate.

Hence the need for new controls: a second line of defence now that the device of bribing a whole stratum "through the market" was becoming both economically difficult and politically unreliable. Put briefly, the answer was to add a set of bribes that by-passed the market and went direct from the state or employers to (or through) trade union leaders and politicians. These were thus able to reach all *organised* workers, including those in unskilled unions, but had the disadvantage of relying upon the manipulation of organisation and leadership (rather than being built into an entire social stratum) and hence tended to generate opposition.

Naturally, the actual process by which these controls were first built up was somewhat more piecemeal and less deliberate. Employers confronted with the new general unions took time to discover the crucial weakness of those unions: that during the lean years of high unemployment their leaders could be persuaded to swap militancy for the closed shop.[15] On the political front the original initiatives came more from the older generation of trade union politicians themselves—now faced with the partial break-up of their old base. They needed solid concessions to be able to answer their socialist critics: the municipal socialism of the Fabian progressive alliance in London during the 1890s, the promises of employers' liability and redistributive income tax in the 1891 (Liberal) Newcastle Programme, and the radical elements in the Tory legislation of the later 1890s. Bit by bit, therefore, the extension of a 'welfare state' interlocked with the creation of a new breed of reformist labour politicians. The emergence of a far more recognisable and independent 'Labour' political identity—now organised on a national scale—went hand in hand with a quite new form of involvement with the capitalist state.[16]

Indeed, very soon the fundamental constitutional innovations demanded by this approach were being sharply debated within the political establishment—all the more so because they overlaid (and to some extent could be used to hide) key changes in the internal ruling class balance between the state, banking capital and the capitalist class as a whole. It is noteworthy that the main supporters of extended state intervention (and the main political allies of the Fabians) were those politicians most closely associated with developing a new global strategy for British imperialism. The Fabians were to provide vital ideological support for the Liberal Imperialists of the late 1890s (Rosebery, Haldane, Grey) in their campaign for a more centralised and expert state machine—typified by the Committee for Imperial Defence—by which political institutions still over-influenced by non-banking capital was being effectively by-passed. And the same was true for the philosophy of imperial federation nurtured by the very self-conscious élite of empire administrators grouped round the South African pro-consul Lord Milner. Here domestic welfare policies and even a degree of state socialism were seen as essential components of a new classless racial unity. Perhaps the clearest demonstration comes after 1908. In these years we find Lloyd George, a populist politician originally oriented to the radical petty bourgeoisie (and petty-bourgeois labour), being forced to shift his base and join Churchill in inaugurating state schemes for health and unemployment insurance. These schemes, modelled upon those in Bismarckian Germany, were carried with the full support of Labour MPs and administratively had the effect of linking the trade unions to the state machine. To this extent "Social Imperialism" was the direct expression of the labour aristocracy at this stage in its development.[17]

However, its most important consequence lay in an altogether different direction: in the way "control through organisation", manipulating leaderships against members, generated its own opposition. Understandably, members reacted by creating new institutions of their own. The engineering industry provides a particularly good example. In the 1897–8 lockout the employers' main objective had been a procedure agreement that would strengthen the authority of the unions' national leadership over its more militant district committees. But once put into practice this agreement had quite the opposite effect. By tying the hands of the local leaderships it slowly but surely called into being an unofficial movement based on the shopfloor. That terror of employers, the shop steward, makes his first but not last appearance.[18] Very much the same happened with the general unions. By the 1900s employer pressure had rendered these bodies almost as centralised and authoritarian as the old skilled unions (and often more palpably corrupt). So not unnaturally, when full-employment conditions returned in 1911, local socialist militants—the vital spark plugs for renewed organisation—directed the movement into radically anti-leadership and "direct action" channels. Syndicalism, though ideologically derived from America and France, was, in a sense, the specific and quite predictable product of this stage in the development of the labour aristocracy.[19] Nor did it stop there. The economy had itself moved into a stage which directly reinforced these tendencies. In certain industries, particularly transport, a virtually national system already existed, and in others, like coal, effective industrial action could only be taken on a national scale. More and more, therefore, a new type of national strike emerged that inevitably drew workers (together with their usually reluctant union leaders) into direct conflict with governmental state power: on the railways and docks in 1911, in the mines in 1912 and even to some extent in cotton in 1913. In these struggles workers could see with their own eyes the contradiction between the increasingly society-wide scale of production and its still private ownership and control. Nationalisation—of docks, mines, railways—now became a slogan of immediate relevance.

Already before the war, therefore, the key structures of the labour aristocracy were coming under strain, and nowhere is the extent (as well as the limits) of the resulting transformation more clearly revealed than among the miners.

Generalisations about mining are always dangerous. Its labour force was very large (over a million by 1911) and was geographically scattered among coalfields which had as radically different internal economies, markets and industrial hinterlands as the Forest of Dean and Fife. Politically it was characterised by extreme unevenness. In Scotland, Lanark was already a base for independent labour politics in the 1880s, while Fife was still committed to Liberalism thirty years later. Both South Wales and Durham switched from old-style liberalism in the 1890s to radical militancy in the 1910s. Even the Miners' Federation presents contradictions. Although destined to become the main core of anti-government opposition in the '20s, it was in 1908 the last major union to affiliate to the Labour Party, and in doing so did much to reinforce that body's subservience to the Liberals.

Nonetheless, some patterns do stand out. First of all, in the *origins* of the labour aristocracy. In mining the process was particularly complex and many-sided—perhaps reflecting the part-skilled, part general union elements in its make-up. It seems originally to have involved granting an enhanced dominance to the hewer or coal-getter, and then manipulating this grade against other sections. It is noteworthy that this was most thorough-going in the north-east, where previously the mining community had taken the lead in working-class struggle, and in this district the bribe went as far as granting hewers a privileged shift system (in the 1860s half the length of that for transit staff). Elsewhere, it was restricted to wage differentials, cultural methods of control (methodism, baptism, the Orange lodges) and a bit later the buttressing of organisation in the way that was to become characteristic of the second phase of the labour aristocracy (both the sliding scale and in some areas the institution of checkweighman seems to have been important here). So despite the miners' radical past, their drastic exposure to market forces—with wages rising and falling up to 50 per cent—and the still spectacular bursts of militancy, their basic class organisation was for a very long period dominated by the privileged patriarchal hewers, often the only unionised section; and though the pioneers of labour parliamentary representation they remained as culturally and politically petty-bourgeois as their archetypal leaders, Thomas Burt and William Abraham.[20]

It was only in the last decades before 1914 that decisive changes began to occur. Geographically two main forces stand out. First, those coalfields working for export markets saw a period of rapid expansion. This involved a big influx of outside labour and a disproportionate growth in non-hewer grades and transit staff. Once unionised, these workers were in a strong position to contest the aristocrats' control. Secondly, as coalfaces became more extended and the rate of re-investment slackened, many of the older coalfields began to suffer from declining profitability and the piecework wages of the hewers fell significantly. Where these two forces came together—as in South Wales and Durham—the old-style leadership came under strong attack. Nowhere was its labour aristocrat base entirely destroyed. A number of districts remained quite untouched. The highly profitable Midland fields—mainly working for the domestic consumer—were still conspicuously collaborationist in 1914. Even where the challenge was strongest the effect was often more to consolidate reformist (ILP) Labour trends in the leadership—hence the ultimately syndicalist reaction of the South Wales reform movement (its 1912 *Miners' Next Step*). But some positive results were achieved. The national orientation of the union did become more industrial, less sectional. A national eight-hour day was won in 1908; the minimum district wage in 1911. By 1914 the first steps were being made towards a Triple Industrial Alliance with the railwaymen and the transport workers—two home market sectors particularly exposed to the economic pressures of the pre-war period (and whose basically right-wing leaders were also under siege from the syndicalist left).

Finally, therefore, to sum up the situation in 1914. The labour aristocracy, as a means of control, was quite different from what it had been fifty years before. Always associated with trade union organisation and to this extent incorporating the gains of previous struggle, it had been compelled to move forward from simply manipulating the sectional bargaining power of the unionised élite to manipulating trade union organisation itself: from selective bribing "through the market" to blanket control through bureaucracy. Each step in this direction meant more politics, a closer, more explicit intervention in the internal struggle for the control of organisation. Each intervention meant a higher price for reformist credibility. By the 1900s a continuous ideological guerrilla war was having to be fought to preserve labour's organisation from radical change, to prevent it reverting once again into a weapon of class unity and struggle. To this degree, the possibility of a new explosion of class consciousness was already there in 1914.

Yet to say this and no more is to miss an ever bigger reality. Although bourgeois dominance had to be continuously fought for, it was nonetheless *maintained.* For a whole half-century labour's class organisation remained virtually under enemy control. The only force that could have broken down the ramified divisions and jealousies that had fragmented the working population since the mid-nineteenth century was used, if at all, to sustain them. It is this crucial fact that is often forgotten. Concentrating on the purely institutional growth of the labour movement we are apt to forget about the wider field of mass consciousness, and are therefore unable to explain the strange contradiction between the relatively rapid unionisation in the five years before 1914 and a working population that still, politically and culturally, identified with the bourgeoisie. Though there are all too few useful studies of what people actually said and did at the time, what exist bring this home all too clearly. In Tressell's classic novel about Hastings building workers the whole dramatic tension rests on the marginal isolation of the socialists, the seeming impossibility of Owen's survival amid a sea of petty-bourgeois prejudice (while the book's biggest weakness is its perhaps not unnatural tendency to see solutions in terms of outside intervention rather than labour's own collective organisation).[21] Similarly with Alfred Williams' description of Swindon or Roberts' memories of Salford.[22] Despite the differing industrial backgrounds, what stands out in both is the almost caste-like internal discipline imposed by each grade within the workforce; the seemingly complete absence of any vehicle for class unity or change. Nor is it perhaps an accident that opening sequences in the autobiographies of both Pollitt and Gallacher describe the mass chauvinism and anti-German hysteria that greeted the eventual outbreak of war. It was this last grotesque expression of bourgeois social dominance that in later years served as a kind of benchmark for measuring what followed.

For war did bring change very quickly indeed. It struck at all the system's most vulnerable points. It brought full employment and hence unionisation to the remaining unorganised sectors (by the end of the post-war boom in 1920 union membership had reached over 8 million). It demanded the massive introduction of women and labourers to work previously reserved for skilled men. It radically altered the distribution of income and authority in the family (Roberts gives a detailed description of its liberating effects on women in Salford).[23] Most fatally, it fractured the trade union movement as an effective instrument of control. Almost all union leaderships were implicated in initial support for the war, and most signed the Treasury Agreements of March 1915 by which union rule books were suspended and strikes made illegal. Coming in a period of rapid inflation, sudden and arbitrary changes in wage differentials and savage assault on workshop practices this would have been bad enough. But at a time when shopfloor workers found themselves in an unprecedentedly powerful bargaining position it inevitably threw up a new unofficial movement radically at odds with the leadership. The use of labour's class organisation had now become effectively illegal, involved open conflict with the state and was only able to operate at local factory and city level under the leadership of usually socialist shop stewards. At last a situation had arisen in which the progressive, unifying class forces so long imprisoned inside the trade union movement could be released.

In practice, not all (or even most) of this socialist potential was immediately fulfilled. The really intense struggles were restricted to those areas where skilled workers still formed a big section of the workforce and where the introduction of semi-skilled labour posed the biggest challenge. This excluded the newer engineering industries of the west Midlands and the south-east and tended to be localised in the heavy industry sectors of Clydeside, Sheffield and South Lancashire.[24] It was only here that we find the most advanced form of the new unofficial movement—the workers' committees—taking over leadership from existing trade union structures. And even in these areas, although the new leaders were usually drawn from one or other of the Marxist groupings and tried to pursue policies of workshop unity and industrial unionism, there was no automatic acceptance of socialist perspectives. Sectional, craft attitudes remained strong to the end of the war. In 1916 the government commissioners were able to hamstring the Clyde Workers' Committee for a whole year by exploiting sectional differences (between shipbuilding and engineering workers) and then arresting the leadership on "political" charges remote from the issue of workshop practice which still preoccupied most workers.[25] Across the country the power of the shop stewards movement tended to fluctuate unpredictably—able to generate wider campaigns on particular issues (like the Manpower Act in 1918) but then losing momentum and falling back to its localised bases when the government started to make piecemeal concessions. Among the miners only the South Wales Federation defied the government with extensive strike action—although unrest in the pits was sufficient to force the government to take control of the industry in November 1916 and to set up Joint Pit Committees in June 1918. Moreover, much of the increase in union membership was in the general unions—the Workers' Union in particular. Generally, the leaders of these unions were (and could afford to be) much more openly pro-war than in the craft unions, and their growing strength was consistently used by the government to wear down craft resistance.[26]

Yet it would be a mistake, and a gravely misleading one, to leave it at that: to concentrate only on the fact that the cases of open struggle were limited, inconclusive and often mixed syndicalist forms with a large dose of defensive craft prejudice. It would have been surprising if this were not so. In fact, the really significant developments seem to have taken place at an altogether lower (but more fundamental) level: in the transformation of mass assumptions about the whole role and purpose of trade unionism.

The change in scale was itself important. Shop stewards' committees now became responsible to all grades, and union membership was no longer seen as the badge of a privileged minority. Key unions like the miners and engineers moved rapidly towards becoming fully industrial. What is more, the change did not occur in a political vacuum. It took place at a time when the working population was coming under unprecedented pressures; when shortages of food and housing, the issues of rents, prices and pensions, were all forcing local trade union branches and above all trades councils into sharp conflict with the local authorities. Whatever the importance of the workers committees in fashioning a new proletarian leadership (and this was considerable), the wartime creation of a locally rooted mass labour movement seems to have been the particular contribution of the trades councils: finally fulfilling their potential—absent since the days of the political unions—of acting as centres of mobilisation and defence for the entire working population. Though there is a serious lack of useful studies, what we have to stress is their key role in organising action which eventually—and town by town—forced the local adoption of food rationing, effective rent control and the scaling down of conscription quotas. And not just this. There was also a vital ideological aspect. Every act in defence of the local population set the trades councils more squarely against the centralised state apparatus in which the old generation of labour leaders (and their Fabian advisers) were becoming increasingly enmeshed. By late 1916 all the pre-war trends towards social imperialism had come together in the Lloyd George coalition. This included the right wing of the parliamentary Labour Party as well as Milner, Churchill and Bonar Law, and its determination to carry through full conscription seems to have been particularly important in pinpointing the class nature of the state as the key issue of ideological division. Even in Birmingham, one of the least militant areas, the Trades Council's opposition was sufficiently firm for the right wing (led by the Workers' Union) temporarily to split away and form a rival Industrial Trade Union Council.[27]

But even these developments are unlikely to have produced any really coherent reorientation by themselves. The pace of events was too slow, the existing ideological trends too diffuse. The vital spark seems to have come at international level. Despite the creation of workers committees, the success of direct action, the growth of a locally rooted mass movement and the exposure of social imperialism, it still needed the conquest of working-class power in Russia to show British workers the full significance of their own struggles. Coming in a form so remote from the vaporisings of Ramsay MacDonald or indeed from the perspectives of any of the socialist groupings in Britain, it seems to have been this direct, simple setting up of Soviets and the destruction of the old capitalist state that finally revealed the common thread running through the many separate, isolated struggles in Britain. It showed that the process by which labour was reforming itself as a class was also preparing, then and there, the organs by which socialist state power could be achieved. Soon the insistent hammer blows of Lenin's logic were ringing out in Britain also. The working class must constitute itself directly as the new state power. The capitalist state must be destroyed, not taken over.

How many heard and understood? It is impossible to make any conclusive assessment. As evidence for the movement's *general* reorientation, one could point to the strikes which erupted in 1919 (particularly the general strikes in Glasgow and Belfast), to the defeat of right-wing officials in the engineering union, to the victories of the Trades and Labour Council candidates in the November 1919 municipal elections (as against the general defeat of Labour Party parliamentary candidates in 1918)—even to the rapidly lengthening reports on civil disaffection from the cabinet's Directorate of Intelligence. But for a more precise political reorientation the best evidence comes from a year later: the local Councils of Action set up from August 1920. These bodies, based directly on the local Trades and Labour Councils (which at that time also comprised the Labour Parties) were called into being to co-ordinate action to halt British military intervention against Russia. This action included a possible general strike. The fact that the Parliamentary Labour Party (together with the Parliamentary Committee of the TUC) felt compelled to take this step is itself a reflection of the feeling already existing among the rank and file. But the real significance of these bodies—which Lenin described (with perhaps less exaggeration than has sometimes been thought) as embryo British Soviets—is what happened to them in the months that followed. A near majority maintained their existence and went on to demand lines of action radically different from those advocated by the national leadership. The records of the national council show that 288 Trades and Labour Councils constituted themselves as Councils of Action.[28] Of these 139 subsequently passed resolutions in defiance of the right-wing national leadership and backed calls—supported by the newly-formed Communist Party—for direct industrial action to end the economic blockade of the Soviet Union as well as force the withdrawal of troops from Ireland. These quite explicitly political resolutions, embodying the principles of both proletarian internationalism and direct action and passed by the official representatives of the local Labour movement, are doubly significant because they came after the threat of outright war had been averted and when renewed unemployment had limited this purely economic base for militancy. It is also important to note that the left-wing councils were concentrated in precisely those urban working-class areas where the wartime pressures for reorientation had been greatest: South Wales, London, north-east, Lancashire and Clydeside (Figure 6). But most important of all is their sheer number. It is clear evidence that by the end of the post-war boom the labour aristocracy was, in any of its forms, no longer the effective instrument it had been six years before: that the ideological guerrilla war so essential to the manipulation and control of labour's organisation was turning dangerously against the ruling class. Lenin was beating the Webbs.

Of course, had British imperialism still been in the same dominant position it was in 1914, these temporary reverses would have been of only limited concern. But, as we saw in the previous section, it was not. In 1920 the banking establishment was only just beginning its long road back to gold. The main assault on working-class living standards had still to come. What is more, it was precisely those sectors that had previously been the mainstay of the labour aristocracy—heavy industry, engineering, coal—that faced the biggest cuts. In these conditions it is not surprising that for the next six years the ruling class was almost exclusively preoccupied with the problem of how to control the labour movement.

3. THE STRUGGLE FOR CONTROL

"In those countries where democratic parliamentary culture is of long standing, the bourgeoisie has excellently learned to operate, not only by means of violence, but also by means of deception, bribery and flattery . . . 'You will train them and we will buy them', said a very clever capitalist lady to Mr. Social Imperialist Hyndman." So Lenin wrote, in July 1919.[29]

Before tracing this process in detail it is worth turning for a moment to theory and examining a bit more deeply what Lenin meant by the "labour aristocracy"—above all, to see how far it can still be applied in the 1920s. Already one thing should have become clear. Lenin never

Figure 6 Councils of Action 1920–1[30]

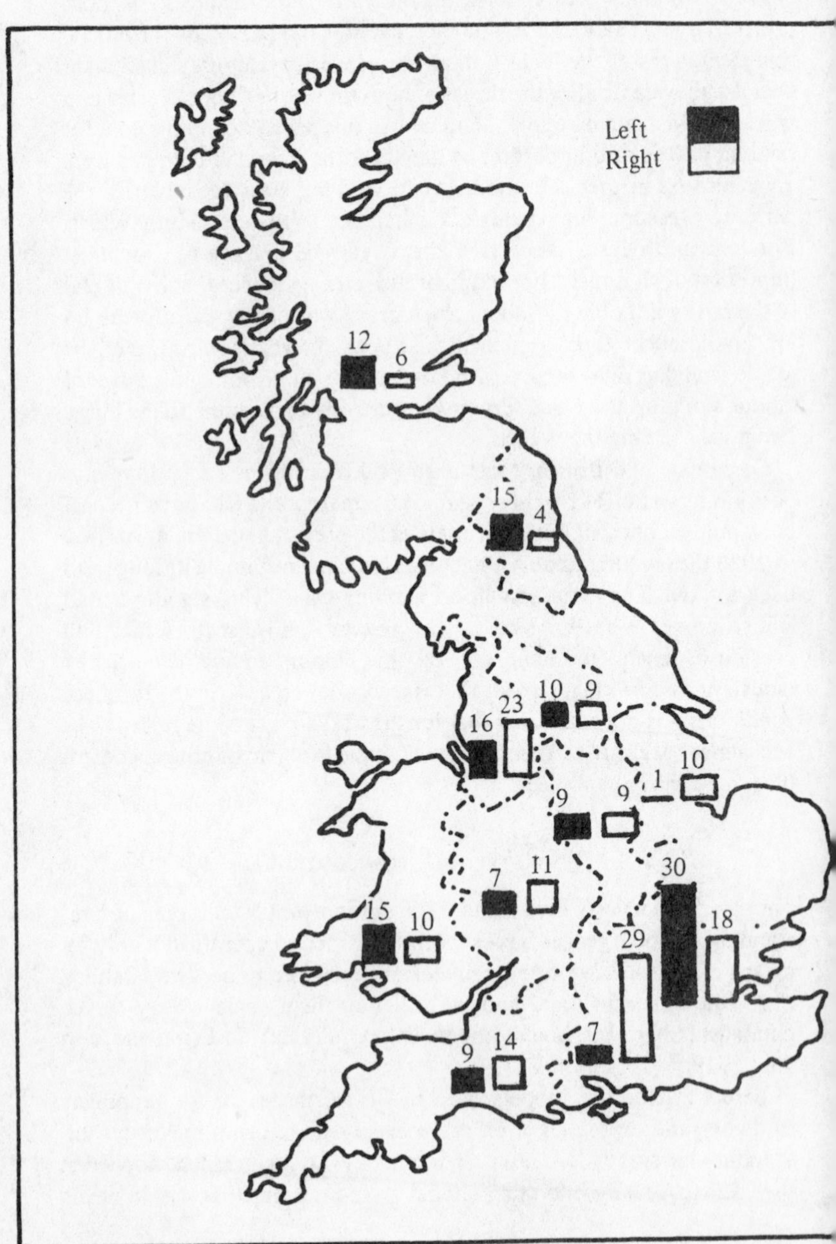

used the term merely sociologically, to describe a stratum within the workforce. He was talking about a historical process, and a very special one: how, *after* labour had formed its class organisations, and *after* the anti-capitalist logic within them had started to become explicit, this "conscious element" was nonetheless excluded and the dominance of bourgeois ideas maintained. It was a labour aristocracy—a form of ideological control appropriate to "democratic parliamentary culture of long standing", and which maintained the "hegemony" of bourgeois ideas—now no longer automatic—from inside labour's class organisation. As we saw, the first attempt to exclude the conscious element took the form of a bribe "through the market". A legal and political framework was created within which the minority of effectively organised skilled workers were free to bargain for their own sectional ends but for them alone—against, not for, the working people as a whole. *Within* this framework only a limited, economic consciousness was possible. Later on, as trade union organisation spread across the labour force and anti-capitalist elements regained a foothold, the emphasis shifted towards capturing the leaders ("people bought by the bourgeoisie") and strengthening their organisational ability to defeat and isolate their opponents. This was the logic behind Lloyd Georgism—the growing together of reformism, Fabian state socialism and social imperialism—which reached its climax during the first world war.

What then happened in the 1920s? At first glance, the whole formation might seem to have collapsed in on itself. The previously privileged 'aristocratic' sections now came under crippling attack. Their local cultural institutions (the backbone of the old "framework" of control) disappeared into the abyss of mass unemployment. Yet to see this as the end would be to miss the whole essence of the labour aristocracy, to see it purely descriptively, in just one of its forms, and ignore its historical role and development: as the active *process* by which labour's class organisation was purged of anti-capitalist elements and made safe for economism and spontaneity. If the first method was now abandoned, the second—which developed out of it—was transformed to an entirely new level.

It is not easy to categorise it precisely. Very great importance was still attached to manipulating trade union organisation and to the battle between "moderates" and "extremists". But if one had to pinpoint what was new, one would probably single out the intensity of governmental concern with the "direction" of labour's new national institutions. By now these were mass organisations. They covered an outright majority of the working population and provided the only readily accepted channel of information. How they were used, the ideological content of their actions, would have a determining effect on whether the process of class mobilisation begun during the war were continued or reversed. This was the challenge that faced the government in 1920 and it has a certain similarity to the situation in the 1840s. At that time we saw that the solution was to surround the labour movement with a loose institutional framework that left it both apparently "free" and "autonomous" but at the same time decisively limited its scope. For the 1920s the response was not dissimilar—except that the framework was now national instead of local and that the containment of the conscious element rested far more directly on ideological and organisational manipulation (and hardly at all on creating distinct sectional cultures). Mainly it seems to have been ideological. A "climate of opinion" would be created by a growing battery of mass influence—newspapers, radio, the church, education and the government itself. The labour leadership would be persuaded to adopt a course of action that would enable it to "win" this public opinion. In doing this the leadership would both endorse the same assumptions within the labour movement and find itself forced into confrontation with those anti-capitalist elements that still opposed. Slowly, attitudes would be remoulded, come into line with those peddled by the establishment—even though remaining distinct and "Labour". The ideological guerrilla warfare of the 1900s became regular warfare waged with heavy artillery support.

To put it like this is, of course, to make it look simpler than it was. But it is certainly undeniable that by 1920 the establishment was explicitly (indeed continuously and obsessively) discussing the problem of ideological control inside the trade union movement—or that on the other side, Lenin and the Communist International saw this as perhaps the most vital issue of the time. Should communists work in right-wing trade unions, and run the risk of being trapped? "Opportunist, social chauvinist trade union leaders are nothing more nor less than 'agents of the bourgeoisie in the labour movement', 'Labour lieutenants of the capitalist class' (to use the excellent and profoundly true expression of the followers of Daniel DeLeon in America). To refuse to work in reactionary trade unions means leaving the insufficiently developed or backward masses of the workers under the influence of reactionary leaders, the agents of the bourgeoisie, the labour aristocrats. . . . Millions of workers in England, France and Germany are *for the first time* passing from complete lack of organisation to the elementary, lowest, most simple and (for those still thoroughly imbued with bourgeois democratic prejudices) most easily accessible form of organisation, namely the trade unions. And the revolutionary but foolish Left Communists stand by, shouting 'the masses, the masses!' and *refuse to work within the trade unions*. There can be no doubt that [the opportunists] are very grateful to such 'Left' revolutionaries. . . . Undoubtedly, Messieurs the 'leaders' of opportunism will resort to every trick of bourgeois diplomacy, to the aid of bourgeois governments, the priests, the police and the courts, in order to prevent communists from getting into the trade unions, to force them out by every means. . . . It is necessary to be able to withstand all this. . . ."[31] It was, as both sides knew, this battle inside labour's class organisations that would determine the larger battle for State power.

Historically, the establishment's solution seems to have been worked out in three stages. From 1918–22 the aim was still to reduce the labour movement to the purely trade union based body it had been before 1914, to prevent the crystallisation of a new political "Labour" identity and so keep the mass of the working population within the old parties. After the Labour gains in the 1922 election this was given up. Instead, attention was focused on "educating" labour, using various forms of ideological persuasion to turn the new political identity into constitutional, reformist channels. Only under the shock of Red Friday in July 1925—when the movement seemed to be reverting back to direct action tactics—were more drastically coercive methods adopted (culminating in the general strike of May 1926).

It was Lloyd George who was the main advocate of the original line. And with good reason. His own political future depended on building up some kind of alternative populist radical party (perhaps with backing from the emerging finance capital conglomerates), and in the meantime he had to keep together his coalition government. The threat of a Bolshevik-dominated Labour Party was, therefore, certainly useful. As long as the Tories saw him—the victorious war leader—as an indispensable focus for national unity, he was safe. In February 1919 he persuaded the cabinet to finance his reconstruction programme (essential both to fuel the post-war boom and to maintain his own reformist credibility) by giving a probably quite genuine description of the direct action threat within the labour movement. At £71 million it was, he claimed, "a cheap insurance against Bolshevism".[32] A few months later he was telling a Tory junior minister that the Labour leaders were prisoners of their left wing; a Labour government would be "Kerensky all over again".[33] And in January 1920 he seems to have been able to work the cabinet into a state of near hysteria over the lack of ready manpower in face of direct action: "Macready said that there were a number of soldiers among the Metropolitan Police who could use rifles and Aukland Geddes pointed to the Universities as full of trained men who could co-operate with clerks and stockbrokers. [During the discussion Bonar Law so often referred to the stockbrokers as a loyal and fighting class that one felt that potential battalions of stockbrokers were to be found in every town.] Horne suggested the preparation of secret lists of reliable men by the Chief Constables and Eric Geddes suggested having the Mayors up, but in view of the number of Labour Mayors and the difficulty of keeping the matter secret, there was opposition to this suggestion." Tom Jones, the deputy cabinet secretary, comments, "throughout the discussion the PM did a lot of unsuspected leg-pulling as he does not believe in the imminence of the revolution . . .".[34]

But plainly Lloyd George would never have been able to do this had the establishment not been fairly widely convinced that the situation inside the labour movement was very fluid. Even before the end of the war Dawson, the editor of *The Times* (who made it his business to cultivate contacts inside the labour movement) was urging Lloyd George to hold an early election to "re-establish the authority of parliament against attempts to 'hold up' the country by unconstitutional methods . . . the case seems to me to be greatly strengthened by the recent Labour troubles which to an increasing extent are said to be due to sheer Bolshevism and not to any genuine industrial grievance."[35] On a number of occasions—in January–February 1919, summer 1920 and again in spring 1921—there seems to have been genuine fears that the direct actionists were making the running. Repeatedly in these years the cabinet was minutely preoccupied with the details of industrial negotiation (above all in the still State-controlled railways and mines) and with debating the long-term psychological effects of particular lines of action.

The miners were, of course, the key group—above all because it was mining that would have to bear the brunt of the return to gold. At the end of the war the miners formed the biggest organised section of the labour movement (and indeed a sixth of the entire male labour force) and were demanding a 30 per cent rise on the wartime minimum wage together with full nationalisation of the mines. They had the formal backing of the other two unions of the Triple Alliance and in some districts were already displacing right-wing leaderships (although Cook did not succeed to the secretaryship till 1924). In February 1919—just five days before Lloyd George asked for his "insurance against Bolshevism"—they voted six-to-one for strike action. The government played for time. A royal commission was set up (stuffed full of Fabians) and in March gave an interim report in favour of nationalisation and a wage increase. The government pledged itself to accept the commission's fiindings and the strike was called off. When in June the commission gave its final report (this time non-unanimous and divided), the industrial boom was underway and the government felt able to use the disagreements to shuffle out of its earlier commitment. The miners appealed to the TUC in the autumn but in the meantime the government's propaganda battery had done its work. They were told to campaign politically for a Labour government. The miners returned to the fight in the summer-autumn of 1920. This was at the height of the Councils of Action campaign and at a time when unemployment was just beginning to bite. The government again temporised, granted a slight wage rise and used the occasion to work up differences between the Triple Alliance unions. Finally in spring 1921 the government felt strong enough to move forward to its ultimate objective: returning the mines to private ownership, ending all national agreements and in doing so opening the way to a decisive attack on wages and conditions. It was a difficult and risky operation. It was calculated to rouse the entire labour movement, demand action by the Triple Alliance, and place the right-wing leaders under acute pressure. But if successful, it could be expected to bring immense benefits. It would decisively weaken and split the movement, discredit direct action, isolate the champions of a wider class perspective and possibly even drive a wedge between the parliamentary Labour leaders and the movement in the country.

Indeed, although at first Lloyd George seems to have made some half-hearted attempts to detach the other unions ("everything depends on the influence that can be brought to bear on the railwaymen and the transport workers. When can you detach them best?"), he seems eventually to have gone for outright confrontation. Very soon J. H. Thomas, the right-wing secretary of the NUR and the government's traditional contact man, was grovelling. By 13 April, a couple of days before solidarity action was due to take place, he was on the phone almost all day to Tom Jones in the Cabinet Secretariat. "9.55 a.m. J. H. Thomas on the telephone. He said he was desperate: that he had striven last night to get the Triple Alliance to go to Downing Street today in vain. As he put it, 'Things were as black as death . . .'" An hour later the phone rang again. "The Subcommittee of the Triple Alliance had met . . . Thomas felt quite sure that they would not seek a meeting with the Government and he urged me to see the PM and try to move him to invite the Triple Alliance. . . . I went across to No. 10 and saw the PM. . . . He said 'I think we had better have the strike. Let them kick their heels for a week or a fortnight. It will help the moderates against the extremists. . . .'" In the end after a couple more days, and somewhat to the dismay of certain cabinet members, Thomas got the other Triple Alliance unions to desert the miners. Tom Jones sums up: "The [Cabinet] strike committee very sick. They had been waiting two years to press the button. They had pressed it. The Strike Books had been issued from the secret banks where they had been concealed; the milk cans were rolling down to Devon, the troops were steaming in ship and train from Ireland, from Malta, from Silesia to defend us from the men of Fife. . . . But Jim Thomas upset it all and despoiled Sir Hindenburg Geddes of the fruits of victory and was being damned as a traitor by the miners and hardly being thanked as a Saviour by the Cabinet. . . ."[36] This was Black Friday—for the miners and the labour movement as a whole. On both sides, it remained a powerful memory in the months leading up to the general strike. Although the government missed out on what they hoped would be the final destruction of the left, it was bad enough. After a grim struggle the miners were defeated, and the way opened for assaults on other sections, notably the engineers who were locked out in spring 1922.

In its handling one can see quite a number of the new elements of control: the constant informal contacts; the crucial go-between role of the Fabian deputy cabinet secretary, Jones (it was this that made him indispensable to a long series of governments); the discreetly visible anti-strike preparations; the co-opting of "moderate" leaders, like Hodges, into taking up "responsible" positions; the carefully orchestrated barrage from "public opinion" (at one point Lloyd George commented, "If I were left without newspapers and without Parliament I would leave the miners alone").[37] But of course more was involved than just this. The context had been well prepared over the previous years. Besides the purely industrial factors—the high unemployment and falling union membership—there was some progress in building up the new framework of ideological coercion. In autumn 1919 the Minister of Labour had instituted a continuing propaganda campaign "to encourage constitutional as against 'direct action' " with an initial allocation of £100,000. At its peak (it continued work for three years) it was distributing articles to over 1,000 newspapers a week and even designing school textbooks.[38] On the other side, steps were taken to make it more difficult for the left to put across its case. In February 1919 the cabinet gave instructions for the systematic prosecution of seditious speeches and began a period of police harassment which limited the freedom of speech more decisively than at any time since the Chartists.[39] In autumn 1920 police powers were extended still further by the Emergency Powers Act. While to an extent these actions —particularly the propaganda campaign—were untypically explicit and not repeated, they did much to set the tone for more informal styles of action, and act as storm warnings for the ruling class generally.

However, this was in the long run. As far as Lloyd George's own immediate future was concerned, none of it did him much good. The apparent containment of the left meant he was no longer indispensable. His own plans to implement a radical reconstruction programme—and then dump his right wing—had been wrecked by Bank of England deflation. Worst of all, the savagery with which the government's industrial and domestic policies had been imposed—particularly perhaps the cuts in unemployment benefit in 1921–2—had done much to consolidate the local hold of the Labour Party. (Indeed, apparently one of Bonar Law's main reasons for pulling the Tories out of the coalition was his fear that it was creating "an amalgamated 'bourgeois block' which leaves the Socialists as the sole alternative".)[40] Moreover, the early twenties had also seen some important longer-term changes in the social orientation of the Labour Party. Coming on top of the Party's success in the 1922 election (it doubled its seats from 75 to 142) this finally convinced at least a number of establishment figures that it was now both feasible and necessary to develop the Labour Party as the constitutional alternative to the Tories.

The forces at work in the Labour Party were still somewhat contradictory. In general the Right was in the ascendant although in certain limited areas the wartime class mobilisation continued —particularly in those mining districts where previous dependence on heavy industry or exports had brought big falls in wages and employment (Scotland, Durham and South Wales). Here the aristocratic stance of the hewers crumbled badly while government tactics in the 1921 lockout did much to bring forward a new generation of often Communist local leaders.[41] Where this was matched by heavy unemployment in the surrounding industrial community—as in the Lanark steel industry—quite fundamental changes seem to have occurred.[42] Equally, in the few areas where the unemployed workers movement and the Labour Party worked together, the struggle over dole also did something to maintain the leftward momentum.[43] But in most places the tide was quite strongly in the other direction. The 1918 constitution of the Labour Party had created a new individual membership that overlaid the previous local structure of Trades and Labour Councils. Of itself this might not have helped the Right (although it did open up the way to influence from outside the Labour Movement). But in conjunction with the Labour Party's post-war breakthrough in local government and its involvement in the politics of rehousing it seems to have decisively tipped the balance in favour of reformist, area-based organisation and greatly weakened links with the local industrial rank and file (a process which was, of course, later helped by the Right's systematic splitting of Trades *and Labour* Councils into separate bodies).[44] In Scotland, and maybe in other areas also, this trend was still further strengthened by clerical intervention. Between 1918 and 1920 the Catholic hierarchy ended its public position of active disapproval of the Labour Party. Partly this was because working-class Catholics were already voting Labour in large numbers (the rent and housing issue seems to have been important here), but it was also done with the quite express intent of counteracting and diluting socialist influence inside the Labour Party (in 1919 the Scottish ILP had temporarily voted to affiliate to the Third International).[45] At all events, by the early 1920s the local influence of the Right was decisively reasserting itself.

Added to this there had been changes in the trade union movement itself. Again not all were negative—at least in form. Between 1920 and 1921 the TUC had established a General Council which went to meet Left demands for a centralised general staff. There was also a spate of amalgamations especially in general unions. The Transport Workers and the General and Municipal Workers both moved into positions of strength. But it was the Right not the Left who got control of the new levers of power. Already the post-war economic pressures were making themselves felt. The forces which had brought together the miners, transport workers and the railwaymen in the Triple Alliance in 1914 were now pulling the other way. By the early 'twenties the miners' natural allies were in heavy industry. The relatively sheltered position of the general and transport unions had reinforced the grip of their right-wing leaderships as well as giving them numerical dominance in the TUC. In that body it was Thomas, Bevin and Dukes who now tended to call the tune—and they were able to do so all the more effectively after May 1922 when the General Council took control of the movement's only paper, the *Daily Herald*.

Hence, the confidence of those establishment politicians who were in favour of "educating Labour" (mainly conservatives like Baldwin, Davidson and Dawson). Both in terms of central organisation and development in the constituencies the Right seemed to be securely in control. Labour's class organisation was now again being used to halt and not develop class mobilisation. The only remaining step was to consolidate the parliamentary party as an active engine of constitutionalism. Already in 1923, while the Conservatives were still in power, ex-Liberals were being encouraged to enter and play a leading role in the Labour opposition. Davidson, the Tory Chancellor of the Duchy of Lancashire (a title generally reserved for ministers in charge of security and anti-strike preparations), wrote to the King's secretary "so far as the Labour Party is concerned it will undoubtedly increase in efficiency as an Opposition under the guidance of that old and very experienced Member, Josiah Wedgwood".[46] MacDonald, now leader of the Party, was also carefully cultivated. When Baldwin lost the November 1923 election (Labour secured 191 seats against 158 Liberals and 258 Tories) most leading Tories favoured putting Labour into office—with, of course, the safety catch of Liberal (and to some extent Tory) support. Obviously, for the Tories this had the party political advantage of eventually leading to the destruction of the Liberals (as well as isolating the remaining advocates of a coalition). Amery, for instance, believed that "the right solution is for the Liberal Party to disappear by one section of it gradually joining with and diluting the Labour Party and the other section coming into line with us".[47] But the decision also reflected more fundamental considerations about social stability. Davidson rejected coalition on the grounds that "any dishonest combination of that sort which means the sacrificing of principles by both Liberal and Tory to deprive Labour of their constitutional rights—is the first step down the road to revolution".[48] Dawson wrote in his diary (4 January 1924): "all my efforts lately have been devoted to combating a very popular view that the Conservatives and Liberals should join hands forthwith to keep Labour out. . . . It comes largely from the middle element in the City (where it is not shared, however, by Monty Norman or any of the more intelligent people)", and earlier in a letter to Robert Cecil ". . . the safest as well as the correct constitutional course is for Baldwin to face parliament and be beaten. The King would then presumably send for Ramsay MacDonald, who would be unable to govern without Liberal support and would therefore (if he undertook the task at all) gain some experience of administration with his wings clipped . . . it is the only way in which you will ultimately arrive at a strong, reasonable constitutional party. . . ."[49] In the event Baldwin and his followers were able to coerce the Liberals into giving Labour support. The final seal of establishment confidence was given when Haldane, the old Liberal Imperialist and architect of Britain's centralised war machine, agreed—after much collective arm-twisting from Baldwin, the Palace, the cabinet secretary and MacDonald himself—to enter the government as chairman of the Committee of Imperial Defence.[50]

In these circumstances it was only to be expected that the Labour Government would be thoroughly constitutional. But just how bad it was only fully came to light with the opening of the cabinet papers. There is the famous instance of what happened to the preceding Tory government's anti-strike preparations. Previously it had been claimed that these were put under wraps by the civil service and never seen. It now turns out that a special cabinet committee (including Henderson, Webb, Wedgwood and predictably Thomas) was actively preparing to use this machine against the dockers and tramwaymen. Still worse, not the slightest attempt was made to change the anti-working class personnel. Even the local Tory dignitaries who acted as chairmen of the eighteen Volunteer Service Committees were untouched.[51] In other areas the situation was little different. In foreign affairs and economic policy the government remained tightly controlled by the senior civil service and MacDonald's informal "bipartisan" contacts with the Tory leadership. MacDonald referred all his foreign office material to Baldwin and according to the King's secretary in October 1924, "[Baldwin] likes and trusts the PM and has had from time to time interesting talks with him and always gathered that the PM would adopt a quite determined opposition to Communism believing that in five years it would die out".[52] Indeed, it is probably no coincidence that it was at the Labour Party's 1924 conference that the right wing began the process of using administrative methods, the bans and proscriptions, to eliminate communists from the Party (previously communists had enjoyed the same constitutional position as members of the Fabian Society).

So when MacDonald left office in November 1924—still more mellow and responsible than when he entered and with a fair number of ex-Liberals neatly tailored into the Party Leadership—Baldwin and his friends could feel reasonably confident that the battle was over. The gamble of "educating Labour" had paid off. Although the mass appeal of the old bourgeois parties had been broken and the bulk of the industrial workforce now identified with its own class organisations, these now seemed to be effectively under right-wing control at every level: in parliament, the TUC and the constituencies. To the victorious Conservatives (who emerged from the November 1924 election with 410 seats) it must have appeared that there were no further obstacles to the final stage in post-war stabilisation: the return to gold. Indeed, this soon followed in April 1925.

It was only when it came to enforcing the economic consequences—"all workers in this country have got to take reductions in wages"—that the government discovered how weak the hold of the right-wing really was. As usual it was the coal-owners who began the attack—but this time the outcome was very different. The miners were able to get General Council backing and faced with the threat of a national sympathy strike, the government was caught unprepared. Its emergency preparations had not been up-dated. It was without adequate arrangements for transport or volunteers.[53] It bluffed for a few days, found its bluff called and finally on 31 July 1925 was forced into the humiliating course of granting the owners a nine month subsidy to maintain wages. For the labour movement this was Red Friday. For Baldwin it was disaster. Not only was the gold standard now in jeopardy but also the whole perspective of social control to which he himself was particularly committed. He found himself under attack from all sides. Churchill and Birkenhead—the disappointed advocates of anti-socialist coalition—now saw their chance to seize the initiative. For the Tory old guard, Lord Salisbury put in a long cabinet memorandum: "The precedent we are setting leads straight to nationalisation. I need not say that to a government pledged as we are, this conclusion is absolutely unacceptable. . . . Is there any ground on which, in our retreat, we could hope to make a stand; and if there be such ground, which I do not perceive, have we the strength to hold?. . . For good reason or bad we retreated because we did not venture to fight. We have not only thought it right to give way to force, but we have condoned the breaking of their contracts by the allied unions, and we have actually agreed to pay a large sum for the arrangement. Whatever our ultimate intentions, there is no doubt that this is how the Trade Unions themselves and the world regard the event. Who will believe us, after the experience of the last few days, when we say we will die in some ill-defined ditch rather than accept the nationalisation of the coal industry, the nationalisation of every other distressed industry? . . . the moral basis of the government seems to me to have dropped out."[54]

Why did this strange reverse take place? Why was it that the TUC stood firm against the government? Even now it remains one of the most puzzling developments of the post-war period. One common explanation is the change in the composition of the TUC General Council—which had indeed been quite considerable. J. H. Thomas had left to take office as a Labour Minister, the increasingly militant Bramley had become secretary and there had been a definite shift towards left-wingers like Swales (engineers), Purcell (furnishing trades) and Hicks (bricklayers). Such an explanation has the merit of emphasising the importance of just who controlled labour's class organisation—of how far it did, or did not, respond to the new framework of control being built up by the establishment. And undoubtedly the General Council's decision in April 1925 to set up a committee to liaise with the Russian trade unions caused the establishment acute distress. It would, claimed Dawson's *Times*, "cause irreparable injury to the Trade Unionism of the continent, which, though with difficulty, is maintaining a bulwark against the westward spread of communism among the workers".[55]

Yet while the change in leadership was important, any consideration of the individuals involved makes it quite clear that the shift would have been impossible without pressure from below. It is this that was the key factor, and a number of forces appear to have been at work. First of all, the steady erosion of wages and employment in aristocratic trades since 1920 was at last making itself felt in terms of a leftward shift in trade union organisation (especially among the miners, engineers and boilermakers). Secondly, the shortlived industrial recovery of 1923–4—plus the overseas demand for coal following the occupation of the Ruhr—had done much to restore the movement's local morale and halt the decline in membership. Thirdly, of course, there was the new offensive against wages brought about by the return to gold. But even these economic pressures are unlikely to have been enough had they not been given political force and coherence by a much higher level of organisational awareness on the left. In August 1924 the Communist Party and other left-wing forces had launched the National Minority

Movement. This body had the objective of campaigning for left-wing policies *inside* the trade unions. And with surprising speed it had managed to regroup what left-wing forces remained from the post-war offensive and mobilise them in formidable campaign for solidarity. The wider role of the NMM and the Communist Party is described elsewhere in this volume. But there can be no doubt that, as far as the government was concerned, it was the Communist Party which was seen as the real cause of their defeat in July 1925. Davidson wrote "we were at this time particularly worried about revolutionary activities in the country. In January 1924 the Communist International had thrown its full weight behind United Front tactics and was prepared to use them in the factories and trade unions, which were the natural link between the Communist Party and the workers . . . we were particularly worried by the strength of the Minority Movement in the mining industry and by the attempts to organise the unemployed . . . MacDonald's failure to act, and the mounting unemployment figures while the Labour Party had been in office, made for a growing disillusion in the Labour Movement that was dangerous. The TUC conference at Scarborough in 1925 seemed to show the growing influence of the movement. . . ."[56]

The story of how the government reacted is well enough known. Within five days of Red Friday plans were in hand for a complete overhaul of the government's emergency machinery.[57] Every ministry was instructed to make its own special preparations. Permanent headquarters were to be established in each of the regions into which the country was divided, and key civil servants seconded to a central headquarters in London. Directions were issued for a gradual expansion of the special constabulary to be ready by the winter. The navy was given responsibility for transporting supplies and, if necessary, troops.[58] Then, a bit on the side and apart from his official duties, the Home Secretary, Joynson-Hicks, took it upon himself to stimulate the formation of a private strike-breaking organisation, the Organisation for the Maintenance of Supplies. By the beginning of October he was able to tell the cabinet that the emergency organisation was virtually complete. The only remaining task was the recruitment of volunteers: "Up to the present no official arrangements had been made for recruiting the persons who carry out the various duties under the general organisation. Various unofficial organisations, however, had been formed for this purpose including the O.M.S., the Chambers of Commerce, the Fascisti and the Crusaders, and it is understood that the persons who volunteered under these unofficial organisations would, in case of emergency, be at the disposal of the government. . . ."[59]

At the same time the Home Secretary also gave details of the preparations made for "keeping under observation the activities and speeches of Communists in this country, with a view to such action as might be considered appropriate at the time . . ." Within two weeks twelve members of the Party's executive had been arrested, and were later convicted on charges that virtually rendered the party an illegal organisation.

Meanwhile the TUC had reverted to its old policy of masterly inaction (J. H. Thomas had returned to the General Council and Citrine had become secretary). Great hopes were pinned on the Royal Commission which the government had set up in September. Despite plain evidence of government preparations and constant warnings from the Left (each issue of the *Weekly Worker* underlined the diminishing period left till the subsidy ran out on 1 May), virtually no preparations were made. Even the very moderate proposals put forward by Citrine at the end of January were cold-shouldered by the General Council.[60] And not unnaturally—for its right-wing leaders had no intention of facing the government in a general strike. Preparations would be provocative. At most they expected a repeat of 1921: some last minute grovelling by Thomas and a face-saving formula taken from the Royal Commission. And in fact this is almost what happened. Two days after the May Day conferences of Union executives had voted strike powers to the General Council (already after the miners had been locked out and a few hours before the strike was due to begin) the Industrial Subcommittee conceded the principle of longer hours and lower wages in the mines.[61] Had the government wished to do so, it could have ended the strike before it even began. The miners would again have been left on their own, the movement divided and demoralised. But the cabinet was not interested. This time its emergency machinery was to be put into action.

What was the government really after? Certainly the miners had to be beaten. This was essential for economic reasons (both in terms of coal exports and industrial fuel costs) and also because it would open the way to a more general attack on wages. But as far as defeating a general strike was concerned, it was far more ambitious: to do by force what the government had previously failed to do by persuasion. The "conscious element"—the communists and the Left—were to be permanently excluded from the movement. The division between "constitutional" and "unconstitutional" trends had to be made absolute, and the right-wing then put in a position where it could demand a total repudiation of the latter. This was the significance both of the government's rejection of the peace offer and its subsequent propaganda campaign to present the strike as an attack on the constitution. The whole concept of solidarity action—the very minimum for any wider class concept of the labour movement—had to be firmly outlawed. On these terms anything short of unconditional surrender was unacceptable. To quote J. T. Murphy, what the government wanted was "to reduce the trade union movement to impotence as completely as they had rendered the Labour opposition in parliament".[62] This was its aim.

4. THE GENERAL STRIKE AND THE WORKING CLASS

In part, and unfortunately there can be no denying this, the government succeeded. After nine days the strike was called off on terms that allowed Baldwin to claim it as unconditional surrender. Still worse, during the course of the strike the government had managed to turn the debate from the miners to the constitution, and the TUC right-wingers, despite all their betrayals, were able to take the offensive against the Left. "Never again" became a by-word for the following generation. Under the 1927 Trades Disputes Act general strikes and most sympathy strikes became illegal. Trade union membership fell by half a million. And parallel to the harassment and victimisation of the Left by the government and employers, bans and proscriptions were launched in individual trade unions. In almost every union right-wing dominance was ensured for the following decade—with all that this meant in terms of neutralising the mass organisations of the working class in a period of acute economic crisis. To this extent the outcome of the strike was a victory for the government and a serious setback for the working class.

Yet at another level the general strike was also an epic victory for the working class—and one which can be said to have changed the course of history.

Contrary to all expectations—at any rate of the government and the TUC—the strike was totally solid. We still lack enough detailed local studies and are woefully short of material that would permit us to compare the regional intensity of the strike. (Indeed, we are likely to remain so until the opening of the vast archive of government files containing the details of arrests, troop dispositions and local police activities.)[63] Yet on the basis of the TUC's own (very good) local reports and the cabinet's daily intelligence bulletin one thing is plain.[64] Almost everywhere the strike was complete and growing in effectiveness as time went on. And this is remarkable. The government had expected some militant action—but localised, in pockets and largely restricted to depressed trades. Elsewhere, in the transport and service industries and the relatively prosperous south, support was expected to be lukewarm and shortlived. Indeed, this was probably also the expectation of Bevin and may explain his otherwise inexplicable insistence (in face of strong opposition of the General Council) that only the transport and general unions should come out immediately and the heavy industry trades be kept back as a "second wave".[65] Such a sequence could be expected to give the right-wing general unions time to consolidate their hold on local organisation before the more militant sectors entered the battle. Yet despite this, despite the almost total lack of official preparations and subsequent instructions that were conspicuously unhelpful (like that to black only "industrial" electricity), the strike was solid. Furthermore, it quickly took on militant class-mobilisation characteristics—so much so that the government found that its own meticulous preparations were breaking down. In the run up to the strike the government had significantly increased the size of the special constabulary, accumulated a home army five times the size of that available in 1921 and positioned a good part of the navy round the coast (Figure 7). Yet on the fourth day of the strike the cabinet had to be told that the use of mass pickets and a shortage of police was seriously hampering the movement of supplies. Certainly this was no incipient revolution. But the situation was sufficiently grave for the cabinet to decide on steps which it had previously resisted: the mobilisation of the Territorial Army into a specially created Civil Constabulary Reserve and a much more open show of military force.[67]

Equally among the TUC leadership the success of the strike was both unexpected and acutely worrying. As the leader of one general union put it, "every day the strike proceeded the control of the conduct of the strike was passing from the hands of the responsible executives into the hands of men who had no authority, no control and no responsibility and was wrecking the movement from one end to the other".[68] Reactions like this made the TUC leadership an easy prey to the government and seem to have been a major factor in inducing the General Council to end the strike so quickly and above all before the "second wave" could be brought into action. Had this happened and the strike continued for another week, it seemed likely that fundamental social changes would have occurred in several parts of the country. However the key thing—and what needs explanation—is not what

Figure 7 Military dispositions April–May 1926[66]

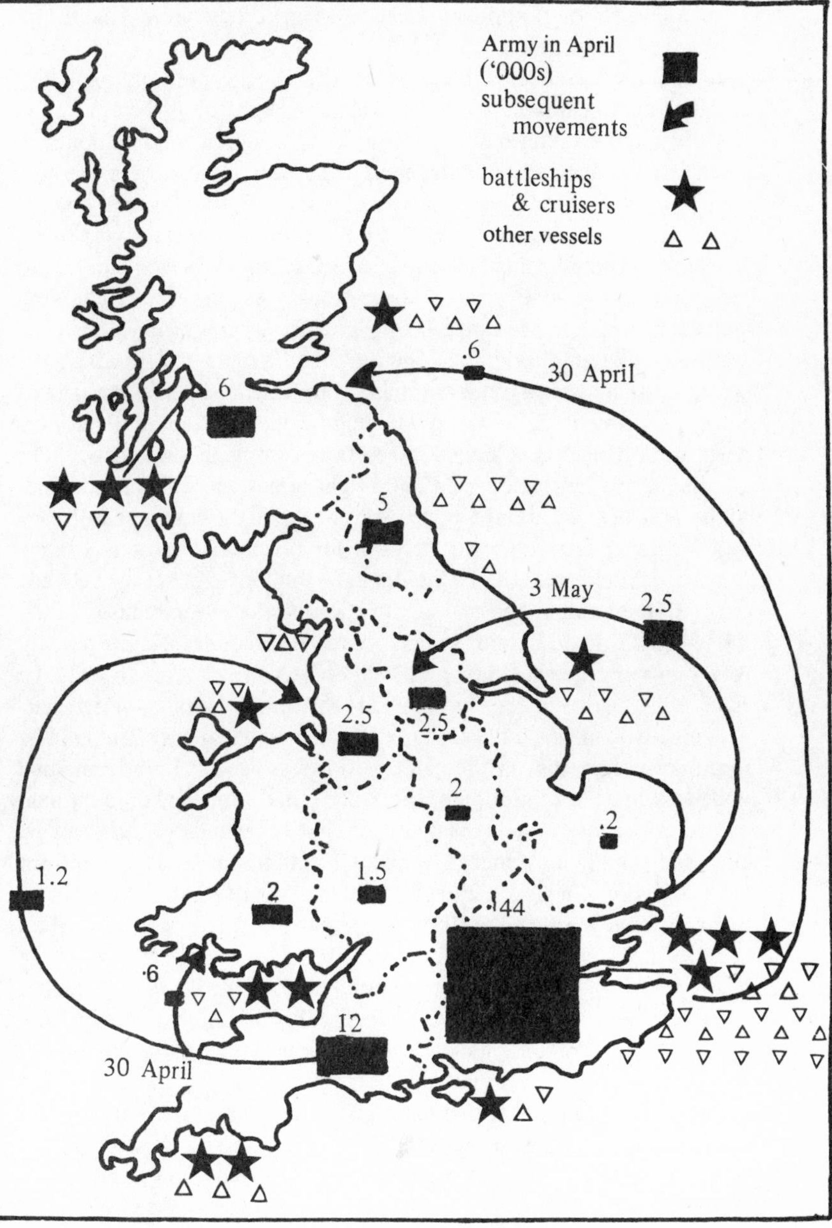

failed to happen but what *did* happen: why all sections responded so well and not just those trades under similar pressures to the miners; why great areas of south and east London seem to have been among the most militant and best organised.[69]

It could, of course, simply reflect the effectiveness of the Left's campaign in the months up to the strike: the clarity and relevance of its slogans and the strength of its industrial organisation. And no doubt to some extent it does. But it is also tempting to suggest that there was also something more fundamental at work: that the fabric of social control had itself partly given way. For although the new system was being developed with sophistication and speed, it was still critically incomplete, still dangerously precarious. As yet the right-wing leadership had not been placed in a position where it could make an automatic response to "public opinion". There remained massive gaps between the language of the organised movement and the language of the establishment. It was only six years since the Labour Party had itself sanctioned the Council of Action campaign on Russia. The administrative separation of left and right trends was only months old. In the Trades and Labour Councils up and down the country the theory and practice learnt in the struggles of the previous decade must have seemed far more real than MacDonald's dubious distinction between constitutional and unconstitutional action. As had been realised at the time of Red Friday, Labour's mass organisation could still quite quickly revert into an engine of class mobilisation. Admittedly even in 1925 the right wing was still well-entrenched and the General Council left-wingers by no means totally reliable. But the sequel to this should not be forgotten either: that in the run up to the strike the Right remained under acute organisational pressure, had to make continual compromises and was repeatedly unable to exclude class struggle slogans from the movement's public declarations. Indeed, had this not been so, the General Council would certainly have surrendered unconditionally before the strike had begun. To this extent the strike's success does seem to reflect both the nature and the *stage of development* of the new system of control: first, the degree to which it relied almost exclusively on the manipulation of organisation and hardly at all on concrete social divisions within the working population; and second, the fact that the largely ideological basis for this manipulation was still at this stage critically incomplete, had not had time to penetrate down into the movement as a whole. Consequently as soon as Labour's national organisations were set in the direction of class mobilisation (or at least no longer impeded it) it was still comparatively easy to draw on existing local traditions of class solidarity and action.

At any rate the government emerged from the experience considerably chastened. Suddenly the ice was found to be much thinner than originally thought. Lord Salisbury's Red Friday memorandum has already been quoted. Six days after the ending of the strike he wrote another which is worth quoting at length. Denying that any legislative ban on general strikes could solve the crisis, he went on: "the causes lie deeper . . . I am convinced that the root of the matter is in the status of the worker and if the situation is not to grow worse it is to this status that a remedy must be applied. In fact there is no hope whether we look at the past, present or future that in this respect the present system can continue. I will not dwell on the familiar history of industrial suspicion and its distastrous effect. . . . [It] is not only widespread but has gradually grown in power, if not intensity, and has now developed into a settled determination to have a change. And this determination to secure a change has since the war assumed a dangerous and therefore urgent character. Up to that date the workers sought their ends in parliament. . . . It is, however, clear that they are beginning to lose faith in that road to relief. The favourite method is now direct action, which is, in its logical development, revolution. . . . Unless Government and Parliament bestir themselves the change of method may become stereotyped: revolution may become a conviction. The worst of it is that unconstitutional pressure and direct action have been proved to be effective and the present triumph of the forces of order is an exception. . . . If we look at the attitude of the workers and at their intentions—no doubt largely subconscious but none the less formidable for that reason—the situation is essentially unstable. [The worker] is no longer content to be merely a hired machine of somebody else to do somebody else's work for so much an hour or so much a week and have no more to do with it. And he will be told, and will partly believe, that if the means of production are nationalised the work will be the Nation's work and therefore as he is part of the Nation his own work. It is this sense of ownership—the most powerful in human nature next to the sense of life itself—that will be appealed to and the only way of counteracting the attraction of nationalisation is by an appeal to the same motive."[70]

Somewhat tamely perhaps after this opening Salisbury went on to demand legislative action to make co-partnership mandatory on all firms. But general cabinet reactions were not all that different. Before the strike had ended Robert Cecil (Salisbury's brother), Amery and Percy had all privately warned of the dangers involved in any further reduction in living standards. As soon as the strike was over, Baldwin found it necessary to make his public declaration that there would be no general reduction in wages, while Churchill spent much of the summer trying to get the coal-owners to settle on more reasonable terms.

On this front, therefore, the strike does seem to have compelled a change of line. In order to carry forward its social control strategy, the government was compelled to sacrifice a number of its economic aims. The drive for "wage flexibility", considered so essential by the Bank of England, had to be suspended. To have gone forward and challenged the other export oriented trades in the same way as coal would have made it virtually impossible to consolidate the ideological position of the Right. For the moment the issue had to be the constitution not wages. So while the general strike may not have been the only factor contributing to the eventual breakdown of the gold standard, it certainly played its part.

Finally, then, to sum up. This essay has tried to do three things. First, show how the general strike *made* history. The strike took place in the context, and to some extent as a result, of the post-1914 crisis of British imperialism. The attack on the miners was part of a general drive to reduce wages, to force all workers to bear the costs of British banking hegemony. As we have seen, the strike did much to halt this process, prevent the stabilisation of British imperialism in its old form, and was to this extent a victory.

Second, there was the problem of mass consciousness and social control—the question of how far the strike was itself part of the process by which ruling class hegemony was re-established. Plainly, the argument here is that was indeed the strike's function, and that it succeeded. At a time of intense legal harassment for the left (there were up to 9,000 arrests before the end of the emergency), the right wing was enabled to polarise debate around the constitution and make use of the defeat they themselves engineered to isolate their opponents.[71]

But how is one to characterise the overall result? One might point to the general unions (or maybe the employed as against the unemployed) as the new "aristocracy". One could perhaps identify the new "bribe" as the decision not to reduce wage levels further—ultimately, after 1931, involving a much more explicitly empire-based economic policy. But to do so (at least without qualifications) would be to foist on the 1920s and

'30s a purely mechanical concept of the labour aristocracy, not to see it in its development and growth. It would seem that in the twenties we are faced with an altogether new *type* of control: that the previous manipulation of labour organisation had so expanded as to take on an altogether new character. It is very difficult to express it precisely. It was in certain ways so subtle as to be almost imperceptible. It incorporated and sanctioned Labour's emergence as a political force; flattered its legitimate pride in governmental action. Yet it was also (to use Baldwin's own, very apt, description) a process of "education": a leading forward within particular set limits and under the threat of very definite punishments and sanctions. A nationally orchestrated "climate of opinion" was set up. The right wing was then forced into positions where it was compelled to reiterate at least parts of this wider ideology, give it credence within its own "Labour" channels of information. Nor can there be any doubt that as a system of control it was very effective. It is significant that the only areas of Britain to see any large-scale development of socialist consciousness in the decade after the strike were those in which the right did not dominate trade union organisation in this way (Fife and parts of South Wales).

However, having said this, we are still left with the problem of ideological *content*: of what particular establishment ideas could be taken over and absorbed. Plainly there were limits—as Ramsay MacDonald found in 1931. The "Labour constitutionalism" that developed after 1926 was by no means as empty as MacDonald's rhetoric. For Labour Party members at local level it contained an intensely held belief that "justice" could somehow be secured through parliament—a justice, moreover, that was concretely expressed in terms of jobs, the means test, unemployment benefit. Plainly, too, although the communists might have been temporarily isolated, they were still present, and the struggles they waged over many issues did limit the scope for right-wing ideology. However, the precise effects of this and the nature of the new labour ideology will be examined in detail in a later chapter.

Lastly, the third—but not least important—aim of this chapter has been to provide a context for what happened during the strike itself: for the immensely rich and varied experiences of class action, solidarity and power which are described in the rest of this volume. Even though this experience was short-lived, nothing could be more foolish than to dismiss as some kind of historical freak—untypical and accidental—and not see it as a specific product of the class forms evolved by the British working class movement over the previous century. Naturally, the Councils of Action and Strike Committees of 1926 were no simple repeat of the class forms of the 1830s. But a continuity was there. Embodied within Labour's class institutions (particularly perhaps in the trades councils) there had long existed embryo forms: starting to reveal themselves in the trades councils during the war, again potentially in the Councils of Action of 1920–1, and finally but not completely in 1926. Similarly for the years that have followed. Much has clearly changed. New forms of struggle have been developed; new types of manipulation and control imposed. But the relevance of what was done in 1926 still remains. Concretely and locally, in towns and villages, working people had started to organise themselves as an alternative power to the capitalist state. They only started. And they were defeated. At a national level, within Labour's institutions, the Right was too strong and the Marxist Left too weak. Yet sooner or later, once these lessons have been learnt, this basic experience will have to be drawn on again.

NOTES

1. Lenin notes Britain's special characteristics in his *Imperialism*: its lack of tariffs and the consequent slow and incomplete development of monopoly before 1914; the paradox of the country's capital wealth and its decaying industry (*Collected Works*, vol. 22, p. 300). More recent material on Britain's capital export can be found in B. Thomas, "International Capital Movements" and M. Simon, "Foreign Investment, 1865–1944" in *Capital Movements and Economic Development*, ed. J. Adler (London, 1967). A. Ford usefully re-examines Imlah's figures for capital export in *Yorkshire Bulletin*, 1965. M. Dobb, *Studies in the Development of Capitalism* (London, 1946) remains indispensable as a general guide to the development of monopoly capitalism.
2. H. Clay, *Lord Norman* (London, 1957), provides the best inside account; S. Pollard, *The Development of the British Economy, 1914–67* (1969 edition), makes an informed analysis.
3. S. Howson, "The Origins of Dear Money, 1920", *Economic History Review*, February 1974. T. Jones, *Whitehall Diaries* (Oxford, 1969), I, pp. 77 ff. W. Reader, *Imperial Chemical Industries* (Oxford, 1970) and C. Wilson, *Unilever*, II (London, 1954), provide examples of monopolies rapidly diversifying after the war.
4. R. Middlemas, *Baldwin* (London, 1969), chapter 10, gives this explanation.

5. D. Moggridge, *The Return to Gold, 1925* (Cambridge, 1969), shows the strength of United States pressure in the winter of 1924–5 and the disquiet this caused even the Treasury and Bank of England.
6. B. Mitchell, *Abstract of British Historical Statistics* (Cambridge, 1962), p. 351 for percentage increase in weekly wages between 1914 and 1924 (taken from A. Bowley, *Wages and Income*); p. 478 for the Board of Trade retail price index for 1914 and 1924.
7. B. Mitchell, *Abstract*, p. 252 (from A. Chapman, *Wages and Salaries*).
8. B. Mitchell, *Abstract*, p. 67 (average of unemployed insured workers for January and July, *Ministry of Labour Gazette*).
9. 1931 Census. Obviously it would have been more useful if it had been possible to distinguish depressed metal trades (especially iron, steel and shipbuilding) from other sectors in the industry.
10. *British Labour Statistics: historical abstract* (HMSO, 1971), p. 307 for numbers registered as unemployed by region (average January, February and March 1926) as percentage of total occupied taken from 1931 census. The figures are therefore only approximate. The *Ministry of Labour Gazette* provides no base figure of its own and its regions are somewhat different from those adopted in the 1931 census (Lincolnshire and Huntingdonshire, for instance, have been moved from East Region to the Midlands).
11. The figures come from L. Hannah, "Managerial Innovation and the Rise of the Large-scale Company in Inter-war Britain", *Economic History Review*, May 1974. Some of the biggest monopoly firms, notably Imperial Chemical Industries, did pursue policies radically at variance with City of London orthodoxy—but, as the failure of the Mond–Turner discussions in 1928 revealed, their industrial base was still comparatively narrow. It is only in the 1930s that decisively new alignments seem to emerge.
12. Lenin, *British Labour and British Imperialism* (London, 1969), p. 75.
13. E. Hobsbawm, "Lenin and the Aristocracy of Labour", *Marxism Today*, July 1970, provides a detailed guide to Lenin's use of the term, while "The Labour Aristocracy in 19th Century Britain", *Labouring Men* (London, 1964), makes some concrete analyses. A valuable discussion of associated political activity can be found in R. Harrison, *Before the Socialists* (London, 1965). I. Prothero, "William Benbow and the Concept of the General Strike", *Past and Present*, May 1974, provides a useful contrasting analysis of pre-existing forms of class action.
14. P. Thompson, *Socialists, Liberals and Labour* (London, 1967), and G. Stedman Jones, *Outcast London* (Oxford, 1972), more or less cover London, although useful additional material can be found in J. Shipley, *Club Life and Socialism* (History Workshop, 1971), and G. Cronjé, "Middle Class Opinion and the 1889 Dock Strike", *Our History*, 61, Winter, 1975.
15. Hobsbawm, "General Labour Unions" in *Labouring Men* is the classic

study and its analysis is largely borne out by J. Lovell, *Stevedores and Dockers* (London, 1968), and R. Hyman, *The Workers Union* (Oxford, 1971).

16. J. Harris, *Unemployment and Politics* (Oxford, 1972), shows the unemployment agitation of the late '80s and early '90s to have played a significant role in stimulating reformist action within both bourgeois parties.
17. The linking of the Fabians and Liberal Imperialists was originally made by B. Semmel, *Imperialism and Social Reform* (London, 1960), and is borne out in detail by C. Searle, *The Quest for National Efficiency* (Oxford, 1971).
18. J. Jeffreys, *The Engineers* (London, 1947), and E. Wigham, *The Power to Manage* (London, 1973).
19. R. Holton, "Syndicalism and Labour on Merseyside, 1910–1914", *Building the Union*, ed. Hikins (Liverpool, 1973).
20. Examinations of the right wing's base in mining have been made (from different standpoints) by R. Page Arnot, *Miners: the Years of Struggle* (London, 1949), and *The Scottish Miners* (London, 1955), who stresses the sliding scale; J. Williams, *The Derbyshire Miners* (London, 1962), on hewers' pay differentials; W. Garside, *The Durham Miners Association* (London, 1971), on the shift differential in the north-east; R. Challinor, "Alexander MacDonald and the Miners", *Our History*, 48, on checkweighmen; A. Campbell, "Lanarkshire Mining Communities", *Bulletin of the Society for the Study of Labour History*, Spring, 1974, who examines ethnic and cultural factors; and L. Williams, "The Road to Tonypandy", *Llafur*, 1973, who emphasises the privileged position of the hewer and its subsequent erosion. R. Gregory, *The Miners and British Politics* (Oxford, 1968), provides a useful, if limited, survey of miners' politics before 1914.
21. J. Mitchell, *Robert Tressell and the Ragged-Trousered Philanthropists* (London, 1969).
22. A. Williams, *Life in a Railway Factory* (David and Charles, reprint 1969). R. Roberts, *The Classic Slum* (Manchester, 1971).
23. Roberts, *Slum*, pp. 33 and 193.
24. J. Hinton, *The First Shopstewards Movement* (London, 1973). Despite a tendency to treat the shop stewards' movement in isolation this study provides a pioneering analysis of its social base and development.
25. Here I. McLean, "The Working Class Movement on Clydeside, 1914–22", Oxford D.Phil., 1972, provides a useful supplement to Hinton.
26. Between 1914 and 1920 the Worker's Union membership rose from 114,000 to 500,000 (Hyman, *Workers' Union*).
27. J. Corbett, *Birmingham Trades Council* (London, 1966).
28. The usual figure of 350 seems based on a guess first made in the draft "Report of the Council of Action August to October 1920" (Labour Party

Library, CA. ADM. 29, i–xi). The typed draft originally contained a blank later completed in ink as "about 350". The records themselves show documentary evidence of only 288 (CA. CON. and CA. GEN. files).

29. Lenin, *Collected Works*, vol. 29, p. 502.
30. "Left-wing" Councils are all those in correspondence with the National Council of Action demanding an extension of the Council's activities to cover Ireland, unemployment and to force trade with Russia and (in November) for a Convention of local councils. Many of these resolutions were in response to a circularisation of all Councils undertaken by the leading left-wing Councils, Birmingham and the North-East District Council of Action, and a positive response is a fair indication of the balance of forces on a particular council. "Right-wing" are all those Councils known to exist but not backing the left-wing resolutions. Labour Party Library: CA. CON. and CA. GEN. files.
31. Lenin, "Left-Wing Communism", *Collected Works*, vol. 31, p. 54.
32. T. Jones, *Whitehall Diaries* (Oxford, 1969), I, p. 80.
33. B. Gilbert, *British Social Policy, 1914–39*, p. 35 quoting Lord Swinton.
34. Jones, *Diaries*, I, p. 101. M. Cowling, *Impact of Labour* (Cambridge, 1971), examines the factions within the Coalition.
35. J. Wrench, *Geoffrey Dawson* (London, 1955), p. 159.
36. Jones, *Diaries*, I, pp. 146–7 and 153.
37. Ibid., p.148.
38. Report enclosed in a letter from S. Walton (who was responsible for this work) to A. Steel-Maitland, 17 June 1926 (Scottish Record Office, GD. 193/109/5). According to Walsh, the scheme was initiated by the cabinet (originally to be under the auspices of the Ministry of Labour), but was almost immediately converted into an ostensibly private organisation. However, very similar practices are reported by Lloyd-Graeme in the Cabinet discussion, 7 April 1921 (Jones, *Diaries*, I, p. 139).
39. Cabinet decision, 7 February 1919 (PRO. CAB. 23/9).
40. As reported by James Hope, Middlemas, *Baldwin*, p. 252.
41. R. Page Arnot, *Scottish Miners*, makes the 1921 lockout the turning point in Fife. In Durham it apparently came a year or so later and was more linked to unemployment: Garside, *Durham Miners*.
42. J. McLean, "Lanarkshire in the 1926 General Strike", Strathclyde BA dissertation, 1975.
43. Notably Poplar in London and the Vale of Leven in Scotland.
44. I. McLean, "Clydeside, 1914–22", sees the post-war housing campaign as crucial in expanding (and politically diluting) the area base of the Labour Party.
45. McLean finds this development in Glasgow and W. Walker in Dundee ("Dundee's Disenchantment with Churchill", *Scottish Historical Review*, 1970).
46. R. James. *Davidson's Memoirs* (London, 1969), p. 141.

47. Cowling, *Impact of Labour*, p. 341.
48. R. James, *Davidson*, p. 189.
49. Wrench, *Dawson*, p. 224.
50. Cowling, *Impact*, p. 368.
51. R. Desmarais, "Strike Breaking and the Labour Government", *Journal of Contemporary History*, 1973. PRO. CAB. 27/259 EC. 24.
52. Middlemas, *Baldwin*, p. 268.
53. The Cabinet minute for 30 July 1925 (CAB. 23/50) makes it clear that lack of anti-strike preparations was the principal factor.
54. CP. 383 CAB. 24/174.
55. Quoted J. Klugmann, *History of the Communist Party*, II, p. 19.
56. James, *Davidson*, pp. 227–8.
57. 5 August 1925, Cabinet minute (CAB. 23/50) and CP. 390, pp. 542–86, CAB. 24/174, with covering note by Joynson-Hicks dated 6 August 1925 for detailed proposals.
58. There is no direct evidence showing Hicks to be organiser of the OMS but Cabinet discussion makes it clear enough that he was seen as the effective originator of the organisation. In particular, see the highly critical cabinet paper from Steel-Maitland, CP. 462, 6 November 1925, CAB. 24/175.
59. 7 October 1925, CAB. 23/51 (CP. 416).
60. W. Citrine, *Men and Work* (London, 1964), p. 145.
61. J. Murphy, *The Political Meaning of the General Strike* (CPGB, 1926), shows this convincingly enough and the opening of Cabinet records provides full confirmation.
62. Same, p. 47.
63. These are the closed files registered in PRO. HO. 46/247 and 252 and cover all the detailed Home Office plans for emergency preparations, local police reports, and interdepartmental correspondence on all matters pertaining to left-wing and communist politics. For 1925 there are around 700 entries; for 1926 somewhat more. It says a good deal for the establishment's order of priorities that these files are still closed while those covering the war with Germany are open to 1945.
64. The TUC reports are in the TUC Library (HD. 5366) and the Cabinet bulletins PRO. CAB. 27/331, 332. Among existing regional studies the most outstanding is A. Mason, *The General Strike in the North East* (Hull, 1970).
65. Citrine, *Men and Work*, p. 179.
66. Disposition of the fleet at end of the strike, 16 May 1929: PRO. ADM. 1/8697. This gives emergency duties. For the army the relevant file on troop dispositions during the strike is closed (HO. 46/252, 17 May 1926: 449000/88) but WO. 73/123 provides regimental strengths for April 1926 by barracks and the absolute number of troops did not significantly change in the interim. The main subsequent movements (shown in the figure) are recorded in CAB. 27/260 for 27 April and 1 May.

67. On Friday, 7 May 1926, there were two cabinet meetings to discuss the situation (CAB. 23/52). The detiled discussions in the Supply and Transport Committee (CAB. 27/260, 5, 6 and 7 May) are even more revealing.
68. C. Dukes in 1926 TUC Annual Congress Report.
69. This comes through both the TUC and Cabinet reports. The mass picket on the Thameshaven petrol depot was one of the most effective in the country.
70. Cabinet Paper 207, dated 18 May 1926 (CAB. 24/180) and papers from Amery, R. Cecil and Percy in CAB. 24/179.
71. The Criminal Statistics for 1928 put the total arrests for the entire 1926 emergency at just under 8,000 for England and Wales. Including Scotland the number must be well in excess of 9,000.

2 MARXISM, REFORMISM AND THE GENERAL STRIKE

by JAMES KLUGMANN

1. FROM RED FRIDAY TO THE EVE OF THE STRIKE

When the first Labour Government fell and, in November 1924, the Tories resumed office, the stage was set for the offensive against the conditions of the British working class. Economic crisis was to be translated into political attack. Capitalism's problems were to be solved, at least in part, at the expense of the workers.

The *Workers' Weekly*, the Communist journal, was soon sounding the alarm: "It should be apparent to even the meanest intelligence that the employing class is preparing a devastating offensive against the Labour movement," it declared on 21 November 1924. "The wage offensive is likely to be accompanied by an attack on the Labour movement itself." But what was apparent to the *Workers' Weekly* was not so apparent to all the workers, still less to some of their leaders. "Will the 'left' awake?" was the title of an article by J. R. Campbell in the first 1925 issue of *Workers' Weekly*. The New Year, he wrote, would be a stormy one. But while the employers were preparing "quietly and determinedly", the workers, while putting new demands to the Union Executives, were "not preparing the machinery for action at all". They were leaving it all to their leaders. Could they afford, he asked, to do that?

After the fall of the Labour Government militant trends were clearly evident in the unions. In the Miners' Federation A. J. Cook replaced Frank Hodges. In the General Council of the TUC a number of leaders were talking "left" on various issues. And now that members of the Communist Party were being step by step excluded from the Labour Party, it was in the unions that their militancy was most felt either as active trade union members or through the medium of the National Minority Movement, founded in August 1924 on Communist initiative.

From its first formation the NMM made it very clear that it was not set up in opposition to the existing trade unions. It aimed at strengthening them by giving them a fighting capacity of which they were being robbed by the right wing. In the resolutions of the first NMM Conference, at which some 200,000 workers were represented, great emphasis was put on the formation of factory committees and the revival of trades councils,[1] but not only on revival. The aim was to make the trades councils "the leading local organs of the class struggle".

The Unity Conference of the NMM, held at the end of January 1925, was on a larger scale.[2] It represented some 600,000 workers. Its leading speakers included men like Tom Mann, Harry Pollitt, Arthur Horner and George Hardy, and the central and recurring theme of them all was warning of the coming employers' offensive. The call for vigilance and preparedness was summed up in the welcoming message to the delegates from Miners' Secretary A. J. Cook: "We are in danger. A united enemy is knocking at the gate. . . . My slogan is—Be prepared." It was no accident that the miners were amongst the most clear-sighted about the impending offensive. British capitalism had long learned the art of taking on its opponents one by one, starting with the most dangerous—in this case the miners.

Throughout the first six months of 1925 warning succeeded warning from miners, Minority Movement, Communist Party. Warning and preparation were central themes at the Seventh Congress of the CPGB held in the St. Mungo Hall, Glasgow, at the end of May 1925, where a militant young communist miner from South Wales—Arthur Horner—called on the delegates "to stand by the miners in whatever struggles their conditions drove them into".[3]

July 1925 was to be the month of decision. On 30 June the coalowners gave notice to terminate the existing Agreement with the miners, which was to run for the month of July and end at midnight, 31 July. On 1 July the owners' organisation, the Mining Association of Great Britain, put forward proposals for a fresh Agreement, with immediate wage reductions and the end of the guaranteed minimum wage. Rejection by the Miners' Executive on 2 July was unanimously endorsed at a special delegate Conference on the following day. On 9 July the miners put their case before the General Council of the TUC, who appointed a "Committee of Nine" to "maintain continuous contact with the negotiations now taking place". With militants much in evidence, the miners actively campaigning, NMM and communists working to capacity, key sectors of industry signified their support.

Complex negotiations at every level—with coalowners, government, cabinet, Prime Minister—were held against a background of growing mass activity. On 30 July a special Conference of Trade Union Executives ratified an embargo on the movement of coal in the event of a stoppage, agreed by the Committee of Nine and the General Council. For the moment the working-class front was solid. And the effect was instant. The cabinet was recalled, and early on 31 July the government agreed to offer a 9-month subsidy in return for which the owners were to withdraw their notices while an enquiry was carried out by a Royal Commission. At 4 p.m. a terse telegram was despatched to District Miners' Federations: "Notices suspended—work as usual—Cook, Secretary". The *Daily Herald* well named the day "Red Friday."

The General Council rejoiced in a letter to all affiliated unions and all trades councils: "The manifestation of solidarity which had been exhibited by all sections of the trade union movement is a striking portent for the future and marks an epoch in the history of the movement." True enough! This was a lesson of what real trade union unity, above and below, backed up by the mass of the working class and by readiness to act, could achieve. But it was not all the lesson. For British capitalism, with its great experience and capacity to manœuvre, had long studied the tactics of temporary retreat. It was a master of division. It knew its opponents' weaknesses as well as their strength.

In the first days of August 1925 the shouting headlines of the Tory press conveyed the anger of the ruling class.

The Home Secretary—"Jix" (Sir William Joynson Hicks)—chanted a traditional Tory war song: "He said that to them, coming straight from Cabinet Councils, the thing was not finished. The danger was not over. Sooner or later this question has got to be fought out by the people of the land. Was England to be governed by Parliament and by the Cabinet or by a handful of Trade Union Leaders?"[4]

The Chancellor of the Exchequer, Winston Churchill, made clear to the House of Commons what would be the role of the State in the coming struggles: "In the event of a struggle, whatever its character might be, however ugly the episodes which would mark it, I have no doubt that the State, the national State, would emerge victorious in spite of all the rough and awkward corners it might have to turn. . . . As the struggle widened, as it became a test whether the country was to be ruled by Parliament or by some other organisation not responsible by our elective processes to the people as a whole—as that issue emerged more and more, and with every increase in the gravity of the struggle, new sources of strength would have to come to the State, or some action, which in ordinary circumstances we should consider quite impossible, would, just as in the case of the Great War, be taken with general assent and as a matter of course."[5]

And such direct threats of force were accompanied by careful preparations for dividing and disarming those whose unity had for the moment prevailed. There were different trends in the ruling class, but all were agreed that the time gained by the temporary retreat must be used to prepare the next round.

In contrast to the basic unity of the capitalists there emerged the utter disunity of the working class.

Ramsay MacDonald, classic right-wing reformist, was angry and scared at the challenge of militant trade union action to reformist methods and reformist beliefs. If some hard-headed (and short-sighted) Tories had railed at Baldwin's "retreat", MacDonald, too, felt betrayed. The government, he lamented at the ILP Summer School, "has simply handed over the appearance, at any rate, of victory, to the very forces that some well-considered thoroughly well-examined socialist feels to be probably the greatest enemy. . . . If the government had fought their policy out, we would have respected it. It just suddenly doubled up. . . . "The consequence has been to increase the power and the prestige of those who do not believe in political action."[6]

Many socialists within the Independent Labour Party and on the left of the Labour Party, socialists of the heart, "sentimental socialists" (an important trend within the British labour movement which plays the role of something like a centre-grouping and deserves careful analysis), expressed their joy at the Red Friday victory, wrote of the "triumph of right and justice", but did not (and could not) analyse the deeper movements beneath the surface of events. They could not see that the victory was one of struggle, unity, mobilisation, organisation, and that the point was not just to rejoice at victory but to prepare for the struggles ahead.

It was the militants in the Labour and trade union movement, above all the miners, and most articulate of all, the communists, who saw that Red Friday—victory indeed—was but a temporary Tory retreat to prepare a further offensive, and that the most essential lesson for the working class was *to prepare*. "This is the first round . . . let us prepare for the final struggle," declared A. J. Cook.[7] "It is only an armistice," warned the Miners' Chairman, Herbert Smith.[8]

The *Workers' Weekly* editorial in the issue that followed Red Friday called for "vigilance". "Behind this truce, and the industrial peace talk which will accompany it, the capitalist class will prepare for a crushing attack upon the workers. If the workers are duped by the peace talk and do not make effective counter-preparations then they are doomed to shattering defeat. . . . The Government . . . will endeavour to break the united front of the workers to make its attack successful."

The government's first line of attack was to strengthen directly and indirectly the machinery of State. Red Friday was hardly over before the OMS was established (the "Organisation for the Maintenance of Supplies", in theory private and voluntary, but destined to be incorporated at the time of crisis with the State apparatus). There followed, in September, the government's division of England and Wales into ten areas each with its own intricate network of officers and committees, and with extended powers under the Emergency Powers Act. Little pretence was made at this time that the purpose was anything else than to prepare a "showdown with Labour", and plans to set up such machinery had been secretly laid much earlier.

But the right-wing Labour leadership continued to maintain its theory of State neutrality, and to remain silent. It was a special merit of the British Marxists in the months from Red Friday to the eve of the General Strike that in the *Workers' Weekly*, *Sunday Worker*, *Communist Review* and *Labour Monthly* there was a continuous effort to explain in general terms the class role of the British State and, more specifically, the class nature of successive steps to extend State powers.[9]

In August 1925, the Communist Party wrote to the Executive Committee of the Labour Party and to the General Council of the TUC warning that the government was preparing to use the armed forces against the workers and suggesting that the workers' side of the case should be put by the Labour Party and TUC to the members of the Army and Navy[10]—a proposal described by J. R. Clynes as a "hysterical demand for a campaign of sedition and disaffection among the soldiers and sailors".[11]

Preparations for the coming struggle by the leaders of the Labour Party and TUC were as vague and ineffective as those of the government were precise and ruthless. Their approach was aptly described by Professor Wilfrid Crook, American historian of the General Strike, as a "studied attitude of unpreparedness". At the inquest on the General Strike held by the TUC, J. H. Thomas explained that it had been impossible to prepare "deliberately and calculatedly" because "the other side would anticipate every move".[12] Three days before the strike was due to begin (1 May 1926) Ernest Bevin acknowledged that no real preparations for it had been made before 29 April 1926.[13]

In what could very roughly be called the centre (particularly within the ILP) many individual socialists had a real sense of impending struggle, but failed to make a collective call to prepare for it. It was left to the miners, to individual militants in different sections of the Labour movement, and above all to the small Communist Party and organisations it influenced like the NMM and the National Unemployed Workers' Committee Movement (NUWCM), to call continuously for vigilance and preparation for struggle, and to put forward practical proposals on how effectively to prepare. The *Workers' Weekly* carried a regular weekly warning, set in a frame, indicating how many weeks remained. On 28 August, for instance:

> 34 WEEKS TO GO
>
> Thirty-four weeks to go to what? To the termination of the mining agreement and the opening of the greatest struggle in the history of the British Working Class.
>
> WE MUST PREPARE FOR THE STRUGGLE

Preparedness was the central message of the Second Conference of the NMM held at Battersea Town Hall on 29–30 August 1925,[14] with Tom Mann in the chair and with 638 delegates representing around 750,000 workers. The two main Conference slogans were: "Prepare for the coming fight". "Solidarity Spells Success". Tom Mann's Presidential Address was built around a call for vigilance. Yes, Red Friday had been a victory of solidarity. But "still we have to ask ourselves: are we prepared to meet the opposing forces when the next round begins?" He stressed the role of trades councils, called for Councils of Action, emphasised the importance of winning the unemployed to the struggle and, therefore, of the NUWCM, and called for vigilance towards incipient fascist and other anti-Labour organisations.

The Conference adopted organisational proposals and endorsed previous proposals for the formation of workshop committees, and reorganisation of trades councils "to make them become local unifying centres of the working-class movement in every locality. It further called for the affiliation of NUWCM and Trades Councils to the TUC, and for the development of a strong General Council of the TUC 'with full powers to direct the whole activities of the unions and under obligation to the TUC to use that power to fight more effectively the battles of the workers'."

The slogan on the General Council should be considered with care. Clearly in this context the "full powers to direct the whole activities of the unions" were demanded only for a General Council "under obligation to the T.U.C. to use that power to fight effectively the battles of the workers".

At that time of the Conference communists and militants had seen on Red Friday the effective potential strength of a united trade union movement with a General Council prepared to take action. A number of prominent trade union leaders had at that time taken up progressive attitudes on a number of issues, including trade union internationalism. Communists and militants throughout this period never separated their call for a militant General Council with increased powers from their appeal for struggles to achieve the strengthening of the movement *from below* with Factory Committees, reinforced Trades Councils, Councils of Action. These struggles to strengthen the trade union movement from below, and for Councils of Action in particular, became more and more the central demand.

But even when this is said, it is questionable whether it was correct to demand increased power for the General Council without making clear that no such powers should be given to a General Council that was preparing to use those powers against the interests of the working class. The slogan was one that demanded great care and precision in formulation which in this period was sometimes lacking.

Something of the militant feelings and decisions of the NMM Conference was taken to the 57th TUC which opened at Scarborough a week later. One proposal, often put forward by the NMM, for arrangements between the TUC and the Co-operative Wholesale Society to ensure distribution of food and other necessities in the case of a strike, was put forward by a delegate of the National Union of Vehicle Builders and strongly supported by A. J. Cook.[15] But the same resolution, which also called for powers for the General Council to call for a stoppage by an affiliated organisation or part thereof in order to assist a union defending a vital trade union principle, was strongly opposed by J. H. Thomas and Ernest Bevin—and by J. R. Clynes with a textbook reformist declaration of faith: "I am not in fear of the capitalist class. The only class that I fear is our own. I think, therefore, it will be better not to divide the Congress by insisting on a vote on this question but that the proposals should be withdrawn, and we should put our trust in our leaders."[16]

Much of Scarborough was militant—the resolution, for instance, against imperialism, on China, on TUC unity, on "Trade Union Aims" (which was seconded by Harry Pollitt on behalf of the Boilermakers Union). Many of the progressive resolutions were moved or seconded by trade unionists from the Communist Party and NMM. But Scarborough also revealed weaknesses and dangers.

Apart from Cook and Swales, the well-known leaders who had often been considered "left" were conspicuous by their silence before the attacks of the right wing. Virtually no practical preparations were made for the impending struggle. J. H. Thomas and Ernest Bevin were elected to the General Council. Right-wing reformists confronted militants and Marxists, and the silence of the centre showed that sentimental socialism could not stand up to reformism.

If the Scarborough TUC was, nevertheless, on the whole a militant Congress, the Labour Party Liverpool Conference which followed it was an undoubted triumph for reformism. The programme adopted—"Labour and the Nation" (a title later used for an even more outright reformist programme)—was a political step to the right, and the Conference's main activity was to speed the removal of communists from the Labour Party's ranks.

It was a good day for profits: "There was a much better tendency in the Stock Exchange, not little due to the decisive defeat of the Communists at the Labour Conference" (*Daily Telegraph*, 1 October 1925). "Investment, evidently, is greatly relieved by the testimony afforded at the Liverpool Congress to the fact that the Reds are not going to have their own way" (*Financial Times*, 1 October 1925).

The ultimate thesis still has to be compiled on the Stock Exchange as reflection of the struggle of Marxism versus Reformism in the history of the Labour movement. But there is no doubt that, as events moved towards the critical moment, consciously and/or unconsciously capitalists and reformists grew closer together. As May 1926 drew near miners, militants and, above all, communists became the main danger for right-wing Labour.

The Times, MacDonald and J. H. Thomas drew parallel conclusions: "The Liverpool Conference has enunciated a principle.

So far so good. A policy must follow.

Communism must not only be condemned; it must be cast out."[17] "The National Executive after the Liverpool decision will no doubt put its foot down heavily upon the offending parties."[18] "Smash the Reds or they will smash us."[19]

At the Tory Party Conference, which followed Liverpool, Baldwin announced that proceedings against the Communist Party were under consideration. And on 12 October, within a fortnight of Liverpool, twelve leaders of the Communist Party, Minority Movement and Young Communist League had been arrested. They were speedily tried and sentenced to six or twelve months' gaol, perhaps the greatest compliment that capitalism could have paid to the role of the Communist Party in preparing the working-class side for the coming General Strike. That a considerable part of the Labour movement recognised this role was shown in the tremendous campaigns of solidarity, the money collected, the 300,000 signatures, the demonstrations of tens of thousands from Clapham Common to Wandsworth Prison, the support of Labour MPs and leading trade unionists. "The Communist Party", wrote George Hicks, President of the National Union of Building Trade Operatives, "is now in the same position as the trade unions were during the early part of last century."[20]

In fact it was from the time of the trial that Communist Party membership, which had increased from around 2,000 in the summer of 1922 to about 5,000 in October 1923, began to rise.

Just before the arrests A. J. Cook had issued one more warning: "I warn the right-wing leaders in our movement to cease their attacks upon the left wing. They are encouraging every effort of reaction in this country to destroy our militant fighters. If these are beaten, the path lies open for the propertied interests to smash those who call themselves moderate."[21] But despite such warnings the General Council of the TUC was conspicuous for its inactivity in the last months of 1925 and the first of 1926. The workers were called to await with faith for the Report of the Royal Commission on the Coal Industry set up under the chairmanship of Sir Herbert Samuel on 5 September. Ramsay MacDonald celebrated Christmas 1925 with a manifesto for "Industrial Peace" in Rothermere's *Answers*.

When the General Council met the miners in January 1926 it was to preach patience and persuade them to wait on the Commission. At the end of January the General Council appointed a Special Industrial Committee, weighted heavy with right-wingers, to maintain contact with the miners. *The Times* noted how skilled this Committee was in being unprepared.[22] In February the leaders of the Co-operative Wholesale Society repudiated any intentions of granting credits in the coming struggle.

The arrest of the Twelve was naturally a heavy loss to the Communist Party, but it stirred up members to greater activity and sense of responsibility and, incidentally, gave greater credibility to the Party's continuous warnings. When during the trial the Twelve were let out on bail they acted jointly with other members of the Executive to select an acting leadership, with an acting Political Bureau, to take over if their absence should be enforced. At a meeting in the house of Francis Meynell (the famous typographer, then a communist), Bob Stewart was elected Acting General Secretary. Hundreds of meetings, rallies and demonstrations were held to call for solidarity with the miners' claims, warn against the contents of the awaited Royal Commission Report, and urge organisational preparation for the inevitable clash in May.

The acting leadership of the Communist Party called an extended Executive meeting on 9–10 January 1926, with some thirty extra invitations to District organisers and members active in industry.[23] Bob Stewart reported on the home and international situation. Arthur Horner, a still young militant from the Welsh pits, opened the session on preparations for the coming struggle. A resolution was adopted in the form of a "Programme of Action". The subsidy and the Commission, it said, meant nothing but a "breathing space" for the capitalists to prepare their offensive. The resolution listed eight principal measures and lines of action to prepare to meet these attacks:

1. The General Council of the TUC to call a Conference of Trade Union Executives.
2. Completion of the formation of the Industrial Alliance.
3. A Working Agreement between the General Council and the Co-operative Wholesale Society to ensure the provisioning of the workers during the coming struggle.
4. The formation of Factory Committees elected by the workers irrespective of craft or sex.
5. A campaign for 100 per cent trade unionism with special attention to recruitment of young workers.
6. The organisation of Workers' Defence Corps, composed of trade

unionists and controlled by trades councils, to protect working-class meetings from fascists and reactionaries, and an effort by the General Council to put the workers' case before the workers in the Army, Navy and Air Force.

7. The formulation of a Common Programme for the whole Labour movement (£4 a week for a 44-hour week) supplementary to the special demands of each industry.
8. Strengthening of relations between the General Council and the National Unemployed Workers' Committee Movement in order to counter capitalist attempts to use the unemployed as blacklegs.

The conflicting approaches of the reformists, on the one hand, and militants and Marxists on the other, became still more apparent when the Royal Commission Report (300 pages supported by three volumes of evidence) was published on 6 March 1926. This was as much a part of the preparation for the General Strike as OMS, Emergency Powers, arrests and mobilised armed forces. Bludgeon and bribe, force and persuasion, lock-out and arbitration were complementary.

The aim of the Commission's Report was to divide the workers before the battle, by providing the right-wing leaders with a platform for deserting the unions.[24] In essence it proposed that whilst the mining industry should be reorganised under private ownership at some indefinite date, wages should come down *now*. Nationalisation was rejected, replaced by a proposal to nationalise Coal Royalties. Continuation of the subsidy was "indefensible". It "should stop at the end of its authorised term and should never be repeated". This was greeted as a victory by the right-wing leaders of the Labour Party and TUC, and most of what might be called the centre, and then used to "tranquillise" the miners, to bid them be "reasonable". Ramsay MacDonald proclaimed it "a conspicuous landmark in the history of political thought. . . . The stars in their courses are fighting for us."[25] The only organisations to expose the Samuel Commission Report for what it was, and to appeal for its complete rejection, were the Communist Party, the NMM and the Miners' Federation, supported by individual militants from the Labour Party, the ILP and the trade unions.

The Communist Party's statement[26] characterised the Report as "a declaration of war against the miners and the whole working-class movement". Two dangers, it argued, now faced the workers. The first was the direct offensive of the mineowners and the capitalists generally, the second the hesitation and trepidation of reformist leaders who called for reconciliation of classes and preached sweet reason.

As the critical month came closer and the contrast of reformist and Marxist approaches became sharper, a clear call for vigilance and struggle came from the National Minority Movement's Conference of Action, held at Latchmere Baths, Battersea, on 21 March.[27] This was the biggest NMM Conference to date, representing around one million workers, and perhaps the most effective action in the whole NMM history.

Tom Mann opened the Conference with a critical analysis of the Samuel Report. Its *real* content was attack on wages, hours and national agreements. It complemented the open attacks like the OMS and the arrest of the twelve communists and, more recently, of Welsh anthracite miners. The Commission hoped that "the reformist elements in the Labour movement will concur with their recommendations . . .". But Labour must "*prepare at once* . . . have our industrial machinery ready for *action* . . . every Trades Council should be genuinely representative of all the working-class organisations in the district, the co-operative guilds as much as the unions. In the shops, factories and mines, and on board ship, committees should be active in every department; this is where the workers have their chance as against all who do not work."

Alex Gossip, General Secretary of the National Amalgamation of Furnishing Trade Associations (NAFTA), moved, and J. J. Vaughan of the Bethnal Green Trades and Labour Council (a leading London communist) seconded, a detailed plan for the "Defence and Maintenance of Trade Union Rights":

(a) To organise the workers on the job into factory and pit committees . . . and to set up Trades Councils where none exist.
(b) To form (through and under the supervision of the Trades Councils) Workers' Defence Corps, in order to protect working-class speakers from bourgeois terrorism, to protect trade union headquarters from Fascist incendiarism, to defend strike pickets against police interference, and, finally, build up a powerful working-class force, capable of defending the political and industrial rights and liberties of the workers.
(c) To demand the repeal of "sedition" and anti-labour laws.
(d) To resist strenuously any attempts by local authorities either

voluntary or at the instigation of the Government to prevent free association and public expression.

(e) To demand the rights of soldiers and naval ratings to refuse strike services.

A resolution on "the capitalist offensive" was moved by Arthur Horner and seconded by Peter Kerrigan, member of the AEU, speaker for the Glasgow District Committee of the NMM. It appealed to the workers to develop, through the trades councils, all-embracing *Councils of Action* to prepare for the struggles ahead. It urged each trades council "to constitute itself a Council of Action by mobilising all the forces of the working class in its locality (the trade union branches, the organised unemployed, the Co-operative Guilds, and the workers' political organisations . . .". Such Councils of Action should work to strengthen the unions, bring in young workers, improve workshop organisation, and establish food and supply organisations (Commissariats) along with the local Co-operatives.

The General Council of the TUC was urged to convene a National Congress of Action and to take steps to secure international solidarity.

From March to the first days of May, right up to the brink, the struggle of the trends within the Labour movement grew daily more distinct and bitter. The miners were not by threat or persuasion to be dislodged from their militant positions. The right wing became more vocal. Thomas' speech at a Monmouthshire meeting of 18 April 1926, typifies their position: "To talk at this stage as if in a few days all the workers of the country were to be called out was rot, only letting loose passions that might be difficult to control, but it was not rendering the best service either to the miners or anyone else . . . instead of organising, mobilising and encouraging the feeling that war was inevitable, let them concentrate on finding a solution honourable and satisfactory to all sides."[28]

On 23 April, the *Workers' Weekly* published a Communist Party call to the miners, railwaymen and engineers under banner headlines: "ALL TOGETHER FOR THE FIGHT", "FORM COUNCILS OF ACTION".

In the last days of April right up to the strike there were talks between the TUC Negotiating Committee, the Industrial Committee of the TUC, and the Conference of Trade Union Executives, and every level of government, trying to arrive at a settlement. The TUC negotiators prostrated themselves before the government in the search for a compromise, which would have been, in fact, a surrender. Thomas, in his own words, was "almost grovelling".[29] But the cabinet wanted a showdown. It declared a State of Emergency, published the names of the Civil Commissions for the different areas, allowed OMS posters to go up and, even while negotiations were still supposed to be in process, forced the reluctant General Council into unwilling action.

On 1 May the Conference of Trade Union Executives accepted the General Council's "proposals for co-ordinated action" by a vast majority of 3,653,527 to 49,911. The masses of the workers, despite threats and manœuvres, were ready for the struggle. The General Council could not withdraw. But it went into the battle backwards, looking for a way out.

On 28 April, the Communist Party had already issued a call to the Conference of Union Executives warning that ". . . official leaders of Labour . . . are straining every nerve to secure a 'compromise' which will mean for the miners nothing but defeat".[30] And on 2 May the Party issued a final Manifesto[31] calling for solidarity between all sections of Labour, warning that the greatest danger was "that the government and the Right Wing may succeed in isolating the miners from the rest of the movement", appealing for the formation of Councils of Action, Workers' Defence Corps and Joint Committees between unions and co-operatives, and for the development of international trade union unity. Two slogans ended the Manifesto: "A COUNCIL OF ACTION IN EVERY TOWN", "EVERY MAN BEHIND THE MINERS".

2. THE NINE DAYS

From the first moment of the General Strike one thing was clear—the mass of the working class was ready for the struggle, responsive to every call for action, irritated only at delay. The first line moved solidly into action. The second line (which the General Council at first kept in reserve) held reluctantly back, demanding to join in. The strike was overwhelmingly solid.

At midnight on Monday, 3 May, only three unions out of some 1,100 had refused to answer the call.[32] In their first communiqué the General Council had to report that the response surprised them:[33] "We have from all over the country reports that have surpassed all our expectations. . . . The difficulty of the General Council has been to keep men in what we might call the second line of defence rather than call them out." The despatch riders sent out by the General Council to take out and gather information returned with heartening reports: "On

Monday night the first batch of despatch riders set out on their journeys: on Tuesday the reports began to come in. They amazed Eccleston Square. Everywhere a solid enthusiasm. Everywhere a realisation of this simple issue, we cannot let the miners down this time. Men with responsible posts and long terms of service had come out as wholeheartedly as any. Villages in which a strike had never been known before were as forward as places believed to be 'centres of disturbance'. As report after report came in, it was clear that what criticism there was, was all in one direction. Why were food permits dealt out so freely? Why were the gasworks and the electric power plants running? Why were carters told off to supply 'black' coal to the 'black' gas works, and work alongside blacklegs? Why were not more trades called out? This last criticism, be it noted, came not from the men who were striking but from the men who were left at work. They too wanted to strike their blow in this great adventure. Day and night, at any hour, the despatch riders found the strike committees at work."[34]

The BBC and the government's *British Gazette*, together with the various capitalist papers reduced to news-sheets, published daily reports of defections, mostly imaginary. Though various groups of blacklegs—almost all from the upper and middle classes—painfully and often dangerously manned a minute proportion of services, working-class defectors were extremely rare.

Day by day the strike became more effective, better organised. By the second week the Councils of Action and Strike Committees were becoming more confident, widening their influence and their political horizons, winning authority. By 10 May (before the bringing out of the second line), the *British Worker*, official organ of the General Council, reported that there were more workers out on strike than on the first day. On 11 May, rudely contradicting its own propaganda, the *British Gazette* had to admit that there was "as yet little sign of a general collapse of the Strike".

In fact, on 12 May, the day of betrayal, when the General Council called off the strike, the number of strikers was at its peak, their enthusiasm at its highest level, and their organisation stronger and more effective than on any previous day.

Whatever minor differences arose in its ranks, when the crunch came the ruling class and its government were united in their intent to defeat the strike and to smash the miners, as the prelude to an all-out offensive against the working class—on wages, houses, established agreements and hard-won trade union rights. The government had prepared and now rolled into action.

On the eve of the strike the export of coal was stopped and emergency regulations on fuel consumption were issued. An appeal for blacklegs ("volunteers") was broadcast on Sunday night (3 May). On Monday night, the Metropolitan Commissioner of Police called on citizens below the age of forty-five to enrol as Special Constables, promising glory, and protection as well as pensions and allowances for widows and orphans in the case of accident in the execution of their duty.[35] All army leave was stopped. Troops were moved to important supply and industrial areas. Hyde Park became a milk distribution centre. OMS came into its own and put its personnel and organisation at the disposal of the State.

On 7 May, the *British Gazette* carried a government announcement that: "All ranks of the Armed Forces of the Crown are hereby notified that any action which they may find necessary to take in an honest endeavour to aid the Civil Power will receive, both now and afterwards, the full support of His Majesty's Government." On 8 May two battalions of Guards, with supporting cavalry and armoured cars, occupied London's docks.

The Navy was assigned special strike-breaking responsibilities graphically described by J. R. Clynes, Cabinet Minister in the First Labour Government: "The mails to Ireland and elsewhere were being carried on naval destroyers. In the Clyde, where rough mining and other elements had caused some trouble, the *Warspite*, the *Comus* and the *Hood* (the world's biggest battleship) towered with their big guns outlined starkly against the sky. Three other warships overawed Liverpool. Destroyers anchored in the harbours of Cardiff, Harwich, Middlesbrough and Portsmouth. In London, the power station was manned by naval ratings. Other naval men worked in the docks, where machine guns were held in case of need."[36]

On 4 May, the BBC became an open propaganda agency of the government, uninterruptedly issuing attacks on the strikers, appeals for scabs, dreamed-up fantasies of mass defections, Red wreckers and Moscow gold. On 6 May the BBC and *British Gazette* refused to let it be known that the Archbishop of Canterbury had put forward proposals for a settlement, including a renewed period of subsidy and withdrawal of the proposed new wage scales. But three days later they reported with relish the declaration of Cardinal Bourne at High Mass in Westminster Cathedral that the General Strike was "a direct challenge to lawfully constituted authority . . . a sin against the obedience which we owe to God . . .", and that "all are bound to uphold and assist the

Government, which is the lawfully constituted authority of the country, and represents, therefore, in its own appointed sphere, the authority of God himself".

The freedom of the mass media was upheld by the publication of the *British Gazette* with the imprint of HMSO, printed by blackleg labour on the machines of the *Morning Post*; by the raid (on 5 March) on the *Daily Herald*; by the government taking formal possession of all newsprint; by Churchill's announcement that supplies of newsprint would be withheld from any papers that attacked the government; and by the widespread arrests of those who prepared, distributed or even possessed bulletins of the Communist Party, Young Communist League, NMM, Councils of Action or militant strike committees.

Arrests began on 4 May, mostly under various clauses of the Emergency Powers Act, with the lone Communist MP—Shapurji Saklatvala—candidate for first place in gaol, on pretext of a speech made on 1 May.

Thus, within a few days of the strike beginning, the line-up was clear. The mass of the British workers were ready and eager to go—solid in support of the strike, and becoming stronger. They faced a ruling class determined to win the strike, outright and unconditionally. But there was this great difference. Despite some tactical differences, the ruling class was solid behind its leaders. The leaders of the working class, on the other hand, for the most part classic reformists, had been pushed reluctantly into a struggle they had desperately tried to avert. And the stronger the strike became the more eager they were to end it.

However much it publicly berated them, the government knew His Majesty's right-wing Labour leaders. It knew they did not want this strike, had seen them "grovel" to prevent it, and knew that they feared a militant political development of the strike and the emergence of new militant leaders far more than defeat.

The government threatened force and used it where it thought necessary. Publicly it attacked the General Council as a subversive revolutionary body, leading an illegal unconstitutional struggle to undermine law and order and bring the country to anarchy. The forces of State were paraded. The General Council was threatened with arrest, imprisonment and unlimited fines. But the complementary approach was to contrive a crafty "compromise" which, while in effect a sell-out, could be construed as an "honourable" settlement.

First came a vigorous process of softening up the TUC leaders.

Already on the Monday before the strike, Prime Minister Baldwin had begun to attack the nerves of the General Council:[37] "I do not think that all the leaders when they assented to ordering a General Strike fully realised that they were threatening the basis of ordered Government, and going nearer proclaiming civil war than we had been for centuries past." On 5 May, in its first issue, the *British Gazette* accused the General Council of direct challenge to ordered government. Day-in, day-out the *Gazette*, the capitalist news-sheets, the BBC, the Prime Minister, the Chancellor of the Exchequer, Lord Balfour, Lord Oxford and Asquith, all of them, raised a chorus of frantic denunciations to the effect that the British Constitution was under attack, and with it the British Empire, Law, Order, Democracy, the Family, Religion and the British sense of fair-play.

On 6 May, Sir John Simon, Liberal leader, former Attorney-General and Home Secretary, informed the House of Commons in the most "authoritative" terms, that the General Strike was illegal, that every striker in breach of contract could be sued in the County Courts for damages, and that every "trade union leader who had advised and promoted this course of action is liable in damages to the uttermost farthing of his personal possessions".[38] Mr. Justice Astbury a few days later gave birth to his *obiter dictum* that participating in this "illegal strike" or inciting others to participate was "not protected by the Trades Dispute Act of 1906".

How could reformists who believed that the State was *their* State, that the law was *their* law, resist such accusations of subversion?

By the week-end of 8–9 May, whilst the softening-up process was operating on those in command, the strike itself was thriving, and the Councils of Action were beginning to come to the fore in many areas.

Complementary action was urgent, a face-saver, a pretext for the General Council to call for the return to work. Sir Herbert Samuel had laid the basis for this *before* the strike, in the Royal Commission Report. Could he not do it again? As MacDonald put it so well, no sooner had the strike started than "peace efforts went on from the trade union side, every attempt was made to discover contacts that had such influence as to give some promise that their opinion and support would mean something, and at last Sir Herbert Samuel was discovered".[39] And as A. J. Cook expressed it, Sir Herbert "returned post haste to England . . . as soon as he arrived . . . he was seen by the Rt. Hon. J. H. Thomas, and discussions began in private. Those who had been unwilling and hesitant to go into the strike were continually seeking some way out of it. . . . These discussions were held simply with a view to creating some pretext to justify calling off the General Strike."[40]

There were surreptitious discussions between Sir Herbert and the General Council—all, at first, unbeknown to the miners. The "Samuel Memorandum", handed to the Council on 11 May, contained *no* concessions, nothing for which the miners were fighting or to secure which the TUC was supposed to be pledged, except a vague "undocumented" hint of a possible renewal of the subsidy. It accepted that, after some specified reorganisation, wages should come down. It was the old Royal Commission Report rehashed—"a new suit of clothes for the same body", said the Miners' President, Herbert Smith. Above all, the Samuel Memorandum had no government recognition, no official status whatsoever.

By 11 May, the eighth day of the strike, the mass of the strikers were more solid and confident than ever before, Councils of Action were spreading and becoming more effective. They were even beginning, under militant leadership, and especially where communists were amongst the leaders, to develop into alternative centres of power insofar as they controlled permits for transport and the distribution of food. There were no signs that the mass of the strikers were overawed by the parade of State power, nor by threats of arrest, nor by accusations of unconstitutional acts. Nor did the majority of Christian strikers believe that they were offending Christ.

But for the refomist leadership of the strike, the advancing political outlook of so many strikers, the extension of their organisations, the raising of their sights, became the most potent reason for calling off the strike.

By 11 May, the General Council, who had been negotiating with Sir Herbert for several days behind the scenes, had definitely decided to call off the strike on the pretext of the Samuel Memorandum. On that day the miners were called in to the negotiations for the first time, and informed by Arthur Pugh, the TUC Chairman, that the General Council had unanimously endorsed the Memorandum and considered it a reasonable basis for negotiating a settlement. On this basis they proposed to terminate the strike.

Again and again the miners asked: *what were the guarantees?* A. J. Cook recounts: "Mr. Pugh was continuously pressed and questioned by Mr. Herbert Smith, myself, and my colleagues as to what the guarantees mentioned were, and who had given them. We got no answer. But J. H. Thomas said to me personally, when I asked him whether the Government would accept the Samuel proposals and what were his guarantees: 'You may not trust my word, but will you not accept the word of a British gentleman who has been Governor of Palestine?' "[41] The miners were unconvinced, angry, and determined to struggle on, if necessary alone.

On the morning of 12 March the General Council deputation unconditionally surrendered to the Prime Minister in the presence of the cabinet—without terms, without any written statement, without guarantees.

Millions of strikers, when the news was first announced over the wireless, could not believe it. They thought it was some new trick of the BBC. When they found that the news was true they were bewildered, bitter and angry, but for the most part could see no alternative to accepting the General Council's instructions.

The miners continued the struggle.

3. THE COMMUNIST PARTY IN THE GENERAL STRIKE

The General Strike was called off just when it was at its strongest. It was not just a question of numbers. Day by day the organisation of the strike had improved—bulletins, pickets, security, control of transport and goods distribution. Day by day organisation developed more and more in the localities around the strike committees, trades councils and Councils of Action. The weaker and more hesitant the General Council became, the stronger, tougher and more united became the *local* leaderships or, at least, the best of them. The gap had widened between the effective forces of struggle in the localities and an ineffective reluctant national leadership. Mass political understanding of the issues was becoming ever clearer. And all over Britain thousands of men and women, whose factory, pit, depot or unemployed committee had been their university, who drew their strength from their class, from their experience of struggle, were becoming acknowledged leaders of the strike.

Many of the effective leaders were militant members of the Labour Party or the ILP. The miners provided a solid core of leaders, and there were no few Marxists amongst them. It is often hard to identify the political affiliations of those who emerged to head the Councils of Action. But when the most effective Councils are examined, those considered dangerous by the authorities, when one studies who were the editors of the most militant bulletins or looks at the lists of arrests, one finds, in numbers out of all proportion to their 5,000 strong organisation at the time, members of the Communist Party, and with them supporters of the Minority Movement.

When the strike began some of the most experienced communist leaders were still in gaol. But in London the Working Bureau met daily.[42] With a cloud of detectives clustered around King Street, the venue was daily changed. A series of special departments were formed—organisation, communications, publicity—with a Bureau member in charge of each, so that a small mobile leadership was established, insufficiently experienced in semi-legal conditions, but learning and improving in the short days of the strike. The King Street headquarters was kept open despite the government's arbitrary attacks and the attempts to brand the Party as an illegal organisation. And on the eve of the strike a number of Executive members, including those who had by then served their six-months' sentences, were sent out to the Districts.

Communications became a central problem.[43] A skeleton courier service was established with a rough plan for contact with the Districts. All Districts and most of the Branches had some or other contact with the Centre. The arrest of the London District Secretary complicated matters, as the District's responsibilities included despatch all over the country of the central *Workers' Bulletin* which served as a basis for extended local bulletins.

On 3 May, the eve of the strike, the Party produced a printed *Workers' Daily* in 40,000 copies, containing, amongst other items, the *Manifesto* of the previous day.

On 4 May the first issue of the *Workers' Bulletin* was published in London, and, apart from 9 May, continued for ten consecutive days. The number of copies thus centrally produced rose rapidly from 5,000 to 20,000. There were plenty of problems. Paper had to be procured, duplicators kept hidden from the police, fresh places of operation found almost daily, copies distributed in London and, from London, all over Britain. With the help of the central Bulletin, many Districts and Branches produced their own, so that total circulation of communist daily bulletins soon rose to 100,000 and then to around 200,000. Police raided many offices and private homes in their attempts to locate the bulletin producers, and made no few arrests.

The task of the Party's propaganda during the strike was not easy. It tried to give the more politically conscious workers a deeper analysis of the strike, to explain the role of the capitalist offensive, to draw lessons on the nature of capitalism in general and the special crisis of British capitalism, to present the long-term socialist alternative. And at the same time, it had to speak to the mass of workers, profoundly influenced as they were by reformism—who saw the strike simply as one of solidarity with the miners on issues of wages and hours, who still looked for leadership to the General Council or the Labour Party—and put before them a line of *immediate* actions which was comprehensible to them, which could unite them, and which could indicate (or at least try to) a path that could lead to victory.

The Party well knew that on the eve of the strike the workers were eager for action, but not in any sense in a revolutionary mood. They were ready to fight on economic issues, to show their solidarity with the miners, to defy the threats of the government—but they were *not* ready to challenge the social system. The Party knew, too, that many of those taking part in this great unprecedented strike, particularly those the most deeply involved in it, could in a few days develop further politically than in years of more "normal" times. Its problem was how to help to organise the struggle, develop the local leaderships of the Councils of Action, lift the level of the strike, put forward, step by step, new lines of action, and prepare, as far as possible, for continued struggle when, as it had so often warned, the General Council capitulated. Not easy!

The 2 May Party Manifesto called for solidarity with the miners, warned against all attempts to isolate them, argued that the employers' aim was lower wages, longer hours, District instead of National Agreements, and appealed for "a Council of Action in every town".[44]

The successive issues of the *Workers' Bulletin* and the local bulletins criticised the conduct of the General Council and warned repeatedly of the danger of a sell-out. The 12 May issue accused the Left on the General Council of being shamefully silent about the conduct of the Right, called on the workers to be ready to take things into their own hands, to call emergency meetings of strike committees and Councils of Action—but by mid-day the capitulation had been announced. That afternoon the Political Committee telegraphed to all Districts a statement along the following lines:[45]

1. The General Council was surrendering at the very moment when the workers were most enthusiastic;
2. The surrender was a betrayal not only of the miners but of all workers;
3. The left-wingers in the General Council, by their policy of cowardly silence, had left the right-wing with a free hand to pursue their active policy of betrayal;
4. The workers themselves must step in where the leaders had failed;

5. The slogan should be "refuse to resume work"—repudiate the Samuel Memorandum, keep the Councils of Action and strike committees in being;
6. The miners should appeal directly to their fellow-workers over the heads of false leaders.

The gist of the telegram was embodied the following day in a Manifesto, *Stand by the Miners*.[46] The General Council's capitulation was characterised as "the greatest crime that has ever been permitted not only against the miners but against the working class of Britain".

It was already clear the next day that there was no hope of keeping the General Strike going. On 15 May the Party called for the organisation of district conferences of Councils of Action with the hope of maintaining them as forms of struggle, and raised the problems of fighting to change the leadership of the Labour movement. It put forward as immediately urgent, support for the miners in their continued struggle and the fight against victimisation.

On 16 May, with the triumphant employers in full attack, with victimisation already rampant, with the workers in a mood of angry bewilderment, with the danger of disillusioned and disorganised retreat, the Party's Political Bureau decided that efforts should be concentrated along three main lines[47]—solidarity with the miners (including struggle for an embargo on the transport of coal, financial aid from the unions and credits from the Co-operatives); the fight against victimisation (including local and district conferences of the Councils of Action and pressure on the General Council of the TUC to call an immediate Conference of Union Executives); efforts to strengthen the unions (involving resistance to withdrawal from the unions, struggle for 100 per cent membership and to replace the leaders who had capitulated with those who were ready, in whatever appropriate form, to fight).

In the weeks and months that preceded the General Strike and, above all, in the nine days themselves, many workers heard the voice of the Communist Party for the first time. On 17 May a call was issued by the Party for recruitment to its ranks. Old members still tell with a gleam in their eyes of the mass attendances at meetings called by the Party in the days that followed the strike, particularly in the mining areas, where the lockout was to continue for six bitter months. Sometimes hundreds of miners joined the Party at a single meeting (in the Durham and South Wales coalfields, for instance). Party membership rose from around 5,000 before the strike to around 12,000 at the end of 1926.

For those who would understand the conflicting policies of the main contestants of the strike a revealing source is a comparison between the three news-sheets or bulletins—the government's *British Gazette*, the General Council's *British Worker* and the Communist Party's *Workers' Bulletin*.[48]

The *Gazette* was printed in full newspaper format, the *British Worker* half newspaper size, the *Workers' Bulletin* roughly duplicated on all sorts of paper, begged or borrowed or "found", harried by the police, reproduced with part local content in many parts of Britain, a "crime" to produce and distribute, and sometimes to possess. "Stencils were cut in several places and printing was moved from place to place. The distribution was done mainly by women, who did wonderful work during the Strike. In distribution, prams came in very useful and many a policeman was passed by a smiling mum with a chirpy baby in the pram sitting atop several quire of our news bulletins. But not all got past, and several of our women were arrested."[49] It was to the credit of the *Workers' Bulletin*, that, of the three, it was, on 4 May, first in the field.

The *British Gazette*, in its first issue of 5 May, warned and stormed: "If Parliament were to allow its considered judgement to be overborne under the cruel assault of a General Strike, the economic disaster would only be a part of a much greater disaster. . . . These men (the General Council), would in fact become masters of the country and the power of Government would have passed from Parliament into their hands." On 6 May, in big bold type, it quoted the Prime Minister. "THE GENERAL STRIKE IS A CHALLENGE TO PARLIAMENT AND THE ROAD TO ANARCHY AND RUIN". On 7 May it fulminated: "There can be no question of compromise of any kind. Either the country will break the General Strike or the General Strike will break the country." On 9 May it prominently printed the government's guarantee that all ranks of the armed forces who aided the "Civil Power" during the strike "will receive, both now and afterwards, the full support of His Majesty's Government", appealed to civil servants of all grades to volunteer for "emergency duties", and flaunted in heavy headline Sir John Simon's declaration of the illegality of the strike.

On the critical day of 10–12 May, the *Gazette* continued its denunciations of the "revolutionary" General Council. On 13 May, the farewell issue, it printed top centre on the front page the King's Message: "Let us forget whatever elements of bitterness the events of the past few days have created. . . ." Had the stony employers' hearts melted? Immediately below these soft and clement words was the government's communiqué with the big bold headline "REINSTATEMENT: NO OBLIGATION INCURRED"; and in a big black box:

EMERGENCY REGULATIONS STILL IN FORCE

The *British Worker*, making its début on the evening of 5 May, replied to Churchill's bloodcurdling rhetoric and to the accusations of insidious preparations for the seizure of power, with reports of "Red Tyranny in Russia" and of a love affair in the parrot house of the London Zoo. There was a deep distinction between the courage of the print workers and staff of the paper who fought consistently to bring it out and keep it going, and the pusillanimity of those who decided its political content.

The first issues did indeed describe the strikers' solidarity. There was an "immediate, unanimous, enthusiastic response to strike orders". It was in its advice on what to do that the reformism of the General Council leaders stood out in sad relief. To the thundering accusations of subversion, of undermining Law and Order, the *British Worker*, No. 1, meekly replied: "The General Council of the Trades Union Congress wishes to emphasise the fact that this is an industrial dispute. . . ." When the support and action of every man and woman was urgently needed for communications, pickets, supply, relief to the deprived, distribution of bulletins, when tasks grew hour by hour, the same first issue of the *British Worker* recorded in bold type the classic appeal: "**The General Council suggests that in all districts where large numbers of workers are idle, sports should be organised and entertainments arranged. This will both keep a number of people busy and provide amusement for many more.**"

The *Gazette* could threaten to crush and to punish, and accuse the General Council of every sort of subversion, sedition and illegality. To this, again and again, the *British Worker*, speaking for the General Council, could only meekly repeat, as on 6 May: "No political issue has ever been mentioned or thought of in connection with it (the strike) . . . at the Special TUC. It was perfectly clear that nothing was in anybody's mind save the industrial issue . . . the General Strike is not a 'menace' to Parliament. No attack is being made on the Constitution. We beg Mr Baldwin to believe that."

The *British Worker*, in the same issue, printed the "Message to Workers", which called on every striker to "be exemplary in his conduct and not to give any opportunity for police interference" and asked pickets "to avoid obstruction and to confine themselves strictly to their legitimate duties". But the police were "interfering" everywhere, protecting blacklegs, arresting pickets and distributors of bulletins. What was "exemplary conduct" in the face of police interference, baton-charges, mobilisation of troops, BBC monopoly, attempted monopoly of newsprint, when the whole State was organised on *one* side, *against* the strike? By 9 May the *British Worker* had not printed one item of news on arrests, though the *Gazette* and the BBC were announcing them daily. Its view of "exemplary conduct" was revealed (9 May) as "special football and cricket matches . . . indoor attractions . . . whist drives". There was the praiseworthy Plymouth example where a strikers' team defeated a police team at football, after the Chief Constable's wife had kicked off. Most "exemplary" of all was the Cardiff Strike Committee's Appeal, approvingly quoted: "Keep smiling. . . . Refuse to be provoked. Get into your garden. Look after the wife and kiddies. If you have not got a garden get into the country, the parks and playgrounds. Do not hang around the centre of the city. Get into the country, there is no more heartful occupation than walking."

There was no clue in the issues of the *British Worker* from 10–12 May that the General Council was deep in discussions with Sir Herbert Samuel. The solidarity of the strike was still praised. Later editions of the 12th presented the sell-out as an honourable settlement.

On 13 May it appealed to one and all to "forgive and forget". At the same time it could not but protest that the employers were doing neither. Victimisation had begun. Beneath the headline "Peace with Honour" (a claim that, at another sell-out 12 years later, was so dishonourably to be reborn) the *British Worker* lamented: "The General Council called off the General Strike in confidence that the Prime Minister meant what he said when he asked for resumption of negotiations towards an honourable peace."

It lingered on to 17 May. On almost the last page of this last issue it discovered that there *had* been some arrests.

The opening leader of the *Workers' Bulletin* in its first issue on 4 May congratulated the workers on the completeness of their answer to the strike call, paid tribute to the print workers for their action stopping the *Daily Mail* and, rather solemnly, warned: "There is of course a danger—and already the Government's policy makes it clear. They build upon the hope that the TUC will be bamboozled into trying to induce (in the interests of peace!) the miners into retreating behind their minimum demands. This the miners cannot and should not do." From this first issue it continued to note, condemn and draw lessons from the massive intervention of the State.

On 5 May the *Bulletin* carried news of mass pickets, of police attacks, of troop movements, of successful efforts to defeat blacklegs and the stopping of private buses manned by scabs. It reported insubordination amongst soldiers of the Welsh Guards and troops at Aldershot. It contained the Party Manifesto—*The Political Meaning of the General Strike.*

Unlike the *British Worker*, there was no attempt to "justify" the strike as non-political, no call to stay at home. "Once the battle has been joined, the only way to victory is to push ahead and hit hard. And the way to hit the capitalist hard is for the Councils of Action to throw out clear watchwords: Not a Penny off the Pay, Not a Second on the Day; Nationalise the Mines without Compensation under Workers' Control; Formation of a Labour Government." On 8 May the *Workers' Bulletin* returned to this question: "The anxiety of the *British Worker* to assure everybody that the strike is a 'purely industrial dispute' is almost pathetic . . . the Government every hour makes more of a political issue of it. Their seizure of the stocks of printing paper is not only evidence that they are driven to extremity, but evidence also, that under EPA the 'Constitution' is just what the Government chooses to make it."

The 12 May issue appeared before the General Council's capitulation had been officially announced. But well aware of what was secretly being prepared, it called for emergency meetings of strike committees and Councils of Action. The 13 May issue contained the Communist Party's call "Stand by the miners". It appealed to the Councils of Action to fight on despite the betrayal, and made it clear that the miners had rejected the General Council's capitulation (a fact that the *British Worker* concealed so far as it could). The last issue, on 14 May, contained the Party's Appeal—"Reform the Ranks and Fight on".

In the course of the General Strike and the months that preceded it the struggle between reformists, on the one hand, and militants and Marxists, on the other, was fought out not just in the field of theory, of policies, but on issues of organisation. In particular, the division of the strikers into two "lines", to be called out one after the other, was essentially a right-wing conciliatory reformist organisational approach, which was much resented by the strikers and weakened the effectiveness of the strike.

In the localities there was a wide difference between a number of the right-wing dominated formal stike committees and the best of the blossoming Councils of Action led by the Left. The Communist Party had already put forward the idea of Councils of Action in 1920, when the National and Local Councils of Action embodied for a moment the strength of the British working class and played a key role in stopping war against the young Soviet Republic. And after Red Friday the Party foresaw the importance of Councils of Action for the coming General Strike and, along with the Minority Movement, began to call for and work for their formation. On the eve of the strike, the formation of Councils of Action was amongst the central proposals of the Party Statement of 23 April and of the 2 May Manifesto. The "Proposals for Co-ordinated Action" issued by the General Council to Trade Union Executives on the night of 30 April, accepted by Conference on 1 May, had defined the role of Trades Councils in the strike: "The work of the Trades Councils, in conjunction with the local officers of the trade unions actually participating in the dispute, shall be to assist in carrying out the foregoing provisions (i.e. stoppage of work in various trades and undertakings, and exceptions thereto) and they shall be charged with the responsibility of organising the trade unionists in dispute in the most effective manner for the preservation of peace and order." But the Councils of Action and effective strike committees that developed in the course of the strike were far more than the formal co-ordinating committees envisaged by the TUC. They went far beyond the normal functioning of Trades (and Trades and Labour) Councils.

In the course of the strike and on the initiative of militants, quite often communists, moribund trades councils were revived and many existing ones broadened to bring in all types of working-class organisations, including political organisations. They became real expressions of the whole local working-class movement—in effect, they were transformed into Councils of Action.

The analysis of Councils of Action made by the Labour Research Department following the strike and collated by Emile Burns,[50] found that many of the most effective were composed of trades council delegates, strike committee representatives from each of the unions or groups involved, representatives of unions not affiliated to the Trades Council, and representatives of political parties and other mass organisations (women, youth, unemployed).

When the right-wing dominated, however, or where there was an excess of craft or local industrial "patriotism", the unity of the Councils of Action tended to be replaced by a series of *separate* union sub-committees, each more intent on vertical contact with its own District or Executive than on militant local unity. In such cases picketing was often organised separately or ineffectively, mass picketing was frowned on, political organisations were not involved and joint mass meetings were discouraged.[51] One of the main proposals made by the Communist Party in its statements and appeals that preceded the strike had been for national and local agreements between the trade union and Co-operative movement, particularly on questions of food supply and credit. This was resisted by the right wing in both the TUC and Co-operative organisations and achieved in only a few areas where the left was strong. There were Co-operative organisations only in five out of the 140 strike committees and Councils of Action examined in the *Labour Research* enquiry.

As the strike developed many of the strike committees and Councils of Action broadened and deepened the scope of their activities. Some were in almost permanent session. Various departments were set up—finance, propaganda, press, information, intelligence, relief, prisoners' aid, picketing, permits, transport and communications, entertainment. Mass pickets (sometimes up to 1,000) proved most effective. The General Council's transport and communication service was unprepared before the strike, and remained very inadequate. Much of the burden of maintaining contact with Headquarters and with their neighbours fell on the strike committees and Councils of Action, who mobilised cars, and both motor and push bikes.

In the same way much of the responsibility for publicity and propaganda fell to the Councils of Action. The *British Worker*, reported to have reached a million circulation by the end of the strike, contributed little to its organisation and fighting spirit. But there were virtually hundreds of local bulletins produced by strike committees, Trades Councils, Councils of Action. About half of those who replied to the Labour Research questionnaire produced bulletins of their own.

Workers' Defence Corps (or "Workers' Police"), a form of organisation constantly proposed by the communists before the strike, developed in the main only around those Councils of Action or strike committees where communists or militants were active. The *Labour Research* enquiry reported their existence at Aldershot, Chatham, Colchester, Croydon, Methil, St. Pancras, Selby, Sowerby Bridge, Willesden. Amongst the most effective was that at Methil in the Fife coalfield.

After the strike the *Workers' Weekly* published a series of reports giving details of communist activity during the strike including their participation in strike committees and Councils of Action.[52]

J. R. Campbell reported in *Workers' Weekly* of 21 May on communist activity in various parts of Scotland. In the West of Scotland a joint committee of the Communist Party and the Minority Movement remained in more or less permanent session throughout the strike, directing the activities of two organisations in the West of Scotland, and keeping contact also with the separate Lanarkshire District Committee of the CPGB. It issued locally the Communist Party Statement of 2 May in some 14,000 copies and 10,000 copies of a Minority Movement Manifesto to Metal Workers. During the first week it published emergency editions of the *Worker* and the *Workers' Weekly* (4 pages, about 18,000 copies)—but then "the night shift was picked up by the police". On the second week it published *The Workers' Plan* (edition of 6,000) with a further issue (10,000) at the end of the strike.

In Glasgow, Campbell reported, there were five Communist Party members on the Central Strike Committee waging a difficult struggle in face of a not very active leadership, trying above all to compensate for the inactivity of the Central Strike Committee by the development of local committees. Communist initiative was largely instrumental in the establishment of fifteen local strike committees, which included many communists elected as trade union representatives. There were active Party groups, for instance, in the Councils of Action at Motherwell and Blantyre. At the Andrie and Coatbridge Council of Action there was a strong Party group which included the Chairman. Here a bulletin was issued (8,000 circulation), a Workers' Defence Corps organised, and mass picketing involving up to 4,000 workers.

In Lanarkshire, all the local Councils of Action linked up on a county basis, composing a committee of forty delegates of whom eight, including the Chairman, were members of the Communist Party. On the Paisley Committee there were four communists, on the Kilmarnock Committee two. The Vale of Leven Central Strike Committee of twenty contained nine communists and was one of the most militant, with functioning sub-committees on organisation, picketing, propaganda, defence and supply. At Falkirk two Party members were on the Town Strike Committee. In contrast, at Greenock, a *new* Trades Council had been formed to counteract the old one's positive attitude to the Communist Party. This new anti-communist Council was virtually dead so far as activity was concerned in the General Strike.

In the East of Scotland the Fife coalfield was very active. The Methil Council of Action, formed by the Trades Council (which accepted a number of communist organisational proposals), seems to have been something of a model.[53] It set up a Workers' Defence Corps, sections on Food, Transport, Information, Propaganda, adding later Prisoners' Aid and Entertainment. A prominent communist miner, David Proudfoot, was appointed Convener for all the sub-committees. Reporting after the strike a member of the Council of Action wrote:[54] "The organisation worked like clockwork. Everything was stopped—even the railway lines were picketed. The Council had a courier service second to none in Britain with three motor cars (and a maximum of six available), 100 motor-cycles, and as many push bikes as were necessary. They covered the whole of Fife taking out information and bringing in reports, sending out speakers everywhere, as far north as Perth." On the Defence Corps, he writes: "After police charges on mass pickets, the Defence Corps, which 150 workers had joined at the outset, was reorganised. Its numbers rose to 700, of whom 400 comradely workers who had been NCO's during the War marched in military formation through the town to protect the picket. The police did not interfere again." A daily bulletin was issued, and the Council of Action took over the Co-operative Hall as its Headquarters. The Communist Party issued its own bulletin and distributed 20,000 of the Party *Manifesto*. It is not surprising that in this, one of the most militant and best organised areas of the strike, arrests were frequent.

J. T. Murphy, at that period a member of the Executive Committee of the Communist Party, reported immediately following the strike on events at Middlesbrough and around Sheffield.[55] At Middlesbrough there were four Party members and a number of close supporters on the Central Strike Committee, an extremely effective organisation.[56] It met daily, kept an emergency committee on duty at night, organised an efficient despatch rider service. Indeed, Murphy reported, it was so authoritative that it secured the withdrawal of all mounted police and special constables from the streets "in the interests of order".

In Sheffield the Trades Council formed its industrial section into a Central Dispute Committee, which refused an official offer of co-operation from the Communist Party but, at the same time, sought the support of its individual members, one of whom, George Fletcher, was in fact Vice-Chairman of the Trades Council and a moving spirit of the strike committee.[57] The Communist Party and Minority Movement organised in Sheffield an unofficial strike committee, which produced a daily bulletin of around 10,000 copies (with the usual hustle to keep the duplicator away from the police). When, after five days the equipment was finally seized, the "special Strike Bulletin", No. 6, appeared on 11 May, prepared secretly from somewhere in the AEU Institute at Stanley Street, which was itself raided the next day. Twelve communists, including George Fletcher, were arrested for their strike activity.

In what was then the Liverpool District of the Party, the District Party Committee remained in almost constant session throughout the strike.[58] It published a Party bulletin, *The Workers' Gazette*, on 10 and 11 May and helped in the production of the daily bulletin of the Merseyside Council of Action. There were six communists on the St. Helens, two on the Garston, one on the Bootle and the Liverpool, two on the Birkenhead and four on the Wallasy Council of Action.[59]

In South Wales the Party gave all its support to the militant system of strike committees and Councils of Action. A Report after the strike[60] commented that: "The Party membership rose to the occasion with a vigour and resourcefulness we could not have imagined in our wildest dreams." The District Committee was in more or less permanent session and there were communists on nearly all the Councils of Action.

In London the arrest of R. W. Robson, the District Organiser, caused some dislocation at first. The leadership met daily at different places and kept contact with the majority of branches. It arranged the production of the *Workers' Bulletin*, and many other bulletins were published in the branches. It fought for comprehensive local Councils of Action and, against strong right-wing resistance or at best inertia, for some form of All-London Co-ordinating Council.[61]

By 8 May, some fifteen Councils of Action were functioning in London. By the end of the strike there were around seventy. When the strike began the London Trades Council called a meeting of Union District Committees and established a very formal Central Strike Committee.[62] It was only after the strike was ended that the first real Conference of Councils of Action was held. The London Trades Council Secretary Duncan Carmichael did his best, however, working day and night, travelling the district by motor cycle, though suffering from an illness which was to cause his death before the year was out.[63] But it was the local Councils of Action, on many of which communists served, that saved London's honour.

Poplar Council of Action (with three communists) edited a regular bulletin which had a 300 circulation. In Stepney there were four Party members on a Council of fifteen. In Bethnal Green there were four communists on the Council of Action, in West Ham eight (four on its Executive). In Battersea there were ten communists on a Council of Action of 124, four on the Executive of seven and a daily bulletin (2,500 circulation). In St. Pancras, the Communist Party Branch published its own bulletin (10,000 circulation) daily and two communists served on the Council of Action, who were mainly instrumental in producing a *St. Pancras Bulletin* (3,000–4,000) daily. This was an effective Council, meeting daily, one of the few where the Co-operative had agreed to supply goods on credit (for a canteen organised by the Women's Committee). An agreement was made with the local Labour Party, ILP and Communist Party to run all meetings jointly under the auspices of the Trades Council.[64] At Islington there were two communists on an Emergency Strike Committee of five members. A Party bulletin had a circulation of around 1,500 and the Council of Action's *Islington Worker*, about the same.

In a number of areas where the strike committees or Councils of Action were most effective, where they really embodied the unity of the local working class, there *began* (only began) to develop in embryo an alternative centre of government, something like an elementary type of "dual power". The beginning of such development could be seen where Councils of Action controlled the granting of local transport permits. The situation was evidenced by the cars and lorries carrying black or yellow labels bearing the words "by permission of the TUC".

An Ashton sheet metal worker, member of his local Permit Committee, wrote in his union journal:[65] "Employers of labour were coming, cap in hand, begging for permission to do certain things, or, to be more correct to allow their workers to return to perform certain customary operations. . . . Most of them turned empty away after a most humiliating experience, for one and all were put through a stern questioning, just to make them realise that we and not they were the salt of the earth."

The Edinburgh *Strike Bulletin* reported the formation of the establishment of a Food Permit system:[66] "There has been a constant stream of applicants at the Offices and many business firms have been on the doorstep. All kinds of businesses are represented. The Committee insist, however, upon certain conditions which many firms find irksome. Permits are only issued to those men who are members of Transport Unions, and no departure is made from this rule. The Committee believe that in a few days practical control of road traffic will be in their hands, and that the O.M.S. . . . will find their occupation gone."

Probably the most effective exercise of power was by the Northumberland and Durham General Council and Joint Strike Committee.[67] The local Trades and Labour Council called a meeting of its delegates on Sunday evening, 2 May, inviting all sections of the working-class movement, including members of the Co-operative Board of Management, officers of the Women's Co-operative Guild, Labour Councillors and County Councillors, and representatives of the Plebs League and of the Communist Party. A detailed, comprehensive (and very militant) "Plan of Campaign" was adopted by the meeting which constituted itself into a Council of Action. The plan of action envisaged from the beginning a challenge to the government distribution of food. "Whoever handles and transports food, the same person controls food; whoever controls food will find the 'neutral' part of the population rallying to their side. Who feeds the people wins the Strike. . . ." On 4 May a meeting of various trade union representatives was held with Will Lawther, a member of the Durham County Miners' Federation Board, and R. Page Arnot, leading communist, one of "the Twelve" who had recently been released from prison (and future historian of the Miners' Union), in his capacity of Director of the Labour Research Department. Here it was agreed to form a local General Council to cover the whole Northumberland and Durham area, as well as a strike committee. Arnot was co-opted on to both.

Even the Civil Commissioner, Sir Kingsley Wood, had to acknowledge the authority of the Northumberland and Durham General Council. Arnot writes:[68] "After forty hours of the general stoppage (Sir Kingsley) came by night to negotiate personally with the Strike Committee. Sixty hours after the Strike began Sir Kingsley Wood, accompanied by General Sir Kerr Montgomery, were once more at Burt Hall, making a plea for 'dual control' of the transport of food. This proposal was immediately rejected by the Joint Strike Committee—we cannot agree to our men working under any form of dual control—which at the same time decided 'that we now use the discretionary powers vested in us by the Trades Union Congress and withdraw all permits today'." The Minutes of the strike committee continued confidently: "On Friday (7 May) the success of the General Strike appeared completely assured. It was clear to everyone that the O.M.S. organisation was unable to cope with the task imposed upon it. The attitude of the population was favourable to the strikers and unfavourable to the Government. There were no disturbances, the trade unionists maintained an almost perfect discipline. There was no change from the ordinary except for the quietness in the streets and the absence of traffic. . . . The situation as a whole was now well in hand."

Authority for transport and for more than this was beginning, just beginning, to pass into the hands of the organised working class. The Councils of Action, or, rather, a few of the best of them, were beginning to develop, just beginning, into something of different quality from a strike committee, to embody an element of power. On the other hand, on the capitalist side before, during and after the strike, no attempt was made to disguise the fact that to crush the strike they were ready to use in every form *the power that they held*. The myth of a neutral State and impartial justice was for a moment dropped. Arrests, mainly under different sections of EPA, had started the previous October with the arrest of "the Twelve".

During the nine days of the strike the figure of arrests rose daily, with communists and miners the principal targets.[69] Considering the 5,000 membership of the Communist Party, a very high percentage of the "casualties" were Party members. It took some months following the strike to compile a "list of honour". The first Executive Committee meeting following the strike had a list of around 100 communist arrests, nearly all for producing, distributing or possessing the *Workers' Bulletin*.[70] Of these, thirty-five were still in prison. Most of the sentences were from two to six months. But as reports flowed in the communist casualty list was seen to exceed 1,000. In the *Political Report* prepared for the Eighth Congress of the CPGB (October 1926), it was calculated that over 1,200 (between one-fourth and one-fifth of the pre-strike membership) Communist Party members had suffered one or another form of government repression for support of the General Strike and of the miners after the sell-out.

Police seizure of duplicators, police raids and searches, detectives clustered outside Party offices and Party homes, the extension of the usual interceptions of correspondence, became the norm. King Street, the Communist Party headquarters, was under a sort of siege. Raids were made on the *Workers' Weekly*, the office of the NMM, the Dorritt press, the Young Communist League, and Party offices up and down the country. It is significant that the chief target was everyone connected with the *Workers' Bulletin*. *Lansbury's Labour Weekly* reported:[71] "The 'Special Department' at Scotland Yard was in full cry after Communists in particular. To be in possession of one of their multi-graphed bulletins was as good as a sentence without the option. Almost any news unfavourable to the Government was 'false' now."

R. W. Robson, the London District Organiser, was arrested for carrying a copy of the *Workers' Bulletin* and sentenced to six weeks. Marjorie Pollitt, wife of Harry Pollitt (still in gaol), was charged as a publisher of the *Workers' Bulletin*, fined £50 and costs (with alternative of three months). T. A. Jackson, Acting-Editor of the *Workers' Weekly*, was given two months "for having under his control matter likely to cause disaffection". R. Stoker of Manchester was charged and sentenced for having in his car a supply of the lone issue of the *Workers' Daily*. John Forshaw, following a police raid on the Party office at Salford, was imprisoned for one month and fined £100 for being in possession of a leaflet entitled "The Great Betrayal". In South Wales Frank Bright, communist miner, Emrys Llewelyn, Daniel and Isaac Lewes (the latter seventeen years old and Secretary of the Porth YCL) were charged with having committed breaches of the Emergency Powers Act "by having in their possession documents which were likely to cause disaffection amongst His Majesty's Forces" (the "documents" included a pit paper and a YCL circular). Twelve Sheffield communists all received fines of £5 to £15 for possession of "seditious literature".[72]

Many members of the Young Communist League were on the list of honour. It was the YCL's pride that it was considered just as criminal to produce, distribute or possess their bulletin, the *Young Striker*, as the Party's *Workers' Bulletin*. YCL members had plunged into every aspect of the struggle. The YCL Secretary William Rust was one of "the Twelve". D. F. Springball, Acting Secretary, was given two months by a Bow Street magistrate for possession of the *Young Striker*. George Miles, one of its publishers, was fined £70 and costs. Sarah and Bessie Span were bound over for a year in respect of copies of the *Young Striker* found in their flat.

So the story could continue. The second favourite charge was "seditious speech", as with the communist MP, Saklatvala, who received two months, and Isabel Brown, a popular mass speaker, charged at Pontefract and sentenced to three months for a speech at Castleford, where she was alleged to have appealed to the forces not to act against strikers. Mass picketers were usually charged with "acts of intimidation", like the fifty Gateshead workers, mostly miners, arrested when holding up blackleg transport.

The direction of the arrests is very significant. The *Workers' Bulletin* and the host of local bulletins of Councils of Action, strike committees and local organisations of the Communist Party were dangerous because they represented the interests and struggle of the working class. The *British Worker*, alas, was not dangerous. The anger and violence of the Law was a compliment, a ruling class recognition of the role of the Communist Party in the General Strike, along with the militants in different sectors of the Labour movement, along with the miners.

4. SOME CONCLUSIONS

No event of British Labour history has been so much studied as the General Strike. As soon as it was over each side and each trend within each side proceeded to hold inquests. Capitalists discussed how to make its recurrence impossible, right-wing reformists how to proscribe it from accepted forms of Labour struggle, Marxists examined the weaknesses on the side of the working class so that these could be overcome in future struggles.

The Communist Party analysed the strike lessons at the Executive Committee meeting at the end of May,[73] again more in detail at its Eighth Congress in mid-October.[74] The Communist International adopted a thesis, "The Lessons of the General Strike"[75]—at a session of the Executive Committee of the Communist International (ECCI) held on 8 June 1926. The strike was examined in a whole number of communist pamphlets.[76] The TUC and the miners held their inquests.

In the few years that followed the General Strike the analysis of its contents, its strength and weaknesses, its significance, became deeply entangled with internal struggles within the international communist movement and within the British Communist Party. Trotsky and his supporters raised within the Communist International above all questions about the characterisation of the General Council and the role of the Anglo-Soviet Trade Union Committee.[77] Often the picture presented of the strike and the estimate of its outcome was adapted by the different contestants in the internal political struggle to fit in with their own particular theory, and throws more light on the contents of the political conflicts of the day than on the strike itself.

It is an indication of the immense political significance of the General Strike that each generation of British workers, and of students of British working-class history, has had to look at it anew and draw from it lessons for their own contemporary struggles. Perhaps, fifty years after, the lesson that still stands out most clearly in relief, is the importance for the Labour movement to come to understand the nature of the State.

The British Labour movement is more than two hundred years old. It has learned very much of organisation, discipline and solidarity. But developing within the framework of what was for so long the centre of world colonialism and imperialism, it came to combine great militancy and effectiveness in the struggle for the defence of its own *immediate* interests, with a widespread acceptance of the political system within which that struggle was taking place. A very low level of political and socialist consciousness was combined with a high level of experience of economic struggle and industrial organisation. And the Achilles heel, the weakest point of the political consciousness of the British working class is, precisely, the lack of understanding of the State, of political power, and the acceptance, central to the whole reformist approach, that the State is neutral, non-political, unbiassed, unpartisan, above classes—that workers and capitalists can share this same "impartial" machinery, that this State will treat them fairly (under capitalism) and even help them to build a socialist society.

In the General Strike, the Tory Government might have set out to disprove reformism and underline the basic truth of the Marxist-Leninist conception of the State.

Baldwin, Churchill and their colleagues took it for granted that *the* State was *their* State, the State of the coalowners, capitalists, employers, to be used for *their* objectives. Army and Navy were rushed into action to defend property, but not the rights of trade unionists. Troops were concentrated in the main industrial areas to protect blacklegs, not strikers. Armed convoys defended government supplies. Security tapped "red", not Tory, telephones. That famous "impartial" Law declared the strike illegal and sentenced those who distributed (or even possessed) the *Workers' Bulletin*, not the *British Gazette*. The BBC served one side only. It appealed to God as an anti-strike Authority, but rejected the God of the Archbishop of Canterbury who called for conciliation. Liberals, like Lloyd George, who criticised the government, found the BBC closed to them, but for fellow-Liberals H. H. Asquith, Lord Grey of Fallodon and Sir John Simon, who denounced the strike as illegal, it was wide open. Even *The Times* waxed indignant when the government commandeered part of its stock of newsprint along with that of the General Council. Its protest was handed by the Prime Minister to Mr. Churchill. "I do not agree", he replied, "with your idea that the TUC have as much right as the Government to publish their side of the case and to exhort their followers to combined action."[78]

The General Strike was political from the outset. The capitalists recognised this and fought it politically, using every political weapon they could including all the powers of the State. The reformists could not understand the nature of the State. It was not within their philosophy.

It was one of the merits of the Communist Party that, before, during and after the General Strike, it sought to explain, and explain again, the *class* nature of the State and the *political* character of the strike.

A minority exploiting class maintains its power not just by direct control of machinery of State, like the police, armed forces, security, judiciary, but by its capacity through a multitude of means—education, religion (sometimes), control of the media, of press, magazines, learned journals, and children's comics—to dominate people's minds, secure their acceptance. British capitalism is old, long-established, experienced, and with age and strength have come cunning, elasticity, duplicity, a formidable capacity to manœuvre, a deftness at division, an aptness at knowing how and when temporarily to retreat in order to transform retreat (provisional defeat) into victory. All these qualities and skills were amply employed in preparing for and coping with the General Strike.

The OMS, District Commissioners, EPA, blacklegs, "specials", armed forces, arrests, declarations of strike illegality, warnings of measureless fines, were aspects of direct force. But the temporary subsidy, the establishment, after Red Friday, of the Royal Commission, its ambiguous formulations, the masterly playing for time, the superbly timed production of Sir Herbert and his misty Memorandum at the critical point of a fast-expanding strike, were the crafty manœuvres of the two-faced tactics and strategy in which British imperialism excels. British reaction used double weapons. Samuel complemented Jix, Thomas and MacDonald complemented Baldwin and Churchill. When it came to the crunch, reformism complemented capitalism.

This last point must be examined with care. It is not simply that reformist leaders are, by nature, conscious personal traitors (though a few may be so). It is that the reformist outlook, quite irrespective of the personal sincerity or insincerity, morality or immorality of individual leaders, leads inexorably to conciliation and capitulation.

The essential political thinking of the leading British reformists in 1925–6—men like MacDonald, Thomas, Snowden and Clynes—moved along well-defined lines. For them the path to socialism was gradual, step by step, within the framework of capitalism, by successive reforms. An essential part of this framework—the British State—was seen as a neutral piece of machinery that would serve with equal fairness all sections of the population, whatever government was elected to office. They denied the division of society into classes and with it the struggle of classes. They believed in "evolution not revolution", envisaged as a gradual series of electoral advances, local and national within the capitalist State. The function of the masses was to vote periodically in such elections. The role of the trade unions was, in a non-political way, to negotiate economic reforms, backed up when unavoidable (but as rarely as possible) by a show of strength, that should not in any way weaken the existing political system.

The leading British reformists were not "revisionists" in the continental sense. They did not (like Bernstein, for instance) "revise" Marxism. They rejected it out of hand, along with all conceptions of revolutionary change in society.

Out of office, in opposition, and particularly at times of relative economic and political "calm", they could speak with a certain militancy, preach socialism, call on the people for support. But at times of crisis, sometimes in opposition, but mostly in office, they would forget their pledges, reject their own programmes, call for the defence of "the nation", which in class terms meant defence of the interests of the dominant minority of the nation—the ruling, capitalist class.

When the capitalist course was relatively smooth, a smooth advance to socialism was smoothly envisaged. But, in capitalist crisis, it was necessary for all good people, including trade unionists and socialists, to rally to the cause of "the nation", to go into "provisional retreat". At such critical moments, capitalism was, for reformism, no longer the enemy. Now it was the militants, those who demanded the fulfilment of previous promises, still more those who still fought to achieve them, above all the Communists, who became the enemy. In order to advance within the existing system, the system itself had to be saved. Betrayal at such times of economic and political crisis was the built-in product of the reformist philosophy. Given the nature of capitalism, its economy, its State, consistent reformists were bound to betray.

Nor should we ever forget that even on the minds of millions of militant workers, trades unionists, Labour Party and ILP members, reformist ideas had a deep and lasting grip.

It is only within this context that we can comprehend the almost incredible "calculated" unpreparedness of the General Council and Labour Party leaders for the impending struggle which the government and employers had openly announced, and of which the miners and communists especially had so repeatedly warned.

Once the strike was over this "unpreparedness" was admitted by all, including the leaders of the General Council. The official Strike Organisation Committee of the General Council explained: "The Strike Organisation Committee desire to emphasise that the organisation was of necessity improvised. The date upon which we were first asked as a 'ways and means' Committee to consider the question in the event of a general dispute, was April 27, and prior to that date, no consideration had been given to the possibility of such an eventuality."[79] Ernest Bevin confirmed at the Conference of Trade Union Executives in January 1927:[80] "With regard to preparations for the Strike, there were no preparations until April 1926, and I do not want anyone to go away from this Conference under the impression that the General Council had any particular plan to run this movement. In fact, the General Council did not sit down to draft the plans until they were called together on April 27th. . . ." In his *Nine Days*, A. J. Cook, Miners' Secretary, described his own failure to push the General Council into taking preparative action:[81] "There were certain leaders who were determined that no preparations should be made. Most notable amongst them was J. H. Thomas, arguing that any preparations would only encourage the Government to make ready, and would lead people to believe that we thought a fight inevitable." The more critical the situation, the nearer the strike became, the more urgent the appeals of the miners and the communists, the more vigorously the right-wing opposed preparation, endeavoured to avoid the strike and, when this was not possible, prepared (yes, at last, *prepared*) the most rapid capitulation.

Before the strike had begun J. H. Thomas had described it as "the greatest calamity for this country".[82] During the strike, on 9 May, he admitted: "I have never disguised that I did not favour the principle of a General Strike."[83] Ramsay MacDonald told the House of Commons, on 3 May, that "with the discussion of General Strikes and Bolshevism and all that kind of thing, I have nothing to do at all. . . ."[84] J. R. Clynes, writing his *Memoirs* ten years later, explained: "No General Strike was ever planned or seriously contemplated as an act of Trade Union policy. I told my Union in April (1926) that such a Strike would be a national disaster, and a fatal step to Union prestige, and such it eventually proved to be."[85] C. T. Cramp, with Thomas leader of the National Union of Railwaymen, avowed to the Conference of Trade Union Executives in January 1927:[86] "We have not to blame the General Council for taking the action they did in calling off the Strike. The pity of it is that it was ever called on."

If such key figures in the TUC, the Labour Party, not to forget the ILP were so drastically opposed to the strike, why, then, was it called? The General Council called it because it could not do otherwise without isolation from the mass of the workers. Ramsay MacDonald admitted this after the strike:[87] "After the conduct of the Government it was perfectly evident that had no General Strike been declared industry would have been almost as much paralysed by unauthorised strikes." As did Ernest Bevin:[88] "It must not be forgotten that apart from the rights and wrongs of the calling of a General Strike, there would in any case, with the miners' lock-out, have been widespread unofficial fighting in all parts of the country, which would have produced anarchy in the movement." Kingsley Martin, later editor of the *New Statesman*, described the TUC as "a combatant in a war which had been forced upon it and which it feared to win".[89]

The more solid, organised and combative the strike became, the more the leadership was passing into the hands of the Councils of Action and local strike committees, and through them into the hands of the more militant side of the movement, the more necessary it became for the right-wing to bring it to an end. The editorial of the first issue of the *Workers' Weekly* to appear after the capitulation[90] underlined this conclusion: "The truth cannot be concealed. We had men at the head of the General Council who were more afraid of winning than losing."

The struggle of Right versus Left trends in the Labour movement was mirrored, not only in theoretical approaches to the strike, but also on questions of organisation. The calling out of workers by their individual unions, and in two "lines" or stages, reflected (as has already been noted) right-wing approaches fearful of unity and of action. Individual union strike committees often overlapped with local Councils of Action or refused to pool their resources. The TUC was scared of the local Councils of Action and strike committees taking into their own hands the allotment of permits. Reformist trade union leaders were reluctant to bring the local Co-operatives into the Councils of Action (as were right-wing Co-operative leaders). Right-wing leaders in the Labour Party (and in the ILP) were equally reluctant to draw in *their* local branches, though there were many honourable exceptions.

When unity develops in working-class struggle the resulting strength cannot be calculated by simple arithmetic. When a dozen local trade union organisations joined in a Council of Action with the left-wing political organisations, including the communists, with sections of the NMM and NUWCM, with women's or youth organisations, maybe with a Co-operative, still more when they began to struggle in a united way, the force that emerged was greater than that of the sum of the component parts.

With the development of the best, most organised and conscious of the Councils of Action, a British form of united action, started in 1920, was taken a step further, entered our history, our tradition of struggle, and left its mark.

While it is true that in the nine days the Councils of Action were moving left whilst the General Council was preparing a sell-out, the experience of 1920, and the relation of the Councils of Action to the miners in 1926, showed that there was no necessary contradiction between the struggle from below through the local Councils and the leadership provided by progressive trade union leaderships on national or local level. The two could strengthen each other. If the strike taught anything it was the need for unity, that reformist ideas would not be defeated by theory alone, though this was essential, but with the aid of theory in the course of action.

The right-wing leaders feared unity like the plague. In the months that preceded the strike and in the nine days they tried by every means to isolate the miners, to take decisions out of their hands.

Still more was this true of the right-wing attitude to the Communist Party. The Liverpool Labour Party decisions prepared the way for the arrest of the Twelve. The trial showed a deep cleft between the right wing and the warm solidarity with those arrested from individuals (and sometimes Branches) of the Labour Party and ILP.

The right wing was scared above all that, as the strike continued, leadership would pass more and more to the Left. Charles Dukes of the General and Municipal Workers, speaking at the January 1927 Conference of Executives, admirably expressed the right-wing nightmare:[91] ". . . every day that the Strike proceeded the control and authority was passing out of the hands of responsible Executives into the hands of men who had no authority, no responsibility . . .". J. H. Thomas explained in the House of Commons on 13 May, the day of the sell-out, how he shared this same obsession:[92] "What he dreaded about this struggle more than anything else was this: If by any chance it should have got out of the hands of those who would be able to exercise some control, every sane man knows what would have happened. I thank God it never did. That is why I believe that the decision yesterday was such a big decision, and that is why that danger, that fear, was always in our minds. . . ."

It has been a tragic feature of British working-class history that again and again, the anger or disillusion that followed on capitulation has been diverted in personal terms against individual betrayers—MPs, Labour Party or trade union leaders—not against the most real enemy—reformist theory, reformist ideas.

In 1925–6 reformism was a very strong influence, not only on the minds of leaders, but on those of millions of Labour Party, ILP and trade union members, including many who had fought courageous militant battles on the economic front. It is hard to assess how far the experience of the nine days began to weaken the stranglehold of reformist ideas. It is important not to exaggerate, because exaggeration breeds illusions and illusions disillusion.

On 4 May the workers were ready and eager to go. They had a deep sense of solidarity with the miners, and many of them saw that *their* wages and living standards were also at stake. But for the great majority this was by no means a revolutionary approach. They were not challenging the political system, though they fought with the determined courage typical of the British working class. They showed an admirable power of improvisation and a tremendous capacity to organise complex operations in the greatest order and discipline. It would be wrong, too, to forget their humour—their capacity to laugh at themselves as well as at their enemies even in critical situations. Their satires, in cartoons, poems, on the picket line, in all-night vigils, in leaflet and bulletin, made fools of Tories, police inspectors, and public school blacklegs, and their laughter gave them strength. But deep-felt solidarity, dogged courage, capacity to organise, self-discipline, humour, great qualities for struggle—are not, and were not, by themselves, enough.

The retiring Communist Party Executive, drafting the *Thesis on the Strike* for the Eighth Party Congress, and having explained the workers' readiness for struggle, added, with classic understatement: "Their determination to win was, however, accompanied with a lack of understanding of the full political implications of the General Strike."[93] Reformism was still the principal influence in the minds of the workers. Many were still political Liberals, many still voted Tory.

It is true that in great struggles ideas can shift more in a few days than in years of more "normal" times. There is evidence that many *began* to shed their illusions, to open their minds, began to understand the political nature of the strike, and something of the class structure of the State, particularly where Marxists were present to help translate experience into more theoretical terms. But this was only a beginning. It was not a level of political consciousness sufficient to reject the call-off by the General Council, and to fight on (like the miners).

The development of some Councils of Action to the point of taking over certain of the functions of government was an important advance; but this, too, was only a beginning. The progress of the strike, with only the relatively small forces of the communists, helped by a number of militant socialists in the Labour Party, ILP and trade unions hammering away at its political explanations, accelerated the political awakening—but nine days were not enough to transform the hatred of the Tories, resentment against the coalowners, anger with the employers, growing disillusion with the General Council, into a revolutionary outlook or a level of political consciousness sufficient to maintain the strike.

Looking back, therefore, after fifty years, at the strength and weaknesses of the General Strike, perhaps the most recurring thought relates to the Communist Party itself.

Hundreds of thousands of militant workers from trade unions, Co-operatives, Labour Party and ILP played, individually, courageous and important roles in the local leadership of the strike. But, with all its weaknesses, only the Communist Party acted as an organised collective conscious force.

Many of the tens of thousands who led the Councils of Action and strike committees had sharp class instincts, hated the old (capitalist) order of things, yearned for a new order which they saw as Socialism. But most often they lacked a real understanding of the nature of capitalism, its growth, exploitation, crisis, methods of maintaining rule, and still more a developed conception of how to advance from capitalism to socialism.

British history in the crowded months from Red Friday to the General Strike "shouted aloud", as it were, for a revolutionary Party, strong enough to give daily leadership on all the immediate struggles, to develop unity of all the progressive forces of the working class and people, to prepare for the coming offensive, to lift the level of struggle at each successive stage, to take to the working class the theory of socialism, socialist consciousness, to build branches in pits, factories, railway depots, in all the industrial areas where the crux of the struggle would come, in close and friendly contact with every militant section of the Labour, trade union and progressive movement. Can it be said that such a leadership was provided by the CPGB? Looking back, it is clear that there were in the Party's approaches many weaknesses. But, in my opinion, on all *essentials* its stand was correct.

The Communist Party told the workers of the coming offensive, exposed the manœuvre of the Royal Commission, put forward the fundamental lines of preparation for struggle, above all the formation of Councils of Action. It withstood the arrest of its own leaders, put its total strength at the disposal of the strike, warned against capitulation, tried (unsuccessfully) to carry on the struggle, turned its efforts to resist demoralisation, victimisation, and above all to support the miners who were fighting on alone.

There have been periods in the history of the British Communist Party when, in my opinion, errors and weaknesses were particularly great—in 1928–31 for example. But from Red Friday up to and including the General Strike the role of the Party, in my judgment was, with all mistakes, overwhelmingly positive.

This was widely recognised. By the capitalists, for example, and their government, who made the communists their especial target; by miners' leaders like A. J. Cook:[94] "I should like to state plainly and emphatically that the splendid solidarity of the miners and the whole working-class movement is due to a large extent to the uncompromising attitude taken by the *Workers' Weekly*. Events since April 30 have proved conclusively that the *Workers' Weekly* was right"; by the thousands of rank-and-file miners who in the months that followed the strike joined the Communist Party's ranks and more than doubled its membership.

Of course, there were many weaknesses. Though the Party held together very well after the arrest of the Twelve, there was certainly insufficient preparation for the semi-legal days that lay ahead. There was ambiguity and inconsistency in the slogans put forward on increasing the powers of the General Council (though all the emphasis was quite clearly on the formation of factory committees and Councils of Action).[95] The Party seemed slow in the critical first days of the strike to answer the government's claims that the strike was illegal and unconstitutional.

These and other errors and weaknesses need to be studied within the context of the contribution made by a Party that before the strike had just over 5,000 members. For the outstanding weaknesses of the Party (and, therefore, of the whole situation of the strike) was that it was *too small*. Despite increasing influence and, for its size, rapid recruitment, it had neither the influence nor the membership to develop a united left that could take over leadership from the reformists. Despite rapidly changing outlooks in some sectors during the nine days, reformist influence was still far too extended.

Looking back fifty years after we can see more clearly that to be successful in the advance to socialism the British working class needs a well-established Party that will bring to the working class and working people a socialist theory, socialist consciousness, that will help the workers to fight on all the immediate struggles that confront them, to co-ordinate these struggles, lift their level, that will give to the most politically conscious workers and their allies a strong organisational basis where they work and live. Such an aim is inseparable from the transformation of every section of the Labour movement, the victory of militant attitudes in trade unions and Co-operatives and of socialist ideas in the Labour Party, and the creation of broad unity of the Left.

The General Strike was defeated, but there can be defeats that contain within themselves the elements of future victory. Such were the Paris Commune, the Russian 1905 Revolution. During those tragic glorious nine days pits were closed, traffic was at a standstill, the capitalist class shouted its anger and shivered with apprehension. That great slumbering giant the British working class showed something of its vast potential power. There was a glimpse of its unbounded strength once it had thrown off the bonds of capitalist and reformist ideas, once socialist ideas were wedded to the great organised mass movement. It was only a glimpse, perhaps, but one that has left its mark that will not be forgotten.

NOTES

1. Resolutions 4 and 5. See Report of the National Minority Movement Conference, 23–24 August 1924, published by NMM.
2. The Conference was sometimes referred to at the time as the 2nd Conference. But later this title was given to that of August 1925. See *Workers' Weekly*, No. 104, 30 January 1925.
3. *Report of the 7th Congress of the CPGB*, CPGB, 1925. The Congress met on 30 May–1 June.
4. Speech at Northampton, reported in *The Times*, 3 August 1925.
5. *Hansard*, 6 August 1925.
6. *Manchester Guardian*, 4 August 1925.
7. Quoted in *Workers' Weekly*, No. 131, 7 August 1925.
8. Quoted by R. Page Arnot, *The Miners—Years of Struggle*, pp. 383–4.
9. See, for example, *Sunday Worker*, 27 September and 4 October 1925; *Workers' Weekly*, 2 October 1925; *Labour Monthly*, "Notes of the Month", July 1925, p. 393.

10. *Workers' Weekly*, No. 133, 21 August 1925.
11. Interview with *Sunday Times*, 23 August 1925.
12. See *The Mining Crisis and the National Strike, 1926*, TUC General Council, London 1927, p. 26.
13. Ibid., p. 10.
14. *Report of 2nd Annual Conference of the National Minority Movement*, NMM, 32 pp.
15. *Proceedings of the 57th Annual TUC, Scarborough, September 7–12, 1925*, p. 382.
16. Ibid., p. 387.
17. *The Times*, 1 October 1925.
18. Ramsay MacDonald, quoted in *Labour Monthly*, "Notes of the Month", November 1925.
19. J. H. Thomas in *Weekly Dispatch*, 11 October 1925.
20. *Sunday Worker*, 29 November 1925.
21. Ibid., 18 October 1925.
22. *The Times*, 30 January 1926.
23. See *Workers' Weekly*, 15 January 1926; Bob Stewart, *Breaking the Fetters*, London, 1967, pp. 168–9; "Political Report of the CC to the 8th Congress CPGB" in *Theses, Resolutions of 8th Congress of CPGB*.
24. *Royal Commission on the Coal Industry (1925)*, Cmd 2600, HMSO, 1926. See also summaries in *Facts from the Samuel Commission*, LRD, 1926; and R. Page Arnot, *The Miners—Years of Struggle*, pp. 401–5.
25. Quoted by Arthur Horner in *Incorrigible Rebel*, 1960, p. 74.
26. *Workers' Weekly,* 9 March 1926. The Report was not available for analysis in the previous issue. See also Emile Burns, "Divide and Conquer" and an editorial article on the Coal Commission Report in *Communist Review*, No. 12, April 1926; and Arthur Horner, "The Coal Report and After", in *Labour Monthly*, May 1926.
27. See Special Supplement of *Workers' Weekly*, 12 March 1926, and *Report of Special Conference of Action*, NMM, 1926.
28. *The Times*, 19 April 1936.
29. *The Mining Crisis and the National Crisis*, TUC, 1926, p. 31.
30. *Workers' Weekly*, No. 169, 30 April 1926.
31. *The Sunday Worker*, 2 May 1926.
32. Postgate, Wilkinson and Horrabin, *Workers' History of the General Strike*, Plebs League, p. 4.
33. Quoted by Allen Hutt, *Post-war History of the Working Class*, p. 136.
34. "The Secret History of the Great Strike", *Lansbury's Labour Weekly*, No. 63, 22 May 1926.
35. *The Times*, 4 May 1926.
36. J. R. Clynes, *Memoirs: 1924–1937*, pp. 86–7.
37. *Hansard*, 3 May 1926, col. 71.
38. Sir John Simon, *Three Speeches on the General Strike*, London, 1926, p. 3.

39. Quoted by R. Page Arnot, *The General Strike*, pp. 209–10.
40. In *Socialist Review*, June 1926.
41. A. J. Cook, *The Nine Days*, p. 18.
42. *Workers' Weekly*, No. 170, 26 May 1926; *Political Report to 8th Congress CPGB*, pp. 10–11.
43. *Political Report to 8th Congress CPGB*, pp. 10–11.
44. *Sunday Worker*, 2 May 1926; *Workers' Daily* (the sole issue), 3 May 1926.
45. *Political Report to 8th Congress CPGB*, p. 9.
46. Full text in *Workers' Bulletin*, No. 9, 13 May 1926, and in J. Klugmann, *History of CPGB*, vol. 2, pp. 210–12.
47. *Political Report to 8th Congress CPGB*, p. 10.
48. The *British Gazette* was published by HMSO, 5–13 May (eight issues, no issue on Sunday, 9 May). The *British Worker*, official strike news bulletin, was published by the TUC General Council, 5–17 May (eleven issues, no issue on Friday, 14 May, and Sunday, 16 May). The *Workers' Bulletin* was issued by CPGB, 4–14 May (ten issues, no issue on Sunday, 9 May).
49. Bob Stewart, *Breaking the Fetters*, pp. 170–1.
50. Emile Burns, *The General Strike—Trades Councils in Action*, LRD, 1926, reprinted Lawrence & Wishart, 1975.
51. *The Reds and the General Strike*, CPGB, 1926, 2nd ed.
52. Clearly, more research into local strike activities is necesssary to complete this report—some of it is provided by other essays contained in this book. I thought it best to confine myself here to information provided by *Workers' Weekly* and other communist and left-wing journals published immediately after the strike, knowing that this would need to be extended and, in some cases perhaps, corrected by the fruits of local research.
53. *Workers' Weekly*, No. 170, 21 May, and No. 173, 11 June 1926.
54. *Workers' Weekly*, No. 173.
55. *Workers' Weekly*, No. 170.
56. Emile Burns, op. cit.
57. Nellie Connole, *Leaven of Life, the Story of George Henry Fletcher*, London, 1961.
58. *Workers' Weekly*, No. 170.
59. Ibid.
60. Ibid.
61. *Workers' Weekly*, No. 171, 28 May 1926.
62. J. Jacobs, *London Trades Council, 1860–1950*, London, 1950, pp. 129–30.
63. Ibid., p. 130.
64. Emile Burns, op. cit., p. 168.
65. *Sheet Metal Workers' Quarterly*, October 1926.
66. Official *Strike Bulletin*, Edinburgh, 7 May 1926.
67. See *inter alia* Emile Burns, op. cit., pp. 152–4; "Account of the

Proceedings of the Northumberland and Durham General Council and Joint Strike Committee" in *Labour Monthly*, June 1926; R. Page Arnot, *The Miners—Years of Struggle*, pp. 436–43; "The General Strike in the North-East", *Our History*, No. 22, Summer 1961; Note by R. P. Arnot in J. Klugmann, *History of the CPGB*, vol. 2, pp. 162–3.

68. R. Page Arnot, *The Miners—Years of Struggle*, pp. 439–40.
69. See Diary Section of R. Page Arnot, *The General Strike*. It starts off with the lone arrest of Saklatvala, communist MP. By 6 May he is reporting sixty-six arrests in Glasgow, twenty-two in Edinburgh.
70. *Workers' Weekly*, 4 June 1926.
71. *Lansbury's Labour Weekly*, 22 May 1926.
72. See J. Klugmann, *History of the CPGB*, vol. 2, pp. 163–9, where detailed references are given.
73. *Workers' Weekly*, No. 176, 4 June 1926 ("Why the Strike failed").
74. *Report of 8th Congress CPGB*, pp. 55–71.
75. See *Communist Review*, vol. 7, No. 3, July 1926.
76. Including R. Palmer Dutt, *The Meaning of the General Strike*, written in June 1926; J. T. Murphy, *The Political Meaning of the General Strike*, CPGB., September 1926.
77. See L. Trotsky, *Writings on Britain*, vol. 2, pp. 187–253, New Park Publications, 1974.
78. *Strike Nights in Printing House Square: an Episode in the History of The Times*, printed for private record, 1926, pp. 32–4.
79. Report of the Strike Organisation Committee, quoted in A. J. Bennett, *The General Council and the General Strike*, CPGB pamphlet, p. 9.
80. See *The Mining Crisis*, TUC, 1927, p. 10.
81. A. J. Cook, *The Nine Days*, p. 7.
82. Quoted in A. Hutt, op. cit., p. 152.
83. Quoted in R. Page Arnot, *The General Strike*, p. 201.
84. Quoted in A. Hutt, op. cit., p. 152.
85. J. R. Clynes, *Memoirs, 1924–1937*, p. 75.
86. *The Mining Crisis*, TUC, 1927, p. 57.
87. Ramsay MacDonald in *Socialist Review*, June 1926.
88. Ernest Bevin in TGWU journal, *The Record*, quoted by A. Hutt, op. cit., p. 134.
89. Kingsley Martin, *The British Public and the General Strike*, Hogarth Press, 1926, p. 58.
90. *Workers' Weekly*, No. 170.
91. *The Mining Crisis and the National Strike*, TUC, 1927, p. 58.
92. Quoted by A. Hutt, op. cit., p. 135.
93. See *Report of 8th Congress CPGB*, "Thesis on General Strike", p. 63.
94. A. J. Cook, in *Workers' Weekly*, No. 173, 11 June 1926.
95. See fuller discussion in J. Klugmann, *History of the CPGB*, vol. 2, pp. 194–5.

PART TWO

REGIONAL STUDIES

1 THE WEST OF SCOTLAND

by PAUL CARTER

The West of Scotland is virtually a country in itself, with more variety in terms of geography, industry and people than several European nations possess. The region contains the heavy industrial and shipbuilding centre of the Clyde, the scarred landscape of the coal-mining counties, the rich farming land of the South West and the lonely beauty of the Highlands. Its people include the experienced and militant Clyde working class, the landed gentry of the country areas and the Highland crofters. This underlying variety gives the region its main interest in the General Strike. Different areas adopted different forms of organisation with different degrees of success.

In the most militant industrial centres the political and trade union sectors of the labour movement combined to form Councils of Action. These exercised almost complete control over their areas during the strike. In other parts of the industrial belt the strike was organised by strike committees, established by the trades councils without direct political involvement. In the country areas, remote from the main industry, the strike was organised by the individual unions concerned, with little or no local co-ordination. The famous "Red Clyde" was, however, only marginally involved, since the engineering and shipbuilding workers were in the "second line", not brought into action until the last day. This tore a gaping hole through the militant solidarity of the industrial West. Glasgow is a story in itself. It was the regional capital and hence the centre of regional strike activity, but at the same time its own strike organisation was weaker than in many surrounding areas.

COUNCILS OF ACTION

Councils of Action were formed throughout North Lanarkshire and the Vale of Leven, two of the most militant districts in the West of Scotland,

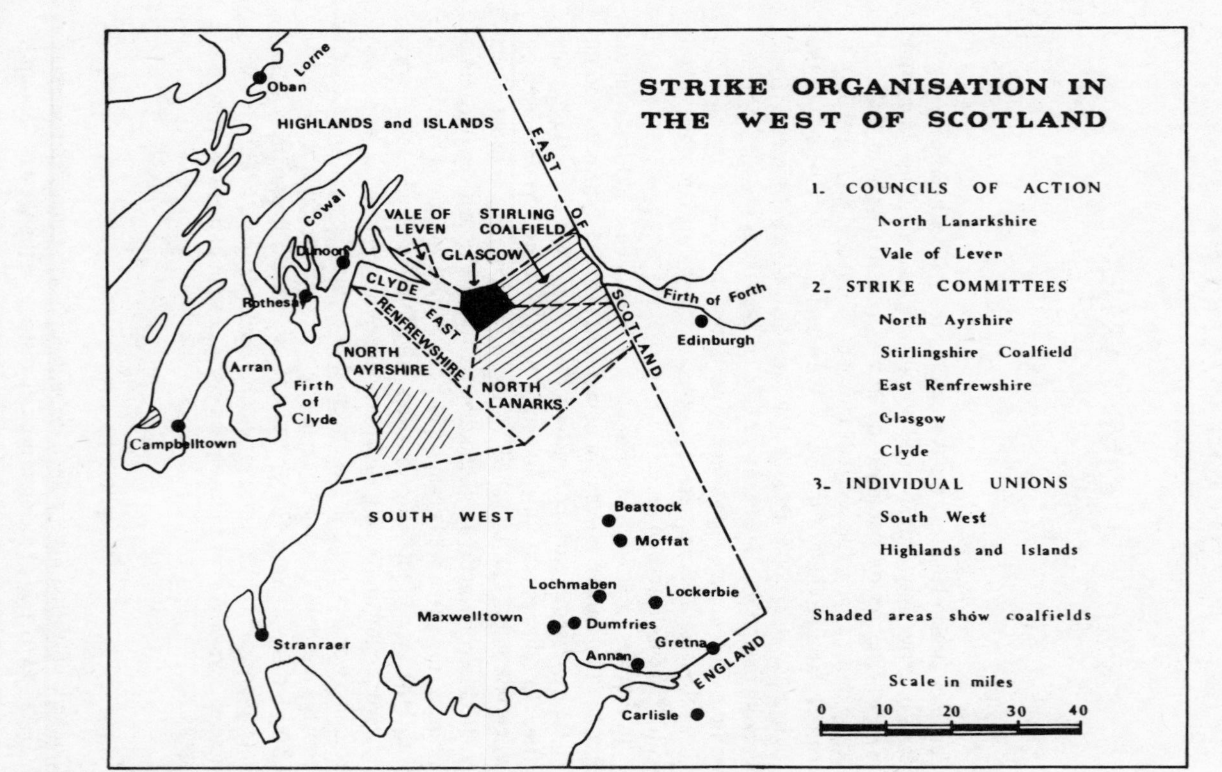
STRIKE ORGANISATION IN
THE WEST OF SCOTLAND
1. COUNCILS OF ACTION
North Lanarkshire
Vale of Leven
2. STRIKE COMMITTEES
North Ayrshire
Stirlingshire Coalfield
East Renfrewshire
Glasgow
Clyde
3. INDIVIDUAL UNIONS
South West
Highlands and Islands
Shaded areas show coalfields
Scale in miles
0
10
20
30
40
Oban
Lorne
HIGHLANDS and ISLANDS
EAST OF SCOTLAND
Cowal
VALE OF LEVEN
STIRLING COALFIELD
GLASGOW
CLYDE
EAST
RENFREWSHIRE
NORTH AYRSHIRE
NORTH LANARKS
Firth of Forth
Edinburgh
Rothesay
Arran
Firth of Clyde
Campbelltown
SOUTH WEST
Beattock
Moffat
Lochmaben
Lockerbie
Maxwelltown
Dumfries
Stranraer
Gretna
Annan
ENGLAND
Carlisle

and was composed of representatives of the trade unions, the working-class political parties, and other working-class campaigning organisations such as the anti-eviction Defence Leagues. As such they represented the most advanced form of local working-class organisation developed during the strike, a coming together of the political and industrial wings into one united body. They typically met every day, and had sub-committees to deal with control of road and rail transport, organisation of mass meetings and issue of bulletins, and picketing of any works which had not already come out on strike.

North Lanarkshire

North Lanarkshire is the main industrial centre of the West of Scotland outside of Glasgow. The towns of Airdrie and Coatbridge, Cambuslang and Rutherglen, Motherwell, Wishaw and Hamilton form the district, together with large mining villages such as Uddingston, Bellshill, Blantyre and Shotts. The area grew up two centuries ago, based on the North Lanarkshire "blackband", a combination of coal and ironstone which could be mined together as one seam. Mining and steelmaking became the area's main industries, and, as industry grew, the native lowlanders were joined by many Irish and Highland immigrants, with a later influx of Polish workers.

A strong Minority Movement existed amongst the miners of North Lanarkshire in the early 'twenties, led by a local communist, William Allen. The MPs for the area were all Labour in the 'twenties, except for Walter Newbold, elected as Communist MP for Motherwell in 1922. The unemployed workers' movement and an anti-eviction Defence League had conducted many battles in the post-war years. Marxist influence in the area dated from the SDF, SLP and BSP branches which were formed in many towns and villages earlier in the century, combining to form the Communist Party in 1920. Labour movement members were steadily taking over more and more seats on the Parish Councils. By the time of the General Strike, North Lanarkshire was at the peak of a sustained period of militant activity.

Twenty-three Councils of Action were set up in the towns and villages of the county. And the weekend before the strike a Lanarkshire Joint Committee of the Councils of Action was formed, with its headquarters at the Lanarkshire Mineworkers Union offices in Hamilton. This Joint Committee played two main roles—communications and relief. It distributed the Scottish TUC daily bulletin and the *Scottish Worker* to the local Councils of Action,

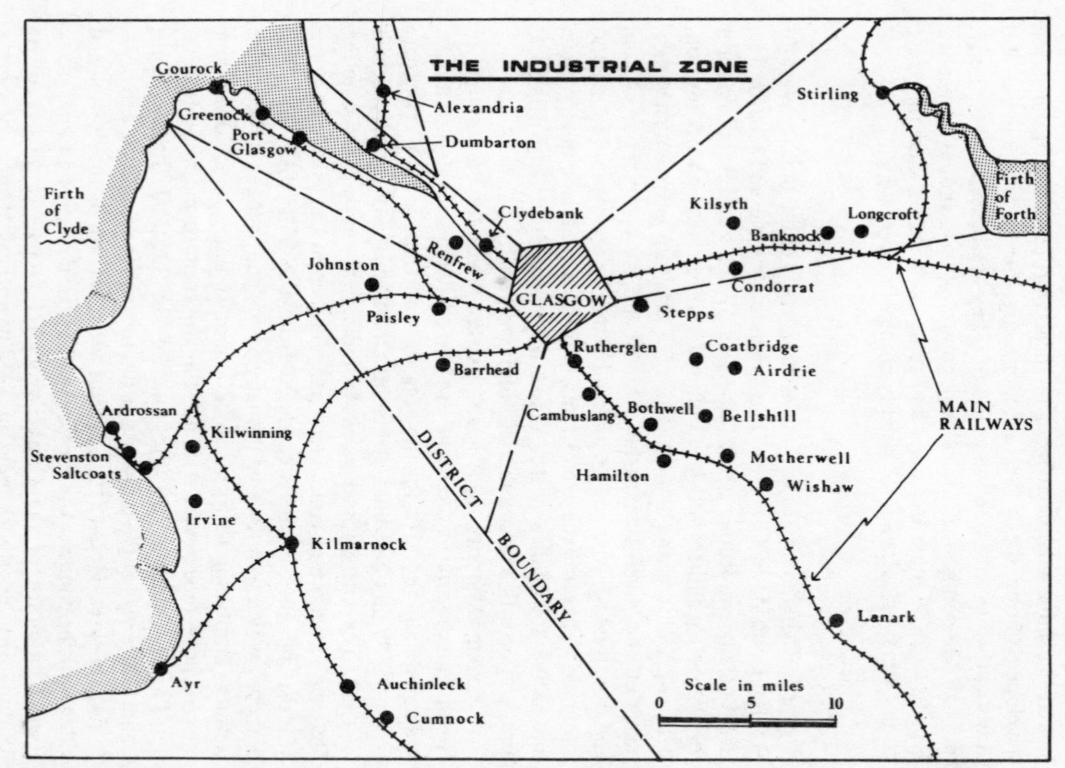
THE INDUSTRIAL ZONE
Gourock
Greenock
Port Glasgow
Alexandria
Dumbarton
Stirling
Firth of Clyde
Firth of Forth
Kilsyth
Longcroft
Banknock
Clydebank
Renfrew
Johnston
Condorrat
GLASGOW
Paisley
Stepps
Rutherglen
Coatbridge
Airdrie
Barrhead
Ardrossan
Cambuslang
Bothwell
Bellshill
MAIN RAILWAYS
Kilwinning
Stevenston
Saltcoats
Motherwell
Hamilton
Wishaw
DISTRICT BOUNDARY
Irvine
Kilmarnock
Lanark
Ayr
Auchinleck
Cumnock
Scale in miles
0
5
10

and issued its own information and instructions. All this was done through a relay system covering the whole county, using cars, motorcycles and push bikes. It also worked to remove one incentive for some of the poorer workers to return to work by organising parish relief to destitute strikers—which was done through local strike headquarters and using clerks drawn from the dole queues.

The main organisational work was, however, left to local Councils of Action. In the twin towns of Airdrie and Coatbridge, for example, where the iron and steelmaking, railway and mining workers provided the main strength on the Airdrie and Coatbridge Council of Action, the Council set up sub-committees to deal with transport, picketing of works, and propaganda. The transport committee issued permits for food transport and organised picketing of road and rail communications. The mass pickets, some of them up to 4,000 strong, were so successful that by the third day of the strike all public road and rail transport in the district had ceased. The committee which organised picketing of the works was also successful: mass pickets several thousands strong were used in the first two days to bring out works which had continued operating, and after this no pickets were required, as the strike was solid. The propaganda committee issued a daily strike bulletin and maintained a courier service with County HQ in Hamilton and Scottish TUC headquarters in Glasgow. Mass meetings were organised in local cinemas and these were always packed out. At one of them William Allen urged the men "not to go without whilst food is in the shops".

By the end of the first week even second line men came out, before being officially called out by the TUC. The strike was so solid that an air of peace and quiet pervaded. This was not to last. Over the weekend the Airdrie magistrates met and decided to restart the Glasgow buses, with police protection. Police raided the transport committee premises where permits were issued and confiscated all documents. On Tuesday, 11 May the County Chief of Police and the Chief Constable of Airdrie supervised the running of a fleet of buses to Glasgow under strong police protection. Large crowds gathered for the buses' return despite pleas by the Council of Action to ignore this provocation. The crowd contained many women and children and was mainly composed of spectators. But all the same, the Riot Act was read, a large body of police made a baton charge and eye witness accounts tell of "men and women smashed at random". The police seem to have enjoyed a bloody revenge for being made to look powerless during the previous week. A

Workers' Defence Corps was formed in response, but never went into action, as the General Strike was called off the next day.

Cambuslang also formed a very strong Council of Action consisting mainly of miners, steelworkers, transport workers and railwaymen. Sub-committees were set up to deal with various aspects of the strike, and transport picketing ensured a standstill of all vehicles without permits. Mass pickets were in evidence on the first day at a few steelworks that kept working and these works were successfully brought out. The Council of Action was in direct daily touch with Scottish TUC headquarters and issued its own twice-weekly bulletin. A mass meeting held in Eastfield Park nearly ended in violence when Mr. Wright, the local Labour MP, suggested that the strike was a great mistake: he was lucky to escape unharmed. The Cambuslang workers felt strongly enough in command on their own ground to lend assistance elsewhere when required. At the request of the Glasgow tramcar workers 500 men marched into Ruby Street depot where students and other blacklegs were spending the night. Violent clashes occurred and twelve men were arrested after a baton charge, and later sentenced to three months' hard labour.

All was quiet during the strike in "Red" Motherwell, the town which had elected a Communist MP four years previously. But it was the quiet of working-class strength. The Council of Action was in total control and all trade unions and working-class parties were represented. Sub-committees were organised for picketing, food, transport and propaganda, and daily open-air meetings were held. Motherwell had the second largest railway depot in the whole of Britain at that time, and not a single engine moved out of the sheds. After the strike the local paper commented: "Motherwell, red and revolutionary Motherwell has been a perfect model of peace and quietness . . . it was also one of the towns where solidarity was the keynote all during the conflict."

Hamilton was the seat of the Joint Committee for the county and thus an important focus of the strike. A major demonstration was held there during the dispute, with thousands marching in from surrounding villages such as Uddingston, Bellshill and Blantyre. The Local Council of Action was successful in stopping all transport which did not carry trade union permits. The government had moved soldiers of the South Staffordshire regiment into the Hamilton Barracks. But the Army's only contribution to the dispute was to play a musical programme in Hamilton Public Park on the day the strike ended.

The industrial villages in North Lanarkshire all had their Councils of

Action, similar to the larger towns. The Bellshill Council of fourteen members was particularly active. Sub-committees dealt with picketing of pits, factories and transport. Permits were issued for food transport. Bulletins were obtained from Glasgow and mass meetings were held regularly on Bellshill Green. On 11 May the transport committee was raided by the police at the Bellshill Miners' Welfare and all papers were confiscated.

The mining village of Shotts had a Council of Action representing fifteen local union and political organisations. A daily bulletin was published. One of the popular pastimes of the period appears to have been hen stealing. As the Shotts police kept a number of hens at the police buildings under strong security, the miners amused themselves by putting out a rumour that they were going to raid the hen farm up the road. They then raided the police hens whilst the police were away up at the hen farm. Other local Councils of Action included Stonehouse, Bothwell, Carluke, Salsburgh, Coalburn, Blantyre, Larkhall and Rutherglen, plus many others.

A major feature of the Lanarkshire Councils of Action was the strong Communist Party influence. The Chairman of the Joint Committee was a Communist, together with seven other members of the forty-man committee. Airdrie and Coatbridge had a Communist Chairman and several other Communists on the Council, as well as some right-wingers. Both the Chairman and secretary of the Cambuslang Council of Action were Communist Party members, and the secretary was also an active member of the Parish Council. Bellshill had a Communist chairman and it was reported that all the Communist Party members in Shotts were on the village Council of Action. Local Communist Party strength appears to have gone hand in hand with a high degree of strike activity in the county.

The strike led to a further radicalisation of the North Lanarkshire working class. The mineworkers, previously right-wing dominated, elected left-wing union officials in what amounted to a landslide. Minority Movement leader William Allen was nominated for Parliament and elected as the county union general secretary, but was kept out of both positions by proscriptions and bureaucratic manœuvring. In the local elections in November there were significant Labour gains in Motherwell, Wishaw, Hamilton, Airdrie and Coatbridge. The one disappointment to the left was Walter Newbold. His continued rightward drift since his election as a Communist MP accelerated after the strike, and he was forced by hostile working-class audiences to abandon a speaking tour during the lockout.

VALE OF LEVEN

The Vale of Leven is a compact industrial area stretching along the river Leven from Balloch on Loch Lomond to Dumbarton on the Clyde. Alexandria (scene of the famous 1973 work-in at Plessey Electronics) is the main town.

The Vale had a long history of working-class struggle well before the General Strike. The early twenties in particular were militant years, with the unemployed workers and anti-eviction movements gathering strength. Mass unemployment arrived in 1922 and Alexandria became the town with the second highest unemployment rate in Britain. The unemployed workers' movement had a system of "street captains" for collecting dues and giving information. Over a thousand workers could be gathered for a meeting at the drop of a hat and the movement had a representative on the Trades Council. Unemployment led to rent arrears, and the consequent attempts at eviction were met with mass sit-ins of 200 people and more, crammed into the victims' houses. Evictions ceased after one year of such campaigning. There were mass demonstrations to the Parish Council to demand increased relief payments. After one such march a local Communist leader, Alan Campbell, locked the Council in the Chamber, and refused to let them out until they came to a decision. He unlocked the doors at midnight.

Militancy in action led to militancy in politics. The working class obtained a majority of seats on the Parish Council in 1922 when Trades Council sponsored members (ILP, Labour Party, and Communist Party) took control. The left-wing parties operated as an alliance, by not contesting each other's wards and by having joint group meetings. As soon as elected, the new council increased unemployment relief to well above normal standards. They were threatened by the Board of Health, refused advances by the banks on the Government's instructions, and each councillor was surcharged £700. However, when the first Labour Government took over in 1924 Willie Gallacher contacted Maxwell and Wheatley, and the "Alexandria File" was mysteriously lost.

So the Vale of Leven workers entered the General Strike with several years' experience of militancy. They formed a Council of Action which contained nine Communists and eleven socialists from the other left-wing parties. The Council of Action then divided into sub-committees dealing with the organisation and picketing, propaganda, commissariat and defence.

Meetings were held in the Communist Party rooms in Bonhill (the

Trades Council had no permanent accommodation) to organise the picketing and propaganda work. But as it turned out, the area was so solidly on strike that no picketing was required. Not a single arrest was made in the Vale. The police, recognising the workers' strength, adopted a low profile, and no workers' defence corps was needed. The Council of Action issued transport permits in certain cases, such as to the Director of Education for the transport of schoolchildren. No attempts were made by the authorities to run buses and there were no blacklegs. A motorcycle courier link was established with Scottish TUC headquarters in Glasgow to obtain up-to-date information. Bundles of the *Scottish Worker* were also collected and distributed throughout the Vale. Propaganda work was the main activity during the strike, with frequent mass meetings being held.

The Vale as a whole was so solid that Hugh McIntyre, Communist leader of the local unemployed workers' movement in the twenties, considered that the strike could have developed into a "bloodless revolution". Its sudden unexplained end was felt as "tragic, as if we had suffered a personal bereavement". However, the Left in the Vale of Leven had grown stronger through the strike and the local Communist-Labour alliance passed through the crisis united. The break between the two organisations was only to come in the mid-thirties, after the Labour Party had been successfully infiltrated by the local Catholic Truth Society. Communist Party membership grew from around 20 in 1924 to over 100 in 1928. Hugh McIntyre went on to become chairman of the District Council in 1930 and later Convenor of the County Council Health Board. He was forced out of public service during the Cold War of the fifties.

STRIKE COMMITTEES

Strike committees were established by the trades councils in most parts of the industrial belt, including the towns of Northern Ayrshire, the Stirlingshire Coalfield and East Renfrewshire. The committees were made up of the local representatives of the unions which were involved. In many cases these consisted basically of the railwaymen, transport workers, builders and miners. There were no representatives of the local political parties or working-class mass movements. Nevertheless, in some areas, such as Ardrossan, the strike committee's control over the local situation was as complete as the control exercised elsewhere by the Councils of Action. At the other extreme the strike committees in towns like Kilmarnock and Ayr made no attempt to impose their authority locally. In much of the industrial belt their effectiveness fell between these two extremes. They found themselves at the head of militant mass movements which were unable to impose total trade union control, but made a strong attempt at doing so. This led to bloody clashes with the police in many areas, such as in Johnstone and near Kilsyth.

NORTHERN AYRSHIRE

The northern half of Ayrshire is the industrial part of the county. The group of five towns on the coast, Ardrossan, Saltcoasts, Stevenston, Kilwinning and Irvine, were dependent primarily on docks, shipyards, a railway depot and the big ICI explosives factory. Further inland, Kilmarnock earned its living from big engineering works and locomotive construction shops. To the south the county town of Ayr was another docks centre. Throughout the whole of northern Ayrshire the industrial towns were set in a sea of mining villages. Some of these, such as Cumnock, had grown large enough to become burghs in their own right. The whole area had a long Labour history. It was a young Ayrshire miner, Keir Hardie, who became Britain's first Labour MP. By 1926 the towns of Kilwinning and Cumnock had ILP Provosts and strong ILP branches existed throughout the county. Communist Party strength in the country was low, though some of the miners' local leaders were members. The Miners' Union county leadership was, however, right-wing and docile, and went out of its way to assure the authorities of its anxiety to co-operate in any way.

The neighbouring towns of Saltcoats, Ardrossan and Stevenston had a joint Trades and Labour Council chaired by Robert Lambie, who is the present Burgh Treasurer and father of David Lambie, local left-wing Labour MP. The Trades and Labour Council formed itself into a strike committee which met every day and night. Sub-committees dealt with railway picketing, docks and road transport. The Trades Council kept official minutes, but the sub-committees were careful not to take minutes—a sensible precaution, but a loss to today's historians. The railways committee had little to do, as the men were out solid—with one exception, and two pickets got 6 months' jail for dispensing some over-rough justice to the latter. Thereafter troops ran one train to Glasgow each day as a token. The docks committee had a novel way of dealing with the mail to the Isle of Arran, which was being conveyed by blackleg labour. Each docker went on to the quay with one large stone. This he threw into the dinghy containing the mails. The weight of several hundred stones eventually sent the dinghy to the bottom of the harbour, and the Arran mails ceased. The transport committee had more work on their hands, but alone amongst strike organisations in the West of Scotland they gave permits for the local buses, since they served "our ain folk". This seems to have been a sign of strength rather than weakness.

One local coal operator tried to operate without the committee's permit. Whilst he was up a close delivering a bag, a committee man unhaltered his horse and sent it cantering off down the road and then yelled "free coal". Within minutes all the strikers' wives were there with their buckets and the luckless blackleg coal merchant had no wares left to sell. The strike committee also saw to the feeding of their own class. The Co-op gave all the credit that was needed to members and to the unions, and all was paid back after the strike. Other local merchants also accepted Trades Council vouchers. Several soup kitchens were run with "as much soup and bread as you wanted". Parades were held every day to the Victoria public park where crowds of up to a thousand or more gathered to hear the speakers. The parades were led by members of the local Orange band, the rank and file Orangemen having broken away from their right-wing leaders during the strike. No strike bulletin was issued, but strike leaflets were issued every day advertising meetings. The *Scottish Worker* was used—fetched from Glasgow by an efficient courier service.

The mining villages around Irvine, Cumnock and Auchinleck sent out mass pickets to ensure that no transport operated without permits. On 7th May crowds of between 200 and 500 gathered in Irvine to stop buses carrying workers to Ardrossan and Irvine docks. Several miners were jailed for up to three months each. Trains, run with blackleg labour on the main Dumfries–Glasgow railway line, were held up at Auchinleck. A crowd of 200 miners obstructed the line and hurled missiles at the few trains which attempted to run. On the day after the strike eleven miners were arrested for stopping buses near Ayr. This was all in marked contrast to the ultra quiet approach favoured by the Ayrshire Miners' Union leadership and the miners' MPs.

The two other main Ayrshire towns, Kilmarnock and Ayr, seem to have had a quiet time during the strike. In Ayr the trams continued working as the workers had broken away from the union during a previous strike. In Kilmarnock many of the men were in the second line and therefore not affected until the end. In both towns the local committees organised daily mass entertainments for the men rather than mass meetings.

The end of the strike came as a bitter blow, and convinced many Ayrshire workers of the need for more political activity. For example, ILP strength on the Saltcoats Council gained rapidly until the Labour Government debacle of 1929 sent it crashing down again, control not being achieved until 1945. In the words of 82-year old Annie Read, secretary of the Saltcoats ILP from 1919 until it was disbanded in 1975, the strike "made you keener than ever to work for socialism, because the workers had been defeated industrially".

THE STIRLINGSHIRE COALFIELD

The Stirlingshire coalfield was one of the major mining areas of Scotland. Coalmining had been the county's lifeblood since the 1850s, working the rich coking coal seams—a high-grade fuel used in the foundries and steelworks of Bonnybridge and Falkirk. The main mining community was the Burgh of Kilsyth, which was the centre of the six-thousand-strong County Miners' Union. Many other mining communities were scattered across the county, ranging in size from large villages to isolated roadside miners' rows. The ILP was growing in strength and Tom Johnston was MP for the area until the "Zinoviev Letter" election of 1924. He was then unseated by a notoriously right-wing Tory, Commander Fanshawe. The County Council and the local town and parish councils were under right-wing Independent (the current euphemism for Tory) control, with a growing Labour representation.

A strike committee was formed in Kilsyth under the leadership of Trades Council chairman James Doherty. The main unions involved were the miners and railwaymen. The strike committee issued food permits, arranged a limited amount of transport picketing, organised a courier service, and held mass meetings almost every day in the local cinemas with upwards of one thousand strikers attending. The miners' leaders, including James Doherty, president Malcolm Turner and agent James Barbour, used these meetings to try to keep the strike on a "respectable" level. As a result there was little organised official picketing in the town.

In the rest of the coalfield the organisation of the strike was carried out directly by the local Miners' Union branches. These tended to have a more militant approach than the county leadership, and road pickets were widespread. The village of Longcroft was the scene of one of the best organised official pickets, led by the local miners' chairman Pat Lafferty—one of the few Communists in the coalfield. The Longcroft picket lasted the duration of the strike, and any lorries or vans travelling without permits were diverted into the Longcroft Thistle football field. The drivers were then sent to Kilsyth or Falkirk to obtain permits. As many as 300 vehicles were impounded at any one time. A system of three eight-hour shifts a day was worked, with ten official pickets to each shift, backed up by a crowd of a hundred or so miners. The local police were prepared to co-operate with the strikers, as the picket was effective but peaceful. But towards the end of the strike a bellicose police chief arrived from Kilsyth, whose intervention resulted in a near riot situation, several accidents and some arrests.

Mass unofficial pickets also occurred. The largest was at the village of Condorrat on the main Glasgow–Edinburgh road. Miners marched to Condorrat in their hundreds from the nearby mining villages, armed with stones and long poles. They successfully prevented most of the traffic getting through for several days, despite several police charges and arrests. One of their main objectives was the Royal Mail, which was reputedly being carried by Rolls-Royce due to the rail strike. This picket earned the accolade of being mentioned in Scottish Office intelligence reports several days running.

In some parts of the county the hooligan element used the strike as a cover for looting. In the village of Banknock a local "bluenose" called Kane trundled several hams off the top of a lorry after it had been stopped by the crowd. The driver had a permit. Not all the men followed Kane's lead and some of the hams were loaded back on again before the lorry was allowed to continue on its journey. In Kilsyth some men earned themselves local notoriety by looting fish waggons from Aberdeen on their way to Glasgow.

The picketing lay heavily on the conscience of Kilsyth strike leader James Doherty, particularly when looting was involved. At several mass meetings he attacked the looters for damaging the workers' cause. But instead of stepping up official picketing and channelling the efforts of the strikers along organised lines he withdrew all official pickets and formed a "peace committee". Kilsyth is a clear example of what happens when right-wing leaders find themselves forced into militant situations which do not square with their lifelong approach. James Doherty, in particular, was a devout Catholic and a member of the parish council and schoolboard. It must have been a bitter irony for him to find himself accused later of being the county "commissar" during the strike, and to lose his JP status for signing transport permits.

The end of the General Strike in the Stirlingshire coalfield marked the end of only the first stage in the miners' lockout. This continued for seven long months, ending in late November with a major defeat. The miners eventually returned to worse conditions than the owners had demanded at the outset. Their union was seriously weakened, and many militants were victimised. But politically, the strike and lockout led to a leftward swing. Important Labour gains on the Kilsyth Town Council in November 1926 culminated in full Labour control in 1929. The new Labour council transformed Kilsyth from the worst housed town in Scotland, to the town with the greatest proportion of council housing. More Labour members were also elected to the County Council in late 1926, including James Doherty. Tom Johnston was re-elected MP at the next general election. The strike and lockout also led to the emergence of the Communist Party as an important force amongst the rank and file, and an active "local" (as Communist Party branches were then called) worked in Kilsyth for several years afterwards.

East Renfrewshire

East Renfrewshire consists of a tightly knit group of industrial towns, Paisley, Johnstone, Renfrew and Barrhead. Engineering was the mainstay of the district and this is still the case today, including the major Chrysler plant at Linwood. This general dependence on engineering meant that the actual strikers formed a minority group, as the engineering workers were in the second line.

Paisley Trades Council formed a Central Strike Committee which had transport, building and engineering sub-committees. The committee adopted a non-militant approach, at least in regard to transport picketing. Several trams and buses ran, and these increased in number towards the end of the strike. This caused discontent among the tramway section of the TGWU, and the engineering sub-committee considered ways of cutting off the tramways' power. The strike committee recognised that their main problem was that the "black squad", the engineers, had not been called out. During the first week the Committee wired the Scottish TUC demanding that these workers be called out, and during the weekend they claimed that "the big battalions of the AEU in the Clyde area are growing restive, and anxious to share in the fortunes of the strike". A strike fund was started, with the workers in the engineering shops each contributing 3*s*. per week.

Paisley's main strike activity was the publication of a daily bulletin from the ILP rooms in Cumbernauld Court. This was a well-produced cyclostyled broadsheet sold at one penny with a circulation of 2,000. It was rich in cartoons and limericks, such as:

When wages to thirty bob fell
The miner said "I'll hae a spell"
So if ye want coal
Go down in the hole
And dig up a ton for yersel.

The bulletin's cartoons have since been reproduced in several books on the General Strike, and the strike committee proudly announced that their cartoonist was a planing machine operator in an engineering shop during more normal times. The bulletin also announced that the Duke of Northumberland drew £84 an hour from mining royalties, whilst the British miner drew 9*s*. 4*d*. for seven hours, with the owners proposing to reduce even this by 3*s*.

Events in the neighbouring town of Johnstone were a marked contrast to the quiet situation in Paisley. Pickets stoned buses in Houston Square on the first day of the strike, provoking a police baton charge. Later in the week a 1,000-strong mass picket intercepted buses. It too was dispersed by a baton charge. The secretary of the Joint Strike Committee recorded: "Never before has such solidarity been shown in an industrial dispute, even our political opponents, Orangemen, being active pickets and taking part in the struggle." The mass pickets, however, proved ineffective in the long run. A mass breakaway of tramcar workers took place towards the end of the strike, with the majority resuming work. The picketing, baton charges and arrests gave Johnstone a brief "red" reputation locally.

Little strike activity has been recorded in Renfrew, which was primarily an engineering and shipbuilding town. Some trams were off, but the buses kept running with little interference. Many specials were enrolled but none were needed. When the engineers and shipbuilders eventually struck work on the last day of the strike, some yards appear to have come out with reluctance. Barrhead presents a similar picture of little strike activity, although ten pickets were later charged with forming part of a mass picket early in the strike.

The shadow of the engineering and shipbuilding industries of the

Clyde fell heavily over East Renfrewshire during the strike. With so many men still at work it is not surprising that the strikers were unable to control their districts as effectively as Ayrshire or the Stirlingshire coalfield, where virtually the whole of the working class was involved.

AREAS WITH LESS STRIKE INVOLVEMENT

Three areas of the West of Scotland were less involved during the General Strike. These were the south-west, the Highlands and Islands, and the Clyde. The first two areas are remote from the major industrial centres, but the Clyde is a major engineering and shipbuilding centre.

The South-West

The south-west of Scotland includes the counties of Dumfries, Kirkcudbright and Wigton together with the southern halves of Lanarkshire and Ayrshire. The area is predominantly agricultural with a little fishing around the coast, and the workers in these industries were not involved at all in the General Strike. The workers who were called out, the railwaymen, printers and building workers, fragmented and isolated in small scattered groups nevertheless formed surprisingly solid islands of strike activity in an area which was otherwise strongly hostile. Strike action was organised by the branches of the individual unions concerned rather than by trades councils or general strike committees.

The railmen were particularly solid. They were out at the main stations of Lockerbie, Beattock, Lochmaben, Moffat and Annan, at each of which up to 100 were employed. One Beattock driver who attempted to blackleg found himself imprisoned in his own house during the strike. Another driver lost his student volunteers after a hostile demonstration. Six student volunteers were employed at Beattock as watchmen and firemen. Railwaymen also demonstrated at Annan against station clerks who had continued to work locally.

The strike presented a great opportunity to one local volunteer, Col. E. P. A. Melville, CBE, of Gillespie. The Colonel had long looked back nostalgically to his youthful Army days driving locomotives in India. According to the *Annandale Observer*, "When he went on duty on Monday the Colonel, attired in his serviceable suit of dungarees, received an ovation by numbers of townsfolk who had gathered in the vicinity." The Colonel had to send his apologies for absence to the next County Council meeting because he was away driving trains. The Council were not at all upset and "Mr. H. Cavan Irving, CBE, of

Burnfoot warmly congratulated Col. Melville on the services he had patriotically rendered in the crisis, a sentiment which the meeting warmly endorsed." The Colonel's activities did not, however, have any material effect locally.

Few transport pickets were active on the roads, and the buses ran throughout the strike. The Provosts of Dumfries and Maxwelltown issued a joint statement calling on citizens to refrain from countenancing road permits, and to report any demands for permits to the police. A call was also made locally for the recruitment of Specials, to allow local regular police to be released for work in the industrial towns. Some political work was carried out by Labour organisations during the strike. An ILP meeting in Stranraer attracted one hundred participants and a large open-air meeting was held by the ILP in Lockerbie Market Square. The May Day meeting of the Gretna ILP pledged support for the miners in the crisis.

Highlands and Islands

The Highlands and Islands are predominantly dependent on agriculture, fishing and tourism. On the "Costa Clyde", tourism is by far the most important industry. Workers in other industries such as the railways, printing and building were even more scattered and isolated than in the south-west. Despite this the transport workers and miners in Campbelltown were out, 100 of the 120 railmen in Oban joined the strike, and at the foot of Ben Nevis the 80 power men at the Lockaber hydro-station came out. The strike was organised by the individual unions concerned, as in the south-west, with no apparent trades council co-ordination.

The area's main involvement in the General Strike was the export of men to serve in the forces of "law and order" in the industrial areas. The Island of Bute loaned a detachment of police to Renfrewshire, a hundred specials were recruited in Cowal and a further fifty in Lorne. Cowal and Lorne are both small mountainous areas, and the large number of recruits suggests that the old clan habits of marauding abroad after a good fight had not yet died. Many of the Lorne men made a point of offering their services to the London police. The Rothesay press covered the sad story of one local girl who had to postpone her wedding as her Navy bridegroom sailed away for duty on the Clyde.

The Clyde

The industrial Clyde, excluding Glasgow, consists of the lower Clyde shipbuilding trio of towns Greenock–Gourock–Port Glasgow,

Dumbarton on the other side of the river, and the Upper Clyde shipbuilding towns of Clydebank and Renfrew—the heartland of the labour movement in the west of Scotland. The modern shop stewards' movement began there during the first world war, its women made history with their successful wartime rents strike, and it was the breeding ground for militants like Willie Gallacher. Of the 100,000 engineering and shipbuilding workers employed in Scotland, 80,000 were employed on the Clyde. But as these men were not called out till the last day, the strike was left to relatively small groups of rail and transport workers, printers and building trade workers, whilst the militant mass of the Clyde workers was held back from the struggle.

Strike activity in the Lower Clyde towns was so slight that the first issue of the *Greenock Herald* published afterwards carried no strike news. However, the Gourock paper reports that some picketing was carried out, and two tramwaymen and a busman were arrested for attempting to stop a bus. The strike committee in Greenock published a strike bulletin which reported that the railwaymen who were involved in the dispute were solid, and only two signalmen remained at work, "one old man and the other under petticoat command". A contributory factor to the Greenock district's lack of picketing activity was the disbanding of the old left-wing trades council prior to the strike. A new Trades and Labour Council was formed by the Scottish Labour Party, purged of any Communist participation. A well-known Clydeside Communist, J. R. Campbell, later reported that the new trades council "was dead during the crisis". The local Communist Party put in a major propaganda effort by holding mass meetings and issuing a daily bulletin.

Dumbarton and Clydebank similarly saw a low level of strike activity. Some picketing was carried out and a number of arrests were made, but the very fact that the engineering and shipbuilding workers used the buses and trams to get to their work had a demoralising effect on the men on strike. On the last Wednesday the 80,000 engineers and shipbuilders of the Clyde joined the strike. But by midday the news that it had been called off was coming through. A few hours later the shipbuilding workers received instructions from their employers that they would only be taken back individually not collectively and the opportunity was taken to remove leading militants. When the Singer workers reported back after one day on strike they were told that they would have to accept a wage cut. A major demonstration was held in Clydebank on the Saturday, following which the works resumed. The management claimed it had been all a big "misunderstanding".

The government had made ample preparation for unrest in the area by despatching a number of warships to the Clyde. These included the *Hood*, *Comus*, *Halo*, *Harmattan*, *Trusty* and *Furious*. The *Hood* landed parties for the protection of the Loch Long torpedo range and the Ardrossan fuel depot. Parties were also despatched to Dalnottar, Old Kilpatrick, Hungryside and Castlecary. The warships *Comus* and *Warspite* were used for strike breaking activities further up the river in Glasgow.

GLASGOW

Glasgow is the metropolis of the west of Scotland and in 1926 contained about one-third of the region's three million citizens. Its people were a rich Celtic mixture of Highlanders, Irishmen and native lowland Scots. The city lived by its docks, shipyards, engineering shops, railway yards and general industry. Socialism had been a rapidly growing movement locally since the turn of the century, and in 1922 ILP candidates had been elected in all but two of Glasgow's parliamentary constituencies. This was, however, partly due to a split between the right-wing parties, and many of the ILP MPs were elected on a minority vote. The Town Council was still right-wing dominated and in 1925 the labour movement just failed to gain 50 per cent of the total vote in the local elections. Organisations to the left of the ILP were stronger than elsewhere in Britain. The Communist Party had about 500 members and controlled the local unemployed workers' movement, as well as having a strong influence in the unions. The Minority Movement was very active in the city and its national weekly paper, *The Worker*, was printed in Glasgow. John McLean's Socialist Workers' Republican Party had been very influential earlier in the twenties but had declined since his death. Left and Right were almost evenly balanced on the Trades and Labour Council, as shown by the 181 to 174 vote in favour of affiliating to the Minority Movement taken in 1925. For a city with such an experienced and well-organised labour movement it comes as a surprise to find that the strike in Glasgow was relatively weaker than in many surrounding areas.

At the onset of the General Strike the Trades and Labour Council established a Central Strike Co-ordinating Committee (CSCC). As its name implies, the main function of this body was to co-ordinate the activities of all the unions involved. They were grouped according to trade, and each group selected its own representatives, thus avoiding the formation of a large unwieldy committee. The trades involved were builders, woodworkers, vehicle builders, iron and steel trades, transport workers, printing workers and miners, with a few engineering and shipbuilding workers. Most of the militant engineering and shipbuilding workers were, however, in the second line. The first line trades tended to have smaller, more right-wing unions. The left–right balance on the CSCC was reflected in its officers. Peter Kerrigan, local Communist and convenor of the Industrial Committee, was the chairman, and William Shaw, right-of-centre full-time Trades Council official was the secretary. The committee acted as a clearing house for information, issued bulletins, established a courier service, handled inter-union disputes and took up complaints with the police. Despite the hard work carried out by the CSCC, it proved to be a frustrating experience for left-wingers who wished to see it adopt a more positive and militant role. J. R. Campbell wrote afterwards that the five communist members of the committee had a "hard fight against the deadweight of do-nothing permanent officialdom".

The sheer size of Glasgow would in itself have made effective central control of the strike difficult. The left wing on the CSCC pushed for the establishment of area strike committees (ASCs) and on this issue they won two important votes. The first was in favour of establishing ASCs throughout Glasgow and the second was against the requirement to have these convened in all cases by local councillors. Seventeen ASCs were formed and were beginning to prove effective by the time the strike was called off. The Govan ASC reported that the strikers' wives had formed a committee to watch prices and maintain order. A strike bulletin was produced by the Partick ASC: they sold 2,000 copies of their first issue at $\frac{1}{2}$*d.* each. The Shettleston ASC formed a strike defence committee, and the Camlachie ASC held meetings at Dennistoun and other tram depots. Springburn ASC wrote to the CSCC to demand that all commercial lighting should be cut off. The ASCs had a considerable correspondence with the CSCC and proved to be the CSCCs eyes and ears, as well as being local strike organisations in their own right.

Control of the strike throughout Scotland was nominally in the hands of the Scottish TUC, which had its headquarters in Glasgow. However, the STUC limited its operations to establishing an efficient courier system and attempting to impose a uniform very non-militant TUC line. The courier system reached as far as Carlisle in the south and Aberdeen in the north. It was used to distribute TUC bulletins, STUC bulletins, and eventually the *Scottish Worker*. The latter was not produced until the second week of the strike, and much of its material was reprinted from the *British Worker*. Reflecting the cautious line of both the TUC and the STUC, it was printed by voluntary labour on the printing press of the weekly ILP newspaper, *Forward*, and created a poor impression amongst many militants. The *Scottish Worker*'s first issue of 25,000 copies was, however, sold out in 40 minutes. In Glasgow the STUC tried to dampen the struggle by attempting to prevent the formation of ASCs. Once this had failed it tried to insist on the ASCs being convened by local councillors. The STUC also tried to ban strike meetings being held on Sundays and to prevent the production of "unofficial" strike bulletins. It was singularly unsuccessful in all these attempts.

An alternative central directing body to the STUC was set up by the Communist Party and the Minority Movement. They established a joint committee which was in continuous session at the Communist headquarters in Salkeld Street. Through its own courier system this committee kept in touch with many of the surrounding districts, directing the work of both the organisations involved. The joint committee also published an emergency *Worker* and *Workers' Weekly* (18,000 4-page copies) during the first week until the police arrested the entire night shift. All were released unconditionally after 24 hours. During the second week the joint committee published a paper entitled *The Workers' Press,* 6,000 copies being published on the eve of the strike being called off and a further 10,000 copies subsequently. The Minority Movement also prepared 10,000 copies of a manifesto for the metal workers, and the Communist Party produced 16,000 copies of a manifesto to all strikers.

The strike amongst the first line trades was solid in the great majority of Glasgow's workplaces. Official Government recognition of this fact was given in a Ministry of Labour memorandum of 12 May. This stated that "There is not the slightest sign of any break whatever in the strike. In fact many of those working now wish to join in."

However, the strike did have serious weaknesses, caused by the TUC decision to leave some men at work, whilst calling others out on strike. This led inevitably to a certain amount of confusion and bitterness. A local AEU branch reported considerable dissatisfaction amongst its members on this point, and wired the AEU executive demanding that all members be called out. The foundry workers were in a similar position and two branches called on their executive to bring all their members out. Confusion also occurred amongst building workers, as the TUC had granted exemptions for work on hospitals, subsidised housing, jobbing work on working-class homes, and some public works. The Building sub-committee of the CSCC had the difficult responsibility of deciding who should come out and who should remain at work. Furthermore the men who were instructed to remain at work had the problem of getting to their workplaces, which meant that many were using blackleg transport. For this reason the striking busmen called for the giant Singers factory to be brought into the strike, as Singers workers were using blackleg transport to a major extent. By the time the second line men were eventually called out, the CSCC had to report that there was some "uncertainty" over their response.

One of the government's main tactics was to try to create a semblance of normality by keeping the public transport system running, chiefly the trams. And in this they were partially successful. A fair proportion of trams ran throughout the dispute, the power station at Pinkston which supplied the trams was kept operating, and the tram servicing centre at Coplawhill was kept open. The strikers saw this as a serious attempt to undermine their solidarity, and a major effort was made to stop the trams. At the beginning of the strike the Corporation Tramways Committee was suspended and its functions were taken over by the Organisation for Maintenance of Supplies (OMS). This organisation managed to get about 200 out of Glasgow's 1,100 trams running by the weekend. The trams were mainly driven by the Inspectors, 95 of the 97 having refused to strike. Some drivers also refused to strike, through fear of losing superannuation benefits. The OMS supplied volunteers, chiefly students, to act as conductors. As a result both the Partick ASC and the Newlands depot workers demanded that the University Labour Club take action against student volunteers. Maryhill ASC reported that the local labour exchange was getting in touch with unemployed tramwaymen. Partick ASC claimed that blacklegs were being brought into the local tram depot in St. Andrew Association ambulances. Most of the strike-breakers were given beds and food in the depots, others were given police escorts to and from their homes.

The Pinkston power station was defended by electrifying the iron railings, and the workers lived on the premises during the strike. The main problem was that the key switchboard men were members of the EPEA. This organisation was not affiliated to the TUC and was against strikes at any time. The remainder of the men were isolated in the works and did not know the situation outside. An instruction to strike was sent by the CSCC to all the union men in Pinkston, signed by the local officials of all the unions involved. After a meeting inside the power station the unionists agreed to strike, but were then persuaded by a management official to remain at work. After that, the CSCC felt it could do little more about this matter, believing that even if the men did strike their positions would in any case be taken over by naval ratings. The Coplawhill car works, which serviced the trams as well as building new ones, presented a similar story. The AEU members refused to strike and they were joined in this by the woodworkers. The Secretary of the Society of Woodworking Machinists wrote to the CSCC saying "Sorry we have failed at Coplawhill Car Works, but we have been recompensed by stopping woodturners engaged in turning policemen's batons at another shop." The vehicle builders at Coplawhill did, however, respond to the strike call, if somewhat reluctantly. Their local organiser warned of a "debacle" if the other trades remained at work. His words were justified. Before the end of the strike his members voted to return as the other tradesmen had not come out.

The attempt to run the trams provoked a great deal of mass picketing. And this in turn led to mass police counter-action. The first big clash occurred at the Ruby Street depot when 500 Cambuslang miners were met with a police baton charge in the early hours of Wednesday morning. The following day police baton-charged strikers in Bridgeton who attempted to persuade two student tram-conductors to stop working. On the same day the local ASC held a mass picket at the Dennistoun depot, leading to another baton charge. Tram picketing caused more mass arrests in Bridgeton on the Friday, and at a tram depot near the University police dispersed Partick strikers demonstrating against student volunteers. Mass action continued on the Saturday in Parliamentary Road and Kinning Park. In Govan the strikers' wives organised themselves into pickets at tramstops to persuade passengers not to embark. Baton charges and mass arrests led to rioting and looting in the Dennistoun, Bridgeton, Western and Anderston areas. By the end of the weekend over 300 arrests had been made, and on the Monday some 100 sentences of between two weeks and three months were passed on the arrested men. The police conduct provoked considerable resentment, particularly against the Specials. The latter were described as being "mad with drink" in Hutchesontown and Bridgeton, and accused of causing rather than preventing riots. The Glasgow Town Council Labour Group decided to press for an enquiry into police conduct, having received complaints of "unwarranted attacks on unoffending citizens". The Trades Council also decided to investigate complaints against the police. Bridgeton was very badly hit by police action. This resulted in a deputation of town and parish counsellors protesting to the Eastern Police Division against the "molesting of unoffending citizens by agitated policemen". The committee was particularly incensed over the case of James Houston. James was a crippled boy who fell during a police charge, was arrested for obstruction, and later fined.

The authorities had far less success in running the other transport services. The subway did not run at all during the strike. Few buses were on the roads. Only about 50 out of the normal 850 passenger trains were reported running from Glasgow. The railwaymen were out solid, and even the Railway Clerks Association had over 2,000 of their 2,400 members out on strike. The railway companies had more success in keeping the railway yards open, against considerable opposition. Employees at the St. Rollox works are reported to have been assaulted when leaving the works, and police protection had to be given to blacklegs at Cowlairs. Sea-going transport proved to be a weak link in the strike. The notoriously right-wing National Seamen's and Firemens Union, led by Havelock Wilson, continued working. However, the smaller Marine Workers Union led by E. Shinwell fought a considerable campaign in support of the strike with some success. They persuaded many National Union men not to sign on for ships leaving the port, and crewmen of the SS *Transylvania* refused to work with blackleg labour. Mass meetings were held by the Marine Workers throughout the shipping area to try to persuade the seamen to show solidarity with the strikers.

The volunteers were an important part of the Government's strike-breaking policy in Glasgow. The OMS claimed that it had enrolled 7,000 volunteers in the city. Only about 300 of these were students, out of a total student population of 5,000. Professor Henderson of the University Chemistry Department was particularly active in trying to recruit student volunteers. He promised that they would be considered as having been on "active war service" for examination purposes. This easy road through the examinations must have tempted many students, and the fact that 4,700 students did not volunteer can be credited to the influence of the strong University Labour Club. The club's 400 members supported the strike. Many young clerks and runners from the city's business houses joined the volunteers. They were encouraged to do this by promises of £5 a week strike-breaking pay over and above their normal salary. To this was added the excitement and glamour of volunteer work, a break from the drudgery of being small fry in the big business world. Many of the volunteers were employed in Princes Dock. They were housed in first class accommodation in a luxury liner, with three free meals per day. About 1,000 tons of goods were moved daily by these volunteers. And strong naval protection was given to them at the urgent written request of the Sherriff of Glasgow. The HMS *Comus* was berthed in the dock and landed two platoons. These were reinforced by 120 ratings from the HMS *Warspite*.

The strikers also had to contend with the anti-strike propaganda campaign. At mass meetings and in local bulletins they were urged to believe only what they were told by the labour movement press, while the CSCC warned against the "lying trash being circulated by the wireless and the local dope press". Few strikers appear to have been influenced by the wireless. The "local dope press" was a reference to the *Emergency Press*. This paper was an emergency strike edition published by a combination of all the Glasgow papers using staff men on the printing machines. Its editorial policy was to publicise attempts to run public services, and to emphasise any breaks in the strike. But one ASC reported that they had stopped campaigning against the *Emergency Press* because local people were ceasing to buy it since its information had proved inaccurate. The paper took the local place of Churchill's *British Gazette*, which contained virtually no references to Scotland after the first few days.

The account so far of the General Strike in Glasgow has dwelt on its weaknesses and on the government's strike-breaking attempts. It is therefore important to recall that amongst the first line trades the strike was by and large effective and solid. Its sudden and unexplained calling off came therefore as a great shock to those involved, and many workers protested strongly against the decision to return. On Peter Kerrigan's motion the Trades and Labour Council recorded its "strong disapproval of the manner in which the General Strike was terminated". This was carried by 149 votes to 36. The Partick ASC held a mass meeting on the Wednesday morning in the local cinema, with an overflow meeting outside. This angry meeting voted to "emphatically protest against and deplore the calling off of the General Strike" which was a "cowardly surrender". They called on the STUC for an immediate resumption of the strike until the mining issue was settled. The Glasgow Southern Branch of the Railway Clerks Association called the termination of the strike an "unprecedented example of incapability displayed by the General Council of the British TUC" and demanded the expulsion of the leaders.

The disorganised resumption of work left the returning strikers wide open to victimisation, of which there was plenty. The Tramways Department told the men that they "could not be loyal to a union and the department at the same time" and suspended 368 men. The *Glasgow Herald*, *Evening Times*, *Bulletin* and *Evening Citizen* refused to reinstate unionists. The Parks Department refused to reinstate many labourers and tradesmen. Dock employers attempted to impose new conditions, and 100 men were dismissed. The rail strike continued for a few days after the General Strike, as the owners tried to impose wage-reductions. Sheet metal workers found themselves excluded from work at Singers, the railshops, Clyde Trust, Finnieston Engineering and Adams. The CSCC attempted to establish a Joint Committee of the unions involved in the victimisation attempts, but was prevented from doing so by the STUC, on the grounds that resumption negotiations were the responsibility of the individual unions concerned.

Politically the strike had a mixed effect on Glasgow's working class. The overall labour movement vote went up to 55 per cent in the November 1926 local elections, topping the 50 per cent mark for the first time. But the increase was very localised. Large increases were obtained in wards such as Hutchesontown, Parkhead and Kinning Park which had witnessed large-scale clashes with the police. In the shipyard wards like Govan, Fairfield and Kingston the vote remained stationary or even slightly decreased. Glasgow's radicalisation was therefore in proportion to the degree of strike activity that had taken place.

SOME CONCLUSIONS

The three main questions that may be asked about the General Strike in the West of Scotland are: How effective was it? How effective were the government's counter-measures? What was the strike's effect on the local labour movement?

How effective was the strike? In some areas the strike was exceptionally solid. This applies in particular to North Lanarkshire and the Vale of Leven. These areas had long histories of working-class struggle, mass ILP branches, strong communist "locals", and few men employed in the second line trades. They formed Councils of Action which united the political and trade union organisations of the working class, and also included the unemployed workers and anti-eviction movements. These Councils of Action were in strong control of their districts for the duration. There was no real strike breaking. Little transport moved without their permits. The position was, indeed, so secure that considerable effort could be put into propaganda campaigns. The strike was also reasonably solid in North Ayrshire and the Stirlingshire coalfield, despite some weaknesses. Both these areas had large numbers of miners, growing ILP movements, and few second line workers. Councils of Action were not formed, but the trades councils assumed similar powers, with similar results. In all these solid areas the strike was truly a *general* strike involving the great majority of the local working class.

Glasgow and East Renfewshire tell a rather different story. Here the strike can by no means be described as "general", and this was its major weakness. Confusion, bitterness and some deterioration of morale were caused by the TUC's decision to make the strike only partial. The failure to call out the engineers and shipbuilders was particularly harmful since these men were the militant backbone of the Clydeside labour force. As a result the strike committees were largely composed of men from the smaller and more right-wing unions. However, despite these weaknesses the mass pickets kept most public transport out of use and the majority of first line trades remained solidly on strike. The decision to hold back the engineers and shipbuilders hit towns lower down the Clyde area to an even greater extent. Strikers in Greenock, Dumbarton, and Clydebank found themselves in a small minority and were therefore powerless to influence events.

In the country districts of the south-west and the Highlands and Islands the working-class communities were too scattered and isolated to exercise any real local control. Despite this the unions involved, chiefly the railwaymen and printers, were remarkably loyal to the strike.

In terms of assisting the locked-out miners in their dispute the General Strike was, of course, totally ineffective. This was not the fault of the local militants who worked so hard for strike solidarity. These militants found themselves undermined by the national leadership's refusal to call out all trades at the outset, and by the precipitate termination of the strike.

How effective was the government? The effectiveness of the government's counter measures also varied from area to area. In areas where the strike was solid the police favoured a low-key approach and strike-breakers were not to be seen. As a result, little violence occurred. The police attitude hardened towards the end, however, and there were raids on two strike committees and a baton charge in Airdrie. The new police line did not lead to any weakening in the strike, but rather to a toughening in the strikers' attitudes.

Government forces had far more success in Glasgow and the Clyde area in general, exploiting the strike's weaknesses there. They succeeded in operating a significant proportion of the local transport services and unloading a fairly large volume of goods from the docks. These actions led to mass picketing, baton charges, looting and mass arrests. Between 400 and 500 arrests were made in the West of Scotland, the vast majority from these areas. A certain amount of weakening of the strike was apparent towards the end.

In the country districts the government forces had no problem in ensuring their control, but still found themselves unable to run more than a token number of trains. These areas provided the Government with valuable sources of regular and special police for the industrial areas.

Anti-strike propaganda appears not to have had an important effect on the strikers, despite Churchill's campaign through the wireless and the *British Gazette*, and the efforts of the local *Emergency Press*.

How did the strike affect the labour movement? The immediate outcome of the strike for the labour movement in the west of Scotland was the wholesale victimisation of militants and a considerable weakening of the unions. But disillusion with the unions led to a greater reliance on the political parties, and this hastened the leftward political swing of the working class, at least in terms of voting Labour. Many more seats were won in the November 1926 elections in the active areas, with Labour control being achieved in many districts before the end of the decade. However, perhaps the most important result of the General Strike was that it provided a brief and unforgettable taste of class power for many young militants. The generation which received its political education in the General Strike went on to fight the historic unemployment and anti-fascist battles of the thirties and eventually installed the first majority Labour Government in the forties.

ACKNOWLEDGEMENTS

I should like to acknowledge the considerable help in terms of research and discussion given by Carol Carter, Jean Dalgleish, John Foster, Eddie Kelly and John McLean.

SOURCES

The sources consulted include some fifty local newspapers, several trade union minute books, the labour movement press, a few strike bulletins, and the correspondence of the Glasgow CSCC. In addition over two dozen interviews of strike veterans were made and these proved to be of great value.

2 EDINBURGH

WITH SOME NOTES ON THE LOTHIANS AND FIFE

by IAN MACDOUGALL

Although primarily a centre of administration, education, law, banking, insurance, tourism, and the church, Edinburgh, which in 1926 had a population of 425,000, was also a centre of industry. As the annual report of the city's Trades and Labour Council put it: "Edinburgh is partly surrounded by coalfields. Its printing industry in all its branches orders the lives of more than 10,000 workers, and gives rise to other and dependent capitalist enterprises. The two great railway companies, the LNER and LMS, have extensive interests in the area, Edinburgh being the chief railway centre in the East of Scotland. The port of Leith, in addition to being one of the leading coal-shipping ports of the country, is also one of the principal grain ports, and is . . . the main eastern gateway to all Scotland for commerce from the northern European seaboard. General engineering and electrical work, ship-repairing, and various other trades all combine with those industrial and commercial factors . . . and convert Edinburgh into a typical centre of capitalist industry."[1]

Yet Edinburgh had some peculiarities of industrial and class structure. There were no great dominating industries comparable with the shipbuilding and engineering of Glasgow, but only some half-dozen leading trades which included, besides those mentioned above, building, brewing and food manufacture. It had a relatively high proportion of professional and middle-class citizens (roughly double that of Glasgow). As the president of the Trades Council noted after the General Strike: "It would be difficult to find a city, comparable with Edinburgh, so heavily weighted with non-industrial activities. . . . From this it will be seen that the working-class movement in Edinburgh is faced with special difficulties."[2]

To the west of the city lay the coal and shale mines of West Lothian; to the east and south-east, the coal pits of East and Midlothian, employing some 15,000 miners; and across the Firth of Forth were the coalfields and the 30,000 miners of Fife. Other important industries in the region were paper-making, agriculture and fishing; while in Fife there were also the linoleum works of Kirkcaldy and the textile factories of Dunfermline and other small towns.

Apart from the absence of iron- and steel-making, the "first line" unions called upon by the TUC General Council to strike from midnight of Monday, 3 May, in support of the miners, were, therefore, fairly well represented in the area, as were the "second line" unions of engineering and shipbuilding trades called out on 12 May.

In the period before the General Strike, Edinburgh had been regarded as "a weak spot in trade union organisation".[3] The total number of trade unionists in the city at the time of the strike was about 46,000, or just over 30 per cent of the total number of employed persons.[4] Sixty unions, represented altogether by some ninety branches, were affiliated to the Trades and Labour Council, the largest affiliations being those of the National Union of Railwaymen (2,600), Shop Assistants (2,400), and Transport and General Workers' Union (1,500). Among unaffiliated unions was the Locomotive Engineers and Firemen.[5] The political wing of the working-class movement in Edinburgh in 1926 was composed of a small branch of the Communist Party, some of whose members were active among the railwaymen at St. Margaret's depot and among the tramwaymen; a branch of the Young Communist League at Leith; seven branches of the ILP, apparently with about 500 members in total; a handful of members of the Social Democratic Federation; ten branches of Labour women's political organisations; a Fabian branch with about sixty members; and a University Labour Party, probably very small.[6] On the Town Council, the six Labour councillors formed a very small minority.[7] Perhaps with some exaggeration, the local weekly Labour paper, *Labour Standard*, had described Edinburgh shortly before the 1926 crisis as "the most reactionary of cities".[8]

In Fife, although it was claimed that the split in the county miners' union a couple of years earlier had resulted in some 10,000 miners being non-unionists,[9] the Left was nonetheless more active than in Edinburgh. David Proudfoot of Methil, the Moffats of Lumphinnans, John McArthur of Buckhaven, John Bird of Bowhill, and other activists in Fife agitated and organised there on behalf of the Communist Party and the Minority Movement.[10]

Since Red Friday, 1925, the two latter organisations, nationally and locally, had been urging preparations for the impending struggle. But in

Edinburgh and the Lothians, as generally it seems elsewhere in Britain, little or no preparation for the General Strike was undertaken by unions until a day or two at most before it began. In Fife, there were two exceptions to this rule—Methil and Lochgelly trades councils. Lochgelly Trades Council, which was not affiliated to the Scottish Trades Union Congress, appears to have been under strong Left influence, and summoned a conference of workers at Lochgelly in the early part of April. This conference arranged for the setting up of a Central Committee of Action for Fife, Kinross and Clackmannan, with local committees, based on existing trades councils, to be set up in Dunfermline and elsewhere in the area.[11] Methil and District Trades Council met on 22 April, probably at least in part as an outcome of the Lochgelly conference, and discussed the setting up of lines of communication and a Workers' Defence Corps.[12] John McArthur, a militant miners' leader in East Fife who was active on Methil Trades Council at the time, recalls that early in 1926, "We felt we would have to have a series of meetings to get our message (about the impending struggle) across. I don't think that many people, because of bitter disappointments in the past, actually felt that the General Strike would take place. A number of us decided to hold a meeting on the Sunday prior to the General Strike at Denbeath Bridge, Methil. We had to cancel it for lack of attendance. But we had a meeting the next Sunday when the Strike was on, and one could hardly see the back of the crowd."[13]

The failure or refusal of the TUC, the Scottish TUC, and unions generally to prepare for the coming struggle, together with a widespread feeling which that failure itself contributed to creating, that some compromise would be reached to enable a crisis to be avoided, explain the lack of preparations on the workers' side in Edinburgh and area, as elsewhere.

On the other hand, there was no such lack of preparation by the other side in the coming struggle. The government's arrangements for dealing with an emergency in Scotland were revised after Red Friday, and were set forth in Circular No. 2,076 of 21 November 1925 from the Scottish Office to local authorities. Edinburgh was to be the headquarters of the Government Emergency Organisation, which would be directed by a minister (the Lord Advocate, William Watson, KC, MP), acting on behalf of the Secretary of State for Scotland. In addition, a district Civil Commissioner (J. W. Peck, CB) was to be based at Edinburgh, as the centre of one of five districts into which Scotland was to be divided. The

Edinburgh district embraced all the Lothians, the southern half of Fife (the northern half was to be under the control of another commissioner based on Dundee), the Border counties, and Clackmannan, Kinross, east and central Stirlingshire, as well as Orkney and Shetland. The Emergency Organisation was to organise transport, food, voluntary workers, petrol supplies, postal services, etc., and local authorities were to co-operate in these arrangements. The whole scheme was to go into operation directly an emergency was declared.[14]

The role of the separate but allied "strictly non-political and non-party" Organisation for the Maintenance of Supplies was to prepare lists of voluntary workers in advance of the crisis, and to hand these lists over to the government's Emergency Organisation directly an emergency was declared. The OMS appears not to have made much headway anywhere in Scotland with its recruitment until shortly before the General Strike began. Although its General Council in Scotland had been formed on 23 February, it was not until 17 April, as its general secretary, Captain A. R. Dunlop, noted in a report after the strike, that the OMS "really came into the open through the appeal made by its President, the Earl of Stair".[15] By that date, the OMS had formed six branches in Edinburgh, which Dunlop considered "a sticky place", and five in Fife and Kinross, as well as several elsewhere in Scotland. On 24 April, the OMS inserted large advertisements in the *Edinburgh Evening News* and *Evening Dispatch*, calling for enrolment for voluntary work. Obstacles to OMS recruitment, according to Dunlop, had included "the almost universal opinion, . . . held up to the last moment, that a general strike would be avoided", and the "suspicion that the OMS was a Tory organisation". By the last day of the strike, the number of registered OMS volunteers totalled 758 in Edinburgh, and 1,330 in Fife and Kinross, excluding St. Andrews.[16]

But the OMS was not the only organisation that recruited voluntary or blackleg labour. Directly the emergency was declared, the government's own Emergency Organisation began recruiting at its office at the Synod Hall in Edinburgh. Still other volunteers were enrolled by the Students' Emergency Council at Edinburgh University, and at St. Andrews.

Both Edinburgh and St. Andrews Universities played important roles in the General Strike as sources of blackleg labour. At Edinburgh, where the Lord Rector in 1926 was appropriately enough Stanley Baldwin, the Students' Emergency Council was set up three or four days before the strike began. All six of the Council's members were drawn from the Students' Representative Council—one indeed was its president, and two others were past presidents.[17] "We have set up this Council ourselves," its members explained in a letter on Sunday, 2 May, to Sir Alfred Ewing, Principal of the University.[18] "We have been particularly anxious to avoid any suggestion that it has any political bias of any kind. We have included the University Conservative and Liberal Associations, and have invited the President of the University Labour Party to come in with us. He has declined to do this. Beyond this we claim to be representative of the different faculties and interests of the University. We have no connection with the OMS, Fascisti, or any other organisation. We have been recognised by the District Civil Commissioner, and are all to work directly under him. We propose to do our recruiting through depots in each of the [student] Unions, and we propose . . . to make it clear we are both non-political and non-strike-breaking. . . . We have made quiet enquiries among various sections of students in the last day or two, and they are eager to be of assistance." The Student Emergency Council's letter then asked if the Senatus of the University would give an assurance that students who volunteered for work during the strike would not as a result jeopardise their prospects of passing the Degree and Professional examinations which were due to be held about a month later.

Even before this letter had reached him, however, Principal Sir Alfred Ewing had already on his own initiative called an emergency meeting of the Principal and Deans' Committee, to consider granting concessions to student volunteers. The Committee decided that student volunteers who were forced to miss classes would not be obliged to follow another course in lieu or to make up the qualifying attendances and, secondly, that volunteer students unable to sit Degree or Professional examinations that term would be allowed to do so in September "or another convenient time."[19] These were remarkable concessions. If the Degree and Professional examinations had been held at their normal time—in June—hundreds of students might have been forced to think twice about volunteering for labour during the General Strike. As it was, encouraged so warmly by the University authorities, the Students' Emergency Council began on Monday, 3 May, greatly to lengthen its lists of volunteers. Out of the total of 3,953 matriculated students, over 2,000 enrolled as volunteer workers, though only about half of these were actually given work to do during the strike.[20]

This display of class bias at the University certainly did not go unopposed or undenounced. Indeed, the reason for the setting up of a separate Students' Emergency Council was the fear on the part of its protagonists that a proposal to make the Students' Representative Council itself a blackleg recruiting agency would automatically cause serious dissension in that body.[21] Evidence is lacking about the corporate action of the University Labour Party, but several students demonstrated in a practical manner their support for the General Strike. Jennie Lee, then a student at the University, records in her autobiography that "When the Strike began a few of us from the University rushed down to the trade union headquarters to ask how we could help."[22] A. D. Mackie, the popular and competent editor of *The Student* resigned from his post in protest against the action of the University authorities, and the Students' Emergency Council declared that the University had "disgraced itself", and refused to participate in "any student buffoonery in future, as this buffoonery is too easily diverted to class advantage".[23] No impression was made on the University authorities and the Students' Emergency Council, declared committees denouncing recruitment of students for work on the railways, or by a deputation of the Edinburgh Central Strike Committee to the Lord Provost to protest against "the use of irresponsible students as strike-breakers".[24] Quite different sentiments about the student volunteers were of course expressed by those opposed to the General Strike, and Thomas Cowan, a Leith shipowner, so admired "the grit and pluck of our University youths", many of whom had worked at Leith docks, that after the strike he donated to the University a cheque for £10,000.[25]

At St. Andrews University, the story was similar: all 650 or so matriculated students, together with many members of the staff, enrolled for voluntary work, and all but a handful were sent to work at the docks at Dundee, or on the railway at Leuchars Junction or Perth, under a promise by Principal Sir James Irvine of generous concessions in class work to all who volunteered.[26]

The two universities were not the only educational institutions in the area that supplied blackleg labour. As at Glasgow and Aberdeen, senior schoolboys and masters from most of the fee-paying schools in Edinburgh volunteered for work as tram conductors, special constables, etc. At least one sixth year pupil at George Watson's College worked at Leith docks during the strike;[27] several senior boys from Edinburgh Academy worked as volunteers, and eleven of their masters as special constables;[28] while that distinguished former Fettesian, Sir John Simon, in the House of Commons denounced the strike as illegal, Fettes College provided "a strong body of special constables" from among its masters;[29] at George Heriot's School "a small corps of volunteers for emergency labour was formed", but was evidently not called out;[30] and at Royal High School, "some of the bolder spirits . . . joined the OMS, and temporarily exchanged the mangling of Homer for the punching of car-tickets".[31] Besides these schoolboys and masters, some students from Heriot-Watt College also volunteered for work during the strike.[32]

If the response by "patriotic" anti-union elements in Edinburgh to the authorities' call for voluntary workers was thus considerable, the response by local members of the "first line" unions called out on strike from midnight on 3 May was certainly impressive. Despite a notice announcing the intention of Edinburgh Corporation to maintain services during the strike, calling on all Corporation workers to remain at work, and warning any who struck work without giving the required notice that they would be regarded as having resigned from their jobs and that their places might be filled up, the mass of the Corporation workers refused to be intimidated. As midnight approached, a mass meeting and an overflow meeting of tramwaymen voted, almost unanimously, in favour of an immediate stoppage, while outside the hall a crowd of several hundred people cheered when they learned the decision. Next morning, it was found that out of a total of 1,180 drivers and conductors employed normally on Corporation trams and buses, all but 196 had struck work.[33] With the aid of office staff, volunteer labour—mainly students—and blackleg regular crews, the Corporation was able to keep running throughout the General Strike a more or less normal bus service, except that it stopped each evening at 7 p.m. But only a fractional service of trams was run. And the Corporation's refusal to cease running blackleg trams led on the first day of the strike to an extension of the stoppage of work, when the 129 workers at Portobello Power Station, supported by other workers at sub-stations, stopped work in mid-afternoon in protest. Edinburgh's electricity supply seemed about to be cut off, for the managerial staff alone could not have maintained supplies for more than a day. But a dozen technical students from Heriot-Watt College were drafted in at Portobello, and these were later reinforced by further college, university and other volunteer labour. Thus electricity supply was maintained, although for the first few days there was a fairly severe restriction of supply to industry.[34]

The response by other workers in Edinburgh called out by the TUC was also generally solid. Drivers and conductors of the privately-owned Scottish Motor Traction Company, which ran most of the country buses in the Lothians, had voted at a mass meeting on 3 May for an immediate stoppage of work. Throughout the General Strike not a single SMT bus took the road. This surprised even the strikers, as the SMT men were not solidly unionised and some were said to hold small blocks of shares in the company. The company had in fact decided that to attempt running a service of blackleg buses through the coalfields of the Lothians would be a costly provocation of the miners there.[35] Their conclusion was certainly borne out by the experience of the railways during the strike, when the stoning of trains was a daily occurrence in the area.

The response of the railwaymen in the region virtually paralysed the railways on 4 May. On the LMS line, only three trains left Princes Street station, two of them suburban trains, and only one—from Glasgow—arrived at the station; while in the LMS goods yards even *The Scotsman* had to admit that work was at a complete standstill. On the LNER line, traffic was merely a fraction of the normal.[36]

At Leith docks, which except for those of Glasgow were the most important in Scotland, the response was particularly solid. All 2,000 dockers, and virtually all the plate-layers, dredgermen, labourers and cranemen, came out.[37] Across the Firth of Forth at Methil, the docks were reported as "deserted".[38]

Printing trades also responded very strongly, although there was some heart-burning among some members of the Scottish Typographical Association at the breach of agreements caused by the strike call.[39] There appears to have been a complete stoppage of the many printing and bookbinding firms in Edinburgh and district. The strike by printers employed on the newspaper press was impressive in its effects. A check through the files of twenty-two of the twenty-nine daily, evening or local weekly papers normally published in Edinburgh, the Lothians and Fife in 1926, indicates that only three were able to continue publishing more or less normally (though admittedly two of these three were the very influential *Scotsman* and *Edinburgh Evening Dispatch*, both non-union); seven appeared either reduced in size, or merely in roneoed form; and twelve (including the one Labour paper of the twenty-nine, the *Labour Standard*) were unable to appear at all during the strike. "For two weeks," commented the Trades Council after the strike, overlooking *The Scotsman* and *Evening Dispatch*, "the city was free from the influence of the numerous and nauseating capitalist publications turned out from Glasgow, London, and elsewhere."[40]

Much the same problems arose in Edinburgh, the Lothians and Fife, as elsewhere in Britain, from the TUC's decision to call out on strike only a "first line" of unions on 4 May, holding others such as the mass of the engineering and shipbuilding trades "in reserve", and from the conflicting or otherwise confusing instructions sent to local members from head offices in England. But locally there appears to have been only one union, and that a Scots one, whose response to the strike call was perhaps less than good, and whose organisation during the strike left much to be desired—the Scottish Horse and Motormen's Association.[41] The *Labour Standard* commented after the strike that "The organisation of the Horse and Motormen as devised by the Glasgow headquarters of that union, was absolutely inadequate to meet the situation here in Edinburgh. There was no local committee, no local authority, and consequently no local initiative; and the position was further complicated by an almost total absence of instructions from Headquarters. The present position is a positive menace to the movement."[42]

One of the problems arising from lack of preparation by the unions before the strike was obviously the need from 3 May rapidly to build up co-ordination of the strike in the localities. In Edinburgh, and to a lesser extent in the Lothians, co-ordination was provided by the Central Strike Committee, set up in the city during the weekend of 1–2 May. The Strike Committee, whose nucleus was the seven-member Industrial Committee of the Trades Council, grew rapidly to include two delegates from each of the unions on strike.[43] The increase in its numbers quickly threatened the Committee with congestion of its work. A system of sub-committees was therefore created shortly after the strike began. Each sub-committee dealt with a particular industry—printing and paper, building, etc. This system made it easier for the Committee to handle the great volume of work that poured into its hands.[44] Correspondence, clerical work and the publication of the *Official Strike Bulletin* issued by the Committee were handled on its behalf by J. P. M. Millar and his staff of the National Council of Labour Colleges, who volunteered their services at the beginning of the strike.[45] Communications within the city and with the surrounding area were facilitated by the formation of a corps of over 100 workers using their own motorcycles or push bikes.[46] The Central Strike Committee, which met in almost continual session at the head offices of the Mid and East Lothian Miners' Association at

Hillside Crescent, had as its chairman Tom Drummond, an experienced member of the National Union of Distributive and Allied Workers. Drummond, a socialist who had been an intimate friend of the Irish revolutionary James Connolly, was in 1926 the representative elected by the trades councils to the General Council of the Scottish TUC. All the other members of the Strike Committee were also socialists, most of them members of the ILP but one, D. Irvine, a communist.[47] Local strike committees existed also to the east of the city at Musselburgh and at Tranent, the latter covering East Lothian and Berwickshire; to the south at Dalkeith, and to the west, at Bathgate, where the Committee was "charged with the duty of overseeing West Lothian".[48] Across the Firth of Forth, surviving records suggest the existence of a Council of Action co-ordinating the strike throughout the area stretching from Alloa in Clackmannanshire to Leven in Fife.[49] But the only Fife trades council or council of action evidence for whose activities survives or is accessible to any extent, is that at Methil. There the strike was clearly well organised, with sub-committees dealing with food and transport, information, propaganda and Defence Corps.[50]

Strike bulletins were issued by the strike committees at Methil and Dunfermline, as well as by the Edinburgh committee.[51] The Edinburgh *Official Strike Bulletin* was published every day between 4 and 13 May. It was a single foolscap sheet, typed and duplicated on both sides, and selling at 1*d.* per copy. The cost of paper, stencils, etc. was met from a special fund raised through an appeal by the Strike Committee which, within the first twenty-four hours of the strike, had brought in £200. The daily circulation of the *Strike Bulletin* was at first between 5,000 and 7,000 copies, but the insatiable demand for news which was a feature of the strike in this as in so many other areas, convinced the Committee that they could "easily dispose of several times as many" copies. By the end of the strike, daily circulation had reached 12,000 copies, and the total circulation of its ten issues was 65,000 copies.[52] On 11 May, the Strike Committee sent a deputation to the General Council of the STUC in Glasgow to ask permission to print the *Strike Bulletin*, partly because of duplicating difficulties, partly because it was felt a printed *Bulletin* would form a more impressive riposte to *The Scotsman* and *Evening Dispatch*. The General Council refused the request, on the grounds that it was contrary to the strike instructions of the TUC, but instead offered to let the Edinburgh Strike Committee reprint the STUC's own strike paper, *The Scottish Worker*, provided there was an Edinburgh printing shop under trade union or Co-operative control.

The proviso could not be met, and with the calling off anyway of the strike next day, nothing more was done.[53]

The *Official Strike Bulletin*, which was distributed through the Lothians by motor cyclist couriers, reported strike news only. It normally contained a commentary on this news, as well as trade and district reports, and it kept up a running fire against *The Scotsman* and *Evening Dispatch*. It showed its initiative in securing a special article by a Scottish advocate, Craigie Aitchison, KC, rebutting the notorious speech of Sir John Simon on the alleged illegality of the strike.[54] Well written and informative, the *Bulletin* appears to have been an important factor in maintaining the strikers' morale.

As in many other areas, there were numerous incidents in Edinburgh, the Lothians and Fife in which strikers and supporters came into conflict with the police. Most of these incidents arose out of the running of blackleg transport, whether trams, buses, lorries or trains. On the second and third days of the strike in Edinburgh tension arose from incidents involving blackleg trams and the breaking up by police of a strikers' procession in Princes Street.[55] By Thursday evening, 6 May, a serious riot had developed in the centre of the city, around the High Street and Canongate. "Thousands of women, and even children swelled the throng, and in the numerous wild rushes which the crowd made to escape from the police, their cries added to the general uproar. At 9 p.m. the crowd around the Tron Church had assumed huge dimensions and at 9.15 nearly all the policemen were withdrawn to the Central Office (in the adjacent High Street). For half an hour the crowd waited in an ominous silence, and then a stampede from the High Street heralded the return of the police. The mounted men came first, galloping down the centre of the street with batons drawn, and they were followed by hundreds of foot police, plain clothes men and special constables."[56] Twenty people were arrested.

At Methil on 10 May, police made "a brutal assault" on a road picket at Muiredge.[57] Methil Council of Action then increased from 150 to 700 the strength of its already formed Workers' Defence Corps, under the control of former wartime army warrant officers and NCOs, "and there was no further interference by the police with pickets".[58] At Tranent in East Lothian on 7 May, a serious fracas took place between a large crowd and the police, arising from a road-picketing incident. The police retreated to the police station, which was then besieged by the crowd of some 1,000 people, and all the windows were smashed.[59]

The running of blackleg trains created a good deal of tension, and in some cases, especially in Fife and mining districts in the Lothians, the strike committees' policy of peaceful picketing was sometimes departed from by excited crowds or over-zealous individuals. Near Cameron Bridge, in East Fife, for example, a train was diverted by miners on to a branch line and pelted with stones.[60] Another train on 5 May from Edinburgh to Musselburgh in Midlothian was said to have "encountered a fusillade of stone-throwing . . . about half a mile from Musselburgh".[61] By the end of the strike, such incidents had become so frequent that troops were stationed on some sections of the LNER line.[62] It was following one such stone-throwing incident that a conflict took place near Newcraighall mining village on the outskirts of Edinburgh, between miners and police. The police were driven off, but returned to Newcraighall after midnight, arrested several miners and, according to local tradition, beat up one or two of the villagers.[63]

The total number of arrests and convictions for offences connected with the strike in Edinburgh, the Lothians and Fife cannot be assessed with complete accuracy. In Edinburgh itself, 108 arrests were made;[64] and it would be safe to claim that scores of strikers and supporters were arrested in the Lothians, where 40 members of the Mid and East Lothian Miners' Association were reported to be in custody by the end of the strike,[65] and in Fife. At Dunfermline Sheriff Court alone on 10 and 11 June, seventeen strikers, almost all miners, appeared charged with offences during the strike. Fifteen of them were convicted, and the aggregate of their sentences amounted to 450 days imprisonment.[66] In Edinburgh, the Strike Committee protested to the Secretary of State for Scotland about the "savage sentences being imposed upon workers", and subsequently the *Labour Standard* described sentences imposed as "monstrous".[67]

The arrest and sentencing of road transport pickets appears to have had little or no adverse effect on the morale of strikers in the area but, on the contrary, as at Methil, contributed to keeping strikers on their mettle. The Edinburgh Strike Committee, like others, operated a system of permits for transport of foodstuffs which the *Official Strike Bulletin* reported on 7 May covered the whole of the Lothians. "The new food permit system," the *Bulletin* added on the following day, "is working admirably. There has been a constant stream of applicants . . . and many businesses are represented. The Committee insist, however, on certain conditions which many firms find irksome. Permits are only issued to those men who are members of Transport Unions, and no departure is made from this rule. The Committee believe that, in a few days, critical control of road transport will be in their hands." It was to prevent this control passing into the hands of the strikers, however, that a "flying squad" of special constables began to patrol roads in the Lothians from 8 May.[68] And it was partly to avoid conflicts of this sort with police, that the General Council of the TUC ordered the withdrawal of all permits by strike committees at the beginning of the second week of the strike.[69]

Was the strike weakening in the area before it was called off by the TUC on 12 May? The evidence, scrappy and conflicting as it is, suggests that contradictory tendencies were at work by that date, but that basically the strike remained solid. On the one hand, some non-unionist carters in Edinburgh were evidently threatening to return to work. Their return may have been prevented by the Strike Committee's recommendation to the General Council of the Scottish TUC that the appropriate union, the Horse and Motormen, should give the men some strike pay on condition that they joined the union.[70] There was, however, evidently a return to work by some Corporation tramwaymen from Tuesday morning, 11 May. Trams ran on some half-dozen routes for the first time since the beginning of the strike.[71] But as the numbers of tramwaymen returning are nowhere published, the implication is that they were not numerous. Four tramway electricians "with whom the ETU have had trouble all along" also returned to work on Tuesday. *The Scotsman* treated this news with the headline: "Normal conditions in Edinburgh: Electricians' Return".[72] The only other reported return to work was by some thirty railway clerks at South Leith station and the docks.[73] But on 10 May *The Scotsman* had admitted: "In the Edinburgh area, no substantial breakaway from the strikers has been reported."

There is no evidence of any breakaway in the Lothians; and in Fife, although at Dunfermline "some sections were showing signs of weakness",[74] the only actual return to work seems to have been by all but two of the members of the Scottish Typographical Association employed at Cupar on the *Fife Herald and Journal*—probably about half a dozen men only.[75]

On the other hand, the strike and its impact on industries not called out by the TUC was broadening by 12 May. A good response was made by the "second line" unions of engineering and shipbuilding trades called out that day. Over 100 Corporation road- and quarry-workers struck work on 10 May. Of the building trade workers, the *Labour Standard* later wrote that ". . . despite the fact that most of their members should, under the TUC instructions, have remained at work, few would tie themselves down to work, and every avenue by which they could find excuse for joining in the fight was explored to such advantage that the first weekend saw practically the whole of the masons, bricklayers, plasterers, plumbers and joiners lined up to resist depression. . . . Speaking on how the trade had responded, Mr. Dalrymple, the veteran Secretary of the Woodworkers, said that in . . . nearly 40 years he had never seen such enthusiasm or solidarity."[76] Moreover, the transport strike reduced or prevented transport of raw materials to or products from factories and works. At Ratho in Midlothian, for example, "the quarries were thrown idle".[77] Some 400 rubber mill workers were laid off because of reductions in electricity supply, and several breweries were forced to close.[78] At Dunfermline, "the effects of the stoppage have been seriously felt by the linen manufacturers",[79] and at Kingskettle, textile workers were put on a three-day week,[80] as were textile mills at Haddington in East Lothian. The local fishing industry was hampered by lack of transport for the catches.[81]

The calling-off of the strike on 12 May by the General Council of the TUC, and its virtually immediate renewal by railwaymen, printers, dockers and other workers faced by employers' attempts to attack their wages and conditions, or impose non-unionism, affected Edinburgh and district in much the same way as other areas. The actual calling off of the strike appears to have taken the Strike Committee by surprise.[82] But if that were so, the feeling of surprise swiftly became a conviction, at least on the part of some activists, that the pass had been sold by the General Council. Jennie Lee, who had been working throughout the strike on the distribution staff of the *Strike Bulletin* at Hillside Crescent, vividly recalled the sense of betrayal felt by many strikers. "That evening, while the Central Strike Committee attended to the last funeral rites on the floor above us, we younger ones were huddled together in a corner of our improvised office, stunned and listless, demoralised by the utter absolute fiasco of it all. We ended the day with a cursing competition. I was shocked by the language I suddenly discovered I knew."[83]

Victimisation of strikers took place in many cases in Edinburgh, and only the SMT bus crews and the Leith dockers appear not to have suffered from it. Records of the District Committee of the Amalgamated Engineering Union reveal a dozen cases among engineers.[84] Bakers who had struck work at Smiths of Hawkhill bakery against supplying bread to blackleg tramwaymen, were victimised. So were bottle workers at Portobello.[85] Eight months after the strike, the Trades Council and the Transport and General Workers' Union were still pressing Edinburgh Town Council to reinstate several tramwaymen victimised during the strike.[86] Drummond Shiels, Labour MP for East Edinburgh, told the house of Commons on 20 May of the victimisation of LNER railwaymen of supervisory grade in Edinburgh.[87] Two inspectors had been offered reinstatement as guards, and a third as a signalman; a woman carriage cleaner with eleven years' service was "still on the street while one with considerably less service was working".[88] In November 1926, the NUR No. 1 Branch secretary criticised "some very shady tactics the [Railway] Company's representative had used to keep Brother Gaynor out of the service". Gaynor, a branch activist, was, however, reinstated a few days later.[89] Of the twelve men blacklisted by the LNER in Scotland, five—four inspectors and a yardmaster—worked in Edinburgh.[90] A mass meeting of railwaymen of the three railway unions was held at the end of June to agitate the case of the five men, and Drummond Shiels tried unsuccessfully to raise it again in the House of Commons. But the most the LNER would concede was that the men be transferred to stations in Glasgow and Alloa. The offer was refused, and apparently the five men remained in Edinburgh working as signalmen or guards.[91]

As two of the three main Edinburgh papers, *The Scotsman* and *Evening Dispatch*, had already been non-union before the strike, printers in the city did not suffer as did their colleagues in Glasgow, Dundee and elsewhere from the imposition by newspaper owners of non-unionism after the strike. In Fife, there was an attempt to victimise "in a most malevolent form" members of the Scottish Typographical Association employed by jobbing firms at Dunfermline; and at Kirkcaldy there seems also to have been some victimisation, while at Cupar a printer who refused to submit to the non-unionism imposed in the local newspaper office had to find work elsewhere.[92]

If the engineers, railwaymen, printers, dockers and some other workers had not remained on strike for a day or two after 12 May to resist the employers' onslaught, no doubt there would have been many more cases of victimisation in the area. Though the General Strike itself had been called off, the working class of Edinburgh continued to support the miners' struggle. The Central Strike Committee organised a relief fund for the miners, and over £10,000 was collected.[93] The Central Strike Committee itself survived the strike, and indeed the

Trades Council agreed that it should "remain permanently in being". Tom Drummond, the Strike Committee's chairman, proposed that it should "draft a skeleton organisation for future use".[94]

Further research is certainly needed on the extent to which working-class consciousness in Edinburgh, the Lothians and Fife was increased by the General Strike. But that it did increase is clear. In Fife, new recruits flocked into the Communist Party.[95] In Edinburgh, there is some evidence to suggest that attendance at union branch meetings increased considerably in the immediate aftermath of the strike.[96] Another small straw in the wind, perhaps, was that the number of Labour councillors elected to Edinburgh Town Council in the municipal elections of November 1926 increased from six to fourteen.[97] Although the working-class movement in Edinburgh, as in so many other areas, was left with the feeling that a great demonstration of working-class solidarity had been betrayed by treacherous or at best incompetent leadership at national level, there was also a feeling of pride in local achievement, in the discovery of ability to organise spontaneously and rapidly the local aspects of the great General Strike. As the *Labour Standard* put it in its first issue after the strike: "We rejoice in the strike as the most remarkable demonstration ever made of the class-consciousness and solidarity of the workers. . . . To those of us who took part in it, however small that part may have been, the memory still lives—a memory of unselfish devotion, of unflinching courage, of unlimited faith in the power of the workers."[98]

NOTES

1. *59th Annual Report, Edinburgh Trades and Labour Council, for year ending 31 March 1926*, Supplementary Report, pp. 21–6.
2. *Programme for Labour Party annual conference in Edinburgh, 1936* (Edinburgh, 1936), pp. 25–9; for other sources, see *Census for Scotland* 1921 and 1931; Nora Milnes, *A Study of Industrial Edinburgh, 1923–34*, (1936); and *Industrial Edinburgh* (1921).
3. *British Worker*, 7 May 1926.
4. *Report of General Council, Scottish Trades Union Congress, 1925: Part I, Extent and Structure of Trade Union Movement in Scotland*, p. 7.
5. *59th Annual Report, Edinburgh Trades and Labour Council, for year ending 31 March 1926*, p. 30.
6. Ibid.; *Labour Standard*, 25 April 1925 and 30 January 1926; Interview,

1959, with Fred Douglas, former organiser of Communist Party in Edinburgh.

7. Russell A. Fox, *Members of the Labour Party elected to Edinburgh Town Council, 1909 to 1971* (Edinburgh, 1971), p. 4.
8. *Labour Standard*, 28 February 1925.
9. *Kirkcaldy Mail*, 25 May 1926.
10. Unpublished memoirs of John McArthur, tape-recorded, 1968–71.
11. *West Fife Echo*, 21 April 1926.
12. *Fifeshire Advertiser*, 1 May 1926.
13. John McArthur.
14. Copy of Circular 2,076 is in archives of Aberdeen Town Council, and was noted in April 1963.
15. Scottish Record Office, H.H.56/18, typewritten report by Captain A. R. Dunlop, dated 28 May 1926.
16. Ibid.
17. *The Student*, vol. XXII, no. 10, 2 June 1926, pp. 242–3.
18. Minutes of Edinburgh University Senatus, 6 May 1926, pp. 301–4.
19. Ibid.
20. *The Student*, vol. XXII, no. 10, 2 June 1926, pp. 242–3; *Edinburgh University Calendar, 1926–27*.
21. *The Student*, vol. XXII, no. 10, 2 June 1926, pp. 242–3.
22. Jennie Lee, *Tomorrow is a New Day* (1939), p. 82.
23. *The Student*, vol. XXII, no. 10, 2 June 1926, p. 234.
24. Minutes of Edinburgh University Senatus, 6 May 1926; *Official Strike Bulletin*, 7 May 1926.
25. Minutes of Edinburgh University Court, 14 June 1926.
26. *St. Andrews University Calendar, 1927–28*; *College Echoes*, new series, vol. XXI, no. 12, 28 May 1926; *St. Andrews Citizen*, 29 May 1926.
27. *The Watsonian*, vol. XXII, no. 3, July 1926, pp. 113–15.
28. *Edinburgh Academy Chronicle*, vol. XXXIII, no. 5, June 1926, p. 84.
29. *The Fettesian*, vol. XLVIII, no. 5, June 1926, pp. 133–4.
30. *The Herioter*, vol. XX, no. 2, July 1926, p. 28.
31. *Schola Regia*, vol. 22, no. 66, Summer 1926, p. 10.
32. Minutes of Edinburgh Town Council, 1 July 1926, Report of Lord Provost's Committee.
33. Minutes of Meeting of Edinburgh Town Council, 1 July 1926, pp. 536–9, and Report of Lord Provost's Committee.
34. Ibid.; *Official Strike Bulletin*, 4 May 1926.
35. *Labour Standard*, 10 April and 22 May 1926.
36. *The Scotsman*, 5 May 1926. Even on the last day of the strike, Gresley, chief engineer of the LNER, complained by phone to the government's Emergency Organisation that "Situation re train transport in Scotland is not nearly as good as in England." Scottish Record Office, H.H.56/21, note dated 12 May 1926.

37. Minutes of Leith Docks Commission, 11 June 1926—Report by Convener of Emergency Special Committee.
38. *Fifeshire Advertiser*, 29 May 1926.
39. Scottish Typographical Association, *Annual Report, 1926*, p. 24.
40. *59th Annual Report of Edinburgh Trades and Labour Council for year ending 31 March 1926*, Supplementary Report, pp. 21–6. Neither the *British Worker* nor the government's organ, the *British Gazette*, circulated in Scotland during the Strike—see *Report of General Council*, Scottish TUC, 1927, p. 8.
41. Ibid.
42. *Labour Standard*, 22 May 1926.
43. *60th Annual Report of Edinburgh Trades and Labour Council for year ending 31 March 1927*, p. 9.
44. Interview with Tom Drummond, 1959.
45. Letter from J. P. M. Millar, 21 October 1959; Agenda and Secretary's Report of General Council, Scottish TUC, 14 June 1926.
46. *Plebs*, vol. XVIII, July 1926, no. 7, p. 255.
47. Interview with Tom Drummond, 1959.
48. *Labour Standard*, 22 May 1926.
49. *West Fife Echo*, 21 April 1926; *Plebs* typewritten and MS. reports on the Strike, in Edinburgh Public Library Reference Department, on microfilm.
50. Emile Burns, *The General Strike, May 1926: Trades Councils in Action* (London, 1926), pp. 143–4.
51. Ibid., pp. 123, 143.
52. Letter from Gerald Crawford, secretary, Edinburgh Central Strike Committee, to TUC, 8 May 1926, in TUC Library—files concerning Local Strike Bulletins; *60th Annual Report of Edinburgh Trades and Labour Council for year ending 31 March 1927*, p. 9; *Labour Standard*, 22 May 1926. A file of *Bulletins* is preserved in Edinburgh Public Library (Edinburgh Room).
53. Minutes of General Council of Scottish TUC, 11 May 1926, afternoon session.
54. *Official Strike Bulletin*, 10 May 1926.
55. *The Scotsman* and *Emergency Press*, 6 May 1926.
56. *The Scotsman*, 7 May 1926. Edinburgh Town Council spent £831 on batons during the General Strike, including £2 10*s*. paid to Woolworths for blind-rollers, to be used as batons (*Labour Standard*, 10 July 1926).
57. *Leven Advertiser*, 25 May 1926, reporting a resolution at Wemyss Parish Council.
58. Emile Burns, op. cit., pp. 143–4; John McArthur, op. cit. Mr. McArthur recalled: "I remember going down to the [strike] headquarters when the first company were going to resume the picketing, and as they came up with their sergeant in front, he shouted, 'Eyes left.' You could see the arms swinging rigidly because they were concealing pokers, hammers, etc. The

picket took up its post on the road. . . . In spite of the fact that there was a big contingent of police they stopped every vehicle that came along. It was a marvellous display of organised, disciplined activity."

59. *Haddingtonshire Courier*, 21 May 1926.
60. *Fife News*, 15 May 1926.
61. *Emergency Press*, 6 May 1926.
62. *The Scotsman*, 11 May 1926. The risk of being stoned was not the only one that passengers faced in blackleg trains. *The Scotsman* reported blandly on 6 May that, "The gates at a level crossing near Prestonpans were run into by a passenger train, the driver having apparently failed to observe that they were shut." The most serious railway accident anywhere in Britain during the strike occurred in St. Margaret's Tunnel, a few yards from Waverley Station, Edinburgh, on 10 May, when a blackleg train passed signals at danger and smashed into some refuse wagons, with the loss of three lives and eight injured. Thirty-six of the rescuers were temporarily gassed by an escape from pipes broken in the smash. *The Thistle*, Quarterly Journal of The Royal Scots, 2nd new series, vol. II, no. 1, July 1926, p. 17.
63. *The Scotsman*, 11 and 12 May 1926; Interview, 1960, with James Blair, a Newcraighall ex-miner.
64. *Annual Report* of Chief Constable for Edinburgh, 1926, p. 16.
65. *Labour Standard*, 22 May 1926.
66. *West Fife Echo*, 16 June 1926.
67. *Official Strike Bulletin*, 11 May 1926; *Labour Standard*, 22 May 1926.
68. *The Scotsman*, 11 May 1926; *Labour Standard*, 22 May 1926.
69. *British Worker*, 10 May 1926.
70. Minutes of General Council, Scottish TUC, 10 May 1926, morning session.
71. Minutes of Edinburgh Town Council, 1 July 1926—Report of Lord Provost's Committee, pp. 536–9, and private information provided by Corporation Transport Department, 1959.
72. *Official Strike Bulletin*, 12 May 1926; *The Scotsman* 12 May 1926.
73. *The Scotsman*, 12 May 1926.
74. Emile Burns, op. cit., p. 123; R. Postgate, E. Wilkinson, and J. F. Horrabin, *A Worker's History of the Great Strike* (London, 1927), p. 32.
75. *Fife Herald and Journal*, 12 May 1926; *Annual Report*, 1926, of Scottish Typographical Association, p. 59.
76. *Labour Standard*, 22 May 1926; *Emergency Press*, 11 May 1926; Minutes of Edinburgh Town Council, 1 July 1926—Report of Lord Provost's Committee, pp. 536–9.
77. *Labour Standard*, 22 May 1926.
78. *The Scotsman*, 6 and 8 May 1926.
79. *Dunfermline Journal*, 15 May 1926.
80. *Fife Free Press*, 22 May 1926.

81. *Haddingtonshire Courier*, 14 May 1926.
82. *Official Strike Bulletin*, 12 May 1926; *The Scotsman*, 13 May 1926.
83. Jennie Lee, op. cit., p. 83; Interviews with Tom Drummond and Edgar Ramsay, Edinburgh, 1959.
84. Minutes of Edinburgh District Committee, Amalgamated Engineering Union, 14 May 1926.
85. *Labour Standard*, 22 May 1926.
86. *Labour Standard*, 6 November 1926, and 15 January 1927.
87. *Labour Standard*, 29 May 1926.
88. Minutes, Edinburgh No. 1 Branch, NUR, 16 and 30 May 1926.
89. Minutes, Edinburgh No. 1 Branch, NUR, 14 and 28 November 1926.
90. *Labour Standard*, 26 June 1926. Even their "respectability" did not save them: three of the five were elders in the Church of Scotland.
91. *Labour Standard*, 3 and 17 July 1926.
92. *Annual Report*, 1926, of Scottish Typographical Association, pp. 59, 61, and 70.
93. *60th Annual Report of Edinburgh Trades and Labour Council for year ending 31 March 1927*, p. 9.
94. Minutes of Executive Committee of Edinburgh Trades and Labour Council, 21 May 1926; *Labour Standard*, 29 May 1926.
95. Recollections of John McArthur.
96. Minutes, Edinburgh No. 1 Branch, NUR, 16 May 1926.
97. Russell A. Fox, op. cit., p. 4.
98. *Labour Standard*, 22 May 1926.

3 MANCHESTER DIARY

by EDMUND and RUTH FROW

At the time of the General Strike, the population of the Manchester and Salford area was over a million. Surrounding the city was the South Lancashire coalfield, but within the city itself the most important trades were metal working and engineering, and transport and distribution generally. As the engineering trades were in the second line and were not called out until the last day of the strike, it was the transport workers who were in the front line.

In his report to the Manchester and Salford Trades and Labour Council for the year of the strike, William Mellor, the Honorary Secretary, said: "Not only was the call loyally responded to, but discipline and order was maintained to a degree that evoked the admiration of friend and foe alike."[1] He warned against the dangers of carping criticism and called for a continuation of the unity that the strike had so amply demonstrated.

Manchester was not a storm centre of the strike, but it has the dubious honour of having been the scene of the first and the last arrests. The comparative calm that prevailed may be partly due to the traditional good humour of the Manchester workers, but also to the fact that the Trades Council had prepared in advance to some extent and, when the thirty thousand workers were called out on the eve of the strike, some organisation was already in being.

The Manchester and Salford Trades Council had formed a Council of Action nine months before the strike was called. Few trades councils appear to have laid plans so far in advance. Because the original Council of Action had representatives of over seventy unions on it, it was the Executive of the Trades Council that actually constituted the operative Council of Action. Manchester was one of the few centres where trouble was anticipated and trade union meetings were held during the previous nine months to ensure discipline. Although a committee representing the miners, railway workers, transport workers and metal workers was formed as the North West Strike Committee and met in the Salford offices of the TGWU on 3 May, the local organisation remained in the hands of the Council of Action. The North West Strike Committee covered the areas of Lancashire, Cheshire, Westmorland and North Wales.

Although by comparison with other parts of the country Manchester was well prepared for the strike so far as the workers were concerned, the government and local authorities were far more so. The North West area organisation was centred in Liverpool, where the Civil Commissioner was Government Whip, Major G. Hennessy, MP. The local mayors, town clerks and chairmen of the smaller authorities met in Manchester Town Hall on 3 May to finalise arrangements for transport, distribution of food supplies and other essential services. Recruiting offices for volunteer strike-breakers were opened at all public buildings, and an Emergency Committee was set up in Manchester under the Emergency Powers Act to supply food and other essential services. The members were mostly councillors and officials of the City Council, although the area which it covered stretched as far as Salford, Altrincham and Stretford.

TUESDAY, 4 MAY, DAY 1

At midnight on Monday, 3 May, the all-night trams stopped running. The evening shift of the print workers caught the last tram home on the Monday night and from then onwards regular newspapers were few and far between. The *Manchester Guardian* was, however, printed throughout the strike in various forms. The *Manchester Evening Chronicle* was duplicated on one-page sheets. According to *The Times* there was a lack of solidarity among the members of the Typographical Association and the Manchester papers were printed on 6 May.

The transport workers, the shock troops of the strike, were solid from the start in Manchester. The first edition of the *British Worker* published a headline, "BUSINESS IN A CLEFT STICK—Paralysing effect of strike at Manchester—Men firm as a Rock". The article quotes the tram-men as "standing firm as a rock" and says that the Salford men were equally so. It also refers to the solidarity of the Electrical Trade Union. All work at the docks was at a standstill and the Ship Canal was not working. When the Lord Mayor refused to allow a meeting to be held near the Town Hall, the workers marched away "in orderly fashion".[2] This disciplined order astonished the employers who had predicted chaos and confusion.

It was on the first Tuesday that the first arrest was made. The

Communist Party had produced an emergency bulletin called *The Workers' Daily* in London. Dick Stoker, a local businessman who owned a car, went to London to obtain supplies for the north-west and Scotland. He arrived at the Margaret Street Socialist Hall in Openshaw with the supplies and was met by a group of Young Communist League members including Mick Jenkins (to whom we are indebted for this story). The bundles were being unloaded into the members' room when the police arrived. While they looked into the car and questioned Dick Stoker, the youngsters took as many bundles as they could from the members' room and hid them under a pile of coke in the cellar—an action which saved some bundles of the broadsheet from the police. Dick Stoker was arrested and next day sentenced to two months' imprisonment. The *Scotsman* of 6 May reported the incident in these terms: "There was a prosecution yesterday at Manchester under the Emergency Powers Act Regulations. William Richard Stoker (40), of Old House Farm, Ringway, stated to be a Company Director, was sentenced to two months in the second division for having attempted to do an act calculated to cause disaffection among His Majesty's Forces and civilian population, and to impede, delay, or restrict measures essential to the public safety. It was stated that the police found Stoker's high-powered car outside a Socialist Hall at Openshaw, ready to proceed to Glasgow with 1,600 copies of the General Strike edition of the *Workers' Daily*, which, the prosecution alleged, Stoker knew contained seditious matter. Notice of appeal was given."

So Dick Stoker, who had been a member of the Socialist Labour Party until 1920, when he became a foundation member of the Communist Party, had the dubious honour of being the first arrest of the strike.

WEDNESDAY, 5 MAY, DAY 2

Although incidents were reported from other parts of the country, in Manchester all continued quiet. The chairman of the Tramways Committee announced that they "had no trouble" with their men. A motion by Labour councillors criticising the principal officials at the Town Hall for "acting as strike-breakers in connection with transport in the City"[3] was defeated at a meeting of the City Council.

The *British Worker* headed its report; "All Joining In—Manchester's force of Strikers growing hourly". It continued: "In addition to stoppage of the traffic, grades work has ceased at the railway shops in Manchester and district, including Newton Heath and Dukinfield. The Amalgamated Engineering Union reports that its men had struck at works where members of other unions had been called out, including the railway shops, newspaper offices, and tramway sheds. The Electrical Trades Union reports that its members are out, with the exception of those employed on building schemes at hospitals. The tramway stoppage in Manchester is complete, only the three oldest drivers in the employ of the tramways department having reported for duty. All is quiet in the City and no disturbances have taken place."[4]

The last statement may or may not be connected with the fact that there were 1,000 "specials" enlisted in the local police.

THURSDAY, 6 MAY, DAY 3

Although the *Manchester Guardian* reported that train services increased on 6 May and that there were trains running to Leeds, Blackpool, Oldham, Glasgow, York and London, Manchester trade was almost at a standstill. The *British Worker* reported that workers in other branches of industry not already involved in the strike were getting restive and demanding that they should be allowed to join in. The short report of activity in the area in the *British Worker* accentuated the need for a local edition.

FRIDAY, 7 MAY, DAY 4

Ellen Wilkinson and J. F. Horrabin sent a report from the Manchester District to the TUC in which they said: "Position absolutely solid, but local movement demanding news. We urged publication of local strike paper which has not been done. NUDAW Head Office has placed private press at the disposal of the Strike Committee."[5]

In his report, the secretary of the Liverpool Trades Council, Mr. Barton, said that a visit had been received from three delegates from Manchester (Duke, Ross and Webb). He said that exchange visits were being arranged between Manchester and Liverpool.

The TUC sent a telegram to the secretary of the Typographical Association at their headquarters, Beechwood, Oak Drive, Fallowfield, telling them to look into the continued publication of a paper in Rochdale.

The four-page report on the North West Region that T. McLean, Area Group Secretary of the TGWU sent on the fourth day, added considerably to the TUC's knowledge of the general progress of the strike in the North-West. He informed them of an attempt at intimidation on the part of the Salford Tramways Committee, which had sent letters to the men. After negotiation, agreement was reached by which the men received their wages but handed in the uniforms which belonged to the Corporation. This was not actually carried out and the men kept their uniforms and the notices were withdrawn.

The Manchester Emergency Committee, in the evening, prepared to move necessary foodstuffs from the depots if the unions refused to handle it. The NUR had issued instructions not to move goods of any kind, including foodstuffs. The Lord Mayor appealed for recruits to drive road transport vehicles if the need arose. He said that private traders were coping with the situation so far, but he wanted to be prepared. The price of milk was rising and the Manchester and Salford Milk Dealers' Association urged that all milk should be sold at a standard 3*d*. a pint.

SATURDAY, 8 MAY, DAY 5

The secretary of the TUC North West District Committee reported that a large number of charabancs and taxis had been trying to run passenger services between the city and the suburbs. He said that it was having little effect on the position.

The efforts that had been made to print a Manchester edition of the *British Worker* began to take shape. Fenner Brockway was sent from London to be the editor. He and H. Skinner of the Typographical Association were to be jointly responsible for the production. As soon as Fenner Brockway arrived in Manchester, he went to the Association's headquarters in Fallowfield to find that Skinner was ill in bed and unable to co-operate. The Co-operative Printing Society was supposed to print the paper, but their London Executive refused permission. At a meeting of unions concerned in the production of papers, it was suggested that the Manchester Co-operative Publishing Society might do the job. Their manager lived at Southport, fifty miles away by road. But transport was laid on, the manager contacted, permission to print was given and the necessary workers alerted. The socialist members of the National Union of Journalists offered help, although the union organisation refused. The National Union of Clerks provided typists and telephonists, NATSOPA accepted responsibility for the accounts and despatch, and the transport workers organised distribution by road as far south as Derby, west to Holyhead, east to Hull and north to Carlisle. Fenner Brockway commented that as the organisation became clear he realised its historical significance: for the first time a British newspaper was being produced under workers' control.

SUNDAY, 9 MAY, DAY 6

During Sunday, plans for the Manchester edition went ahead and the first issue was due out on Monday afternoon.

Many people went to outdoor meetings to hear Labour leaders and, according to *The Times*, the weekend passed "without an incident of an untoward character". The Lord Mayor said that they were "going very nicely and everyone appears to be cheerful and good-tempered".[6] One incident was reported in the *Manchester Guardian*—a man had been arrested for attempting to interfere with a lorry-load of flour at Sutcliffe's Mill in Hulme, Manchester.

The destroyer, *Wessex*, arrived in the Ship Canal. This was correctly interpreted as evidence that the government intended to enforce the unloading of grain and other vessels in the docks. The North West Strike Committee reported that they had received "authoritative information" that 2,000 beds, blankets and pillows had been taken to Salford docks for the purpose of strike-breaking. "Wire instructions", they requested.

It was estimated that 20,000 people marched into Platt Fields to hear Miss Mary Qualle of the TUC General Council and Rhys Davies, MP. Two brass bands of tramway workers played them on to the field. Other meetings were held in Gorton and Blackley.

MONDAY, 10 MAY, DAY 7

The first Manchester edition of the *British Worker* was produced in 50,000 copies. Fenner Brockway commented: "We could have sold three times as many, but we have only paper for 300,000. The paper caused a great sensation in the streets. Only tiny sheets have so far been printed in Manchester. Conversations with the TU officials here show that the men are wonderfully solid. The Manchester TA office is underneath a bridge outside Exchange Station. Two trains passed on Saturday! Realisation of the success of the strike is much completer than in London. At Westminster one was conscious of the power of the Government. Here the men are absolutely on top."[7]

TUESDAY, 11 MAY, DAY 8

In the Tuesday issue of the paper, the Manchester report said: "The situation in Manchester, as a whole, is splendid. The contrast of the streets with their ordinarily crowded condition is remarkable. It is like a deserted city. Usually the streets are thronged with lorries and the procession of trams is continuous. Now there is not a tram and the lorries are very rare. I walked three miles this morning and saw three! There are a few private buses—during the day I have seen two."[8]

The paper was issued in a larger edition of 100,000. Fenner Brockway said: "We have now got paper for 800,000 copies, so I risked an edition of 100,000 this morning. Yesterday afternoon's edition was largely confined to Manchester. Webb's transport service has got today's issue to Derby, Liverpool, Preston and Colne. The phone is ringing all day for more. We are rationing supplies to districts, but it is difficult to face the bitter disappointment."[9]

He quoted an announcement in Lewis's window to the effect that since the working class had gone on strike to prevent attacks on their wages, the firm was prepared to guarantee not to reduce wages for three years.

Five hundred volunteers were escorted from Cavendish Road Police Station in Salford, to the docks, where they were to unload foodstuffs from the ships in dock.

Workers at the Co-operative Wholesale Society flour mills joined the other milling employees on strike, and the men at the grain elevators at the docks were also out. Volunteers, however, unloaded the grain, took it to the mills and then delivered it throughout the city. The Emergency Committe expressed itself satisfied with the ability of its services to meet all demands.

The Manchester Tramways Committee gave the men until 10 a.m. on Wednesday, 12 May, to resume work if they still wished to continue in their service.

The second line of strikers, the engineers and shipyard workers, were called out by the TUC. This obviously brought Manchester fully into the national picture as there were large numbers of engineering workers in the city, 4,000 at Metropolitan-Vickers in Trafford Park alone.

The students at the Hartley College sent a telegram to the TUC and the Prime Minister urging a resumption of negotiations between Parliament, the TUC and the government. They thought that the

General Strike should be called off and the mineowners should withdraw their lockout notices.

In his report to the TUC, J. A. Webb, secretary of the North Western District Committee, complained that the members of URTWA had not "played the game". He said that repeated complaints had been made about them from all the towns in the area. He also mentioned the excellent position on the docks where the workers were refusing to react to the provocative behaviour of the Ship Canal Company and the local authorities by introducing blackleg labour. He said: "There is no doubt about the morale of the crowd, and I am perfectly satisfied that there will be no resumption of work here until such time as instructions have been received from the TUC."[10]

During the day a burning lorry was seen in the centre of Manchester, in Market Street. It had been overturned by a hostile crowd, set on fire and destroyed. It contained bedding and empty milk churns and was driven by student volunteers.

WEDNESDAY, 12 MAY, DAY 9

The Wednesday Manchester edition of the *British Worker* gave no indication of the shock that was to come during the day.

Fenner Brockway was among the thousands who could not at first credit the news of the termination of the strike. "I was warned from London to be ready for a 'special' and just after midday the news came through," he said. "At first it was meagre. The TUC was assured that a satisfactory basis of negotiation had been reached, the miners had expressed gratitude for the support of the other workers, and the executives were arranging for their men to return. That was about all. I took the news to the N. W. Committee. They had had word over the wireless that the strike had been called off, but were incredulous and were proceeding with their business unmoved. I handed the chairman one of our roneod 'specials', and he held up the spokesman of a deputation, seeking permission to call out further men, to read it. Still they were incredulous. Was I sure that I had not been hoaxed?"[11]

When more definite news was received and it was realised that the terms were only an arrangement with Herbert Samuel and that the miners lockout was to continue, the confusion and anger grew. The comments of the compositors as they set the type of Thursday's *British Worker* were an indication of the reaction to be expected by other workers.

The Manchester tramwaymen had been ordered to present themselves for work at noon. Out of a force of 5,000 only 29 did so. The others went to the Hyde Road depot to gather in strength and then to march through the city. Other strikers joined the procession until it stretched for over half a mile. The news of the ending of the strike was conveyed to the demonstration and many of the men returned to work and a full service was resumed next day. The Salford tramwaymen held a mass meeting in the evening and decided not to go in to work because the management was only prepared to take back the workers as and when required.

THURSDAY, 13 MAY, DAY 10

Although the headline in the *British Worker* was "Strike Terminated", there were two columns of news headed "Last News of the Strike". In Manchester there was no general resumption of work and, according to Brockway, there was "chaos".

The North West Committee had innumerable reports of victimisation and the general picture was one of determination to stay out. Fenner Brockway reported that the railwaymen had had a procession of 25,000 through Manchester and were not returning to work. The dockers from Manchester down to Liverpool were staying out until the threat of victimisation of the railwaymen was removed. The printing trades remained out because of victimisation at the *Daily Mail* and Thomson's. The men in the flour milling trades were also still out. The feeling was that the local committees and unions had to take the initiative because the TUC was in such indecent haste to ensure a resumption of work that they had ignored the instruction that there would be no end of the strike until all trade union agreements had been honoured.

So solid was the local action against victimisation that Stanley Baldwin was forced to issue a statement that he would not countenance any attempt by the employers to force down wages or launch an attack on trade unionism.

FRIDAY, 14 MAY

The North Western District Strike Committee sent a strongly-worded telegram to the TUC:

"This Regional Strike Committee, representative of all the organised workers in the Manchester and North Western Area, urgently directs the attention of the General Council of the TUC to the very unsatisfactory position resulting from the calling off of the General Strike. Employers, with but few exceptions, are declining to reinstate employees, and in those cases where reinstatement is offered, it is only on the basis of lower wages and worse terms of service.

"This Regional Strike Committee strongly and emphatically protests against this action on the part of the employers as a gross violation of the spirit of the agreement as announced between the Prime Minister and the TUC. They call upon the TUC immediately to demand a withdrawal of such action and notices, and that the Government insist upon the maintenance of the 'status quo'."[12]

In spite of this determined stand, by the Thursday the workers were returning to work thoroughly disheartened and disillusioned. Brockway asked a number of pertinent questions to try to understand the thinking behind the TUC's betrayal and eventually accepted the simple explanation, "The General Strike has been led by people who don't believe in it, and they—not the workers—cracked."[13]

The *Manchester Evening Chronicle* was printed on the 14th and there were several items of local news. It was announced at a mass meeting of Manchester tramwaymen at midnight that eleven timekeepers and two ticket collectors who had been suspended were reinstated. The meeting then decided to continue working. The strike cost Manchester £45,000 in tramway revenue and Salford £15,000. There was also an announcement that Salford Police had raided several premises and made seven arrests of men who were alleged to be communists.

A meeting organised by *Lansbury's Weekly*, due to be held in the Free Trade Hall on the Friday night to call for the release of prisoners taken during the strike, was postponed because the authorities had withdrawn permission to use the hall. Ticket-holders were advised to retain their tickets and await further announcements.

The arrests that were mentioned in the *Evening Chronicle* were in connection with a leaflet that the Communist Party issued nationally and sent to the localities for reproduction and distribution. It was headed "The Great Betrayal" and it called on the working class to refuse to return to work until the government guaranteed that the miners would receive no wage reduction. No copy of the Salford version of the leaflet is known to have survived, but the *Manchester Guardian* of 17 May printed a partial text:

"The General Council of the Trades Union Congress has unconditionally surrendered to the Government. Without any guarantees the General Council has called off the General Strike and abandoned the fight against wage reductions for the miners. This is a betrayal, not only of the miners, but of the whole working class. . . .

"The Communist Party, which until now wholeheartedly supported the General Council, feels it their duty, in face of the miserable surrender of that body, to call upon the whole of the working class to refuse to return to work until a guarantee has been obtained from the Government that for the miners there shall be no wage reduction. We call upon the dockers who have returned to cease work, and to convene conferences of Strike Committees to decide upon action in support of the miners."[14]

Jack Forshaw was the Branch Secretary of the Salford Branch of the Communist Party. After the Party lost the William Horrocks hall, they decided to obtain other premises and had been collecting for that purpose for some time. The money was in a Post Office account in Forshaw's name. He decided that it would probably be safer if it were banked under his daughter's name. At the end of the strike he wished to withdraw the money from the Post Office. While he was out of the house, the police entered and carried out a search in the course of which they found copies of the leaflet and a duplicating machine complete with stencil. They arrested Jack and confiscated the £100 which he had in his pocket. Under the Emergency Regulations, he was charged at Salford Police Court the next morning, 15 May, with having at his premises a certain document headed "A Great Betrayal" which was likely to cause disaffection among the civil population. He was found guilty but remanded in custody, judgment being deferred until the Monday. Jack Forshaw was a diabetic and in poor health, but he was, nevertheless, put into a cold cell, refused the special diet which was essential for him and also refused the services of a doctor. On the Monday he was fined the exact £100 that had been found on him when he was arrested and he also received a month's prison sentence. A few days later, the Workers' International Relief obtained bail, but Jack had contracted pneumonia and died while on bail. After his death, the Recorder at the Salford City Quarter Sessions refused to allow the appeal, saying he had no jurisdiction to do so.[15]

There were six other men arrested with Jack Forshaw on the same charge. They were later bound over in their own sureties. Thomas Hamer of Altrincham was less fortunate. He was sentenced to six months' imprisonment.

These cases were almost certainly the last that were heard under the Emergency Regulations. So Manchester, which was exceptionally quiet during the strike, saw the first and the last arrest under the Regulations.

Why was the strike called off? The last word should come from the miners who were left alone to struggle for nine more hungry months. A. J. Cook, the secretary of the Miners' Federation and the well loved voice of the rank and file miners put it this way:

"This is all we know of the tragic decision, arrived at in our absence, to call off the General Strike. The verbatim report of the interview with the Prime Minister speaks for itself. No statement seemed to have been made by anyone except Bevin regarding the raising of the lock-out and the protection of our men. It seemed that the only desire of some leaders was to call off the General Strike at any cost, without any guarantees for the workers, miners, or others.

"By this action of theirs, in 'turning off the power', the miners were left alone in their struggle.

"A few days longer and the Government and the capitalist class, financiers, parasites and exploiters, would have been compelled to make peace with the miners. We should thus have secured in the mining industry a settlement which would have redounded to the honour and credit of the British Labour Movement, and would have been a fitting reward for the solidarity displayed by the workers.

"They threw away the chance of a victory greater than any British Labour has ever won.

"That is the history of the Nine Days which gave an unexampled display of the solidarity of the workers. It is quite evident that some of the TUC were afraid of the power they had created; were anxious to keep friends with the Government and not to harm the employing class. They did not understand the task—at least a great many of them did not—and there were others who were determined to sabotage the General Strike to justify their repeated declarations, 'that it would not succeed'.

"First they declared the rank and file would not respond to a sympathetic strike. Then after the rank and file had responded they continued to try and prove that it would not succeed.

"They are still trying to prove it, but while some leaders have declared 'Never again', and others have tried to say—as the leader of the Labour Party did in 'Answers'—that the strike is a useless weapon, those of us who saw the shattering effect it had on British capitalism and the strike forward in solidarity made by our own people realise that the General Strike did not fail."[16]

NOTES

1. Manchester and Salford Trades and Labour Council, 59th Annual Report for the year ending December 31st, 1925.
2. *The British Worker*, no. 1, Wednesday evening, 5 May 1926 (London edition).
3. *Manchester Guardian*, 6 May 1926.
4. *The British Worker*, no. 2, Thursday evening, 6 May 1926 (London edition).
5. Typescript of material in TUC Library, HD 5366.
6. *The Times* 10 May 1926.
7. A. Fenner Brockway, "A Diary of the Great Strike", *Socialist Review*, June 1926.
8. *The British Worker*, Tuesday, 11 May, Manchester edition, no. 2.
9. A. Fenner Brockway, op. cit.
10. Typescript, TUC Library, HD 5366.
11. A. Fenner Brockway, op. cit.
12. *The British Worker*, Friday, 14 May, Manchester edition, no. 5.
13. A. Fenner Brockway, op. cit.
14. *Manchester Guardian*, 17 May 1926.
15. Letter from Clara Forshaw, and *Manchester Guardian*, *Manchester Evening News* and *Manchester Evening Chronicle*, all of 15 May 1926.
16. A. J. Cook, *The Nine Days*, ND (1926) pamphlet (reprinted in R. and E. Frow and Michael Katanka, *Strikes, A Documentary History*, 1971).

4 THE EAST MIDLANDS

by PETER WYNCOLL

In 1926 most of the industrial activity in the East Midlands was concentrated in a well-defined belt stretching from the Yorkshire border southwards to Derby and Nottingham, and down through Leicestershire to the boot and shoe factories of Northampton. This central industrial axis was flanked on east and west by predominantly agricultural areas, though towns situated on the border of this area like Rugby, Burton-upon-Trent and Lincoln all earned part of their living from manufacturing industries.

In common with the rest of Britain, this area was enduring grim conditions in 1926 when the General Strike broke out. The mining community, of course, was suffering the most deprivation. But as Dan Mahoney, a member of the Nottingham Strike Committee, has pointed out, the labour force of a whole range of industries had suffered "all round reductions".[1] In Nottingham during April 1926 the town's unemployed numbered 6,143, whilst another 1,447 were on short-time or stood off.[2] Other large centres like Derby and Leicester had many unemployed too, but it was in the coal-mining centres like Mansfield in Nottinghamshire, Coalville in Leicestershire or Codnor in Derbyshire that conditions were perhaps the worst.

Some idea of the appalling conditions prevailing in the pit villages can be gleaned from the following account. "Food was scarce, bread and thinly spread dripping twice a day, and we youngsters raided fields and allotments for vegetables . . . bread and butter pudding, margarine of course with five raisins, one in each corner of a slice, one in the centre, watered down milk, if any, or a small teaspoonfull of condensed milk well watered."[3]

George Hamilton who worked at Bestwood pit tells of having to leave school because, with nine in the family, the money he could earn as an errand boy was vital to the family exchequer.[4] George's case is typical of thousands of others; without a welfare state the poor had to rely on each other, or face the Board of Guardians and the workhouse. A good example comes from Rugby: "There was one very interesting character, an inveterate poacher. When he knew a family was up against it . . . they would be woken in the early hours by a banging on the door and a voice would come up out of the darkness . . . 'its for the children. You can't let the little buggers starve' . . . When they went down they found a sack . . . he'd been raiding a potato clamp and he'd leave a couple of rabbits to go with them."[5]

Against the background of such conditions the months leading up to the General Strike followed a long period of sharpening class conflict. By early 1926 the whole British capitalist class was convinced of the need for a major showdown with organised labour, and quickly began the task of creating the organisational weapons with which to fight the battle. The government itself took rapid steps to organise for a major confrontation, and in the East Midlands their decision to set up strike-breaking machinery on a divisional basis was quickly carried through. Captain H. Douglas King, MP, was named as Commissioner for the district. His object was to maintain all essential services and on 3 May, immediately prior to the strike, he issued a statement that "The public can be assured that all preliminary steps have been taken to ensure the maintenance of supplies."[6] In fact, a great deal of work had gone into setting up elaborate strike-breaking machinery. There were offices in every district to enlist volunteers, and the area was divided into eight districts each with a chairman, and road, coal, postage, haulage, food and finance officers. The class background of these gentlemen is made obvious by the fact that three more of Captain King's staff were recruited from the military, whilst the rest came from the business community. On the eve of the strike in Nottingham a Volunteer Recruiting Office was opened. In Leicester a special office was opened in the Town Hall for potential blacklegs, whilst in Northampton the Earl Spencer, Lord Erskine and Lord and Lady Horne were among a reported five hundred volunteers.[7] As the ruling classes' organising centre Nottingham's response to the call for volunteers was disappointing. At a meeting on 30 April it was stated that in some parts of Nottinghamshire doors had been slammed in the face of Organisation for the Maintenance of Supplies canvassers.[8] Captain H. C. Serbrooke, DSO and Mr. H. D. Cherry-Downes both felt that many people refused to sign on with the Organisation because they feared reprisals. However, Captain Turner reported that the Organisation's headquarters was disgusted that so little had been done in Nottingham, whilst Cherry-Downes advanced the view that the unions had passed the word to have nothing to do with the OMS.

The activities of the OMS were paralleled in Nottingham by the Volunteer Service Committee under Major Stuart Hartshorn, CBE. This committee was active in recruiting special constables, amongst whom was Sir Ernest Jardine who personally marched 130 of his staff to the Guildhall, where they were sworn in. Jardine's friend, A. W. Kirkaldy, President of the Chamber of Commerce, was appointed officer commanding one of the volunteer forces, and the strike-breaking role of the Chamber is further emphasised by the appointment of its secretary as one of the superintendents of the volunteer forces.

In fact, the organised blacklegging of the Chamber of Commerce in Nottingham was very highly developed. During the strike its transport department maintained a regular service to and from London. Its vehicles carried food, lace, hosiery, tobacco, medical supplies and other products of the town's factories. The Chamber took over a warehouse in the Lace Market which it used as a clearing house whilst maintaining a daily service to London, Birmingham, Liverpool and Manchester.

Throughout the East Midlands business-dominated city and town councils were prepared to back strike-breaking activity to the hilt. Town clerks had received letters marked "Secret" asking them to co-operate with the government in various ways.[9] The local authorities, even where Labour-controlled, willingly assumed the responsibilities the government imposed on them. In Chesterfield, for instance, the mayor claimed, "they represented the whole of the ratepayers and their position should be entirely neutral . . . they were acting on specific instructions from the Government".[10] Leading members of the Nottingham Council, like Alderman Sir Bernard Wright and Alderman Albert Ball, were appointed to take such steps as they considered necessary to deal with the strike situation, whilst in Leicester Sir Arthur Hazlerigg, the Lord Lieutenant, joined with the Mayor of Leicester in appealing to the county's citizens "to conduct themselves so that when the settlement does come Leicestershire can still boast of being in the front rank of law-abiding people".[11]

In contrast to the speed and relative efficiency with which the local representatives of capital made their preparations for the coming confrontation, the labour movement's battle preparations in the area were slow and hesitant. The situation in Nottingham seems typical. At the September 1925 meeting of the Trades Council it was reported that a Council of Action had been formed, but at the October meeting the secretary reported that the activities of the Council were being held up because of his inability to obtain information from the national leaders.

In December the position was worse, with the secretary reporting that the Council of Action machinery had now seized up altogether, owing to lack of guidance from the central bodies concerned; and Dan Mahoney tells of the opposition of some trade union officials in the area to the efforts of himself and other communists and progressives to create a united movement in the area.[12] In 1926 very few of the town's trade unionists showed much sign of a realistic political consciousness. Billy Lees of the Distributive Workers was the most politically motivated of the Trades Council leadership; an early supporter of the Communist Party, he was the only one of Nottingham's leadership to be arrested and imprisoned during the strike.

The left wing in the East Midlands major centres of population was variegated. The Labour Party, the Independent Labour Party and the Communist Party all had active groups. Since the war the area's socialists had increased their numbers considerably. Many of these converts had come to the left through admiration of the new Russian State, and many more through bitter periods of unemployment in the period leading up to the strike. Frank Treble of Rugby is typical of many: "I got my politics from my father, it was born in me . . . the conditions in which we lived . . . the struggles which we had and the lessons which my father gave me."[13] Laura Johnson of Hucknall, whose father had been victimised in the miners' strike of 1898, read *The Ragged Trousered Philanthropists* before joining the Labour Party and later the communists,[14] whilst a Derbyshire miner who entered the pits in 1904 before losing a leg at the age of seventeen writes: "What would you have done, chum? . . . Yes, I took up trade union work and became a warm Socialist."[15] The Labour Party was of course the strongest political group, although there was a strong Independent Labour Party in Leicester and over 500 ILP members in Nottingham.

Many of the Labour Party's best activists had, however, left it when the Communist Party was formed in 1920. To many on the left the Labour Party was already being seen as a reformist body. Jack Charlesworth, for instance, remembers the Nottingham Labour Party as "really reactionary";[16] Cyril Goddard would agree with this view and he remembers the Party's leaders as being careerists of one sort or another. "The majority were out for a career, if they hadn't been in the Labour Party they would have been in the Tory Party if it offered them a career."[17] The political work of the Nottingham Socialists was based on the ILP hall, and on rooms used by several groups in the William Morris Institute. These rooms were used by the Socialist Sunday

School, Clarion Supporters, ILP and Communist Party supporters, as well as the Labour Party, for a variety of social and educational activities which bore fruit in what Arthur Statham described as a "nightly hive of activity".[18] Throughout the East Midlands, but particularly in the mining areas the labour movement press had never been so widely read and appreciated. The *Herald*, the *Clarion* and *Reynolds's News* were all popular, and there are many veterans throughout the area who can remember selling Labour papers in Market Squares and outside cinemas, whilst others helped to build up circulation by door-to-door sales.

Most of the political activists in the East Midlands were also active in the trade unions, and these links were well demonstrated in the 1926 May Day meetings and demonstrations. Taking place only a day before the strike began, these meetings were large and enthusiastic. In Leicester a huge crowd in the Market Place heard Pethick-Lawrence claim, "this strike is forced on the Labour Movement by the policy of the ruling class".[19] In Derby the secretary of the Trades Council told the May Day meeting, "We are all ready, every one of us. I don't think we will have a man who will remain at work."[20] In Nottingham the May Day demonstration was the biggest for years. Assembling on the Forest several thousand workers heard Arthur Hayday, MP for West Nottingham, declare that the trouble represented the breakdown of modern capitalism. This meeting took place in the afternoon, the morning had seen a procession which eclipsed all previous records for size and display. It took nearly half an hour to pass, and "drew applause even from those who had little sympathy with the ideals of those taking part". A touch of humour was supplied by a humble pram labelled "The Workers Daimler" and a derelict motor car dragged by two cart horses in which sat a miner carrying a placard declaring "both broke". The procession was led by bands playing the Red Flag. Perhaps the most popular tableau was one which featured a hearse carrying the label "Death of Capitalism", followed by a vehicle on which the "Birth of Socialism" was illustrated.

In the evening several more meetings were held. At the ILP rally the chairman warned, "The war in which we are about to engage might not bring bayonet and shell but it will bring sorrow and danger."[21] At another evening meeting J. H. Hayes, MP, told his audience, "Do not play the enemy's game, don't allow yourself to come into conflict with the OMS or the Fascisti, treat them with contempt." At the Communist Party's pre-strike meeting Cyril Goddard remembers: "The Party was fully alive to the fact that the Government was organising and the TUC was doing nothing . . . at our meeting I remember the speaker, Harry Webb, the 'Mighty Atom' we called him, making the point 'watch your leaders' . . . and by God they took some watching."[22] At the Mansfield meeting the Sherwood colliery spokesman told a huge crowd of miners and their families, "Our confidence in A. J. Cook has not been misplaced; he has given all his services and nearly all his life for us."[23]

Unfortunately, as the strike progressed the buoyant optimism of these meetings was to change into a mood of depression as it became obvious that all but Cook of the national leadership had been prepared to betray the strike. Meanwhile, however, on the day before the strike began, the labour movement of the East Midlands enthusiastically looked forward to the coming struggle.

Despite the confusion of the pre-strike period the area's trades councils acted quickly on 3 May. In Leicester the Trades Council quickly formed an Emergency Committee. In Mansfield a Council of Action consisting of fourteen pit representatives, Labour Party and Trades Council delegates was set up. In Derby a well organised Action Committee was set up by the Trades Council, and smaller mining centres like Ilkeston, Ripley and Chesterfield quickly followed suit. The Ilkeston committee was particularly active, sending a message to the TUC daily, and other committees throughout the area were quickly busy, picketing the roads and factories in an attempt to prevent vehicle movement or the carrying on of unauthorised work. In Nottingham the Trades Council convened a meeting by telegram at which a strike committee was set up which met every day, as did the sub-committees which it appointed to deal with the questions of permits, publicity, meetings and pickets.

The rank and file response to the strike call was magnificent. The TUC's official report records the fact that Nottingham was amongst the towns where the response was "unexpectedly fine".[24] In Leicester 6,000 walked out on the first day. Boot and shoe towns like Wellingborough, Kettering and Northampton were quickly affected. Pit villages and towns like Coalville in Leicestershire, Hucknall in Nottinghamshire, or Alfreton in Derbyshire, were, of course, solidly behind the strike. The strike call was answered first by transport workers and those employed in heavy industry, leading the walk out. In Nottingham huge meetings of road transport workers and railwaymen were held, the mood being summed up at a meeting of the three rail unions where W. Halls the NUR organiser said, "We knew this day was bound to come sooner or later, and we ought to be glad. It is a day we have hoped for and prayed for and looked forward to . . . we ought to be delighted."[25]

Meanwhile the permit committees of the area strike committees had swung into action. Through these committees the power and authority of the workers was dramatically demonstrated. The Nottingham strike bulletin for 6 May reported, for instance, "The area food controller has undertaken to move no food except by permission of the Strike Committee. He does not recognise the OMS."[26] In Chesterfield only lorries with labels such as "All Food Supplies" or "Urgent Medical Supplies" were on the streets. The Nottingham Committee checked all applications for food permits and had absolute power. Dan Mahoney, who was a member of the committee, gives the following examples of its work. "A man wanted wire netting to put round a wheat field to keep out rabbits eating the wheat, which he claimed was food . . . granted. A tailor wanted a roll of cloth to make a suit for a funeral . . . not granted."[27]

As the strike continued, the strain which it placed on the social fabric created many explosive situations. In Nottingham both the bus and tram services were idle, and the few private buses which ventured into the town were attacked and overturned. During one demonstration the private car belonging to a local bus proprietor was turned over. This man made a determined effort to run his buses with non-union labour, but after a great deal of trouble with pickets, who removed the carburettors of his buses, he discontinued the effort. Private bus proprietors in Ilkeston tried to run a normal service to Nottingham, but were stopped, passengers having to walk back. At Clowne private buses were stoned and the service had to be discontinued.[28] Crowds at Mansfield Woodhouse smashed the windows of trams attempting to run a service, whilst in Derby strikers filled the seats of private buses and then refused to pay the fare. In Nottingham strikers toured the Queen's Drive area demanding that work should stop at local factories. An eye-witness remembers, "Queen's Walk was undergoing a re-surfacing and immediately in front of our house was a steam roller, a tar-making machine, a lorry and various tools and implements. I remember seeing a huge mob of men surging from the direction of the station. They were headed by a man who had a pole on which was tied a huge red sock . . . a great shout went up and they proceeded to overturn the steam roller, the tar-making machine and smashing such things as the picks, shovels and buckets."[29] Later this same group halted a motor lorry and successfully removed its load of beer and groceries before the police arrived.

Predictably, the class forces opposed to the workers did not take kindly to this kind of activity. The Nottingham evening paper ran an editorial on 4 May which spelt out the attitude of the establishment; "We now wish to record our protest against the use of the General Strike as a weapon with which to settle a sectional dispute . . . we imagine there is very little enthusiasm for a General Strike amongst the vast majority of workers. . . ."[30] The writer of this editorial found out how wrong he was when on 5 May his own printers walked off the job. The owners of the local press were predictably outraged, and on resuming publication published the usual editorials calling for "the unqualified support of every man and woman who values the English birthright of personal liberty and freedom of the press".[31]

Although the Nottingham newspapers were brought to a halt by the strike, newspapers in Derby, Leicester and Northampton continued to be printed by blackleg labour. Nevertheless newspapers were scarce, and distribution difficulties formidable. The *Derbyshire Times* reported at one stage, for instance: "Belper is completely isolated as far as news is concerned . . . not a single paper of any description was on sale after Tuesday."[32] The strikers answer to lack of news, or blackleg news sheets, was to produce their own strike bulletins. With the help of what Dan Mahoney called "Comrade Duplicator", sheets were turned out in Nottingham, Derby, Ilkeston and Chesterfield. Issue number one of the Nottingham bulletin warned workers to ignore "any Government or anti-strike propaganda inspired to mislead the public and break the General Strike".[33] In Chesterfield the third bulletin reported, "The whole life of London, the hub of British capitalism, is gradually being brought to a standstill. Troops stationed in Hyde Park refused to act against the workers. The Welsh Guards likewise took up the same course of action. Blood is thicker than water, as the trite saying goes. The ruling class can don our class in soldiers' clothes, but the working-class heart pulsates beneath."[34] The Chesterfield bulletin printed news which was brought in by twelve despatch riders who toured Derbyshire, and this system was developed in Nottinghamshire too. Throughout the area, in fact, ILP halls, Labour Party rooms and miners' welfare halls were quickly turned into communication centres from which issued the instructions which over the nine days of the strike challenged again and again the assumptions of generations of the ruling class.

As the strike developed every facet of life became affected. The most exciting incidents were mostly concerned with the various attempts to reopen some kind of transport service. At all Chesterfield bus stops messages were chalked on the pavements, "Please do not ride on the buses. Blackleg labour."[35] In the important railway centre of Rugby, "the railway came to a complete standstill".[36] Railwaymen in Derby, too, were solid, and building workers in the town came out as well. In Loughborough the large Brush works came to a standstill. By 5 May 12,000 were out in Leicester, hosiery factories in Hinckley came out, and even market towns like Melton Mowbray were affected. Earnest supporters of the establishment did their best to organise a private transport system by using volunteers owning private cars. Miss Kentish Wright in Nottingham was able to boast that she had organised a service from Basford, Bulwell, Daybrook, Sherwood, Netherfield and Bridgeford into the centre of the city. The attempt to maintain a rail service, of course, involved volunteer blackleg labour. Many of these blacklegs were out for a lark, but others knew full well the implications of what they were about. A navy-trained gentleman at Leicester wrote: "I immediately volunteered for the Great Central Railway . . . sleeping happily on 3rd class carriage seats and jeered at by the bloody-minded mutineers . . . we were the naval train with a Lieut. Commander as driver, a naval chief stoker and myself (a reserve officer) to assist him. Our driver carried a revolver which he said he would use if we were attacked."[37] Starvation forced some workers to join the middle- and upper-class blacklegs, as one writer from Nottingham tells: "I have a confession to make, being of a large family, which required every farthing to exist, I became a blackleg and continued to work until the end."[38]

This blackleg, like many others, had to run the gauntlet each time he turned up for work. "Each day we were bombarded with bricks, chunks of wood and whatever was handy for the pickets, which also included women and girls."[39] A Coalville miner who worked at Whitwick pit remembers, "There were a few blacklegs who went to the mines with police escorts, and women and children would surround them and tin-pan them to and from the pit. These blacklegs were taken by the police on different routes but the tin panners were always there banging their tins and chanting BLACKLEGS."[40] A Ripley miner remembers "Scab" being chalked on doors, and one street having the words "Scab Row" painted over the street sign.[41] Blackleg labour trying to drive a train at Loughborough overturned oil wagons and ripped up the track after one train had crashed into another, whilst Dan Mahoney remembers "a train driven by student volunteer labour taking 8½ hours to travel 21 miles".[42]

It was because of blacklegging attempts of one sort or another that the disturbances which broke out from time to time during the strike were provoked. In Nottingham, for instance, a crowd of about 500 went to the Player's factory to encourage the workers to join the strike, and when they were met by a force of police with drawn batons a serious fight broke out. Several of the strikers were felled to the ground, stones were thrown, and one man arrested. Later there was a running fight through the town's main streets before police managed to disperse the crowds. Scenes like this demonstrate the strain being put on the social fabric. Throughout the area workers were taking the law into their own hands. On 7 May, for instance, a fuel raid at Whitwick removed a ton of wood from the colliery yard: "Hundreds of men, women, and children entered the yard last night and carried away a large quantity of wood of all descriptions, huge poles, railway sleepers and props were siezed. Children's pushchairs were used for haulage, and groups of children were seen pulling large logs along by means of ropes."[43] A similar incident happened at Beeston near Nottingham; "Word got around that there were loaded trucks of coal in the sidings and men, women and children came from all over the place to help themselves, bringing an assortment of containers to hold their loot, prams, pushchairs, buckets, barrows, bags and sacks . . . only to be met by the police who confiscated their various containers before summoning them."[44]

The need for fuel throughout the coalfield led to a great deal of scavenging for coal on the pit tips. From Ripley comes this memory: "I remember sliding down these tips on a shovel bringing home the bags of pickings on carts made from pram wheels and old boards."[45] From Derby a miner remembers: "We used to go from about 10.30 p.m. until 4 a.m. without the cops to drive us away."[46] In Mansfield, too, miners combed the slag heaps for minute pieces of coal: "Grownups and us gleaned at least ½ cwt. a week to keep the living room fire burning."[47] Women, too, scavenged for coal: "My sister and I set out to the tips at the back of Clifton colliery via the canal and waterlogged land; we took a sack each and managed to dig some small coal and took it back on an old pushchair . . . the next time we were not so lucky because the police were waiting for us when we got back to the canal and we had to empty our sacks into the water."[48]

Other miners, desperate for fuel, began outcropping on quite an extensive scale. One boy miner at the Summit Colliery near Kirby in

Ashfield remembers: "Shop windows were broken, railway wagons overturned, fields and woods dug up to get outcrop coal to keep the fires burning."[49] From Ripley there is a memory of a father sinking a shaft in the back garden to get at coal which according to his mates was "just below the surface". After twelve feet he did find a seam of about eight inches and managed to bring a few bags to the surface.[50] Nottingham miners, too, were industrious outcroppers: "I remember sticking my pick in the ground through a great lump of coal . . . two passing men saw this and helped us fill our wheelbarrows . . . we told our fathers, and that night every man and lad were there most of the night, getting coal". At Church Gresley in the south of the county "small shafts were dug and coal was brought up by a small pulley, a rope and bucket".[52] "My husband and two friends were the first persons to put a spade in Church Gresley common to start federationing coal and were arrested for it . . . but lots of miners went and demanded them out as the common didn't belong to anyone so they weren't trespassing; so they came back and started again; and hundreds of miners heard and came and joined in, from Coalville and Whitwick and all the surrounding districts."[53] A Nottingham Federation miner writes of outcropping in a small copse, "carrying out our digging throughout the night, with the aid of candles, and one hurricane lamp. . . . Of course we did not go to any depth, and coal excavated was crumbly and small and bagged as slack. Further along the Trowell Road a gang of three miners had dug a shaft of about twelve feet, and used a tripod, pulley and block method of extraction. Unfortunately, having exhausted the coal at the bottom, they commenced to mine into the seam side along the seam. Alas, although they had timbered up, it was not strong enough to hold the weight of the overground, and at about 3.30 a.m. one morning one of their party came to us in a state of partial collapse to tell us that the roof had collapsed and buried his mate . . . it was next morning before he was excavated. Needless to say he was dead, and that caused police picketing of the whole area."[54]

Tragedy of this sort was made worse by semi-starvation. The constant search for enough food to keep body and soul together calls forth heart-rending memories from retired workers. From Brinsley in Nottinghamshire comes the following: "One day I was so hungry I crept through a hedge and stole a stick of rhubarb and one potato which I ate raw because we'd no means of cooking it . . . one day I sat crying not knowing what to do when a knock came at the door; when I answered not a soul was to be seen, but on the doorstep was a plate with fish, white sauce and mashed potato . . . I never did find out where it came from."[55] Soup kitchens were common throughout the coalfield. A Coalville collier remembers: "Soup kitchens, concerts, parades, parties. . . ." An old resident of the Meadows in Nottingham tells: "They had to open a soup kitchen in the Wilford Road, people went round the shops asking if they could spare anything for this purpose."[56] One Mapperley woman's mother organised a local soup kitchen. "She and grandmother used to light the old brick copper in the big kitchen, and made coppers full of pea-soup. She also made jam pasties, and boiled great big iron saucepans of potatoes. At dinner times there would be a queue of miners' children with jugs . . . my mother used to do this for free."[57] One child who tasted soup made in this way at Bulwell remembers it as the "nicest I've ever tasted".[58] Other workers, like those in the Leicestershire coalfield, poached the Charnwood woods and fields, which were keepered "with big lurcher dogs on duty 24 hours a day".[59] Against this kind of background it is not surprising that a great fund of bitterness built up. From Sandiacre a woman who remembers eating "hasty pudding" (flour and water boiled together and served with a blob of jam) writes: "Some old geezer, a nutrition expert, was paid a few thousands to assess the vitamin contents of carrots and a bit of scrag end to prove that the child of a miner could be kept for 2*s*. 6*d*. per week."[60] In Derbyshire many lived on a staple diet of what was called "soakie", a "basin of tea and bread, the top of an egg if we were lucky, and bread and lard with sugar on".[61] This kind of diet was part of an overall poverty which has deeply scarred the memory of those who experienced it, like this retired Coalville miner: "It was heartbreaking to see people selling their treasured possessions before they could qualify for parish pay . . . several families in the locality were taken to the Ashby workhouse . . . miners marched from Whitwick to Ashby to beg for money to help their families."[62]

To offset this kind of misery there were a great many meetings, and a variety of home grown entertainment. In Hucknall, for instance, meetings were announced by the hand-bell of "Mother Wheeldon" and the George Street Jazz Band helped to boost morale. In Derbyshire the mayor of Chesterfield appealed to cinema proprietors to allow their premises to be used for Sunday concerts, and the Miners' Welfare Committees arranged short talks, lectures and concerts in Derbyshire and Nottinghamshire. At Pinxton in Nottinghamshire comic football and other games and concerts were held.[63] At Ironville, "different picture houses would lend their premises, and local talent would entertain us".[64] At Mansfield an industrial disabled pensioner remembers that during the strike, "processions took place every day, marching into the middle of a field, speeches were given and the Red Flag sung with gusto. We were not old enough to understand the speeches, but enjoyed ourselves by pinching vegetables from cultivated fields and stuffing them inside our jackets."[65] At Ripley, "there were meetings in the Co-op Hall when the Labour Party and miners' leaders lent their voices to the cause".[66] On 3 May, thousands of miners together with their wives attended such a meeting in the Grand Cinema at Coalville, and as the strike continued similar meetings were held throughout the region, helping to boost the optimism of the rank and file. In between meetings, and between incidents like the one involving a large crowd of miners who on 5 May blocked both sides of the Coalville High Street level-crossing gates to boo and jeer at the engine driver and fireman of the 11.5 to Leicester, most workers would work on their gardens or allotments. And many of the miners would pay visits to their favourite pit ponies, as they did at Mansfield: "The miners came and shouted them by name, put their hand through the wooden railings and fondled them, sometimes bringing them a tit-bit."[67]

The sharpness of the struggle between the opposing class forces led to many arrests. At Ashby in Leicestershire a miner was sentenced to two months after being charged with using violent language to compel a carter to stop work. In Northampton two men were arrested after an attempt to stop a tram. At Kimberly Thomas Bird, a miner, was given three months' hard labour for putting a log across the road to stop a bus. In Nottingham a miner was given six months for assaulting a policeman. Four other Nottingham strikers were fined after threatening to put a Mills bomb on a blackleg bus. A striking bus driver was fined for pushing a blackleg off his bicycle, whilst yet another worker was sentenced to three months for inciting a crowd of Nottingham strikers.

Over the period of the strike something like a dozen arrests were made in Nottingham—some under rather frivolous circumstances. George Hamilton, for instance, remembers the following incident involving miners scavenging for coal: "Best laugh I ever had. They were on Cinderhill pit bank, they'd got roughly eight bags of coal, and of course the police pounced on them. The lads had got a nice donkey and cart, and when the police arrived they said, 'come on load the bags', the lads said 'not bloody likely, you want them on, you put them on yourself', and it was worth the fine to see the police struggle to put them on. Well, the donkey belonged to a rag and bone man and it would only move for either him or a boy who worked with it, but he'd seen police coming and made his escape. Anyway they got the bags on and it was 'Gee up Neddy' but it wouldn't have it, so anyway it finished up with one policeman at its head and three shoving, and they had to shove him right to Bulwell. When they got to where the rag and bone man lived, the police knocked at his door; 'course he was in bed, so he put his head out of the window and said, 'Go on, lock him up same as the rest'; but as soon as the donkey heard his master shouting he sat down and started braying. By this time there was a big crowd, laughing at the police and enjoying themselves. Anyway, they had to shove the donkey into the police yard and next day they fined them 2*s*. 6*d*. apiece."[68]

Arthur Statham, too, had personal memories of the police and the arrests they made. Arthur's cousin was employed at a brewery as a carter and he came into the office in which Arthur was working in a very agitated state. "He burst in shouting, 'Arthur they are trying to take out beer, I'm going to see about this'. And off he went, you see. Anyway when he got there he was arrested and he went to Lincoln prison, like Billy Lees, for three months." Arthur was able to remember the arrest of Billy Lees, since the two men were working together when Inspector Castle made the arrest. "Billy was a lively character and he said to Castle in a joking way, 'I've been expecting you.'"[69]

The arrest of Lees together with that of Thomas Kilworth were probably the most significant of the Nottingham arrests. Lees was a communist and a member of the Trades Council Executive, and Kilworth was a defeated Labour candidate in the municipal elections. He was sent to prison after a speech in which he was alleged to have said, "I would say to the miners, stick out, fight for your rights, and I hope that when the national strike comes in about two years we shall have the good old red flag flying over Buckingham Palace . . . next Sunday I am taking a crowd outside the prison to sing the Red Flag."[70] Instead of being outside the prison, however, Kilworth found himself inside. And so did Lees after a speech in which it was claimed he said, "I am a member of the strike committee. One of our trade union leaders, there is no need to mention his name, says the Chief Constable wants law and order. Well, during the last two or three days he has shown how he wants law and order. He will have amongst you two or three plain clothes men and if there are groups of people some of whom are expressing their views, one or two are pointed out. Down comes the van full of coppers, you are struck with a lump of wood, thrown into the van and away to the police station. But you wait until our comrades have to take a more active part in holding up transport. It will give the Chief Constable the chance to come amongst you and show how pretty he is."[71] Despite the fact that Lees had three witnesses willing to speak for him, he was convicted and sent down for three months.

In Mansfield, too, a well-known local communist was sentenced to three months hard labour after an incident round a lorry. After sentence he told the Court that he was "acting under the instructions of the whole Mansfield labour movement. . . . I would bite, scratch, or kick in defence of my class again if under the same provocation."[72] In Chesterfield Albert Williams, a Mosborough miner, was charged with committing an act calculated to cause mutiny, sedition or disaffection among members of HM forces and among members of the civilian population by printing and publishing the local strike sheet. S. Walker, the Deputy Town Clerk, stated in Court on 11 May that Williams "held strong Communist views" and had come to Chesterfield with the intention of creating disturbances. Williams was found guilty and sentenced to prison for two months with hard labour and fined £5.

Williams in Chesterfield and Lees in Nottingham stand out as being two amongst a very small minority of the area's leadership to fully understand the potential of the strike. In the end local militants like these were betrayed by the class-collaborationists who were taking the decisions at national level. Behind the scenes the National leadership had wavered from the very beginning, but nevertheless it came as a great shock to the strikers when on 12 May newspapers came out with enormous banner headlines: "GREAT STRIKE TERMINATED". Among the ruling class congratulations seemed to have been the order of the day, and as the workers struggled to comprehend the extent of the betrayal, members of the establishment rushed to pat each other on the back. In Nottingham the town's ruling group were profuse in mutual congratulations. The local press congratulated the government on standing firm, and Sir Charles Starmer, the Managing Director of the *Journal*, received a letter of thanks for his efforts during the strike from Asquith of the *Westminster Press*. The Lord Mayor quickly appealed for thanksgiving contributions to the local police fund, and this was answered by £500 from Boots, £250 from Shipstone's Brewery, and £150 from Raleigh.

Meanwhile the strikers remained shocked. Of the capitulation Jack Charlesworth remembers, "I heard it on the radio, it was a most pitiful story . . . they took their caps off, and this of course is how the commentator at the time reported it, they really apologised and wanted to get the country back on its feet . . . it was a shocking statement."[73] Cyril Goddard remembers "utter dismay", and George Hamilton has memories of "real gloom cast over everything".[74] In Rugby Frank Treble remembers a "stunned silence in the Trades Hall, everything went dead."[75] During the strike Frank had plastered the slogan "Watch Your Leaders" all over the town, and after the capitulation he remembers . . . "most railwaymen . . . their language regarding J. H. Thomas . . . Citrine was known as Latrine . . . Bevin was one we knew we'd got to watch."[76] One old Derbyshire miner still talks of "Judas H. Thomas who sold we miners for less than thirty bits of silver".[77]

The area's capitalists were quick to push home their class advantage. In West Bridgford this meant that more than half the transport department workers employed by the council had their jobs filled by blackleg labour. Seventeen of the motormen at the Nottingham brewery were not allowed back. Only 80 per cent of the Cammel Laird workers were re-engaged. Notices posted by Blackburn and Sons, Stevens and Williamson, and the Standard Company stated that shortage of work would mean staff "alterations", and notices issued by Ericsons stated that it would not be possible to restart all its workers at once. The Midland Red bus company banned any dealings with the trade unions at its Coalville depot, and the railway companies and town transport departments attempted to get returning workers to sign a document promising that they would not "at any time withdraw service except after seven days written notice".[78]

Despite Baldwin's plea to let bygones be bygones a great deal of bitterness remained. On 13 May several men in Leicester were concerned in removing a pin from an LMS lorry, scattering its contents on the road. At Bulwell a group of miners pulled up a convoy of coal carts and removed the pins holding the tail boards, pitching the coal into the roadway.[79] At a Nottinghamshire bus depot the following scene summed up much of the bitterness: "I well recall the union representative named Jimmy Matthews—the firm, Trent Motor Traction, employing about 250 men. Jimmy was a small, slight man aged about fifty, he was a devout trade unionist, he was a man of undoubted sincerity and integrity . . . the strike pickets were placed outside the picket door . . . a small door in the large sliding garage doors. Jimmy was constantly coming and going, giving the latest news and quiet advice . . . within a few days the first few broke the picket line, these men were later given their reward, their 30 pieces of silver, the private hire and tours that gave extra time and tips. Gradually more and more signed on until all had reported except the one solitary figure at the gate, Jimmy Matthews. When the strike had officially been called off, Jimmy reported for duty and I remember him coming out of the manager's office and I asked him when he was starting back to work. I shall never forget the look he gave me and his quiet voice informing me that he had been sacked: any amount didn't get their jobs back . . . I remember an old miner who told me that after the strike the owner said to them, 'Yes, you've been on strike for so many months now I'm going to make you eat grass'; and he did make them eat grass as well."[80] George Hamilton remembers six or seven committee men from Bulwell pit being sacked after the strike, and he himself was sacked in 1929: "They'd had their eyes on me for years, I could have told you the names of those who would go."[81]

As things began to return to normal people began to take stock. In purely material terms the NUR and ASLEF had paid out over £10,000 in strike pay to their members in the Nottingham area. The miners' financial plight remained perilous. On 17 May the Derbyshire miners agreed to help their Nottingham comrades with a grant of £10,000, but on 19 May it was reported that the Nottinghamshire miners' strike fund stood at only £4,000, with 23,000 eligible for strike pay, and that the bank had had to be approached to advance £11,000 in return for the deeds of the union's property. In Leicester three branches of the Boot and Shoe Union decided to make the Leicestershire miners a grant of £10,000, whilst in Nottingham the National Union of Distributive and Allied Workers levied 1¾ per cent of the wages of members in work to help the distressed. Despite generous gestures like these, distress continued to increase. Towards the end of May a fifth of the population of Mansfield were receiving outdoor relief. In Chesterfield the Guardians had to deal with 5,000 cases of distress among miners, and hungry men who had walked long distances were fainting as they waited for hours in queues.[82]

Taking stock, the General Strike in the east Midlands can be seen as being in the very best working-class tradition. But let down by the national leadership, the strike was a defeat for the workers. The miners managed to stop out for some months, but in the end were forced back to work. Jack Charlesworth sums up the whole experience well: "The workers were ready, there is no doubt that with proper leadership we would have gone over the top, the spirit was magnificent, magnificent."[83] Certainly the eagerness and enthusiasm with which the workers answered the call were in the same tradition which the great struggles of the nineteenth century had been fought, so that even today men who were there remember, "I see the banners carried by the marchers, gloriously emblazoned with the colliery head stocks, the clasp of hands, and the words encircling, *Together we stand, divided we fall.*"[84]

NOTES

1. "My Personal Account", handwritten notes by the late D. W. Mahoney.
2. *Nottingham Evening Post*, 1 May 1926.
3. Private correspondence.
4. George Hamilton, tape recording, 9 January 1969.
5. Frank Treble, tape recording, 11 January 1969.
6. *Nottingham Guardian*, 3 May 1926.
7. Northampton newspaper, 15 May 1926.
8. *Nottingham Guardian*, 30 April 1926.
9. 188, H.C. Debs. 53, 553.
10. *Derbyshire Times*, 8 May 1926.
11. *Leicester Mercury*, 3 May 1926.
12. "My Personal Account", D. W. Mahoney.
13. Frank Treble, tape recording, 11 January 1969.
14. Laura Johnson, tape recording, 13 September 1973.
15. Private correspondence from T. E. B., Sheffield.
16. Jack Charlesworth, tape recording, 12 January 1960.
17. Cyril Goddard, tape recording, 12 January 1969.
18. Arthur Statham, tape recording, 11 January 1969.
19. *Leicester Mercury*, 3 May 1926.
20. *Derby Express*, 3 May 1926.
21. *Nottingham Journal*, 3 May 1926.
22. Cyril Goddard, tape recording, 12 January 1969.
23. *Nottingham Guardian*, 1 May 1926.
24. TUC General Council, "The Mining Crisis and the National Strike", 1927.
25. *Nottingham Guardian*, 4 May 1926.
26. *Nottingham Strike Bulletin*, no. 1, May 1926.
27. "My Personal Account", D. W. Mahoney.
28. *Derbyshire Times*, 8 May 1926.
29. Private correspondence from P.L., Derby.
30. *Nottingham Guardian*, 4 May 1926.
31. *Evening Post*, 10 May 1926.
32. *Derbyshire Times*, 8 May 1926.
33. *Nottingham Strike Bulletin*, no. 1.

34. *Derbyshire Times*, 15 May 1926.
35. *The Derbyshire Miners*, J. E. Williams, Allen & Unwin, 1962.
36. Frank Treble, tape recording, 11 January 1960.
37. Private correspondence from R. J. P., Leicester.
38. Private correspondence from F.R., Nottingham.
39. Private correspondence from F.R., Nottingham.
40. Private correspondence from A.K.W., Ripley.
41. Private correspondence from A.K.W., Ripley.
42. "My Personal Account", by D. W. Mahoney.
43. *Leicester Mercury*, 7 May 1926.
44. Private correspondence from Mrs. J. E. S., Beeston, Nottingham.
45. Private correspondence from A.K.W., Ripley.
46. Private correspondence from R.P., Riddings, Derbys.
47. Private correspondence from A.L.C., Leicester.
48. Private correspondence from Mrs. A., Clifton, Nottingham.
49. Private correspondence from H.T., Lenton, Nottingham.
50. Private correspondence from A.J.W., Ripley.
51. Private correspondence from W.T.T., Nottingham.
52. Private correspondence from W.B., Burton-upon-Trent.
53. Private correspondence from Mrs. A. S., Burton-upon-Trent.
54. Private correspondence from F.R., Nottingham.
55. Private correspondence from A.H., Brinsley, Nottingham.
56. Private correspondence from T.W., Coalville and M.L., Nottingham.
57. Private correspondence from Mrs. M.B., Mapperley, Nottingham.
58. Private correspondence from N.L., Arnold, Nottingham.
59. Private correspondence from T.W., Coalville.
60. Private correspondence from Mrs. F.W., Sandiacre, Nottingham.
61. Private correspondence from A.K.W., Ripley.
62. Private correspondence from G.L.W., Coalville.
63. Private correspondence from W.D.H., Pinxton, Nottingham.
64. Private correspondence from R.P., Riddings, Derbys.
65. Private correspondence from H.L.C., Leicester.
66. Private correspondence from A.K.W., Ripley.
67. Private correspondence from J.H., Mansfield.
68. George Hamilton, tape recording, 9 January 1969.
69. Arthur Statham, tape recording, 11 January 1969.
70. *Nottingham Guardian*, 10 May 1926.
71. Ibid.
72. *Nottingham Journal*, 13 May 1926.
73. Jack Charlesworth, tape recording, 12 January 1969.
74. George Hamilton, tape recording, 9 January 1969.
75. Frank Treble, tape recording, 11 January 1969.
76. Ibid.
77. Private correspondence from T.E.B., Sheffield.

78. *Nottingham Journal*, 14 May 1926.
79. Private correspondence from J.D., Ravenshed, Nottingham.
80. Cyril Goddard, tape recording, 12 January 1969.
81. George Hamilton, tape recording, 9 January 1969.
82. *Derbyshire Times*, 29 May 1926.
83. Jack Charlesworth, tape recording, 12 January 1969.
84. Private correspondence from A.K.W., Ripley.

5 THE BLACK COUNTRY

by GEORGE BARNSBY

The working class in the Black Country had undergone massive structural changes and experienced important class battles in the years before 1926. This accounts for the fact that, while not the strongest area in the country in terms of trade union membership, the response to the General Strike was remarkably solid.

From 1875 to the 1890s the Great Depression ravaged the Black Country aggravated by the fact that its basic industries of coal and iron were in decline. The wonderful 10-yard seam of coal, exploited in an incredibly wasteful way, was virtually exhausted and the whole coalfield becoming like a waterlogged rabbit warren. Wrought iron, the pride of the Black Country, was being replaced by Bessemer steel and, with the exhaustion of both local coal and iron ore, most of the great ironworks either closed or moved to the coast. By 1900 the typical Black Country worker was no longer the miner or puddler, but the engineer. About this time, large factories began to appear, a development shared with Birmingham.

These changes in the structure of the working class together with the poverty and actual starvation of the Great Depression had fostered the re-emergence of socialist ideas for the first time since the demise of Chartism in the 1860s. Branches of the Social Democratic Federation and Socialist League were formed in the main Black Country towns such as Wolverhampton, Walsall and Dudley in the 1880s. The Socialist League degenerated into anarchism, however, and members of Walsall Socialist Club were convicted of making bombs in 1892. In the middle 1890s the Independent Labour Party appeared and in the early years of the twentieth century the local trades councils were transforming themselves into Trades and Labour Councils as they brought Labour Party branches into existence. Leading up to the first world war was the great period of unrest, 1910–14. This saw not only the organisation of the unskilled but the organisation of women who played a leading role in immense industrial struggles in the Black Country. During the war the increasing size of factories led to the further growth of trade unionism. From 1916 conditions on the home front deteriorated and dissatisfaction with the war grew. This led to a further development of trades councils—Dudley Trades Council was formed at the beginning of 1916—and the growth of the Shop Stewards' Movement.

After the war, Socialist and working-class organisations radiated from Birmingham and had their counterparts in the Black Country. There were the branches of the Labour Party, invariably formed by the trades councils, and the trade unions and the shop stewards and workers' committees. There were the socialist parties, the largest being the ILP, followed by the British Socialist Party and the Socialist Labour Party, together with a rump of the SDF. There were broad organisations such as the National Union of Ex-Servicemen. The "Hands Off Russia" movement was formed at the end of 1919 and the National Unemployed Workers' Committee Movement was formed about the same time. There were the Herald Leagues organised around the *Daily Herald*, which merged into social and cultural organisations such as Clarion Clubs and the Clarion Choir which was particularly important in Birmingham under the influence of Rutland Boughton who became a member of the Communist Party in 1926. Finally, in 1920, the BSP, SLP and large sections of the ILP merged in the newly-formed Communist Party. Such variety of organisation gave a broadness to the working-class movement which is lacking today. However, the effectiveness of the working-class movement depended on its unity of action, and key issues for the working class after the war were its attitude to the Russian Revolution (and hence to the formation of the Communist Party and affiliation to the Third International) and the question of reformist or revolutionary trade unionism. Birmingham, and to a lesser extent the Black Country, played an important part in the struggle for a revolutionary movement. The shop stewards' committees were the basis for the strong development of the Minority Movement in the area, and the Birmingham ILP was, for a long time, the most militant ILP branch in the country. This is shown by the role it played in the development of the *Sunday Worker*. This was an attempt to maintain a broad, militant, weekly newspaper to supplement the mass daily circulation of the *Daily Herald*. The editor of the *Sunday Worker* was the Communist William Paul and the paper was strongly supported by the Birmingham ILP. Their members included Joseph Southall, the well-known artist, Fred Longden, who organised the Left-wing Movement which grew up all over the country in support of the paper, and Fred Sylvester (who had originally come into the Communist Party with the Birmingham BSP) who organised the Midlands groups. The Left-wing Movement was active in Black Country towns like Wolverhampton and Walsall, its main basis being the co-operation of ILP and Communist Party members.

But despite such left-wing developments, the working-class movement in Birmingham and the Black Country was dominated by reformist leaders. Militancy among workers continued, however, right up to 1926. There was considerable strike activity, notably at such key motor plants as Sunbeam in Wolverhampton. The large-scale unemployment (the national average for 1923–6 was about 11 per cent and Black Country jobless only slightly less) led to a rapid development of the Unemployed Workers' Movement. The Minority Movement was influential in the trade unions and there was the considerable influence of the Communist Party, despite its small numbers.

Such was the political and economic background to the Nine Days in the Black Country.

There are no surviving trade union sources for the strike in the Black Country, and so Emile Burns' collected reports in his *The General Strike, May 1926: Trades Councils in Action* provide much of our information for this area.

From Burns' report for Wolverhampton we learn that no preparations had been made, and a Special Executive Committee of the Trades and Labour Council met only on the first day of the strike (3 May), when an Emergency Committee of three men was appointed to sit continuously with full powers to co-ordinate the activities of the unions involved. The first wave of workers called out consisted of 3,500 transport workers, and an unspecified number of members of the Typographical Association, NATSOPA, ETU, some AEU and Allied Trades and Building Workers.

The Emergency Committee consisted of representatives of each affected union. It first met the next day, Tuesday 4 May, and was faced with the question of interpreting the general circular sent by the TUC while waiting for instructions from the individual unions to cease work. The Committee was divided in its opinions as to its function, some thinking that it had the power to call all men out. The majority view, however, was that the job of the local Emergency Committee was to carry out the wishes of the TUC and obtain concerted action locally on that basis. But this presented problems, since different unions were sending different instructions to their branches, this being most evident in the building trades. The central Emergency Committee met every afternoon in the Labour Rooms. A separate strike committee was formed of the railway groups (there were important railways shops in Wolverhampton) which met daily at North Road Club, with a sub-Emergency Committee meeting in the Labour Rooms consisting of four Trades Council representatives, a representative each of the building trades and the North Road joint committee.

To overcome the lack of reliable information, lines of communication were established south to Birmingham, north to Manchester and beyond, and west through Shrewsbury to North Wales. Volunteer dispatch riders were appointed to act for the TUC in every town between Dudley and Oswestry, receiving reports each day from each strike committee, sending out official information from the TUC, supplying them with speakers where necessary and forwarding information to London to the General Council.

A local bulletin of 500 each issue was published for six days from 5 May. Open-air meetings were arranged every day at the Market Place, with a good supply of local speakers assisted by the miners from Cannock. There were national speakers at the weekend. A meeting on Sunday, 9 May, packed the Theatre Royal with 2,500 people with an overflow meeting of 1,100 at the Co-op Hall. Even with these two halls packed, thousands were unable to obtain admission.

As in the rest of the west Midlands, there were differences of opinion as to whether car workers were included under transport and therefore among those called on to strike. In Wolverhampton this matter was settled when the Vehicle Builders received definite instructions to withdraw their labour. The other unions involved then acted on the principle laid down by the TUC, that where one section of labour was called out in a given factory then all should strike. Thus the important car industry was closed down.

All building workers, except those engaged on housing, hospitals or sanitation, were ordered to strike. This caused dissatisfaction in Wolverhampton where "the whole of the industry was determined to stand by the miners". The Strike Committee therefore had the greatest difficulty in keeping within the TUC instructions and on Saturday, 8 May, a meeting of building workers instructed local officials to send a telegram demanding the withdrawal of all building trade workers.

The town's power supply from the Commercial Road power station received a great deal of attention. The TUC requested that local arrangements be made to supply houses, hospitals, bakeries, etc., but the management refused to negotiate with a deputation and instructions were eventually received to withdraw all men from the power station.

From figures provided by the manager of the labour exchange on Monday, 10 May, it is estimated that 35,000 workers took part in the General Strike in Wolverhampton.

The only other Black Country report published by Emile Burns was a short one on Wednesbury. Here the strike was organised by the Trades Council acting with its affiliated trade union branches. It issued a bulletin each Sunday, the first selling 750 and the second 1,000 copies. The position on 12 May was given as "No weakening. The position was magnificent. The trouble has been since the termination."

This can be supplemented with information from the only discovered number of the *Birmingham Worker*, the broadsheet of the Communist Party, of 7 May. This stated that the Council of Action which had been formed was in continuous contact with Tipton, Darlaston, Walsall and surrounding area. "Even non-unionists are affected by the spirit of working-class unity and are on the streets with the organised workers. Mass demonstrations are being held and enthusiasm runs high. The formation of a Workers' Defence Force is contemplated. The unemployed, who are rendering valuable assistance, are seeking representation on the Council of Action."

The *British Worker* carried two reports on the strike in the Black Country. In its first issue of Wednesday evening, 5 May, it reported the stoppage in Birmingham and district as complete. Not a man on the railways or in other transport was working. The biggest trouble was to keep at work those who were not involved. The 7 May issue reported that the West Bromwich situation, according to the local Trades Council, was regarded as eminently satisfactory. Councillor Guest, the agent, stated that the response to the call to cease work had been complete. The main difficulty had been to keep men and women in who wanted to strike in sympathy. The opening of the new Labour headquarters had been of great advantage to the local strike committee.

In the TUC library there are reports from Wolverhampton and Walsall, and also a report of Ellen Wilkinson and J. F. Horrabin of their tour through the Midlands. The latter report gives valuable testimony of the position in Wolverhampton towards the end of the strike. It states that there was a ready and unanimous response to the call in every occupation. Public opinion was strongly in favour of the strikers. Not a tram or bus was running. Some attempts had been made by the local Council and Chief Constable to intimidate tramway and busmen, without success. Three Midland Red buses had tried to run, but were withdrawn by inducements. The typographical men had been persuaded to go back by the editor of the local paper, *Express and Star*. Police and strikers were on good terms. Food was supplied by road and there were no shortages. In Wolverhampton, Wilkinson and Horrabin had addressed two open-air meetings on the Market Patch of 6,000 each. The figures they give for the indoor Sunday meetings are 4,900 at the Royal Theatre and 2,000 at the Co-op Hall. In the area between the Black Country and the Cannock coalfield they had addressed an open-air meeting of 2,000 at New Invention. In Bilston 1,500 had listened in Oatmeal Square. Their general observation was that they had been immensely struck by the complete stoppage and the peacefulness of the workers in every town through which they had passed. The response was "magnificent" everywhere.

A report to the TUC from Walsall of 6 May was on special notepaper headed "Walsall Trades Council National Industrial Crisis Committee". The secretary was John Whiston and the chairman A. H. Fox. They reported the position in Walsall as "splendid". A wonderful demonstration had been held with a huge meeting. All were out who had been called out. In addition, several thousand engineers had decided that they were really on transport work and these were out. The local strike committee was very efficient and was publishing a local newspaper. Public opinion was on the side of the strikers.

The recently released Cabinet papers on the strike are disappointing. Police intelligence was no better in 1926 than it had been during the nineteenth century. The Midlands reports are sparse and refer mainly to Birmingham. A survey of reports from the police to the Home Office at noon Tuesday, 4 May, gave the position at the begining of the strike. All towns were reported quiet. Stoppage of trains was almost complete. All tram and bus services were suspended. There was no mention of food supplies except at Birmingham, where the Trades Council reported that they were taking control of the situation and had set up a committee to consider applications for the handling of food. The next day only two trains had been reported as having run and canal boatmen had stopped except for perishable goods in transit. The Ministry of Labour reported that "iron and steel works were stopped generally in the Midlands". This affected particularly Brierley Hill and Bilston in the Black Country. Newspapers were practically all suspended except for a few scrappy publications.

The Home Office report for 6 May stated that in Wolverhampton journalists were on strike in sympathy with the printers. The *Express and Star* was publishing a foolscap sheet with volunteers. About 2,500 men had come out at the Sunbeam Works. McManus was expected to hold a Communist meeting in the town on Saturday, but the police would not allow him to speak. There had been some interference with working railwaymen who were being given police protection.

On 5 May there was a report from the Engineering Employers' Federation stating that AEU members in Birmingham and Coventry were out. The Home Office report for 7 May stated that in Wolverhampton more engineers were out and that 400 police specials had been enrolled, with more coming forward. The electrical workers might come out, but in that case the power station would be run by volunteers. The Home Office summary for 10 May reported a tendency among Shropshire railwaymen to complain because they had not been asked to ballot, and also that there were signs of secessions from the ranks of the miners. A patrol had found a detonator on the GWR line near Cradley Heath.

Turning to the local press, the *Express and Star* ran a badly produced, duplicated 1*d*. sheet on 4, 5 and 6 May. The first reported hopefully that arrangements were being made for charabancs and buses to be run in certain districts under police protection and that it was hoped to run a skeleton GWR train service from Wolverhampton to Birmingham. A Communist meeting of about 800 had assembled at the Market Place and had been immediately dispersed by the police. The bulletin reported pickets at the garage of C. F. James in Sweetman Street and the stopping of one of his charabancs in Stafford Street, police arriving in time to prevent a disturbance. Such contrasting snippets of national news were reported as the arrest of the Communist M.P. Saklatvala in Hyde Park for a "seditious" speech and the arrival of the Prince of Wales in Paris from Biarritz. Local news on Thursday, 6 May was that engineers and bodybuilders at Black Country motor works were out and that all was quiet in Dudley, Darlaston, Walsall and Willenhall.

By Friday, 7 May, the *Express and Star* was producing a two-page printed sheet with more local news. Wolverhampton tramways were still firm. The Star Engineering works at Bushbury and Frederick Street were closed although only 50 per cent of the men were trade unionists. The Sunbeam, Moorfield Road works were at a standstill. Guy Motors had 500 to 600 men out and 200 men in. At A. J. Stevens (AJS) 50 to 60 AEU members were out, but the firm was carrying on. In Brierley Hill

2,000 men were out in iron and bricks. In Walsall between 1,000 and 1,300 hands were idle, but all large works were able to continue. In Bilston, the Springvale steelworks was closed and hollow ware workers would have to go on short time next week. In the Rowley Regis area 6,000 workers were idle, but at Halesowen all workers were continuing. In Dudley all was quiet with 300 men out. At Brierley Hill 1,500 men were out at the Earl of Dudley's Works, 300 at the Harts Hill Ironworks and 90 at the Brettell Lane Ironworks. About 150 men were out at the J. T. Price and Ketley Brick Works, but other brickworks were in production.

On Saturday, 8 May, the *Express and Star* printed four pages. An advertisement from Beattie's, the large department store in the town, showed that they at least had prepared for the General Strike. It stated that the strike had been threatening for months and that the store had ample stocks to meet all demands for three months. In Wolverhampton, the paper reported the continued total absence of trams and buses, but otherwise the town was normal. Bushbury parish church had given over its Institute to the strikers (mainly railwaymen) and these men had decided to march in a body to church on Sunday. AEU men had stopped work at Clyno, but this car firm was carrying on. A short service of prayer for industrial peace was being said at St. Peter's Church in the town centre every day at 12.30 p.m. The Grand Theatre would be closed the following week because the company, which was to have produced "The Jazz Marriage", had "transport difficulties". In Willenhall most factories were on a three-day week because of shortage of fuel. At Dudley on Friday night there had been an attempt to stop a charabanc taking workers home, but despite a large crowd the vehicle had got through.

On Monday, 10 May, another four-page issue appeared. There had been no peace moves over the weekend and the position remained the same. Many Black Country works were still managing to keep open. At Harper Sons and Beans three works with 2,500 men had to be closed at Dudley, Tipton and Smethwick because finished cars could not be dispatched; 3,700 men had signed on at Dudley Labour Exchange since the strike began. Joseph Ball, a miner of Cross Street, Dudley, was given one month's hard labour for allegedly assaulting two police officers and committing an offence against the Emergency Powers Act. He incited a crowd by shouting, "Come on lads, let's have a go! We're not frightened of you!" The crowd rushed the police who drew their staves. Several women said, "Cheer up, lad!" when sentence was passed. Sunbeam and

Star were still at a standstill. At A. J. Stevens it was said, "There is a sort of ebb and flow at our works, but we are still able to carry on. About 800 are on duty and 600 still on strike." At Wednesbury two MPs, A. Short and C. Sitch, had addressed a Labour meeting on Saturday. Halesowen steelworks was closed down and Sitch had addressed 3,000 workers at Cradley Heath on Saturday evening. Two hundred men were on strike at Henry Meadows, leaving 38 at work. In Tipton the roadmen were on strike, and at W. G. Allen in the same town an unsuccessful attempt had been made to prevent a steam wagon loaded with iron plates from entering the works. This issue of the *Express and Star* found space for a remarkable Red scare story: a Paris paper had published a letter from its German correspondent stating that the General Strike in Britain had been planned in secret many months before in Moscow.

On the last day of the strike, the *Express and Star* reported the Wolverhampton situation little changed. Strikers were still coming out—for instance, 129 at ECC, and other works were closing "because of lack of transport". At Bilston lorries leaving goods stations still had to have police guards. At Walsall the Board of Guardians had published their scales of relief for the families of strikers. These were—for wives 10*s*., for wives with one child 14*s*. 6*d*. with 3*s*. 6*d*. for every additional child. Rent relief of 50 per cent could also be allowed. Half of the relief was to be paid in cash and half in kind.

The *Express and Star* voiced the opinions of the employers and much of its reportage was mendacious or misleading. An example is the paper's report of 10 May that at Guy Motors a secret ballot in the presence of two trade union officials had given a 75 per cent vote in favour of a return to work. This issue also reported that at Bayliss, Jones and Bayliss the men were returning to work. The next day the paper reported that 87 men had reported for work at Guy's while between 500 and 600 men were "affected" by the strike and 250 had been "outside" (picketing) when the firm opened. Guy, the managing director, admitted that the meeting at which the ballot had been taken was "not largely attended" due to the fact that pickets had told workers that no meeting was being held. Guy was a particularly active employer in attempting to break the strike. Even this amended version of the Guy story is likely to be only an approximation to the truth and the facts of the so-called "return to work" at Bayliss, Jones and Bayliss are now never likely to be known. Another clear example of misleading reporting was an item in the 12 May issue headed "How men were going back to work before the good news came". Here the whole country was scoured for news of men returning to work before the end of the strike, but all that could be found was such items as "Birmingham—a 12-minute train service to Dudley" or "Stoke-on-Trent—A number of tramway and omnibus employees have returned, but the response is extremely limited." Nevertheless, the press is cowardly as well as venal; while the capitalist system is under attack the endless direct strictures on workers are suspended. But when profits and property are once more secure editors again thunder against the wickedness and criminality of striking workers. This was so in 1842 when Chartists controlled the Black Country in the general strike of August that year, and so it was with the *Express and Star* in 1926. The 12 May editorial spoke only of "Unbounded relief" at the ending of the strike. But the following day it was, "The Law Victorious" and, "Did the TUC ever consider the legality of their action? . . . It can hardly be imagined in any way a victory for the unions. . . . The forces of law have triumphed as they always will in Britain." Much more of this sort was to follow in the days and weeks ahead.

The General Strike of 1926 is the most important event in the history of the trade union movement in Britain. Employers had wanted and provoked the strike in order to curb the power of the trade unions and to bring all wages down. The right-wing Labour leaders feared the strike, had tried to avoid it and wanted it brought to an end at the earliest possible moment before it got "out of hand". To hundreds of thousands of workers, however, the strike came as a revelation. It showed with the starkest clarity that society only existed through the labour of working men. During the strike trades councils exercised powers of decision and control normally carried out by employers and police. Thus the strike taught lessons of democracy and workers' control. It was also a magnificent example of workers' solidarity and comradeship, contrasting with the selfishness of capitalism. Above all, in a society of mass poverty, deprivation and high unemployment a successful conclusion to the strike held the promise of fundamental changes in society. Most strikers realised therefore, however dimly, that the project on which they were engaged was of great significance. Hence the Nine Days had an atmosphere of gaiety, solidarity, determination, militancy, and mass participation which is rarely captured by strike reporting. Some observers, however, did begin to catch this atmosphere. Here is John Strachey writing in the *New Leader* after the strike and referring to the Labour Parliamentary candidates who left London for their Birmingham constituencies on the Saturday before the strike began:

"When they reached the headquarters of their divisional Labour Parties they found unexpected crowds gathering round the banners of local parties and trade unions. As they marched with their comrades through the streets of the city, unprecedented masses of people lined the route and followed them to the park where the May Day demonstration was being held. They did not realise that, almost literally, these great crowds were not to disperse until fourteen days later when they were dismissed at another demonstration. The whole city swayed with the quiet vibrations of these impressive masses."

Ellen Wilkinson also wrote graphically in *Lansbury's Labour Weekly* of 22 May of her experiences in the Midlands:

"We got to Coventry that night to find the town in the hands of the local Soviet. We spoke to one of the biggest open-air crowds I have ever seen. The engineers were very disgruntled at not being called out. . . . Wolverhampton, not on our list, demanded a meeting and in one hour we got a large crowd to listen despite pouring rain. They and Walsall were in the same position as Coventry. . . ."

Much of this mass participation went unrecorded, but it is quite certain that almost every urban area saw meetings and demonstrations perhaps larger than these places had ever seen before and certainly larger than anything since the Reform Bill or Chartist times in the nineteenth century. Immediately before the strike, there had been the mass demonstrations of May Day. The following weekend again saw massive meetings. Then there were the demonstrations of the weekend following. Throughout the strike, the hunger for news and desire for mass communication was such that enormous meetings could be held during the day. Often these were Communist meetings which the police promptly broke up. The solidarity of the strike made mass picketing possible and overwhelming public sympathy was manifest at crucial moments.

In view of the particular efforts that were made to break the strike at what was considered to be its weakest point, namely transport, this atmosphere of solidarity might be illustrated by detailing the determined efforts made in Wolverhampton to get buses back on the road. On Monday, 10 May, it was decided to attempt to run ten buses manned by volunteers. At 6.30 p.m. when the attempt was to be made, a crowd, estimated by the *Express and Star* at 1,000, assembled at the Cleveland Street depot. Police, including mounted specials, cleared a way for the volunteers and it seems that some of the buses got away. At 9 p.m. the crowds "still numbered several hundreds". At 7.50 a.m. the next day, the first bus, manned by three men in plain clothes and one uniformed policeman, set out. It was later claimed that ten buses were running. All that day "strikers in Queen Square thronged the pavements as densely as if waiting for a royal procession". On Wednesday, the *Express and Star* returned to the events of the previous day. "The first day of the volunteer bus service will be long remembered," it reported. The story went on to tell of huge crowds in Princes Square during Tuesday night and photographs confirmed the enormous numbers who protested against this attempt to break the strike. The transport workers of Wolverhampton remained firm until the end.

In Bilston, too, masses of workers demonstrated, although we only have the reports of the *Express and Star* to go by: "Bilston tramway and railway workers gathered in fairly large numbers on Monday 10th when attempts were made to remove supplies from the railway depot to various factories. A number of volunteer lorry drivers, including several undergraduates in plus fours evidently enjoyed the experience. There was no attempt at molestation."

In the great pre-strike May Day demonstration the festive mood was shared by Wolverhampton's communists but this did not prevent arrests taking place. Albert Darke and John James Foster were charged with having worn service uniform "in such a way as to bring it into contempt". Darke wore RAF uniform with a red band. On the shoulders he wore red badges. Foster was in the uniform of a line regiment and he was similarly decorated. The case was heard after the strike had ended. Inspector Churchward gave evidence that on 1 May the Labour Party was holding a demonstration from St. James' Square. As the procession moved off Darke joined it with a placard reading "Don't shoot". At 7.45 the same evening, at a Communist Party meeting, Darke was similarly attired and Foster carried a red flag. The two communists were defended by Randle Evans, a noted Labour Party progressive solicitor, who submitted that his clients were wearing uniform in the course of a *bona fide* military representation forming part of a tableau. They were not there to bring contempt upon the uniform. The Chairman of the bench of magistrates (consisting of W. H. Pritchard, Sir Charles Marston and Alderman T. Frost) said that the court could not tolerate that HM uniforms should be used in a contemptuous manner. Albert Darke was fined £6 and given time to pay, and Foster was fined £1.

Further information regarding the role of Wolverhampton Communist Party during the strike comes from a personal interview of the author with Ralph Prescott who joined in 1924, but is not now a member of the Party. He states that the Communist Party had considerable influence on Wolverhampton Trades Council; Albert Darke, the Party secretary, was a delegate. The most important way of exerting the Party's influence during the strike was through mass meetings on the Market Patch. These were invariably broken up by the police. He particularly remembers one meeting at which he was chairman. He spoke from the steps of the old Market Hall which formed an excellent elevated platform. He had not been speaking long when the police hauled him down. Albert Darke jumped up and took his place. As Prescott was taken away to the Town Hall, mounted police dispersed the crowd with batons in the fiercest struggle he had ever seen. Prescott and Bill Smith, another Communist arrested with him, persisted in asking what they were charged with, but the police would make no charge and they were both released after the crowd had been dispersed. When the strike ended the Party directed its efforts to raising money for the miners. Cannock was at the heart of this struggle and miners' choirs came to the Market Patch to sing and raise funds. The Communist Party came out of the strike with increased prestige, Prescott says, and it exercised influence far greater than its numbers, a fact of which the police were well aware. At this time, however, there were only about nine members of the Party in the town and it was not strong enough to be a decisive influence on the strike.

As in other parts of the country, the first reaction of some to the call-off of the strike was a feeling of elation, for they supposed they must have won. But disillusion was swift and was followed by the struggle for a return to work. In Wolverhampton the Emergency Committee met on the afternoon of the 12th and had posters displayed in front of the Labour Rooms advising men not to return to work until instructions to that effect came from their unions. This caution was well justified. The railways, Guy Motors, the ECC and Midland Red buses were requiring men to "sign documents which would take away the whole of the rights which their fathers and forefathers had fought so dearly for, and it is quite evident that the employers of this country were prepared to use this crisis as a method of breaking down trade union bargaining". Some employers would take men back "only as work became available". Apart from the railways, it is not known to what extent victimisation occurred in the Black Country.

In evaluating the strike, Postgate, Wilkinson and Horrabin classified areas into four classes. Class I was towns where response was near to

100 per cent. Class II was where the strike was wholly effective but with weaknesses in some sections. Class III was towns with serious weaknesses. And Class IV towns where the strike broke down. Of Midland towns, Birmingham, Kidderminster, Lichfield, Stafford, Stoke, Worcester and Wolverhampton were in Class I. In Class II were Coventry, Shrewsbury, Smethwick, Stourbridge, Walsall and Wednesbury. No Midland towns were in the other two classes. The Wolverhampton Emergency Committee summed up the strike as follows: ". . . the trade union movement are indeed to be congratulated upon the splendid stand made on behalf of their more unfortunate brethren, the miners, and with very little exception, the whole of the workers stood solid and were prepared to fight to the bitter end, so that when the news came through on Wednesday May 12th, that the strike was over, it came as a shock, as the situation then looked as though it would last indefinitely."

On Sunday, 19 May, Wolverhampton Trades Council held a meeting at the Market Place. The *Wolverhampton Chronicle* informs us that there was a crowd of 300, "but this increased after the first half hour". Allport, the chairman of the Trades Council, said they met, "to offer thanks for the solidarity of the working class". Dan Davies, the local election agent of the Labour Party, said that "if the strike had lasted another week we would have entered another era of the struggle". This latter statement is highly significant. The day before the strike ended the TUC had called out the second wave of workers, all the engineering and shipbuilding workers not already affected. This call was just beginning to take effect in the Black Country. The solidarity of the strike from start to finish suggests that this unique chapter in working-class history would have ended very differently had the strike continued.

BIBLIOGRAPHY

Books

R. Page Arnot, *The General Strike* (Labour Research Department, 1926).

Emile Burns, *The General Strike 1926: Trades Councils in Action* (Labour Research Department, 1926, reprinted 1975, Lawrence & Wishart, London).

Ellen Wilkinson, J. H. F. Horrabin and R. W. Postgate, *Workers' History of the Great Strike.*

Papers

Cabinet Papers, PRO. CAB. 27/331 at the Public Records Office, London.
TUC Records: The General Strike in Wolverhampton and Walsall, HD 5366 at the TUC Library, London.

Newspapers

National: *Lansbury's Labour Weekly*
New Leader
Out of Work
Sunday Worker
Workers' Weekly

Local: *Birmingham Worker*, no. 3
Birmingham Gazette
Express and Star
Wolverhampton Chronicle

6 BIRMINGHAM

by R. P. HASTINGS

By 1926 the peculiar economic, and social structure of Victorian Birmingham which had helped to make "the greatest industrial city of the Empire" the political province of Liberal Unionism and the Chamberlain family,[1] had largely ceased to exist. "Cloth-capped Chamberlainism", however, persisted. Political canvassing was apt to reduce Labour workers to despair and caused Margaret Newboult to bitterly compare the mental attitude of the contemporary Birmingham worker to that of the village labourer twenty years before.[2] On a City Council of 120 members there were only 19 Labour representatives and even in 1923, when Britain elected the first disastrous Labour Government, Birmingham remained obstinately loyal to tariff reform and twelve Unionist MPs. The General Election of 1924, however, suggested that some of the Birmingham socialists' post-war propaganda work was starting to take effect and, with the eclipse of the Liberals, the Birmingham Labour Party had begun to challenge for the first time the Unionist political hegemony. Labour votes increased from an insignificant 30,000 in 1918 to 120,000, and at King's Norton Bob Dennison, a Glaswegian socialist, broke the Chamberlain "ring" by narrowly defeating his Longbridge employer, Sir Herbert Austin, to become Birmingham's first Labour MP.[3] Neville Chamberlain, who had succeeded his father, Joseph Chamberlain, as leader of the Birmingham Unionist caucus, kept his seat at Ladywood against Oswald Mosley, at that time one of Labour's most promising young men, by only 77 votes. At Deritend, Duddeston, Aston and Erdington "safe" Unionist majorities were greatly decreased. Even so a poll of 190,000 secured the Unionists 11 MPs, four of whom were appointed to key cabinet positions.[4] Trade union organisation, however, had not kept pace with this political advance. The old cry of "No politics for the trade unions" still persisted in the city, and prominent Conservative trade unionists remained a symbol of Joseph Chamberlain's success in securing the allegiance of a large proportion of the working class.[5] Birmingham was "at least ten years behind the best organised areas"[6] and on the eve of the strike Walter Lewis, District Secretary of the ETU, was forced to admit that the city "reeked with non-unionism".[7]

The local authority in Birmingham, as in other towns and cities, took full advantage of the nine-months' truce provided by the Samuel Commission to prepare an elaborate organisation to counter strike action. Upon receipt of Circular 636 from the Ministry of Health in November 1925, the City Council began the preparatory steps "to secure the maintenance of public services . . . during an industrial crisis". In January 1926 its General Purposes Committee appointed an Emergency Sub-Committee consisting of Aldermen Sir David Brookes, Gregory, Sayer and Martineau, and Councillors Lee, Muscott and Shakespeare. The Lord Mayor and Alderman Williams were made *ex officio* members. Brookes, a Birmingham solicitor, was leader of the City Council Unionist Group. Colonel Ernest Martineau was another solicitor, a former Lord Mayor and a prominent Birmingham industrialist.[8] Lee was a retired building contractor, and Williams a chartered accountant and Chairman of the Finance Committee. Of the working-class members Councillor Shakespeare, a railway guard, resigned when the Strike began,[9] although Alderman Joseph Gregory, a former organiser of the National Union of General Workers, had no such scruples.[10] The greatest controversy, however, was to be created by the presence upon such a strike-breaking body of Birmingham's first Labour Lord Mayor, Alderman Percival Bower, one-time president of the Borough Labour Party and a former official of the Associated Blacksmiths and Ironworkers' Society.[11]

The function of this Emergency Sub-Committee was to supplement the efforts of the existing Council Committees in maintaining gas, electricity, water, refuse collection, transport and the distribution of coal and food. Nevertheless, it had full power to act without specific Council authority, and its chairman, Sir David Brookes, was chosen by the Government. Allan Granger, Chief Inspector of Weights and Measures, was made Special Coal Officer. His duty, in conjunction with a Coal Committee, was to regulate supplies to dealers and distributors. Permits for handling coal were printed for issue at the Council House. Householders requiring fuel were to secure permits from the Weights and Measures Department at the Town Hall, or from issuing offices in the suburbs. The domestic ration, except in special circumstances, was fixed at 1 cwt per week regardless of house size, while to avoid forgery a weekly colour change for permits was prepared. For trading purposes priority in supplies was arranged for those concerned with municipal depots, milk supply, milling, baking, cold storage and fried fishshops. Special attention was also given to hospitals and similar institutions. Provision was also made for the preparation of hot meals by a number of bakers and the management of fifteen hot water centres by Girl Guides, although, in the event, the continuation of gas supplies made these arrangements unnecessary.[12]

While the Local Emergency Sub-Committee was making these plans a Birmingham Area Branch of the OMS, chaired by Unionist Councillor Egbert P. Booth, and "maintained by the generosity of a few patriotic citizens",[13] had since February 1926 been independently compiling a list of persons willing to assist in the maintenance of supplies under the headings of Protection (Special Constables), Workers, Transport and Messengers.[14] On the evening of 2 May, although negotiations between the Cabinet and the TUC had not then terminated, the Emergency Sub-Committee upon the directions of the Home Secretary also appealed for volunteers.[15] Car and motorcycle owners prepared to offer their vehicles and their services were asked to register at Birmingham AA or RAC branch offices, and other volunteers, under sixteen different classifications, at a Volunteer Registration Centre at the Town Hall. Several organisations, including the Midland Branch of the National Union of Manufacturers, the Birmingham Chamber of Commerce and the Engineering and Allied Employers Association, placed their staffs completely at the Committee's disposal. One hundred skilled volunteers enrolled from Austin's motor works were placed at the call of the Corporation in the event of strike action by gas and electricity employees. Another three hundred were sworn in as special constables and organised into a force for protection of the Longbridge Works.

At Birmingham University the Senate promised to protect the academic interests of student volunteers, but final year students were advised to continue their studies. On 3 May, upon the instructions of the OMS National Council, Booth placed himself, his committee, and its registered personnel at the disposal of the Emergency Sub-Committee. Similarly C. Spencer Woollard, Commander of the Birmingham Group of the British Fascists, also handed over his organisation to the authorities and all members were ordered to report immediately to their office in Livery Street for instructions. By midnight on 3 May volunteers numbered 1,105. Nine days later they had grown to 11,876 although only 1,990 of them were called upon during the strike. All those utilised were paid the recognised rate for the job and dismissed with a two-day bonus. The Chief Constable also appealed for temporary constables "preferably with police or military experience", who would be paid 10*s.* a day, and for "patriotic and law abiding citizens" to enlist as special constables during the emergency. Almost 2,000 of the latter were eventually enrolled, although several railwaymen and tramwaymen who became "specials" were refused strike pay by their unions and an unemployed man who registered was refused the "dole". On 10 May it was also decided to form a Civil Constabulary Reserve directed by the Chief Constable but administered by the military authorities, whose express purpose was to avoid the use of the Army against strikers.[16]

In contrast to this elaborate organisation, the Birmingham trade union movement was virtually unprepared. A special emergency committee had been created at a "rank and file" conference on 14 July 1925, prior to Red Friday, and a Joint Council of Trade Unionists and Co-operators established about the same time.[17] Both appear to have lapsed, and it was not until the evening of the traditional May Day demonstration, which had attracted some 25,000 marchers and 100,000 spectators, that the Birmingham Trades Council empowered its Executive to create machinery to direct the coming strike. On 2 May 1926, the Executive called a meeting of full-time trade union officials from whom nine representatives were chosen to sit with the Executive as a Birmingham Trade Union Emergency Committee. The Committee consisted of a typical cross-section of Birmingham trade union leaders. Its chairman, vice-chairman and secretary were J. E. Corrin, a full-time official of the T & GWU, W. T. Cardinal (Workers' Union), and F. W. Rudland (Typographical Association), who were president, vice-president and secretary respectively of the Birmingham Trades Council. J. Stuart Barr, its minute secretary, was Midlands Organiser for the National Council of Labour Colleges and a parliamentary candidate for Tynemouth. The other Trades Council Executive members were H. Dawson (Brassworkers), S. L. Treleaven (Life Assurance Workers), C. J. Mann (NUDAW), Jarrow-born George Haynes, district secretary of the Operative Bakers and Confectioners' Society, and the young Walter Lewis who had become district secretary of the ETU in 1923. The full-time officials representing the Birmingham trade union movement included A. E. Ager, district secretary of the AEU, James Crump, Area secretary of the T & GWU, C. Augur (NUR), Charles Brett (Sheet Iron Workers), T. C. Pearson (Printing and Paperworkers), Jabez Hall (Iron and Steel Confederation), and Charles Spragg, district secretary of the National Society of Painters since 1920, and secretary to the National Federation of Building Trades Operatives from 1924. Lastly, and perhaps better known than the others, there was the veteran Eldred Hallas, former president of the Amalgamated Society of Gas, Municipal and General Workers, and an official of the NUGMW, and George Geobey, an organiser of the Workers' Union. Hallas, a lecturer-journalist and trade union leader for many years, had been a councillor for Duddeston and the Nechells from 1911 to 1919, and National Democratic Labour Party MP for Duddeston from 1918–22. The diminutive Geobey was a noted negotiator with a wealth of practical experience in the engineering trades. During the strike the Vehicle Builders, Sheet Metal Workers and Woodworkers also unsuccessfully sought representation on the committee. Since, however, the Committee contained so many full-time officials who were involved in the strike and had large areas to cover, substitutes were allowed at meetings. Thus H. Ayres (NUR) deputised for C. Augur, R. Edwards for T. C. Pearson, and T. Hurley for Eldred Hallas, who fell ill in the early stages of the strike as a result of his exertions and died a month later.[18]

Politically the composition of the Emergency Committee was far from revolutionary, as might be expected from a body which contained four of the handful of Birmingham Labour magistrates (Brett, Hall, Haynes, and Rudland), a councillor (Crump) and an ex-councillor (Ager), and a former Coalition MP. The majority were longstanding trade union officials of maturity, responsibility and moderation. Ager was chairman of the Birmingham Borough Labour Party, and with the exception of Cardinal and Barr none were seemingly associated with the "left wingers" whose bitter struggle with the moderates rent the Birmingham Labour Movement in 1927–8.[19] Cardinal, initially associated with the ILP, was involved in a number of post-war leftist groupings such as the Herald League and the League Against Imperialism. In 1919–20 he was secretary of the Birmingham "Hands Off Russia" Committee and in 1921 became a founder member of the Birmingham Communist Party, which he left about 1928.[20] F. W. Rudland, a printer until 1918 when he became secretary to the Trades Council, had something of a similar background. Secretary to the Birmingham ILP Federation in 1904 he had been president of the "Hands Off Russia" Committee in 1919. His views, however, which had involved him in considerable controversy during the war,[21] were of a left-wing pacifist and anti-conscriptionist variety and he was quite loyal to the Birmingham Labour Party in whose post-war development he played a leading role and to whom he was also for a while party secretary.

George Geobey had played a prominent part in the successful Black Country strike for the minimum wage in 1913 but, this apart, with the exception of the rail strikes of 1911, 1913, and 1919 and abortive strikes of police and ironfounders in 1919, Birmingham, with a long tradition of conciliation, arbitration and industrial peace, had been affected by no other major twentieth-century industrial dispute. In view of this inexperience the complex nature of the machinery hurriedly established by the Emergency Committee is surprising.

Throughout the strike the Committee met daily at the Trades Council offices at 262 Corporation Street to direct operations and keep contact with the TUC General Council whose often ill-defined instructions it had to interpret. It was also linked with joint strike committees in all Birmingham districts and with trade union advisory committees established for specific industries such as the public utilities and the building, furnishing, electrical and engineering trades. In order to function smoothly it set up sub-committees for propaganda and publicity, communications, interviews, vigilance and transport and permits. The last committee, consisting of a railwayman, a transport worker and G. Haynes of the Bakers' Union, was empowered to grant permits for the release of food and the use of union labour in continuing essential work. The task of the Publicity and Propaganda Committee, headed by Corrin and Rudland, was to organise meetings and provide speakers. Distribution of the *British Worker* also fell to one of its members, T. C. Pearson of the Printing and Paperworkers. W. J. Chamberlain, Quaker editor of Birmingham's Labour weekly, *The Town Crier*, was additionally co-opted, but production of the committee's strike bulletin was largely the work of John Strachey, Labour candidate for Aston, and of Oswald Mosley. On the Communications Committee Allan Young, Borough Labour Party Organiser, was responsible for liaison with the Divisional Labour Parties, communication with the districts and a courier network which linked Birmingham with London and the area covered by the Midland Federation of Trades Councils. In its Diamond Jubilee Year the Trades Council therefore managed overnight to fashion an organisation to conduct a strike which was to bring into the open "a deep chasm in outlook within British society".[22]

Birmingham's response to the strike call surprised even the most experienced trade unionists. At midnight on 3 May 6,000 members of the T & GWU, some 90 per cent of those employed in the tram, omnibus and waterways service, stopped work. Only safety men and those engaged in the distribution of food supplies stayed on with union consent.[23] Similarly, after the midnight trains had left Snow Hill and New Street all railwaymen completed their shifts and went home, leaving the stations empty and silent. A Central Railway Strike Committee of the NUR, ASLEF and RCA undertook the feeding of goods depot horses.[24] The absence of morning transport brought total confusion. Normally the GWR brought 10,000–15,000 people into Birmingham and the LMS even more. Now thousands of pedestrians mingled with streams of cyclists and numerous cars. Impromptu services by charabancs, cars and lorries from tramway termini, however, continued to link most areas despite a union suggestion that "blacklegging" should be countered by a stoppage of petrol supplies.[25] While West Bromwich Corporation maintained a bus service to Birmingham manned by volunteers, the Birmingham authorities, despite strong criticism from the *Midlander Daily Bulletin*, did not introduce any regular improvised service. Until bus services resumed on 10 May pedestrians were forced to rely largely upon private motorists, who were issued with RAC stickers stating "If you want a lift please signal". Special transport was arranged by the AA for late duty Post Office and telephone workers.[26]

The response of Birmingham's transport workers was paralleled elsewhere. "Everything in Birmingham is proceeding satisfactorily" the Trade Union Emergency Committee reported to the TUC on 5 May. "The extent of the stoppage is much greater than anybody anticipated and all road, passenger, and carrying traffic has been stopped . . . on the railway the stoppage is complete . . . in the factories the difficulty now is to keep the people at work. All are anxious to be out and in the fight. Newspapers have failed to appear . . . We are issuing daily bulletins . . . Birmingham has full confidence in the General Council; we accept their decisions and await victory."[27] TUC strategy was based upon a strike in "waves", which it was hoped would produce a satisfactory compromise before a total stoppage occurred. The first "wave" consisted of transport workers, printers, building workers, except those employed upon housing and hospital work, metal, iron and steel and heavy chemical workers. Electricity and gas workers were to "co-operate" with the object of ceasing to supply power but not light—a technical impossibility. Individual unions were left to interpret the TUC call in their own way. As a result, workers in the building, engineering and metal trades were only partly called out and confusion reigned. On 5 May the Emergency Committee received requests from the Vehicle Builders, Plumbers and Engineers to ratify branch meeting decisions and order the whole membership on strike, and next day Walter Lewis, leader of the Electricians, who had already been withdrawn from the tram sheds, reported great difficulty in keeping his other members at work.[28]

Accurate assessment of the number of strikers and their effect upon local industry is made difficult by the contradictory claims of the capitalist press and trade union officials. The TUC policy of withdrawing only certain categories of labour from a firm meant that not all work would straightaway cease. The *Birmingham Gazette* estimated the number of strikers at under 20,000, although it calculated that many more were left workless by lack of coal, raw materials and transport.[29] Local membership of the printing, transport and rail unions, whose response was all but unanimous, amounted to some 18,000 workers, excluding the ETU, whose membership was partially withdrawn. AEU members in shops where fellow trade unionists had struck were also ordered to strike. This completed the closure of tramway and bus depots and railway works, while the withdrawal of 2,000 men from the Birmingham Wagon Co. Ltd., and 2,000 from the Metropolitan Wagon Works left these totally idle. Striking vehicle builders and AEU toolmakers reduced Wolseley Motors to chaos, and seriously affected the Austin Longbridge Works. Joseph Lucas Ltd., BSA, Avery's, Lanchester Motors, and New Hudson, despite the loss of varying numbers of employees, continued some form of production. At Cadbury's 1,000 engineers and sundry members of the manufacturing and distributive departments answered the strike call, but a considerable number of workers, perhaps influenced by a Works Council with strong managerial representation, remained at work in the factory which continued as normal. The Dunlop Rubber Company, which was given police protection, and the GEC also stayed open for the time being with a two-thirds complement. Woodworkers were the only strikers at J. B. Brooks & Co., while Kynochs' management claimed only 200 strikers among 3,000 employees and provided free transport for "loyal" workers. A military guard of 90 men was mounted at the latter "to protect arms and explosives" and a similar precaution was demanded at the BSA.[30]

The TUC General Council had apparently intended that the workers themselves should continue the distribution of food and other essentials.

When the government emphatically refused "to enter into partnership with a rival government"[31] the existence of two rival emergency organisations brought in many places an actual if not purposeful assumption of dual control.[32] This showed itself particularly over the issue of permits. On 4 May the Birmingham Trade Union Emergency Committee undertook to issue permits "to trade union labour to load, unload and distribute goods and foodstuffs". A request to carry drainpipes to a contract housing job was refused unless union labour was used. On 5 May permits were issued to transport workers to carry coal to local hospitals. A further bid to win public support through permits was made when one was granted to the firm of Bowen & Son to make safe excavation work at a local girls' school. On the other hand Cadbury's, which had been granted a permit for the transport of cocoa and chocolate, had it withdrawn when it was found that administrative staff there were "blacklegging" in the power house where ETU members had stopped work. On 6 May the Committee decided that all vehicles with permits should also carry notices stating they were moving with union consent and using union labour. The Birmingham Co-operative Society was allowed to use ten men to move 1,000 tons of coal, but permission for the release of cement for the Charles Nelson Co. was withheld for a week. A permit for the removal of 15 cwt. of brass dressing was refused, but the British Soap Company was allowed to move one hundred gross of soap bars to the Public Baths because they were for public use. The anomalous situation in which the Committee was placed over permits culminated on 7 May when a permit was granted for the transport of a theatre company to Manchester, an assumption of the right to grant long-distance permits never intended by the TUC. A deputation to London on 10 May for a ruling on permits reported that transport of food in bulk was a government responsibility and no permits for such should be issued. The same afternoon a telegram from Ernest Bevin instructed all transport workers to strike except Co-operative employees delivering bread and milk to members. On the following day all permits except those to Co-operative Societies were withdrawn.[33] During the period when they were granted, the Trade Union Emergency Committee had in fact taken over the powers of the elected municipal government.[34] This was quickly recognised by the Chief Constable who declared permits illegal.[35] Nevertheless it is significant that many shopkeepers and industrialists needing to transport materials had applied not to the City Emergency Committee but to the Trades Council offices.[36]

If the issue of special permits represented an attempt to win public sympathy, trade union propaganda on the whole was far less effective in 1926 than during the 1919 rail strike. Suppression of the press was perhaps the greatest TUC blunder. The government remained in control of broadcasting and issued its own organ, the *British Gazette.* In Birmingham, the capitalist press continued to appear in some form. Yet the socialist *Daily Herald* and *Town Crier* were the only papers not published, and an excellent opportunity was thus lost of placing the Labour press in the hands of workers previously uninfluenced by it. Moreover, dissemination of the TUC's case was totally inadequate to counter government propaganda. Some 215,000 copies of the *British Worker* were distributed through Birmingham newsagents by T. C. Pearson's circulation committee during the strike.[37] The Emergency Committee's cyclostyled *Birmingham Central Strike Bulletin* and the *Birmingham Railway News*[38] sold as fast as they could be produced. The Communist *Birmingham Worker*, which also published issues in Derby and Wolverhampton, was suppressed after only three editions under the Emergency Powers Act. The total circulation of all these papers was insignificant compared with some 3 million emergency sheets produced by the local press.[39] The *Birmingham Post* was published in duplicated broadsheet form from 5 to 7 May; the *Birmingham Gazette* from 5 to 10 May; the *Birmingham Mail* from 4 to 8 May, and the *Evening Despatch* from 4 to 12 May. After these dates smaller but otherwise normal editions were again issued in print. The self-styled imperialist and anti-socialist monthly, *The Midlander*, also produced a daily bulletin, and distribution of the *British Gazette* was undertaken by the Birmingham Chamber of Commerce at the request of the Civil Commissioner for the Midland Counties. Printed in London, it was brought overnight to Birmingham by private car. Some newsagents called at the Chamber for their supplies, and the remaining papers were distributed by volunteers. On 6 May, the first day of issue, some 35,000 copies were handled. This figure increased to 45,000 copies on subsequent days, and reached 70,000 copies on the final day of the strike.[40] Editions of the Continental *Daily Mail* were also flown into Birmingham from Paris until this source was counteracted by a strike of Paris printers. In the absence of a regular press many individuals throughout the country seized the opportunity to print newsheets of their own consisting partly of wireless news and partly of propaganda, and "the remarkable bulletins published by patriotic persons in London's West End"[41] were paralleled in Birmingham by

The Moseley Village Gazette, produced by Mathias Watts, a prominent member of the Birmingham Business Club.

Members of the Union of Postal Workers were unaffected by the strike although all postal services were hard hit by the paralysis of transport. Packets weighing over 8 oz. were accepted by the Post Office only for local delivery, and the public was asked to use postal, telegraph and telephone services as little as possible.[42] The position of the Post Office was neutral, but union complaints were made concerning the use of AA members in the movement of mails and of civilian motor drivers to blackleg on railwaymen by making long distance journeys. Criticism was also made of delays in the receipt of important telegrams from London by the Trade Union Emergency Committee and of the inefficiency of the telephone service.[43] These things apart, life in Birmingham continued as near to normal as the crisis allowed. There was no shortage of petrol and carefully guarded special petrol trains continued to arrive from Portishead. Appeals were made for economy in the use of food, gas and electricity. Long queues of applicants for coal permits formed at the Town Hall, where by 7 May 20,000 had been issued plus a similar number at the district offices. Coal prices remained fixed at 2*s*. 3*d*. per cwt., since overcharging was a fineable offence. Prices of foodstuffs rose somewhat owing to increased transport costs, although milk trains were still allowed to run by the TUC and in Birmingham the standard rate of 6*d*. per quart was maintained. In the case of other foodstuffs road transport proved an efficient substitute for rail, and there was no shortage of basic necessities.[44] Schools and theatres stayed open. Space in strike bulletins was always devoted to cricket, and play continued in the Worcester Golf Union after competitors had "patriotically offered their services to the Lord Mayor of Birmingham".[45] A more sinister interpretation was placed, however, by trade unionists upon the continuation of a military tattoo at Kings Heath Park for which several thousand troops had encamped on 28 April, and whose stay was subsequently extended from 3 to 10 May. When Colonel F. G. Danielson later claimed that the tattoo had "maintained a peaceful atmosphere during the . . . strike by concentrating a large reserve of troops in the district", many felt that their suspicions were well-founded.[46]

Although Julian Symons lists Birmingham among the cities where "there were more or less serious riots",[47] outbreaks of violence were rare and much less serious than incidents during the 1911 rail strike, when pitched battles were fought between police and strikers, and railway stations guarded by a heavily armed battalion of Munster Fusiliers.[48] Speakers were warned to orate with moderation and strikers recommended to relax in the countryside and public parks. In the latter the Divisional Labour parties organised concerts and entertainments as well as public meetings since, as Oswald Mosley remarked, "The General Strike was in danger of collapsing through sheer boredom. . . ."[49] Demonstrations were only allowed if authorised by the Trade Union Emergency Committee,[49] which the police admitted "wanted to do all in its power to keep order".[50] Most of the trouble that erupted was closely inter-related with transport and picketing.[51] On 5 May, for example, strong contingents of Staffordshire and Birmingham police with reinforcements of special constabulary released seven Midland Red buses from Bearwood Garage in an attempt to run a skeleton service between Quinton and Birmingham. The buses were immobilised, however, by strikers in Broad Street, who deflated their tyres.[52]

In the first cases tried under the Emergency Powers Act a tram driver was fined £5 for impeding a West Bromwich Corporation bus driven by a volunteer; five men were also fined for obstructing vehicles in Spring Hill and two railway pickets convicted for stopping a horse and dray from leaving Lawley Street Goods Station.[53] While blackleg vehicles provoked violence there were also instances of deliberate damage to cars bearing the "TUC Transport" label. One had its petrol tube cut, and a second was attacked by Fascists.[54] Other fines imposed on strikers were for intimidation, damage to tramcars and "speeches likely to cause disaffection". Members of the Communist Party were suppressed with particular rigour. J. Trotter, a Trades Council delegate, was given three months hard labour for a Bull Ring speech, while for publishing a statement in the *Birmingham Worker* that troops at Aldershot and naval ratings in London had refused to obey orders James Gardner, Secretary of the Birmingham Communist Party, was fined £10, and Thomas Lowe, Margaret Clarke, Thomas Gee and John Hesketh £5 each.[55] On the other hand, complaints of police provocation were made to the TUC and Lord Mayor by the Trade Union Emergency Committee, and the Chief Constable was asked to withdraw one of his officers from any scene of action since he had been inciting trouble.[56] That Birmingham witnessed no scenes parallel to those in Poplar, for example,[57] was perhaps in part due to the mediatory action of her churches. Digbeth Institute and various church halls were offered to strikers for recreational purposes and compromise settlements were recommended from numerous Anglican and Nonconformist pulpits. At a special intercessionary service at Birmingham Parish Church on 9 May, conducted by Canon Guy Rogers and attended by the Mayor, Town Clerk and a number of Corporation members, an inter-denominational resolution from 150 Birmingham clergymen was read suggesting a basis for a settlement, and later taken by a deputation to the Trade Union Emergency Committee.[58]

Although it has been claimed that nationally the strike was reaching its peak when called off on 12 May by the TUC, in Birmingham that peak appears to have been reached much earlier. On 8 May the Welsh MP, Morgan Jones, and Mrs. Adamson, wife of the member for Cannock, were sent by the TUC as special speakers to help stiffen morale.[59] On Sunday, 9 May, enthusiasm was still high enough to attract some 5,000 strikers to a Calthorpe Park rally which Jones and Mrs. Adamson addressed together with Oswald Mosley, Labour Councillor Percy Shurmer, the Rev. J. Lewis of Broad Street Presbyterian Church, and local trade union leaders.[60] Some signs of disintegration were, however, already visible. On 8 May an order to return to work by the executive of the Central Ironmoulders had had to be nullified by the Trade Union Emergency Committee.[61] At 6 a.m. the same day a strong force of police had escorted a body of volunteers to Tennant Street Garage, where the pickets who had been on duty since midnight on 3 May were cleared under the supervision of the Chief Constable. The buses had been placed in positions which made them difficult to move, but a regular four-minute service was resumed.[62] This raised "public morale" but damaged that of the strikers. On 9 May J. E. Corrin reported to the Trade Union Emergency Committee that the previous evening the transport workers' representatives had voted by 18–7 to return to work. It was also reported that while the Sheet Metal Workers and the ETU were still "solid" other workers were wavering. A deputation from Cadbury's stated that in the Manufacturing and Distributive Departments members of the Workers' Union, and of the Shop Assistants, Warehousemen and Clerks had agreed to return to work on 10 May. Rumours of other departments re-starting coupled with the influence of departmental chiefs were said to have been decisive factors.[63] Corporation tram and bus inspectors also agreed to return on 10 May when more transport services were restored.[64] Pickets were removed from Dawlish Road Tramway Depot and a regular service recommenced between Selly Oak and the City. Elsewhere services resumed to Moseley Village, The King's Head, Hagley Road, Yardley

Wood and Handsworth Wood, predominantly residential suburbs where least opposition would be expected and from whence criticism of the Tramways Committee had been strongest. Drivers were mainly "regulars" and the conductors volunteers.[65] Police rode on the tramcars but no interference was reported. Only at Washwood Heath was the depot opened in face of opposition and three people appeared before the Birmingham Stipendiary as a result.[66]

Sensing the turn of the tide, the Tramways Committee, after a special meeting on 10 May, issued a postal ultimatum to their employees. Unless they resumed work by midday on 12 May they would be "deemed to have left the service" and must return their uniforms forthwith.[67] Other employers were quick to follow this lead, sending letters to strikers containing a mixture of cajolery and threats and accompanied usually by a copy of a government-issued guarantee of superannuation, pensions and other benefits. The action of the Tramways Committee and the ability of the Corporation to run an increasing number of trams and buses seems to have been decisive. Transport workers returned in increasing numbers and by noon on 11 May it was announced that vehicles were running on practically all routes and that with the exception of a hard core at the Washwood Heath and Coventry Road depots all tramway workers had returned to duty. The return of a number of Midland Red busmen on 12 May enabled resumption of services to Langley, Quinton, Sutton Coldfield, Redditch and Walsall. The city transport strike in Birmingham had therefore collapsed before the General Strike was officially terminated. "When we were in Birmingham [Tuesday, 11 May]", reported W. A. Robson, J. Wedgwood and Kingsley Martin to the TUC, "both corporation buses and trams . . . were running". Next day the Trade Union Emergency Committee admitted that "many of the men have reported back for duty and . . . the tramway service has been restarted on a fairly extensive scale. . . ."[68]

Confusion among the strikers intensified on the afternoon of 10 May with the arrest of the entire Birmingham Trade Union Emergency Committee as a result of a statement in the *Birmingham Central Strike Bulletin* that the government had been defeated in Parliament on a motion concerning the Emergency Powers Act. This erroneous information had been received in Birmingham by the Railway Joint Strike Committee from NUR headquarters at Coventry where it had been copied from a London bulletin, *The Cricklewood Workers' Gazette*. A motion had in fact been brought forward, but the voting figures had been transposed. Consequently police raided the Trades Council and Borough Labour Party offices. Typewriters, duplicating machines and a printing press were confiscated, and all committee members, together with Allan Young, John Strachey, and L. Plummer, who were responsible for actual production of the *Bulletin*, were arrested. Street sellers of the *Bulletin* were also taken into custody and Oswald Mosley alone avoided arrest. Whether the authorities deliberately took advantage of the Emergency Committee's blunder to attempt to destroy the Birmingham strike leadership is not known, but there is other evidence in the closing days of the strike of a hardening in the Government's attitude, noticeably an increasing number of arrests of pickets and strike leaders and more widespread use of the Emergency Regulations.[69] A deputy Emergency Committee was immediately appointed to take control if the trial resulted in imprisonment,[70] but the action was unnecessary since on May 12th the strike was called off.[71]

In a belated attempt to counter the collapse of the transport strike the Birmingham trade unions attempted to cut off electric power. The TUC had already instructed its second "wave", including the engineering and shipbuilding trades and ETU power workers, to strike on 12 May, but in Birmingham it was seemingly too late. On the morning of 11 May Birmingham trade union spokesmen at strike headquarters stressed to visiting TUC delegates that Birmingham was still "astonishingly solid" and "that there was hardly any drifting back", but in the afternoon some doubts were expressed. Next day the key industries were still claimed to be standing firm and the equalisation of strike pay for unions unable to pay according to rule was urged upon the General Council.[72] Even so in the larger factories, where trade unionism had its strongest hold, the disposition to return to work was increasing. Engineers returned to the GEC works and Fort Dunlop re-opened on 10 May. At Bournville where by 11 May many strikers had also returned and other workers, especially girls, had refused to strike, George Cadbury, junior, informed the TUC delegates that he believed the strike "would generally peter out in this way".[73] About 1,700 engineers struck on the morning of 12 May but, despite the claims of Oswald Mosley that in Birmingham power workers responded better than elsewhere to the strike call, on the last day[74] there is no evidence that the TUC edict had any marked effect. The Corporation had already claimed on 8 May to have sufficient skilled volunteers to maintain all essential services including gas and electricity. There was strong feeling in the ETU against coming out, partly because the men were under contract to give seven days' notice and feared the penalties.[75] Notices issued by the Corporation Gas and Electricity Committee warned that the jobs of strikers would be permanently filled. The strike of power workers was crucial. Only by cutting off power could the failing tramway strike be made effective and greater pressure be brought to bear upon industries using electricity. Yet the Trade Union Emergency Committee was "unable to secure anything like a complete withdrawal of labour". Dale End electricians refused to strike, while at Summer Lane Power Station a meeting of ETU members only agreed to strike by 64 votes to 50 after a long and angry discussion.[76] At Coventry members of the ETU and Workers' Union employed by the Electricity Department struck and were replaced by volunteers. In Birmingham the strike did not materialise. ETU members already out and assembling to picket the Dale End, Nechells and Summer Lane Power Stations in the evening, were greeted with the news that the strike had been ended by the TUC. The emergency staff at the Town Hall were demobilised on the night of 15 May, and by 18 May industrial conditions were "almost normal".[77] The railways, where the strike continued for a further three days, took longer to recover because of the continued stoppage in the coal industry.

At first Birmingham trade unionists claimed a workers' victory. A "Victory Bulletin" was issued by the Trade Union Emergency Committee, and in a celebration demonstration at Summerfield Park on 16 May Mosley pronounced "they had whipped the government".[78] Only slowly did it dawn that no guarantees concerning reinstatement had been secured. Most Birmingham employers emulated their MPs Neville Chamberlain and Sir Arthur Steele-Maitland, who in the Cabinet had consistently supported a policy of demanding the unconditional surrender of the strikers.[79] An exception was Joseph Lucas Ltd., where a message of goodwill from the management was read to 500 returning brassworkers and engineers. The workers were paid for the time occupied by the meeting, and the proceedings closed with cheers for the management. Elsewhere, however, it was "the turn of the employers to strike". The dispute had disorganised all trades. Coal stocks were low and local unemployment figures substantially swollen. In such conditions employers were able to enforce their own terms.

Many concerns insisted that men should return on minimum rates, losing up to 5*s*. a week.[80] Avery's and Tangyes dismissed strikers who had not reported back, and accepted only individual applications for resumption.[81] The Engineering and Allied Employers' Federation refused to give the engineering unions any assurances upon re-engagement,[82] while railwaymen were informed that they could return only in order of seniority and grade and upon the understanding that they were not relieved of the consequences of their breach of contract. Those refusing to return except upon the old terms were locked out of Curzon Street and Lawley Street Goods Stations.[83] At the Dunlop Rubber Company, where trade unionism had been struggling with a managerially-dominated Factory Council since 1925, strikers were only reinstated on the "open shop" principle. The Midland Red Omnibus Company endeavoured to promote a form of company unionism,[84] and in the building trades and at the BSA, Austin Motor Company, Lanchester Motors, Metropolitan Wagon Company, Guest, Keen and Nettlefold, the Birmingham Wagon Company and the GEC, strikers were found work only as conditions allowed and the companies required them.[85] Nothing but a wave of rank-and-file resistance avoided complete disaster. The printers and compositors, like the vehicle builders at Kyotts Lake Tramway Works, refused to return except on an "All in" or "All out" basis. The Tramways Department which refused to recognise the T & GWU was confronted with a deputation from the Emergency Committee which threatened guerrilla warfare unless the Corporation acted honourably.[86]

Inevitably strike leaders and trade union officials came under severe pressure. The Trade Union Emergency Committee pledged its support to victimised trade unionists, but the result of its members' trial on 14 May for creating disaffection served only to imperil their own future. In proceedings seemingly pressed against the recommendations of the Home Secretary,[87] eighteen of the twenty arrested were found guilty, ten being fined £10 and the rest bound over. Afterwards H. Ayres of the NUR found his job in jeopardy and F. W. Rudland, secretary of the Trades Council and Labour Party, was removed from the magisterial bench.[88] G. F. Sawyer, "Birmingham's George Lansbury", a railwayman, Labour councillor for Nechells and Duddeston, Poor Law Guardian and member of the Watch Committee, was arrested for describing special constables as traitors. Although the charge was dismissed he was prevented from resuming work for a week after his fellow workers.[89] More serious were the cases of Councillor Percy Shurmer, a Post Office engineer, and Miss Clarke, a teacher at Bournville Day Continuation School. Shurmer was dismissed after a £10 fine for inflammatory speeches. Miss Clarke, fined for her part in the publication of the Communist *Birmingham Worker*, was subsequently discharged by Birmingham Education Committee.[90]

Continuation of the coal stoppage until 26 November seriously affected employment in Birmingham industries. The *Ministry of Labour Gazette* showed an increase of 20,725 unemployed and 16,058 working short-time between the weeks ending 26 April and 17 May alone. More severe, however, was the long-term damage to the morale, membership and finances of the Birmingham trade union movement. The total expenditure of the local authority upon emergency organisation amounted to £1,170, of which half was paid by the government.[91] In contrast, the Birmingham Co-operative Society cashed cheques or IOUs worth £28,000 for some thirty-six trade union branches during the strike, leaving them on the verge of bankruptcy.[92] When the Trade Disputes and Trade Union Act followed, the first consequence was the compulsory disaffiliation of seven branches of the Union of Postal Workers and three branches of the Post Office Engineering Union from the Trades Council, with a loss of £70 per annum in fees for the latter.[93] By 1929–30 affiliation fees to the Trades Council, which had been £470 before the strike, had fallen by £120.[94] The call-off of the strike, moreover, crushed the upsurge of class consciousness which had briefly defied Birmingham's old Victorian social philosophy. It also resurrected the temporarily-submerged conflict between right and left within the Trades Council and Borough Labour Party. The result in both organisations was a purge by moderate and orthodox Labour of its more extreme and militant elements. Not surprisingly, such strikes as took place in Birmingham between 1927 and 1936 were unofficial.[95] Disillusioned by trade union weakness, by sectarian strife and by economic circumstances many Birmingham workers returned to their original state of apathy. In 1934 less than half of them were members of a trade union and as late as 1937 the organisers of a Birmingham Trade Union Recruitment Campaign could still report that the fears and humiliations of May 1926 were unforgotten.[96] Until the trade union revival of the late 'thirties Birmingham was notorious not only for its non-unionism, but also as a centre of sweated industry in the light engineering trades and an ideal centre for the introduction of the notorious Bedaux System of time-and-motion study.

The strike, however, had also affected political beliefs and shown the folly of a working-class electorate supporting so wholeheartedly the Unionist Party of its employers. Three weeks after the strike at a municipal by-election in the Ladywood Ward, regarded as a Labour weak spot in the Ladywood Division, C. Augur, a railwayman and strike leader, secured an 1,146 majority over a Unionist opponent. A month later Neville Chamberlain significantly announced that owing to pressure of work he would be contesting in the next general election not Ladywood, but the Unionist stronghold of Edgbaston. His departure was justified in September, when in another municipal by-election in the Ladywood Division at Rotton Park Ward a Unionist majority of 1,294 was converted into a Labour majority of 1,002.[97] The November municipal elections brought eight further Labour gains and all seats defended were held. Three of the newly-elected councillors—Corrin, Lewis, and Mann—had been members of the Trade Union Emergency Committee. A fourth member of the Committee, A. E. Ager, was later elected at a by-election at Small Heath. The year culminated with a Parliamentary by-election at Smethwick in which Oswald Mosley increased a Labour majority of 1,253 in 1924 to 6,582.[98] By 1928 Labour representation on the City Council had increased from 19 to 36 seats. The high-water mark of the Birmingham socialist advance was reached in the hard-fought general election of 1929 when the Birmingham contests provided the best results for the Labour Party in the country. Labour gained six of the twelve seats and polled approximately 42 per cent of the votes cast. Kings Norton reverted to Unionism by a majority of 491, but at Erdington Sir Arthur Steele-Maitland was beaten by 113 votes. Sir Austen Chamberlain held West Birmingham by the slender margin of 43 and at Aston, Deritend, Duddeston and Yardley former Unionist majorities were converted to substantial Labour ones. Neville Chamberlain's worst fears were justified at Ladywood, which succumbed to the Labour Party by 11 votes. The press was quick to comment upon this change in the balance of political power. "In Birmingham the Labour Party has at last achieved the breach in the old Unionist tradition . . . for which it has worked unremittingly and in face of heavy discouragement for years . . .", admitted the *Birmingham Mail.*[99] "Birmingham's desertion to the enemy", commented one South African journal, more sensationally, "is a real portent in the political heavens."

The triumph was short-lived. The world economic crisis and the defection of MacDonald paved the way for the panic election of 1931. Birmingham again became solidly Unionist and remained so until the Labour landslide of 1945. But the precedent had been created. In its political reaction to the General Strike the city had reverted, if only briefly, towards its former role as a centre of radicalism.

NOTES

1. See T. R. Tholfsen, "The Artisan and the Culture of Early Victorian Birmingham" in the *University of Birmingham Historical Journal*, vol. 4, no. 2, 1954. Also R. P. Hastings, *The Labour Movement in Birmingham, 1927–1945*. (Unpub. Birmingham University M.A. thesis, 1959.) Chapters 1–2.
2. *Town Crier*, 17 July 1925.
3. Eldred Hallas had been returned unopposed as a Coalition Labour candidate at Duddeston in 1918.
4. Sir Austen Chamberlain (West Birmingham), Foreign Secretary; Neville Chamberlain (Ladywood), Minister of Health; Sir Arthur Steele-Maitland (Erdington), Minister of Labour; L. C. M. S. Amery (Sparkbrook), Secretary of State for the Colonies.
5. See *Birmingham Gazette*, 22 January 1932. A. R. Jephcott, for example, a member of the AEU, and a former president of Birmingham Trades Council was Unionist MP for Yardley Division from 1918–29.
6. John Strachey in *The Socialist Review*, June 1926.
7. *Town Crier*, 17 July 1925.
8. Proceedings of the City Council, 5 January 1926. *Town Crier*, 8 January, 5 February 1926. Bibliographical details are available in Cornish's *Birmingham Year Books*, *The Stock Exchange Year Book*, the *Directory of Directors*, and *Kelly's Directory of Birmingham.*
9. *Town Crier*, 14 May 1926.
10. Gregory had already quarrelled with the strong pacifist element in Birmingham Trades Council over conscription in 1916. See J. Corbett, *The Birmingham Trades Council, 1866–1966* (Lawrence & Wishart), pp. 112–13.
11. See public statement by Bower in *Town Crier*, 4 June 1926. He was expelled from the Labour Party in April 1932. Bower incurred the wrath of the more obdurate employers for his protests against police interference with pickets. He won the odium of some trade unionists for the use of volunteers in the transport and social services.
12. *Birmingham Post*, 4 May 1926. Notes of Birmingham Retail Coal Prices Committee, Fuel Control Leaflets issued during the strike, and correspondence relating to emergency organisation. BRL 520446.
13. Booth in an address on "The Objects and Aims of O.M.S." given to the Birmingham Business Club, April 1926. See *The Businessman*, May 1926.
14. *Birmingham Evening Despatch*, 1 May 1926.
15. See miscellaneous posters and literature issued in Birmingham relating to the General Strike. BRL 331861, fol. 1926.

16. *Birmingham Post*, 3, 4, 8, 10–14 May 1926. *Birmingham Gazette*, 12 May 1926. *Town Crier*, 9 October 1925, 11, 18 June 1926. *The Midlander*, 1 June 1926. *Austin Advocate*, June 1926. Proceedings of the City Council, 27 July 1926. PRO. CAB. 27/331. Home Office Situation Report, 8–10 May 1926. I am indebted to Dr. G. Barnsby for his kind assistance with this source and also with the TUC records.
17. *Town Crier*, 17 July, 31 July 1925.
18. See Minutes of Birmingham Trade Union Emergency Committee, 3–18 May 1926. *Town Crier*, 14 May 1926. Biographical details are from the *Birmingham Post Year Books* and the columns of the *Town Crier*.
19. See R. P. Hastings, op. cit., chapters 4 and 6.
20. Obituary in *Birmingham Journal*, October 1954. *Town Crier*, 31 October 1919.
21. J. Corbett, op. cit., pp. 112–13.
22. Margaret Morris, *The British General Strike, 1926* (Historical Association, 1973), p. 5.
23. *Birmingham Mail*, 3 May 1926. *Birmingham Post*, 4 May 1926.
24. *Birmingham Gazette*, 4 May 1926. *Birmingham Post*, 4 May 1926.
25. *Birmingham Gazette*, 3 May 1926. *Birmingham Post*, 8 May 1926. The *Midlander Daily Bulletin*, 5 May 1926. Minutes of Birmingham Trade Union Emergency Committee, 7 May 1926.
26. *Birmingham Post*, 10, 11, 22 May 1926.
27. TUC Records. General Strike in Birmingham, HD 5366, District Report, 5 May 1926. Minutes of Birmingham Trade Union Emergency Committee, 5 May 1926.
28. Ibid., 5–6 May 1926. PRO. CAB. 27/331. Ministry of Labour Bulletin, 4 May 1926.
29. *Birmingham Gazette*, 10 May 1926.
30. *Birmingham Post*, 8 May 1926. PRO. CAB. 27/331. Home Office Situation Reports, nos. 4, 7, 5 May 1926, 8 May 1926.
31. Winston Churchill, *Hansard*, 3 May 1926, col. 123.
32. For a discussion of this problem in Newcastle-upon-Tyne where it has been suggested that the government representative offered the Strike committee a share in the maintenance of food supplies, see A. Mason, *The General Strike in the North-East* (University of Hull Publications, 1970), pp. 55–65 and J. Symons, *The General Strike* (Cresset Press, 1957), pp. 124–32.
33. In return for its preferential treatment the Birmingham Co-operative Society granted credit for strike pay to the unions. Co-op charabancs transported pickets, and union messengers travelled on BCS vehicles. Nevertheless, its own business virtually came to a standstill for ten days. See T. Smith, *Seventy Years of Service: Story of the Birmingham Co-operative Society Ltd., 1881–1951* (1951).
34. Minutes of Birmingham Trade Union Emergency Committee, 5–10 May

1926. PRO. CAB. 27/331. Ministry of Labour Bulletin, 4 May 1926. Permits in Birmingham are also discussed by J. Symons, op. cit., p. 139 and W. H. Crook, *The General Strike* (1931), pp. 404–6.

35. *Birmingham Post*, 10 May 1926.
36. J. Corbett, op. cit., p. 126.
37. Ibid.
38. Railway strike bulletins were published in several towns where railway trade union branches were strong. See E. Wilkinson, R. Postgate, J. F. Horrabin, *A Workers' History of the Great Strike* (1927), p. 65.
39. *Town Crier*, 14 May 1926. PRO. CAB. 27/331. Home Office Situation Report, no. 7, 8 May 1926. The *Birmingham Worker* sold 2,000 copies of its second issue. See PRO. CAB. 27/331. Home Office Situation Report, 6 May 1926.
40. Report of the General Purposes Committee of Birmingham Chamber of Commerce. May–June 1926.
41. Kingsley Martin, *The British Public and the General Strike (1926)*, pp. 66–7.
42. Regulations issued by the Birmingham Postmaster General. *Birmingham Post*, 4 May 1926.
43. *Birmingham Gazette*, 11 May 1926. Minutes of Birmingham Trade Union Emergency Committee, 11 May 1926.
44. *Midlander Daily Bulletin*, 6 May 1926. *Birmingham Post*, 8 May 1926. PRO. CAB. 27/331. Home Office Situation Report, no. 5, 6 May 1926. Board of Trade Petroleum Bulletin, 10 May 1926.
45. *Midlander Daily Bulletin*, 6 May 1926. *Birmingham Post*, 8 May 1926. *Birmingham Mail*, 15 May 1926.
46. *Town Crier*, 23 July 1926.
47. J. Symons, op. cit., p. 102.
48. *Birmingham Post*, 18–21 August 1911.
49. Oswald Mosley, *My Life* (Nelson, 1968), p. 192. Minutes of Birmingham Trade Union Emergency Committee, 2 May 1926.
50. *Town Crier*, 21 May 1926.
51. See A. Mason, op. cit., pp. 65 et seq.
52. *Birmingham Gazette Bulletin*, 6 May 1926. *Town Crier*, 28 May 1926.
53. *Birmingham Post*, 8 May 1926.
54. *Town Crier*, 21 May 1926.
55. *Town Crier*, 28 May 1926.
56. Minutes of Trade Union Emergency Committee, 9 May 1926.
57. See W. A. Hutt, *The Post-War History of the British Working Class* (Gollancz, 1937), pp. 161–2.
58. Minutes of Trade Union Emergency Committee, 10 May 1926.
59. Minutes of Trade Union Emergency Committee, 8 May 1926.
60. *Birmingham Post*, 10 May 1926.

61. Minutes of Birmingham Trade Union Emergency Committee, 8 May 1926.
62. *Birmingham Post*, 10 May 1926.
63. Minutes of Birmingham Trade Union Emergency Committee, 9 May 1926.
64. *Midlander Daily Bulletin*, 10 May 1926.
65. It is interesting to speculate as to what proportion of the "regular" drivers were in fact inspectors.
66. *Birmingham Gazette*, 12 May 1926. TUC Records: General Strike in Birmingham, HD 5366. District Report, 11 May 1926.
67. *Birmingham Post*, 11 May 1926.
68. *Birmingham Post*, 13 May 1926. TUC Records: General Strike in Birmingham, HD 5366. District Reports, 11, 12 May 1926.
69. See A. Mason, op. cit., pp. 74–5.
70. J. Corbett, op. cit., p. 128.
71. Minutes of Birmingham Trade Union Emergency Committee, 11 May 1926. *Birmingham Post*, 12 May 1926. *Town Crier*, 21 May 1926.
72. TUC Records: General Strike in Birmingham, HD 5366. District Reports, 11, 12 May 1926.
73. Ibid., 11 May 1926. PRO. CAB. 27/331. Home Office Situation Report, no. 9, 10 May 1926.
74. *Town Crier*, 4 June 1926.
75. PRO. CAB. 27/331. Home Office Situation Report, no. 7, 8 May 1926. TUC Records: General Strike in Birmingham, HD 5366. District Report, 11 May 1926.
76. *Birmingham Post*, 12 May 1926. TUC Records: General Strike in Birmingham, HD 5366. District Reports, 11 and 12 May 1926.
77. *Birmingham Post*, 17–18 May 1926.
78. *Town Crier*, 4 June 1926.
79. J. Symons, op. cit., pp. 114, 183, 187–8.
80. *Birmingham Gazette*, 14, 20 May 1926.
81. Minutes of Birmingham Trade Union Emergency Committee, 13 May 1926.
82. *Birmingham Post*, 14 May 1926.
83. *Birmingham Post*, 14 May 1926. *Birmingham Evening Despatch*, 13 May 1926.
84. *Birmingham Post*, 14 May 1926.
85. Ibid.
86. Minutes of Trade Union Emergency Committee, 13 May 1926.
87. See *Hansard*, 2 June 1926.
88. *Town Crier*, 21 May 1926. Minutes of Birmingham Trade Union Emergency Committee, 14, 17, 18 May 1926. *Town Crier*, 16 November 1928.
89. *Town Crier*, 31 May 1926.

90. *Town Crier*, 9, 23 July 1926.
91. Proceedings of the City Council, 27 July 1926.
92. *Town Crier*, 11 June 1926.
93. Annual Report of Birmingham Trades Council, 1927–8.
94. Ibid., 1926–30.
95. R. P. Hastings, op. cit., chapters 4 and 6.
96. *Town Crier*, 26 February 1937.
97. *Town Crier*, 3 September 1926.
98. *Town Crier*, 24 December 1926.
99. *Birmingham Mail*, 31 May 1929.

7 SOUTH WALES

by HYWEL FRANCIS

Do you remember 1926? The great dream and the swift disaster,
The fanatic and the traitor, and more than all,
The bravery of the simple, faithful folk?

(Idris Davies, *Gwalia Deserta* VIII, London, 1938)

The . . . jazz bands . . . were formed to take our minds off the real struggle. . . . They were all dressed as Harem ladies, veils on their faces and the beads, etc. . . . We had slaves in front . . . and behind them was a slave driver with a whip. . . .

(South Wales Miners' Library, interview with Reg Fine (Mardy), 2 July 1973)

. . . the political understanding of the workers in this country was nowhere near as high as their class consciousness and (they) saw therefore the opportunity of the strike as being a reflection of their class ideas. But when it came to the prosecution of the strike, now that became a political matter . . . and their leadership was absolutely floundering. The biggest error in the 1926 strike . . . was that we had not concentrated on the education of our members politically.

(SWML, interview with D. D. Evans (Ystradgynlais), 5 December 1972)

Once you sit back and organise concerts and jazz bands and just wait for something to happen then you are going to be defeated. There was a realisation within our movement that immediately there was a strike (because we all knew there was going to be a strike in 1972) we must go on the offensive, we must attack. . . . It was almost a military campaign that we undertook.

(SWML, interview with Emlyn Williams, then Vice-President of the South Wales Area of the National Union of Mineworkers, 3 February 1973)

Within the confines of the mining valleys of South Wales, the General Strike was even something of a non-event. For indeed the Emergency Powers Regulations and the Organisation for the Maintenance of Supplies (both weapons to be used to bolster central government in the event of such an industrial crisis) were hardly invoked in the valleys during the Nine Days. It was as if the authorities stood to one side and seemed temporarily to allow the mining communities to carry on much as they wished. The valleys were so overwhelmingly dominated by the miners and their families, in numbers and political influence, that to contemplate not joining the strike would have been to commit social suicide. When, for instance, it was rumoured that a militant railwayman was about to be arrested at the start of the strike, the Aberdare Central Strike Committee merely passed a vote of confidence in him: he was not arrested until after the strike was called off.[1]

Indeed it was not a question of *dual power* but almost one of transference of power in some valleys. If Bedlinog or Mardy were typical, then the strikers virtually ran their villages unchallenged for the Nine Days.

This was not the case in the large coal-exporting ports to the south of the coalfield. The more "revolutionary" and broader based Councils of Action of the Valleys gave way to the TUC-style Central Strike Committees at Newport,[2] Cardiff, Penarth, Barry and Swansea, based on their respective trades councils. The miners having hardly any presence at all in such towns, the nature of the stoppage was fundamentally different. It was a question of loyalty to the TUC's call, even though there was considerable sympathy for the miners, particularly amongst workers closely associated with the coal trade such as railwaymen, dockers and coaltrimmers.[3]

The authorities were also more seriously concerned about transport and communications to and from the ports: so much so that troops and a naval presence were thought to be necessary. The HMS *Simoon*, HMS *Tetrarch*, HMS *Caledon* and HMS *Cleopatra* (along with a submarine at Cardiff) were seen as vital to free the ports from the stranglehold of the Strike Committees.[4] Yet the Strike Committees were either unaware of their visitors or had not fully appreciated their role, for there was hardly a voice raised in opposition. Indeed, the miners to the north were almost certainly unaware of the situation, for they would have been more than vocal in their protests.[5]

When the Cabinet set up its Supply and Transport Committee, the movement of food and the control of major communications in the regions were judged to be of paramount importance. The Civil Commissioners and the Food Controllers must have realised that if they failed to move supplies then power would slip from their grasp and into the hands of the Strike Committees and Councils of Action. Despite the claims of the authorities that a skeleton service did exist on the Great Western Railway with only 81 per cent on strike, most of the 19 per cent at work were clerks.[6] The reality was that normal road and rail services throughout industrial South Wales were paralysed.[7] The situation was only relieved by "volunteer" and "free" labour which kept a constant flow of food supplies throughout most of the district from the early days until they began to be challenged by the permit systems of the strikers' organisations during the second week.[8]

The strike in the South Wales ports was more akin to the Home Counties than to the coalfields. In Cardiff and to a lesser extent, Swansea and Newport, there was a substantial "loyal" middle class, eager for the jape of playing at being workers or enlisting as special constables. During the Nine Days, bitter clashes occurred in Cardiff and Swansea (and surprisingly at Pontypridd, which had some of the features of both societies). But there was no open warfare in the valleys where the miniscule middle class either identified itself totally with the miners' cause or kept a discreet silence for fear of the "tumbrils".[9]

The defiant standard-bearer of the South Wales industrial middle class and mouthpiece of the coal-owners was the *Western Mail* which achieved the impossible in publishing an eight-page daily throughout the strike,[10] although much of its sales were restricted to queuing Londoners who paid 6*d*. per copy for it.[11] Without any intended irony and seemingly without any awareness of the great national issues involved at the time, the *Western Mail* told its readers of the trivial yet revealing occurrence where "a prominent Cardiff man spent Monday morning taking joy rides between St. Mary Street and the Pier Head in order to show his appreciation of the volunteer workers. He has not yet counted up his expenses."[12]

Such was the scene in 1926 in the largest coal-exporting port in the world, which had grown fat on the unbridled exploitation of the miners inhabiting the valleys to the north and who were now once again challenging their Cardiff "yoke". This uneasy relationship between Cardiff and the Valleys often focused itself upon the antipathy shown by the miners towards the *Western Mail*. *The Rhondda Workers' News Service* on 6 May notified its readers that "Britain is firm but not the Britain referred to in the *Western Mail*".[13]

The significance of Cardiff as the financial, industrial and geographical focal point of the region was not lost on the authorities. The Civil Commissioner for South Wales, the Earl of Clarendon, was provided with temporary accommodation at the Department of Health. The early arrival of troops and naval ratings indicated this awareness. A battalion was stationed on the outskirts of the city and, although it was never used, it made its presence clearly felt by "marching through the streets daily for exercise".[14] There seemed a determination from the outset on the part of the government to make some challenge to the strike in Cardiff (and to a lesser extent at Newport and Swansea). A Home Office Report on the first day of the strike in Cardiff neatly crystallised what appeared to be a calculated provocation: "All continues quiet. It is hoped to run the Corporation buses in Cardiff tomorrow. A submarine arrived in Cardiff today and a cruiser is expected tomorrow. Several potato boats are to be unloaded by non-union labour: adequate protection has been arranged."

The preparations were indeed justified. Communications were paralysed. It was reported that 41 cans of cream and 17 boxes of fish were on hand in Cardiff on 4 May, but the Food Controller was unable to distribute them. The cream was sold locally and the fish was placed in cold storage.[15] On the second day (5 May) two hundred specials were enrolled in Cardiff, the cruiser HMS *Cleopatra* arrived and coincidentally three potato boats were unloaded with police protection, privately run transport increased and "volunteer labour" manned the buses.[16] The following day, under *Cleopatra*'s watchful eye, foodstuffs were freely distributed, three more potato boats arrived, 40 tons of fish left Cardiff by road and 31 wagons of foodstuffs were moved again by road, to Neath and Swansea.[17]

But this challenge did not go unanswered. The initial euphoria amongst trade unionists was giving way to what was interpreted by some as a "gloomy and sulky" attitude in certain South Wales districts.[18] The Cardiff Central Strike Committee pleaded with the TUC to rebut all the "untrue statements by the BBC" that Cardiff docks was "in full swing".[19] Then, between 3 p.m. and 5 p.m. on 6 May, a solicitor tried to man a tram but was held up in Queen Street by angry trade unionists including striking tramway workers. A baton charge ensued and one girl was injured. The crowd eventually dispersed with the help of additional foot and mounted police.[20]

Further conflict occurred the following day when six regular tramwaymen and more "volunteers" attempted to provide a transport "service". The Civil Commissioner was pleased to report that the mounted police were very effective in clearing the streets, that two hundred specials of "the good type" were sworn in and that an attempt by strikers to stop a bus in St. John's Street had failed. Two were arrested and six injured.[21] Ultimately, four men and one woman were gaoled in Cardiff under the Emergency Powers Regulations for offences committed during the disturbances.[22]

But as if to emphasise the unreal and confusing predicament in which some found themselves, on the very afternoon of the last serious transport disturbance in Cardiff (7 May), the tramway workers played the railwaymen at football at Roath Park, in another part of the city.[23]

By 10 May the *British Gazette* was claiming that the main streets were being patrolled by foot police "but there had been *no serious hostile demonstrations*". The city, it further claimed, was being provided with an almost normal tramway service. But the service was being manned by a glut of "volunteers" and the tramwaymen were solidly defiant in refusing to return their uniforms, nor were they prepared to collect their wages.[24]

The difficulties for the Central Strike Committee were compounded not only by the problems of watching over the wide range of trades in the city but also by the unsympathetic insistence of the City Council in providing a transport service at all costs.[25] The Council must have been encouraged by the Conservative member for Cardiff South, Captain Arthur Evans, who assured the House of Commons that "public opinion" in South Wales was behind the government and that the NUR members at Cardiff docks had no sympathy with the strike. As far as the Strike Committee was concerned, Captain Evans was speaking only for the "members of the Baltic Exchange at Cardiff Docks".[26]

Despite all the attempts at breaking the strike in Cardiff and despite all the reports from 10 May onwards that there was an early return to work, the Cardiff labour movement remained loyal to the TUC until the strike was called off. On the Wednesday evening of 12 May, a big demonstration at Cathays Park was clearly hostile towards the strike settlement, particularly the contingents of tramwayworkers and railwaymen. The tramwaymen indeed refused to return unless they were all reinstated (the City Council was refusing to discharge those taken on in the strike), while dockers and some other unions were prepared to support them. The demonstration agreed not to sign on until all members had consulted their branch secretaries. By the late evening of 13 May there had only been a negligible return, with the men insisting on going back on their own terms. The Cardiff Chief Constable was forced to swear in 150 more specials because the employers were worsening the situation by demanding "unconditional surrender". The GWR was, for instance, insisting on strikers signing new contracts which would wipe out all past service.[27] But unlike the other South Wales ports, resistance seemed to crumble quicker in Cardiff.

A similar pattern emerged at Newport where "strike-breaking" activities commenced only with the arrival of the naval ratings. The Central Strike Committee met in continuous session and from the outset all work in factories, docks and on tramways and buses was suspended. Only one train was arriving daily and only gas and electricity supplies were unaffected in the town.[28]

On the first day of the strike, the town was "like Sunday with the shops open". A curious crowd assembled at the station but there was nothing to see except a train in a siding. Yet it was claimed that a "good percentage" of railway clerks remained at work although the Central Strike Committee considered their response to be "splendid".[29]

The various unions were organised into trade groups which were then attached to the Central Strike Committee. The Central Committee published a regular bulletin to its members which included extracts from the *British Worker*, held public meetings and organised entertainments "to keep men clear from streets".[30]

On the second day of the strike, the dock authorities were demanding Naval protection ("simply to police the docks") because the Chief Constable could not spare any men.[31] By 6 May, 160 naval ratings had arrived and were working at the local power station and acting as sentries at the dock gates and the pierhead.[32]

Although the Central Strike Committee was fulsome in its praise of the workers in its 10 May bulletin,[33] by the following day it was revealing to the TUC that the attitude of the Newport Town Council was "causing uneasiness to some of the weaker men out". The Council had decided that they could supply essential services such as electricity without union labour.[34]

Again, in Swansea, once the destroyer HMS *Tetrarch* arrived on 6 May, attempts were immediately made to break the strike by employing "volunteer unloading" at the docks whilst the police then actively encouraged "potato profiteers" to run the gauntlet through the picket lines en route for Birmingham. Despite the police advice of "drive through" the pickets, the Strike Committee prevented this distribution and the lorries were unloaded by the pickets.[35]

However, unlike its counterpart in Cardiff and Newport, the Swansea Committee, with 35 unions representing 35,000 trade unionists, managed to be much more in control of the whole situation. Even local newspaper boys struck for 4*d.* a day. Such was the feeling against "blackleg or OMS labour" being used in some factories that many workers walked out against TUC instructions.[36] One of the few major problems at Swansea was the confusion over conflicting telegram instructions. It was strongly suspected that the government was responsible.[37]

And yet, even at such a local level, there seemed to be some mild interpretations of the issues involved. Local leaders congratulated themselves on running the strike with "good humour all round" and organising "the whole thing without collision with the authorities". They found credit in the strike ending as it had begun, "in the best possible spirit, all based upon principle and showing very little *passion*" (my emphasis).[38]

The unquestioning loyalty of the Newport, Cardiff and Swansea Central Strike Committees, strengthened by frequent despatch rider contacts, reports to the TUC by visiting Labour MP's and the arrival of the *British Worker* (especially in Cardiff), was typified by the letter from Allan Robson, Secretary of the Cardiff Committee: "The bearer of this communication is a Despatch rider under our instructions. Will you please hand to him all the latest information and instructions. Everything is going well in Cardiff. We are an enthusiastic, disciplined army working under instructions from the T.U.C. General Council. We appreciate all you are doing."[39]

Such, however, was not the situation in Llanelli. Unlike the other major South Wales ports to the east, it was without a naval presence during the Nine Days (presumably because it was not so strategically important) and was much closer politically, temperamentally and in terms of its social structure to its coalfield hinterland. It was also unique in that the Communist Party was already quite well established in the town (and succeeded in trebling its membership during the strike). The mercurial steelworker, Enoch Collins, chairman of the local Trades and Labour Council, was a foundation member, and it was he who was largely responsible for converting the trades council into a Council of Action. As chairman, he assumed almost dictatorial powers. The Council went beyond TUC instructions in immediately calling out steel, gas, electricity and brewery workers. All "essential services" were stopped. The police stations and market were commandeered. Food was distributed from the market to the needy whilst the police received instructions from the Council of Action and actually conformed to their orders for the turning back of lorries of blacklegs. The docks were taken over and a regatta was held there to raise funds for soup kitchens. Public meetings were organised where on one occasion Tom Griffiths, Labour MP for Pontypool, shared a platform with leading Communists Arthur Horner of Mardy and the newly-released political prisoner Ernie Cant. The extent of the Council's influence was such that the local Board of Guardians made the unprecedented decision of relieving all strikers at full rates.[40]

Although the General Strike ended on 13 May, the situation was sufficiently grave in Newport and Swansea for the *Cleopatra*, *Caledon* and *Tetrarch* to remain for some days. At Newport, as late as 18 May, dockers, tramwaymen and transport workers remained out in a "disgruntled mood".[41] At Swansea, a settlement governing conditions of re-employment for railwaymen and dockworkers was not achieved until 20 May. Swansea printworkers were also dissatisfied by the widespread victimisation in almost every office, despite promises of "no reprisals".[42]

Just as the navy was about to slip out of South Wales on 19 May as quietly as it had arrived, an ominous message was sent to the Admiralty, not unlike the frantic messages which must have been sent to the Home Office in 1839, warning of the Chartist March on Newport: "S.N.O. Newport reports strikers returning to work and police have information regarding a march of disgruntled miners of surrounding Districts due to arrive at Newport at noon today, Wednesday, and request him to be prepared to render armed assistance if necessary."[43]

The crisis passed with the miners (unaware of the panic they had created) being halted by the police outside the town boundaries and the leaders later being summonsed. With the situation reported normal, the remaining vessels, *Cleopatra*, *Simoon* and the submarine *H24* departed for Plymouth.[44] A major clash had been temporarily averted. But the abandoned South Wales miners, seemingly so passive during the Nine Days, were to show their "passion" in the coming seven months' lockout. It was the events in the lockout which irrevocably changed the social and political face of the South Wales coalfield and not those Nine Days which preceded it.

The trade union movement in the coalfield and in the coastal ports belonged to two rather different historical traditions. The ports had been unionised in a burst of "new unionism" between 1889 and 1892 with a host of often conflicting large and small craft and unskilled organisations emerging and yet with no dynamic, uniform independent *political* outlook emerging up to 1926.[45] On the other hand, although late in grasping the news of "new unionism" (the South Wales Miners' Federation was not formed until 1898), the trade union and political experience of the miners was unique, relatively homogeneous and sophisticated.

It was a single union operating in single-industry communities and was the largest regional union in Britain in 1914. Although always dogged by non-unionism, it was a monolith which made its presence felt in every facet of coalfield society right down to 1926. "The Fed", as it became known to its members, was the focal point of the community and, by its very nature, the lodge (the union branch) was vested with considerable independence. This encouraged a healthy "anarcho-syndicalist" rank and file outlook towards industrial and political problems.[46] Commencing in Mid-Rhondda with *The Miners' Next Step* (1912) and encouraged by the built-in latitude provided by the Federation at its base, a miners' rank and file quasi-syndicalist movement consistently evolved through the Unofficial Reform Committee, the Plebs' League, the Rhondda/South Wales Socialist Society, the Communist Party of Great Britain and finally the Miners' Minority Movement. The South Wales coalfield was undoubtedly the spiritual home of the MMM for it was there that it obtained its greatest support between 1924 and 1926 largely because of the groundwork already achieved since 1912.[47]

By 1926, the SWMF embraced most of the Minority Movement's programme while the grass roots action of its pit papers and pit-groups and the agitational work of its leading propagandists, Horner, Cook and S. O. Davies, ensured a committed militant position for the SWMF in the affairs of the MFGB.[48]

All these developments took place against a background of unprecedented Marxist educational work in the coalfield undertaken mainly by the Plebs' League and later the Central Labour College and the National Council of Labour Colleges (to say nothing of the more transient and localised bodies like the Socialist Sunday Schools, the Irish Self-Determination League, the Proletarian Social League and the SLP). One contemporary enthusiast could claim that ". . . to those who are conversant with the inner life of the . . . area covered by the South Wales Coalfield, there can be no two opinions as to the extraordinary familiarity to thousands of miners, railwaymen, steelworkers and other organised workers of the doctrines contained in the writings of Karl Marx . . . they have become household words. . . ."[49]

Allied to this was the building of over one hundred miners' institute libraries mainly between 1890 and 1920 and containing many socialist texts (often from Kerr of Chicago). The existence of this phenomenon on a universal scale was peculiar to the South Wales coalfield. There was no comparable educational institution generated almost entirely by a proletarian culture anywhere else in the world.[50]

These unusual educational patterns go some way towards explaining the intensity of support for the advanced political and industrial position held by the SWMF: many of its new young leaders at local, regional and national level had been weaned on these heady waters. The trade union and class consciousness was such that a Carnegie Trust Report was breathing a sigh of relief in 1929 that the period of the "prolitcult—a culture based on (the miners') needs as workers and fostered by means of the classes organised by the N.C.L.C." had definitely passed.[51]

These educational and "syndicalist" movements proved to be fertile ground for the growth of the Minority Movement. The pre-eminence of the MMM in the affairs of the SWMF ensured that the demands of Arthur Horner at the National Minority Movement Conference in March 1926 for the setting up of all-embracing Councils of Action in readiness for the coming "general capitalist offensive" were met throughout the valleys in the first week of May.[52] (In contrast to this, the lack of MM influence in the South Wales ports meant that the same call went largely unheeded.)

It is difficult to assess the worthwhile preparatory work undertaken in South Wales for a general strike. Certainly in the spring and summer of 1925 the MMM organised unity committees involving railwaymen in the Afan, Garw, Maesteg and Ogmore Districts whilst a Council of Action embracing road and rail unions was set up for the Aberdare and Pontypridd areas.[53] Quite apart from the national warning signals of "Red Friday" in July 1925, the localised strike of the West Wales Anthracite miners (to save their Seniority Rule custom) in the same summer gave the situation more than an air of expectation. The whole district, according to a colliery official, "was in a state bordering on rebellion"[54] with a *Defence Corps* formed in the Amman Valley. The imprisonment of fifty-eight anthracite miners, coinciding with the Communist Twelve, were indicators which could not have gone unnoticed.[55]

In the run-up to the General Strike at least some work was begun one month before in the larger centres like Aberdare and Merthyr. In Merthyr, for instance, the Executive of the Trades Council held itself in readiness for orders from the TUC General Council from early April onwards. The Executive also obtained powers from the Trades Council to co-opt the Dowlais Co-operative Society, the Merthyr and Troedyrhiw Co-operative Society, Shop Assistants, Bakers, Transport Workers and the NUGMW. From 2 May "interviews were obtained in order that the workers' interests should be safeguarded, and that any wanton incitement to disorder might be prevented".[56] The Rhondda District of the SWMF could well have been typical in mid-April in entering into preliminary negotiations with local Co-operative Societies for the extension of credit in the event of a prolonged dispute.[57]

It would, however, be more accurate to describe the valleys as being only mentally prepared. The whole British trade union movement had not considered the possibility of defeat and the implications of defeat. The fundamental question of the miners fighting on alone, protected by a financially and a numerically weak union and at the worst possible time of the year with vast coal stocks in the country, had never been entertained. In the twelve hours preceding the General Strike, there was an unchallenged and unbroken flood of coal by rail pouring out of such areas as the Anthracite District to be stockpiled elsewhere. The GWR alone could claim on 1 May that it had 48 days normal supply of coal for locos, 10 days for industrial purposes, 58 days for power stations, 53 days for steam boats and 33 days for gas-making and the docks.[58]

Neither had anything been done about effectively freezing the stocks. The Communist Party on 28 May was belatedly and unsuccessfully calling for the blacking of all coal movement.[59]

The main organisational feature of the General Strike (with the exception of the larger coalfield towns where preliminary co-ördinating work with other unions was necessary) was the remarkable improvisation and spontaneity seemingly within days or even hours of the call. At the colliery-village level, strike committees or Councils of Action were formed with the core being provided by the miners' lodge (because it was often the only substantial trade union organisation in the locality). Such was the response to the strike in some areas that a few lodges took no exceptional organisational steps and a handful appear, according to their minutes books, not to have met at all during the Nine Days.[60]

There was such a willingness to co-opt outsiders on to all the strike organisations that the different titles used are misleading. At Mardy, there was no Council of Action, but its Strike Committee was far more revolutionary in every aspect of its work than any of the other Councils of Action elsewhere. Similarly the Central Strike Committees in the bigger coalfield towns had some of the features of the Councils of Action in their approach to outside bodies, issue of permits and food control.[61]

Apart from the decidedly inactive role of the police in the coalfield during the Nine Days, what strengthened the strike as much as anything else was the isolation of the mining communities from each other and of the whole coalfield from the outside world. Baldwin's broadcast and all the pro-government BBC news bulletins were simply not heard in many areas. Not one wireless set existed in three villages at the head of the Dulais Valley.[62] Despite despatch riders, there was also virtual isolation from the TUC, with the *British Worker* hardly being seen. No copies had arrived at all in South Wales until 9 May. Although some Councils of Action were anxious to receive the bulletin, most seemed unperturbed and appear not to have contacted the TUC throughout the strike.[63]

It is difficult to gauge the atmosphere in the coalfield in those fateful days in May 1926. The *Western Mail*, never a newspaper near the heart or the pulse of the Welsh miner, and always willing to caricature him as a gullible moron repeating "mechanical incantations",[64] unwittingly came near the truth. A special correspondent touring the eastern valleys of Monmouthshire detected an air of indifference: "On Saturday and Sunday there were few smiling faces in the district I visited; today there was scarcely a face that was not smiling. Perhaps the Summer sun helped. Between Cwmbran and Pontnewydd a ring of young fellows were too deeply intent on playing cards to pay much heed to me. . . . Gardening was the chief hobby that the freedom from work was fostering."[65]

But the correspondent could not see in his own report that 4 May had come as the long awaited mental and physical liberation. Positive response took many forms and varied from miner to miner and from community to community, reflecting the rich social and cultural mosaic of the valleys. But for the few who travelled the coalfield, the attitude which struck them most was the totality of support and the overwhelming self-assured discipline which frightened some but uplifted others. Tom Griffiths, Labour MP for Pontypool, sent the following report to the TUC on 9 May: "Observations made when passing through Rhondda Valley, Aberdare Valley, Taff Valley and Neath

Valley showed every appearance of calm and orderliness. . . . At 11 p.m. when passing through Glyn-Neath crowds . . . were singing *Hen Wlad fy Nhadau*. . . . We observed throughout that there was no feeling of bitterness shown by any of the strike committees—a quiet feeling of confidence and determination prevailing everywhere."[66]

The most profound impact of the strike on the coalfield was the way in which it began to clarify and then polarise class loyalties, a development which deepened irrevocably during the Lockout. Within a community under siege, the miners and their families, armed with their essentially proletarian institutions of the "Fed", the "Co-op", the Institute and the Chapel along with the local branches of the ILP, Communist Party, Labour Party (both "left" and "right") and the remainder of the trade union movement were ranged against the Government, the coalowners and their officials, the police, the judiciary and the blacklegs. But the new dimension in the situation was that some of the petit-bourgeois—the lower middle class, the professions, and the shopkeepers—were forced (or voluntarily chose) to merge "downwards" or slip into total passivity.

In Glyn-Neath, local tradesmen purchased a loud-speaker for the use of women and children in the evenings, and cinema proprietors handed their halls over to the Strike Committee.[67] In the Aberdare Valley, it was the young teacher Emrys Hughes who addressed the angry crowd when a railwayman was arrested immediately after the Nine Days.[68]

Perhaps the most notable indication of this development was the example of the Cwmgwrach Congregational minister, the Rev. Edward Teilo Owen, who was fined £20 (or a two-month sentence) for apparently stating in a Welsh sermon during the strike: "We have been squeezed. It is time to rebel. I have turned rebel." He was also bound over for telling an assistant teacher that her services were not welcome if she rode on a blackleg train.[69]

Much of these changes were epitomised in the small remote village of Bedlinog, tucked away in the hills of north-east Glamorgan. Its Council of Action was spontaneously formed on 4 May by miners and shopkeepers, who had earlier been influenced by a Minority Movement meeting at the local Church Hall. Four out of the five shopkeepers were Communists, and the only way they could involve themselves in the strike was to form a Chamber of Trade and affiliate to the Council of Action.[70] It also involved the whole village through miners' lodges, local women, the local post-office, woodworkers, the NUR, the NUT, the unemployed, the Dowlais Co-operative Society and its employees, the

Labour Party, the Communist Party and the various religious bodies.[71]

Having a motorcycle in stock, a Communist ironmonger arranged with his colleagues on the Chamber of Trade to present it to the Council of Action. Contact was thus maintained with other Councils by a despatch rider whose main route extended through Treharris, Ystrad Mynach, Senghenydd, Caerphilly, Pontypridd and on to that other "Red" village, Mardy. The news collected en route was collated at Mardy, and cyclostyled notices were produced which were then distributed on the return journey.[72]

The organisation of the strike at Mardy was a much more intense affair. Visiting journalists who dared run the gauntlet of what one called "the red reign of terror . . . in lawless Mardy" came out convinced it was "Little Moscow".[73] Personified in their illustrious checkweighters, Ablett (up to 1918), Horner and Dai Lloyd Davies, the miners of Mardy had earned for themselves the reputation of being the pace-setters of the British miners. The Federation lodge had the distinction (unbeknown to it) of being the only trade union branch in Britain to have one of its circulars placed before the Cabinet during the May crisis. Such was the concern that Mardy generated.[74]

A tight rein was kept by the Strike Committee on the vital spheres of work, food, transport, coal and the press. Only the watchman was allowed to work at the colliery,[75] whilst the coal-owners (Lockett's Merthyr) were prevented from moving coal out of Mardy when miners "knocked all the bloody doors out of the trucks; . . . formed a committee and everybody was getting their ration out of the wagons".[76]

All requests for the use of charabancs were scrutinised by the Committee. The Methodist churches were refused use of any for their Gymanfa Ganu (Singing Festival), but one was allowed for a funeral. Newsagents were reprimanded for distributing the "yellow press" and only bona fide trade union printed newspapers were allowed in the Institute. The lesser hall of the Institute was put at the disposal of feeding adults and children and eventually the Institute and the Lodge took joint financial responsibility for a communal kitchen.[77]

The most controversial act undertaken by the Strike Committee in the Nine Days (and for a short time afterwards) was to remind the local tradesmen of their moral and public duties. A "reign of terror and violence" swept Mardy.[78] For the Strike Committee laid down strict instructions to the tradesmen on maximum prices and sales of certain provisions.[79]

Bedlinog and Mardy were by no means typical in their approach to the strike. The larger towns had more sophisticated Central Strike Committees. In Merthyr, there were six sub-committees dealing with food, finance, communications, sports and entertainments, intelligence and permits: there were also the four district strike committes which in turn had their own sub-committees.[80] In other areas, such as Tredegar, the Council of Action worked on a much more *ad hoc* basis with little committee work.[81]

In at least one town the initiative to form a Council of Action was taken by the Labour Party. At Maesteg, where there was no trades council, Communists, still at that time operating within the Labour Party, were responsible for the Council's formation, but this was against the wishes of the local miners' MP, Vernon Hartshorn.[82]

But it appears that the effectiveness of all the organisations was uniformly high.[83] The solidity of the strike was such that very little blacklegging occurred: only "volunteer" tramwaymen in Pontypridd[84] and railway employees in the Vale of Neath[85] and the Abersychan area.[86] There was thus little evidence of violence towards life or property. Nevertheless it was found necessary to wreck a potential blackleg's lorry at Crumlin,[87] and burn a store of hay at Abercrave colliery.[88] The most outrageous act inevitably occurred at Mardy, whilst police were trying to raid a house: ". . . when they got out their car had been set on fire. They didn't need names. . . . I mean, you only need look at the village, it was all of 'em done that."[89]

And yet, largely because the strike was so overwhelming, there was probably not a single prosecution during the Nine Days. Ablett was the only one to get into difficulties when he was arrested in London for a seditious speech at Battersea.[90]

Only one case can be found of a miner trying to blackleg in South Wales during the Nine Days. He was hospitalised for the remainder of the strike after trying to work at Oakwood Colliery, Maesteg. The blow to the chin was delivered by the son of Nat Watkins, Secretary of the Miners' Minority Movement.[91]

The Labour Party played its part by providing speakers for the many public meetings. George Hall, Tom Griffiths, Will John, Vernon Hartshorn and Dai Watts Morgan were local MP's who were particularly engaged in such work. Mrs. Andrews, the Women's Labour Officer, helped organise women's demonstrations especially in the Glamorganshire valleys.[92]

The Communist Party played rather a different role which was shortly afterwards "recognised" by the authorities. With the dispersal of the Communist leadership to the regions, Ernie Cant was sent to South Wales. Along with Horner, he toured the coalfield, by motor-bike, speaking, recruiting, organising, agitating, giving the warning "watch your leaders"[93] and probably distributing the *District Strike Bulletin* and the *District Strike News*. The Communist Party was particularly active in extending the power of the Councils of Action, some of which they controlled and on most of which they claimed to have some representation.[94]

When the General Strike was called off there were some attempts to resist, especially in the Rhondda and Pontypridd areas: tramwaymen and railwaymen were particularly hostile to the settlement.[95] Even though resistance soon collapsed, some Councils of Action continued to exist for some time: in Bedlinog until 13 August and in Ystrad Mynach until at least 15 September.[96] Fears of resistance must have been entertained by the authorities, for on the following weekend leading Communists were arrested for offences under the Emergency Powers Regulations: in the Rhondda (4), Maesteg (3), Aberdare (3), Aberavon (1), Neath (1) and Abercarn (1), all of whom were imprisoned. There were also some arrests of non-Communists, notably Merfyn Payne of Pencoed who was fined £50 and was accused of trying to control the movement of buses in his locality.[97]

Having had their most potent weapon eliminated, the miners in every coalfield seemed to entrench themselves. Already on the defensive through lack of resources and weak organisation, they were in no position to escalate their action. It was now a question of physical and mental survival or immediate surrender. There was something in the dignified political and psychological make-up of the miner which required him to resist what appeared to weaker spirits the inevitability of defeat. Yet the resistance was doomed to failure from the outset because it was a static struggle with no prospect of escalation or wider support. When the decision, on South Wales initiative, was finally taken to withdraw safetymen, it was merely a gesture, for many had already returned and a temporary breakaway had occurred in the heartland of militancy, the Rhondda.

Enormous energies were therefore directed in trying to hold the fabric of the community together, but this had nothing to do with the elusive victory.

What distinguished the South Wales miner from his brothers in the other coalfields was the manner and intensity of resistance. An alternative social and political culture based on class discipline (resulting often in open warfare), resourceful illegality, direct action and humour, gradually emerged whereby whole communities for seven long months came to terms with the overwhelming odds and met them head-on. The distortion of social life took many forms: "I saw two grown men in their thirties, fighting each other to the point of unconsciousness over two marbles. Because we had to get something for currency, and with marbles you could buy thirty for a penny. . . ."[98]

The most desperate problem from the very beginning of the lockout was the provision of relief. The cabinet was being warned as early as 21 May that distress in South Wales was acute and that there was a fear of serious disturbances. Relief notes by local Boards of Guardians were growing enormously. Local grocers could not negotiate them for some weeks and wholesalers were therefore not prepared to supply to the grocers.[99] The totally inadequate relief resulted in illness and death: ". . . and we had a daughter, so it was a family of three then, existing on thirteen and six a week (relief). The child was born in November 1926, and of course it died as a result of malnutrition, it suffered from meningitis, and the doctor reckoned it was due to the fact that she was carrying the baby through the strike."[100]

"My mother died of pernicious anaemia which . . . is a polite name for starvation . . . which could be attributed to the awful conditions in 1926 and just after."[101]

Most, however, did manage to survive. They pressurised their Boards of Guardians with mass demonstrations to maintain or improve relief.[102] Some were too proud to ask for relief[103] while most were sustained not by the Guardians but by sporadic Federation strike pay and the communal kitchens supported by funds from the Federation, lodge reserves, Institute investments and local "benefactors".[104] Only limited support was given by the co-operative societies because most of the debts from the 1921 lockout had not been recouped by 1926.[105] Some maintained that they actually lived better during the lockout, especially those in the semi-rural west where farmers presented lambs and tons of vegetables to strike committees because they knew that otherwise they would be stolen.[106] The more urbanised and proletarianised valleys to the east were not fortunate enough to have a large rural hinterland. Their plight therefore bordered on despair.

Touring parties of choirs and bands with SWMF authorisation also raised substantial sums.[107] A section of the Gwaun-Cae-Gurwen Silver Band toured north, west and mid-Wales. Having been given a terrific welcome in the quarry areas of the north, especially by their keen rivals the Nantlle Vale Silver Band, they were not too discouraged by the hostility of the spa town of Llandrindod Wells when a retired colonel was told that the Band was playing "The Death of Nelson": ". . .'If they were playing "The Death of Cook", I'd give you something'. And the bugger didn't give me anything either."[108]

The band returned to South Wales in August to win the Class A competition at the Swansea National Eisteddfod. As if to answer the Monday Presidential Address by Admiral Heneage Vivian in his call for harmony in the industrial life of the nation, miners' bands and choirs won all the available competitions. The silky façade of the Eisteddfod was shattered by the crowned bard, Dewi Emrys, whose winning ode described his own life as a vagrant. To the horror of the Welsh Establishment, he later apparently committed the unpardonable sin of pawning his crown.[109]

If food was the most pressing issue, footwear was the most humiliating. In October, 141 Glyncorrwg children attended school barefooted whilst 91 were absent owing to lack of boots. The situation could have been a lot worse without the miners' co-operative boot centres. Ynysbwl alone in three weeks repaired 782 children's boots and 347 adults' shoes.[110]

The fit and healthy young miner could survive by competing in Powderhall sprinting or boxing: "Jack Morgan of Tirphil the famous welter-weight and I we fought in the Abertyswg little Town Hall, and we fought in the New Tredegar Empire, and there we had five shillings each. We agreed to go light with each other because we were friends but our styles always suited and we came out cut to pieces. But we had five bob each. When I fought the boy Nash from Bargoed in the '26 strike, I had seven and six, but for Dick James 'Cowboy' ten shillings. It was all money but every place we went to we would have the five shillings or the seven and six or the ten shillings plus a cooked dinner for yourself and two seconds, after the fight was over. And so we used to go to the places where they would supply butter beans, everyone had a craving for butter beans, and butter beans in the dinner was always given at Bargoed so we'd take anybody on."[111]

If the alternative culture was seen anywhere it was in the jazz and comic bands which proliferated, in particular in the more desperate proletarianised areas of the Rhondda and were sometimes considered a threat to the established cultural pattern. An Aberdare Primitive Methodist bitterly complained of "A most vulgar spectacle—indeed a most indecent spectacle. It was immoral and blasphemous. One jazz band had the audacity to carry a card upon which was the writing: 'I am the bread of life'."[112]

But the escapism of the Seven Sisters *Black Natives*, the Mardy *Harem Band*, the Blaenllechau *Long Row Spuds*, the Gelli *Toreadors*, the Cwmparc *Gondoliers*, the Ystrad *Zulus* (later *Old Spuds*), and the Treorchy *Zulus* (1926 South Wales Tableau Champions), with a whole way of life evolving around them, became as important as the Federation in maintaining morale. One banner, showing the humour and perhaps the aspirations of the miners, proclaimed: "The Graig Miners Perfect Musicians: As Played Before Dai Lossin And Other Crowned Heads: 10,001½ Medals and Diplomas."[113]

But the enormous energies poured into such activities betrayed the static nature of the lockout. They were not organising for victory; they were merely delaying defeat.

The focal points of the day-to-day resistance was the Federation Lodge, its strike committee and the physical centre of the village, the miners' institute. Regular concerts were held with raffles for trousers or sacks of potatoes becoming the order of the day.[114] The Institute's Library also provided a haven for many. At Cymmer Institute (Porth) lending increased from 29,238 (1925) to 49,161 (1926) although stocks could not be replenished.[115]

Demoralisation, of course took its toll. Families emigrated, young men joined the Army, young girls left for domestic service in the Home Counties. Families were shattered: "So I went to see my mother and she started to cry, naturally, there were four children in the house, and I was the head. Lord knows what would have happened if I'd gone up to London . . . and I wouldn't come back."[116]

And gradually there was a slow trickle of a return to work from August onwards. But unlike the other coalfields the resistance turned to open warfare. Miners actually called a "Council of War" in the Afan Valley and elsewhere.[117] There were eighteen serious disturbances caused by protection of blacklegs by imported police. The worst occurred in the upper Afan Valley where the striking miners in three separate riots in October attacked police, overturned lorries, assaulted blacklegs and stoned their houses.[118] The coalfield resembled a battlefield with an "army of occupation" (in the form of imported police) attempting to break the spirit of a hostile and turbulent population.

In that twilight world which was neither criminal in the normal sense nor orthodox political activity, many South Wales miners delved in an underworld of anonymous intrigue which we are only now beginning to rediscover. To carry out "effective" picketing, Ystradgynlais miners indulged themselves in historical gymnastics and disguised themselves as *Scotch Cattle*,[119] whilst miners at Ynysybwl were protected by their lodge secretary who wrote their names in the lodge minute book in his own secret shorthand.[120] It became a disciplined society in which "nobody named anybody".[121] It was also a society in which class loyalties were so polarised that there was no middle ground. Arthur Jenkins, the respectable mild-mannered miners' agent, very much a reluctant martyr, found himself being treated in the same way as Alec Geddes, the Clydeside revolutionary, who delivered seditious speeches in mid-Glamorgan. The heavy sentences given to both indicated a definite hardening of attitudes on the part of the police and judiciary.[122]

The miners' wives played a leading part in the defiance, often "white shirting" blacklegs. When sentencing Mrs. Elvira Bailey of Treorchy to two months' prison, the Stipendiary D. Lleufer Thomas said: "You threw the first stone at the police constable and you set a very bad example to the women of the district. I find that the women have been taking too prominent a part in these disturbances and I must impose a penalty that will be a deterrent to others."[123]

The resourcefulness of the mining communities extended as far as "thoroughly briefing" the accused before the mass trials which, at Swansea alone, took three weeks to complete. One witness was asked to imagine at her trial that she was a Hollywood actress to "impress" the court. Wearing a borrowed coat, skirt, hat, fur and gloves, she was cross examined in the witness box by the Judge: "She drew herself up to her full height and takes off one glove and puts it on the ledge, takes off the other glove and puts it on the ledge, she said, 'Your Honour', she said, 'I am fully aware that I am here in the presence of my God.' "[124]

She succeeded in getting a reduced sentence, but the heavy sentences on dozens of miners and their wives were as inevitable as the final defeat.

With total submission in December, only a skeleton remained of the community which had sacrificed everything in the "war between poverty and opulence"[125] The "Fed" was smashed for nearly a decade, union officials and militants were victimised, blacklists abounded, a rival scab union reared its head[126] and the migration of population out of the valleys accelerated. All the assets painstakingly built up by the mining communities—the institutes and their libraries, medical schemes, chapels, football teams—lay in ruins.[127] Enormous family debts needed to be repaid and some were still outstanding when the triumphant 1972 strike began.

The lockout had been a catastrophe, but something could be claimed from the wreckage, for "it taught us to know our enemies". And the political consciousness which was lacking among the leaders and the led during the Nine Days began to evolve in the coalfield in the lockout.[128] In the following decades children were to be reminded of Dic Penderyn and of how "we won in 1926".

It appears that the defeat in the lockout was catalytic in turning many miners towards conventional Labour Party politics and away from the quasi-syndicalism of industrial action. But something much more subtle occurred. The Labour Party strengthened its hold on the valleys, but a pattern developed simultaneously at ground level which often ran counter to Parliamentary politics. A semi-guerrilla warfare, often harnessed by the growing Communist Party appears throughout the coalfield for the first time during the lockout.[130] A generation was now growing up in which a political prisoner had some significant status and prestige.[131] This extra-parliamentary tradition based on a frighteningly intense community and class consciousness, takes root in 1926, the thread reappears in the mid-1930s with the revival of militancy and direct action and finally comes into its own in 1972. The memory and the received memory of 1926 was sufficiently strong in 1972 for the defiant voice of that "anonymous" arrested Maesteg miner in October 1926 to have more than a little relevance to the miners hammering at the Gates of Saltley: "It's only a matter of principle, mate. I'm out to kill the blacklegs and you [the police] are out to protect them."[129]

The young men who faithfully marched in their comic jazz bands were finally vindicated by their "flying picket" grandsons who wore their pit boots at Saltley.[130]

APPENDIX 1

Mardy Distress Committee[131]

Miners' Institute (1)
Unemployed (NUWM) (2)
ILP (2)
CP (2)
YCL (1)
Women's Labour Section (2)
Miners' Minority Movement (2)
Wesleyan Church (2)
Bethania Chapel (2)
Seion Chapel (2)
Siloa Chapel (1)
Ebenezer Chapel (2)
Carmel Chapel (2)
Spiritualists' Chapel (2)
Salvation Army (1)
Teachers (1)
Miners' Lodge (1)

Mardy Strike Committee[132]

Miners' Institute (2)
Miners' Lodge (2)
NUR (1)
Signalmen (1)
Unemployed (NUWM) (2)
Colliery Examiners
No. 1 and No. 2 Labour Section
CP (2)
YCL (1)
Women's Guilds (2)
ILP (2)
ASLEF (1)

APPENDIX 2

Choirs, parties and bands on tour with the authorisation of the SWMF. During the Miners' Lockout.[133]

Apollo Party (Monmouthshire)
Apollo Party (Tonyrefail)
Bargoed Male Voice Choir
Caerphilly Male Voice Choir
Cwmfelinfach Octette
Dulais Warblers
Glynrhedynog Glee Party (Mardy)
Glamorgan Glee Men
Harmonic Glee Men
Mountain Ash Male Voice Choir
Nine Mile Point Silver Band
Oakdale Glee Party
Pontypool Prize Singers
Pontypridd and District Party
Gwalia Glee Singers (Pontypool)
Plumes Glee Society (Rhondda)
Rhedynog Glee Party
Rhondda Celtic Glee Party
Ynysboeth Brass Band
Glyn-Neath Glee Singers
Garndiffaith Glee Party
Penrhiwceiber Silver Band
Afon Glee Party
Dowlais Glee Party
Gilfach Goch British Legion Party
Tylorstown Brass Band
Neath Silver Band
Talywaun Glee Party

Total collected by 30 August 1926: £2,117 5*s.* 11*d.*

Note: Others went under Trades Councils authorisation (e.g. Gwaun-Cae-Gurwen Silver Band).

NOTES

1. SWML, Interview with Max Goldberg (Aberaman), 6 September 1972.
2. Although in reply to the Labour Research Department Questionnaire, Newport claimed it had a Council of Action (Emile Burns, *The General Strike, May 1926: Trades Councils in Action*, p. 150).
3. At a Special General Meeting of members of the Cardiff, Penarth and Barry Coaltrimmers Union on the second day of the stoppage the following motion was passed unaimously: "This mass meeting of trimmers pledges itself to support the miners in their struggle against a reduction in wages and promises them all the moral and active support they are capable of rendering." (UC Swansea Archives, Coaltrimmers Collection, Minutes 1926.)
4. See Public Record Office Admiralty Papers 1/86997/70 for daily Admiralty reports of assistance to Civil Authorities and naval parties sent to assist Police.
5. There is only one passing reference to the navy's presence in all the Strike Committee Reports to the TUC from South Wales (see TUC Library file HD 5366).
6. PRO Cabinet Papers 27/331, Ministry of Transport Report, 4 May 1926.
7. Ibid. Summary of Reports from Police to Home Office, 4 May 1926.
8. *Western Mail*, 12 May 1926.
9. See below the examples of the silent shopkeepers of Mardy, the "Red" shopkeepers of Bedlinog and the Cwmgwrach Congregational Minister who urged open rebellion.
10. Although in doing so it earned for decades a feeling of endearment towards it in the valleys second only to the miners' feelings for the Powell Dyffryn Coal Company. It was subsequently banned from many miners' Institutes and on at least one occasion was ritualistically burnt on the mountainside (see Michael Foot, *Aneurin Bevan*, vol. 1, p. 71). The Cardiff Central Strike Committee had advised the *Western Mail* reporters to cease work because of their "inaccurate news". (TUC, op. cit., Cardiff Report to TUC, 8 May 1926.)
11. *Western Mail*, 8 May 1926.
12. Ibid., 11 May 1926.
13. SWML, Gwen Ray Evans (Porth) Collection.
14. TUC, op. cit., HD 5366. (Report to TUC from Tom Griffiths, MP, 7 May 1926.)
15. PRO. CAB. 27/331. Home Office Situation Report, no. 3, 4 May 1926.
16. Ibid. Home Office Situation Report, no. 4, 5 May 1926.
17. Ibid. Home Office Situation Report, no. 5, 6 May 1926.

18. Ibid. Board of Trade Daily Bulletin, no. 5, 7 May 1926.
19. TUC, op. cit., HD 5366. (TUC Intelligence Note, 7 May 1926.)
20. Ibid.; see also HO Situation Report, op. cit., no. 5, 6 May 1926.
21. Ibid. HO Situation Report, no. 6, 7 May 1926.
22. PRO. CAB. 27/332. HO Situation Report, no. 9, 10 May 1926.
23. *Western Mail*, 8 May 1926. (The same issue chose, however, not to publish any news of the disorder.)
24. *British Gazette*, 10 May 1926.
25. PRO. CAB. 27/331. HO Situation Report, no. 6, 7 May 1926.
26. TUC, op. cit., HD 5366; Cardiff Railway Unions Joint Strike Committee, News Bulletin, no. 10, 11 May 1926.
27. *Western Mail*, 13 May 1926.
28. PRO, op. cit., HO Situation Reports, nos. 11 and 12, 12–13 May 1926; *British Worker*, 6 May 1926.
29. *South Wales Argus*, Coal Crisis Emergency Issue, 6 May 1926; TUC, op. cit., Newport Central Strike Committee Report, n.d.
30. Ibid.
31. PRO, op. cit., HO Situation Report, no. 4, 5 May 1926.
32. Ibid. HO Situation Report, nos. 5 and 6, 6 and 7 May 1926.
33. TUC, op. cit., Newport Industrial Council Central Strike Committee Official Bulletin, no. 5, 10 May 1926.
34. Ibid., Report for TUC General Council from Arthur Leveson, Secretary Newport Central Strike Committee, 11 May 1926.
35. PRO, op. cit., HO Situation Report, no. 5, 6 May 1926; TUC, op. cit., report by Tom Griffiths, MP, 9 May 1926.
36. Ibid., Swansea Central Strike Committee Daily Bulletin, no. 10, 11 May 1926.
37. Ibid., report by Tom Griffiths, MP, 9 May 1926.
38. *Swansea Labour News*, 22 May 1926.
39. TUC, op. cit., letter from Robson to Walter Citrine, 7 May 1926.
40. Interview with Enoch Collins (Llanelli) by Hywel Francis, 6 November 1969; TUC, op. cit., report by Tom Griffiths, MP, 9 May 1926.
41. PRO ADM.1/8697/70. Message from C.-in-C. Plymouth to Admiralty, 17 May 1926; message from SNO Newport to Admiralty, 18 May 1926; message from Admiralty Devonport to Admiralty, 19 May 1926.
42. *Swansea Labour News*, 22 May 1926.
43. PRO, op. cit., message from Admiralty Devonport to Admiralty, 19 May 1926.
44. Ibid.
45. See L. J. Williams, *The New Unionism in South Wales, 1899–92 (Welsh History Review*, vol. 1, no. 1, 1963).
46. See W. Paynter, *The Fed* (*Men of No Property:* Historical Studies of Welsh Trade Unions, 1971).
47. See M. Woodhouse, *Rank and File Movements Amongst the South Wales Miners* (unpublished D.Phil., Oxford, 1970).

48. Ibid., pp. 316–24.
49. John Thomas, *The Economic Doctrines of Karl Marx and their Influence on the Industrial Areas of South Wales, particularly among the Miners* (unpublished essay submitted to the National Eisteddfod at Ammanford, 1922).
50. South Wales Coalfield History Project, *Final Report* (1974), p. 233.
51. Workers' Educational Association (Cardiff) Records, *Minutes of the Joint Committee for the promotion of educational facilities in the South Wales and Monmouthshire Coalfield, 1929* (financed by the Carnegie Coalfield Distress Fund).
52. James Klugmann, *History of the Communist Party*, vol. 2, 1925–1926, p. 103.
53. See M. Woodhouse, op. cit., p. 341.
54. The South Wales Institute of Engineers, *Presidential Address* by D. Ivor Evans, 1946.
55. See my *Anthracite Strike and Disturbances of 1925* (*Llafur*, vol. 1, no. 2, 1973).
56. See M. Goldberg interview, op. cit.; TUC Library File HD 5366, *Merthyr Tydfil County Borough Souvenir of the General Strike.*
57. UC Swansea Archives, Ferndale Lodge Minutes, 28 April 1926.
58. PRO. CAB. 27/331. Ministry of Transport Report, 3 May 1926; BBC Wales Television Archives, *Eira Ddoe* (a two-part Welsh language account of the General Strike and Lockout, broadcast 2 and 9 February, 1975).
59. J. Klugmann, op. cit., p. 235.
60. See UC Swansea Archives, Caerau, Coegnant, Ferndale and Brynhenllys Lodge Minutes, 1926.
61. For details of the Mardy Strike and Distress Committees see Appendix 1.
62. This is confirmed by conversations with old miners in the Dulais and Swansea Valleys who maintained that even if Baldwin had been heard, scepticism about the reliability of the "machine with earphones" and instinctive hostility towards a Tory Prime Minister would have been such that response would not have been unlike that shown towards Edward Heath's unsuccessful television style in 1972 and 1974.
63. TUC, op. cit.
64. A phrase actually used by the *Spectator* during the General Strike to describe Cook's popular slogan "Not a penny off the pay, not a minute on the day".
65. *Western Mail*, 4 May 1926.
66. TUC, op. cit.
67. Ibid.
68. Max Goldberg interview op. cit. (Emrys Hughes later became Labour MP for South Ayrshire.)
69. *South Wales News*, 5 June 1926.

70. Interviews with Edgar Evans, the Chamber of Trade representative on the Bedlinog Council of Action, 31 March 1969 and 14 July 1973. (The communist butcher claimed direct descent from another radical tradesman, the Chartist John Frost.)
71. SWML, *Bedlinog Council of Action*, Minutes, 1926.
72. Edgar Evans, op. cit.; BBC Wales Television Archive, *Eira Ddoe*, op. cit.
73. See *South Wales News*, 25–8 May, 1–2 June 1926.
74. PRO, CAB. 27/332, Board of Trade Daily Bulletin, no. 20, 22 May 1926.
75. UC Swansea Archives, Mardy Lodge minutes, 5 May 1926.
76. SWML, interview with W. Picton, 18 May 1973.
77. UC Swansea Archives, Mardy Lodge minutes, 8 May; Mardy Institute minutes, 18 May 1926. For a list of the bodies on the Mardy Strike and Distress Committees, see Appendix 1.
78. *South Wales News*, 25 May 1926. Such reporting was repudiated by officials of the Mardy Conservative Workingmen's Club (*South Wales News*, 27 May 1926).
79. Mardy Lodge minutes, op. cit. The circular to the tradesmen was referred to the cabinet, see above note 72.
80. See *Merthyr Tydfil County Borough Souvenir of the General Strike* (n.d.).
81. SWML, interview with Oliver Powell (Tredegar), 29 November 1973.
82. Interview with Idris Cox by Hywel Francis, 8 June 1975.
83. See the analysis provided by R. W. Postgate, E. Wilkinson and J. F. Horrabin in *A Workers' History of the Great Strike* (1927), p. 30.
84. Pontypridd Public Library, Pontypridd Trades and Labour Council minutes, May 1926.
85. *South Wales Daily News*, 5 June 1926.
86. Ibid., 24 May 1926.
87. SWML, interview with Len Jeffreys, 20 September 1972.
88. PRO, CAB. 27/331, Mines Department Daily Bulletin, no. 3, 6 May 1926.
89. SWML, transcript of tape-recorded conversation between Ernie Cant and Peter Wyncoll, 9 January 1969.
90. *Western Mail*, 12 May 1926.
91. Idris Cox interview, op. cit.
92. TUC, op. cit.
93. Ernie Cant, op. cit.
94. J. Klugmann, op. cit., pp. 158–9.
95. Pontypridd Trades and Labour Council minutes, op. cit.; SWML, Gwen Ray Evans (Porth) Collection, Joint Strike Committee Notice (n.d.).
96. SWML, Bedlinog Council of Action minutes; UC Swansea Archives, Penallta Lodge minutes, 15 September 1926.
97. See *South Wales News*, 14 May, 17 May, 18 May, 20 May, 24 May, 31 May 1926.

98. SWML, interview with Jim Evans, 29 November 1972.
99. PRO, CAB. 27/332, Board of Trade Report, no. 19, 21 May 1926. The question of the role of the Board of Guardians in the miners' lockout is thoroughly discussed by Paul Jeremy in *The South Wales Mines and the Lockout of 1926* (unpublished M.A. dissertation, Warwick, 1970).
100. SWML, interview with Ned Gittens, 4 April 1975.
101. SWML, interview with D. C. Davies, 4 April 1975.
102. See for example, *South Wales News*, 22 May 1926.
103. SWML, interview with Mavis Llewellyn, 20 May 1974.
104. The vast donation of the Russian trade unions justified at least one Lodge (Nine Mile Point) calling the strike-pay "Russia Money". The Workers' International Relief presented the Mardy Distress Committee with £200.
105. See Ferndale Lodge minutes, op. cit.
106. Interview with Evan John, by Hywel Francis, 2 June 1975.
107. See Appendix 2.
108. SWML, interview with Jack Evans (translated from the Welsh), 19 September 1974.
109. *Western Mail*, 3–7 August 1926.
110. Paul Jeremy, op. cit; UC Swansea Archive, Lady Windsor Lodge minutes, 5 October–20 November 1926.
111. SWML, interview with Jim Evans, op. cit.
112. *Aberdare Leader*, 24 July 1926. There must be some historical significance in the great resurgence of jazz bands (a world inhabited now by children not young men) in the South Wales Valleys in the 1970s at exactly the same time as the revival of trade union militancy, and renewed confidence symbolised in the successful *Call to the Valleys*. Their very names—the Crynant *Toreadors*, Treherbert Town *Spaniards*, Coity *Saints*, Bargoed *Toy Soldiers*, Glyncoch *Swingers* are not too dissimilar from those of 1926.
113. J. G. Davies (Pontypridd) photographic collection.
114. Mardy Institute minutes, op. cit.
115. SWML, *Report on the Condition of Workmen's Libraries in the Rhondda Urban District* (n.d.).
116. SWML, interview with Glyn Williams, 21 May 1974.
117. *Sunday Worker*, 17 October 1926.
118. Ibid.; *South Wales News*, 15–16 October 1926.
119. Conversations with Ystradgynlais miners, May 1975.
120. Lady Windsor Lodge minutes, op. cit.
121. Glyn Williams interview, op. cit.
122. See reports of South Wales trials in *South Wales News*, *Western Mail* and *Sunday Worker*, November–December 1926.
123. *South Wales News*, 3 November 1926.
124. SWML, interview with Mrs. Anne Thomas, 28 November 1973.
125. A phrase used by Tom Richards, General Secretary of the SWMF (UC Swansea Archives, SWMF Circulars, 17 December 1926).

126. For an admirable account of this see D. Smith, *Company Unionism in the South Wales Coalfield* (*Welsh History Review*, June 1973, Special Welsh Labour History Number).
127. For instance the Aberdare AFC in the Third Division in the Football League folded after the lockout.
128. Conversations with the late Dai Dan Evans during the 1972 miners' strike.
129. *Western Mail*, 18 October 1926. These feelings of hostility were reciprocated by the police. For example, the Chief Constable of Cardiff wrote, on 4 December 1926, to the Head Constable of Brighton: "I am delighted that your splendid fellows have got home safely. You did indeed send us a capital lot. . . . They were easily top-dog in every encounter they had with the strikers and the way they detected and captured the ambush at Pencoedcae was certainly a high-class performance. I little thought that men trained in a fashionable resort like Brighton would have adapted themselves with such alacrity to the rough fighting of the Rhondda Valley and to such places as Blaenllechau, etc. As a result of the way they dealt with the rioters at Ferndale the day before I got there we have had very little trouble from the 'Little Moscow' gang." (This citation is reproduced by kind permission of Andy Durr, whose forthcoming *Brighton in the General Strike* contains a collection of such letters.)
130. The Mardy Lodge in 1926 intended marching over thirty miles to Pencoed to picket the first breakaways by blacklegs in South Wales, but it proved too far for them (Mardy Lodge minutes, op. cit.).
131. C. Swansea Archives, *Mardy Distress Committee*, Minutes, 1926.
132. UC Swansea Archives, *Mardy Lodge Minutes*, 8 and 13 May 1926.
133. UC Swansea Archives, SWMF Circulars, 1916–26.

BIBLIOGRAPHICAL NOTE

I would like to thank Mr. David Smith and Mr. David Egan for helpful suggestions in the preparation of this essay. Mr. Paul Jeremy and Dr. Michael Woodhouse were both generous in allowing me to consult their unpublished dissertations. I have also benefited from the availability of manuscripts and tape recordings collected by the South Wales Coalfield History Project between 1971 and 1974 (financed by the Social Science Research Council). These materials are now housed at the South Wales Miners' Library and the Library Archive at University College Swansea. I have intentionally included an impressionistic discussion of the lockout which is by no means exhaustive but attempts to liberate the *anonymous voices* of ordinary miners who tend to be overlooked by all of us in our rush from one conference report to another. I have tried to look at unusual (but significant) socio-political developments which have been hitherto largely ignored. It is hoped that the argument will be given a fuller treatment in a forthcoming joint effort with my colleague, David Smith entitled *The South Wales Miners: from Defeat to Vindication.* (The book will be a follow up to Robin Page Arnot's pioneering two volumes covering the period from 1898 to 1926.)

8 DEPTFORD AND LEWISHAM

by JOHN ATTFIELD and JOHN LEE

Deptford's industry in the 1920s still rested on foundations laid by the old naval dockyard, which had existed from the sixteenth to the nineteenth century and was now a cattle market. Though itself only a distant memory, the dockyard had spawned a whole complex of dockside and industrial development in the borough. The Surrey Commercial Docks in neighbouring Bermondsey employed a thousand dockers from Deptford; the army and navy victualling yard in Deptford (the Royal Victoria Yard) was also a big employer. A big engineering industry grew up in the borough in the nineteenth century, based initially on marine engineering, and the skilled engineers from Stone's and other large local firms formed the core of the Deptford working-class movement. More recent developments were the growth of metal trades, such as Lloyd's and Francis' tin-works, largely employing unskilled female labour. Transport was also an important industry in Deptford: there were three NUR branches in the borough based on the Southern Railway with its extensive carriage sidings at New Cross; the Metropolitan Railway extended an arm down into New Cross from north of the river. There was an LCC Tram Depot at New Cross.

South London population movements between the wars have been described as "always moving down the map".[1] Although the general standard of living in Deptford was above that of some of the poorer boroughs of Inner London and the East End, it still contained some of the worst old slum dwellings in London, especially in the area around Deptford High Street and Church Street. Some slum clearance had taken place in 1926, and more was to follow soon as new housing developments took place further out, notably in Lewisham. Deptford's population fell by 6,000, and Bermondsey's by 8,000, during the 1920s, while 40,000 people from the two boroughs were rehoused on the Downham and Bellingham LCC estates in South Lewisham, against the opposition of the Tory-controlled Lewisham Borough Council.

If Deptford was old, Lewisham was new. Largely rural in character until the mid-nineteenth century, it had been a select suburban area of large houses and spacious gardens, followed by an extremely rapid process of in-filling, since 1891, with smaller dwellings for the secure working class—foremen, postmen, clerical workers. The LCC developments gave this process an added impetus, but Lewisham still had a higher proportion of middle-class inhabitants than any other London borough in the twenties, as well as a large retired population. It was very much a dormitory borough—over half its workers left for jobs in the City and Westminster every morning, while only a few thousand came into the borough to work. It had practically no slums—less than 5 per cent of Lewisham's population was estimated to be living in poverty in 1928, compared with nearly 15 per cent in Deptford.[2] When Charles Bowerman was elected MP for Deptford in 1906, he became one of the first small group of Labour MPs in the country; the first "Labour" councillors were elected in Deptford in 1900. By contrast the Labour Party never even contested a parliamentary seat in Lewisham (East) until 1922, and did not contest Lewisham West until 1924.

The organised labour movement had its roots deep in Deptford's community life. The Deptford and Greenwich Trades Council had been set up in 1898, mainly on the initiative of the local branches of the Amalgamated Society of Engineers; it had, itself, then taken the lead in organising the Labour Representation Committee in Deptford, in 1900, quickly achieving the election of local councillors and the MP.[3] In 1926 the Trades Council had 14,000 affiliates. The Labour Party in addition had 1,700 individual members and 8,000 Co-op affiliates. The Labour Party in Deptford received the highest vote in council elections in the whole of London.[4] Recent political memories in Deptford centred on the great unemployed struggles of the early 1920s. There was a strong branch of the National Unemployed Workers' Committee Movement, with both men's and women's sections, which fought for trade unionism among the unemployed to prevent blacklegging during strikes, as well as campaigning for higher relief scales. A rival organisation regarded by the local NUWCM as "scroungers", was set up in Deptford, and went round with collecting boxes. In the end, the Labour-controlled Borough Council called a Town's Meeting in Central Hall, Deptford, packed from top to bottom, which took an overwhelming vote to support the NUWCM. After that, the Council set up the Unemployed Movement in an office, directly opposite the Labour Party rooms, with a typewriter, chairs and tables, and gave them use of the Town Hall for a mass meeting once a week. They held their ordinary meetings in the Engineers Club, owned by the local branch of the AEU.[5]

The Deptford and Greenwich Trades Council initiated its strike organisation on Tuesday, 4 May 1926, setting up a Joint Strike Committee in conjunction with the Deptford Labour Party. The Committee set itself up in the Labour Party rooms in New Cross Road, and these offices remained continuously manned, day and night, throughout the nine days of the strike. Delegates to the committee, which numbered about twenty, were not taken on a trade union basis. Three represented the Trades Council, three were from the Labour Party, and additional delegates came from the Unemployed Workers' Movement (including its local Women's Section), from the Deptford ILP, and from the local Co-operative Guilds. The Committee was officered jointly by the Trades Council and Labour Party: Dick Peek, Secretary of the Trades Council, and Walter Green, Secretary of the Deptford Labour Party, were Joint Secretaries; Colin Blanchard and Councillor Ross were Joint Chairmen by the same token.[6] Jack Waldon, who was "Literature Secretary", estimates that the left had a majority on the Committee, represented by the Trades Council and Unemployed Movement delegates, as against Wally Green and the other Labour Party machine men. Dick Peek was a Communist Party member, as were probably some of the Unemployed delegates. Colin Blanchard had built up a left-wing reputation during the unemployed struggles of the early 'twenties, and led the fight against Green within the Deptford Labour Party, only later becoming an elder-statesman of the local right wing.

The Joint Strike Committee immediately set about making the strike as effective as possible in Deptford. The workers' response to the strike call was as good as they could have wished—Deptford was one of the many areas where the response was described in Raymond Postgate's report for the Plebs League as "unexpectedly and amazingly fine". The dockers and road and rail transport workers came out solid right at the start, as did most of the workers in local iron and tin works. The militant London District of the Amalgamated Engineering Union did not wait for the TUC's "second-line" instructions but called out all engineers in the first week except those engaged in health, sanitary and social services.[7] This initiative was of great importance in giving the strike its backbone in Deptford, where engineers from J. Stone's and other large local firms were traditionally leading forces in the local labour movement.

The strike committee placed mass pickets at all factory gates, and by Monday, 10 May, was able to report that "every industrial establishment in the borough worth notifying is out". There is no doubt that the response in Deptford and neighbouring boroughs was overwhelming. The naval Victualling Yard in Deptford came out partially for the first time in its two-hundred year history, while an even larger government establishment, the Woolwich Arsenal, caused some surprise by coming out solid against the instructions of its union, the Workers' Union. Port of London clerks in the Surrey Docks also came out for the first time ever, as did TGWU members on the Woolwich Free Ferry. At the United Glass Company's bottle works at Charlton, 750 men and women joined the TGWU, set up a new branch and came out on strike, refusing an offer of a bonus from the management.[8]

Naturally the strike in the locality never reached 100 per cent effectiveness: the Arsenal workers were ordered back by the TUC after the weekend since they had not been instructed to come out; motor drivers at the Army and Navy Stores returned to work in the second week; and some transport men and operatives at Robinson's Flour Mill in Deptford also went back early. But there is no doubt that the strike in Deptford was more solid on the last day of the strike than on previous days. One NUR branch in the borough signed up 85 new members during the strike, and the branch withdrew its pickets after the weekend, "being quite unnecessary".

In Lewisham, too, where the strike organisation was much more makeshift, the response to the strike exceeded expectations, as it did at Bermondsey, Woolwich, Eltham and other neighbouring boroughs. Indeed, it is worth making the point that the firmness of the initial response in south-east London was uniform, independently of the quality of the strike organisation. In Lewisham both the Trades Council and Labour Party were militantly left-wing—the Labour Party branch was active in the Greater London Left Wing and was refusing to expel individual Communist Party members; while the Trades Council was a supporter of the Minority Movement and actively campaigned for the release of the twelve Communists jailed the previous October.[9] But Lewisham was essentially a middle-class dormitory for City workers, and the Trades Council could reasonably have expected formidable problems in setting up an effective strike organisation. "What there is to do in this dead-and-alive hole I don't know," remarked Frank James, the Trades Council Chairman, when the proposal for a Council of Action was mooted. In the event, Lewisham also had its share of problems—such as the government plant where, due to a confusion over strike orders, the men came out and went back three times in the nine days. But as in so many other places, Lewisham's main headache was in keeping in the workers not called out. A large number of building workers were employed in the borough, largely working on the new Downham LCC Estate, and Frank James had to continually chase down to the sites to urge the men, against his own inclinations, to stay at work. "Lewisham steadily closing rank", he reported to the TUC with satisfaction, on 10 May.[10]

In Lewisham, as in Deptford, the strike committee made some attempt to broaden its base outside the representatives of the unions on strike. Leslie Paul, not an active trade unionist, was called on to the committee because of his involvement in youth organisations—an action applauded by the Young Communist League's paper, the *Young Worker*, of 6 May. The Lewisham strike committee's relationship with the Unemployed Workers' Movement was less cordial, however. No Unemployed delegate was invited on to the committee; but Johnstone, the local Secretary of the NUWCM, according to Leslie Paul, had aroused the suspicions of the activists—so much so that a security pass system was introduced at the strike HQ expressly to keep out the unwanted office helper. When this man committed suicide a few months later, both his wife and his mistress signed affidavits declaring that he had been for a long time in the pay of Scotland Yard as a spy within the Unemployed Movement; he killed himself when his informers' pay stopped coming.

Relations with the local Co-ops also presented a problem in both boroughs. In Deptford the strike committee took delegates from the co-operative guilds, the political side of the co-operative movement; but there is no evidence that the trading arm of the local Co-op, the Royal Arsenal, gave any assistance to the strike at all. Indeed, the general line of policy of the Royal Arsenal Co-op management during the General Strike can probably best be illustrated by the report from Woolwich to the TUC on 10 May: "A five-ton lorry of coke was seen going into the Royal Arsenal Co-operative preserve factory labelled 'coke for hospital'. It came out with 'coke for hospital' rubbed out, but still visible."[11]

The Deptford strike committee gave short shrift to the often confused and restrictive directions from the TUC Headquarters. As well as broadening their organisation to include political and Unemployed delegates rather than simply representing the unions on strike, and organising strong mass pickets, they urged the TUC to call out all municipal workers, "as in our opinion the voluntary workers should do the dirty work as well as the clean".[12]

"Volunteer strike-breakers," commented the Official Strike Bulletin, "would be ideally employed in dust-collecting, street-sweeping and in the sewers—especially in the sewers." The Deptford Official Strike Bulletin, which appeared for eight issues from the first to the second Wednesday, and which was described by the TUC Intelligence Committee as "good", also cut across the TUC's instructions by appearing four times in printed format. Deptford was full of small jobbing printer's shops, and there was no difficulty finding a local firm willing to produce the bulletin. Deptford's veteran MP, the seventy-five-year-old Charles Bowerman, himself a compositor and President of the National Printing and Kindred Trades Employees Federation, sent congratulations to the strike committee for their efforts in bringing out the printed sheet: "It is more than we can do in the House of Commons," he wrote.

Twenty-nine-year-old Jack Waldon, who was active in the local branch of the National Unemployed Workers' Committee Movement, was in charge of distributing the strike material. He gathered together a small group of sellers, who used to collect the papers at 5 o'clock in the morning, and go out with them around Deptford; usually the bulletins were all sold out by 8 a.m. He paid the sellers with something like a packet of cigarettes each, and by the end of the strike they had made £45 clear profit on selling the 1*d.* and ½*d.* bulletins and the *British Worker*. Probably written by Walter Green, the Deptford bulletin never strayed much beyond the cautious line favoured by the TUC. Seven of the eight issues carried the General Council's message emphasising the status of the strike as an "industrial dispute" and warning against "disturbances". "Everybody must understand," stressed the Saturday issue, "that this is an industrial, not a political dispute. It concerns wages, decent conditions of life, fair methods of negotiation; not the Constitution, nor the Government, nor the House of Commons."

Walter Green was certainly the key public figure in the local strike leadership. Aged forty-eight, he had been Secretary of the Deptford and Greenwich Trades Council in 1908; was a Deptford Borough Councillor since 1909, being Mayor in 1921–2; he was Secretary of Deptford Labour Party, and a member of the Executive Committee of the London Labour Party since 1923. He was currently campaigning to become secretary of the Political Purposes Committee of the Royal

Arsenal Co-operative Society. A local man, having been educated at an LCC Elementary School in New Cross and an apprenticed engineer in Stone's, he carried great prestige in the Deptford Labour Movement, and had worked with the Unemployed Workers' Movement for a time in the early 'twenties.[13] He must have irritated the active Communist Party branch members on the strike committee by pronouncing, in the Friday bulletin: "The Home Secretary is reported as stating that he had forbidden a procession into the City by the Deptford Branch of the Communist Party. As no such application could well be made, seeing that no such Branch exists, 'Jixs' must have had another of those delusions which make his brain their home." None the less, Jack Waldon recalls of Green that, "he was right-wing, but he had a way with him, he kept the right and left all together". While the strike was on, he did his best to keep the strikers in Deptford as firm as possible. "For the sake of the future status of all our workers, fight now to win. All the forces of tyranny and reaction will be ranged behind the government. The worker in the mass, with faith in a righteous cause, is greater than them all." Green roped in all the prominent local Labour Party figures to give messages of support: the bulletin carried encouraging messages to the workers of Deptford from the MP, Bowerman, from John Speakman, Deptford's LCC Councillor, and from the Mayor of Deptford, Alderman Frank Trew, as well as from national personalities such as Cramp and Harry Gosling.

The strike committee anticipated trouble from strike-breakers—all the students at nearby Goldsmith's College were considered to be fascists, according to Jack Waldon, and Colin Blanchard used to take his dog into the strike HQ for the night duty, as a precaution. Deptford Broadway was in any case a hot-spot for fights between the police and the populace, even in normal times. The mass picketing could not occupy everyone; so the committee was always arranging events of various kinds during the nine days, to keep the people together rather than just hanging around on street corners. A series of cricket matches was arranged on Blackheath between the different labour organisations; concerts were held; and mass meetings both outside in Deptford Broadway and indoors in the various local halls. On Sunday, 9 May, as part of the TUC's publicity campaign, the strike committee staged a huge rally in the New Cross Empire music hall, with A. J. Cook, Charles Cramp of the NUR, Alonzo Swales of the TUC's Negotiating Committee, and Dr. Marion Phillips, Chief Women's organiser of the Labour Party, as speakers.

But although Jack Waldon, looking back, considers the committee's arrangements reasonably effective in keeping the strikers out of trouble, they were unable to prevent a fairly high level of casual violence in the usual Deptford riot-spots, and the days during and after the strike saw a steady flow of riot cases in front of the Greenwich Magistrates. In the worst of these, on Saturday, 8 May, Arthur Redden, a young merchant seaman, managed single-handed to start a fierce mêlée when the police tried to move him on from outside a pub in Deptford Broadway, and he called on passers-by for protection; a crowd of one thousand immediately gathered and attacked the police, leading to fifteen arrests and five court appearances.[14] Redden himself was not even on strike. The magistrates generally handed down sentences of one to three months for this sort of thing. It is astonishing how quickly crowds of this kind could form in Deptford and how spontaneously they took sides in any contest. On 7 May there was a fight between strikers and men still at work in a bottle works in Church Street; instantly a crowd gathered, and began to shout "Blacklegs!" at the men in the factory. A labourer, moved on from a pub by the police, as in Redden's case, appealed to the passers-by for help, and a big crowd "immediately adopted a threatening attitude", so that the PC had to call for assistance to make his arrest.

On Friday, 7 May, a police inspector complained to the court that "things are getting worse; we are having a rough time!" Someone must have been itching to have a go in return. On Saturday evening an audience coming out of the New Cross Empire was set upon for no apparent reason by a large posse of police, who laid about them with truncheons at everyone in sight, causing many injuries.[15]

There were few openly political trials in Deptford during the strike. But on 12 May a local motor driver, Henry Aldridge, was given one month's hard labour for chalking on a wall "USA Workers on strike in sympathy with British Workers"—an act thought likely to cause disaffection among the populace. And on 14 May Thomas Edwards, a miner and Communist Party member, was arrested in Greenwich for selling the *Workers' Bulletin* containing the "false news" that blacklegs had crashed a train. He declared, "I am selling the organ of the Party which is the only vehicle of expression of the aims, ambitions and desires of the working class in this country! We are out to establish a republic of the workers!" Fortunate in his choice of magistrates, he was fined 40*s*. with the option of fourteen days. Edwards took the fortnight in jail.

The Deptford Borough Council was one of several London councils that refused to co-operate with the government's anti-strike arrangements. The Tory-controlled Lewisham Borough Council, of course, fell over themselves to co-operate with the government. The Home Secretary, rather smugly, expected the recalcitrant councils to eventually co-operate in a national crisis,[16] but in fact all the Labour-controlled East London riverside boroughs held firm and refused to implement the government's emergency arrangements. The Deptford strike bulletin on Thursday, 6 May, reported the policy of the Labour majority on the Council as "a definite and absolute refusal to assist the government in any way in their attempt to defeat the present General Strike. So far no office or officer of the Council was assisting the government, nor would such happen so far as the Council could prevent it." This was followed up by a refusal to appoint a Coal Officer and Coal Committee for the borough. With the Town Hall closed to government activity, the Labour Councillors put the question of permits for food and coal in the hands of the strike committee, who began to issue them from their HQ in the Labour Party offices. "We thought, we'd got control of it now," says Jack Waldon. "If they'd have been able to have done that all over the country, we'd have been able to take control of the strike, practically out of the TUC hands."

It is not clear how concerned the authorities were, while the strike was still on, at the possibility of the left wing capturing control over the strike organisation in Deptford. They were sufficiently worried to send a battalion of the Scots Guards into Deptford on Thursday, 6 May, to guard the Emergency Food Depot in the old Cattle Market in the docks.[17] But the government seems to have been most concerned, in its own review of the emergency organisation after the event, with those London borough councils that withheld electric and power supplies.[18] This applied to Poplar, Stepney, Bethnal Green and West Ham, north of the river, all of which ran municipal electric undertakings, as did Bermondsey and Woolwich. Deptford Borough Council did not operate a power station, and the government did not regard Deptford as one of the "most notable" instances of non-co-operation. Whether it would have been able to overlook its exclusion from Deptford Town Hall, and the entrenched position of the strike committee, if the strike had lasted much longer than nine days, is another question.

The problem of supplying electric power to London was one of the major points of concern for the cabinet's Supply and Transport Committee during the strike.[19] ETU members struck solidly at most power stations in London, including the London Electric Supply Co.'s station at Deptford, and the Greenwich Power Station, which supplied the current for the LCC tram system. Technical staff belonging to the Electrical Power Engineers Association stayed in and the government continued to work these power stations with naval ratings. Over 400 ratings were used in London generating stations during the strike.[20] Reopening the municipally-owned stations was more difficult, because the government did not expect to get co-operation from the technical staff, and the Bermondsey Power Station was a continual headache to the Supply and Transport Committee throughout the strike.

The re-opening of the Port of London was another central problem for the government, in view of its importance in ensuring control of food supplies for the capital and home counties. The dock workers in London came out solid from the first day of the strike to the last, and beyond. At the Surrey Commercial Docks, which employed some two thousand dockers including a thousand from Deptford, a total of seven dockers turned up for work on the first morning of the strike. Lock gate staff continued to work normally, and electric and hydraulic power was kept going by one foreman, but there were no tugs operating, and three ships with food-stuffs were held up with no one to unload them. As a bonus, the Transport and General Workers' Union reported a response of "wonderful solidarity" from Port of London Authority clerical and supervisory staffs in the Surrey Docks—their first-ever strike.[21]

The response of the London dockers to the strike call was such that on the first day only 29 PLA dockers reported for work out of a total 4,300 normally required, while the privately-employed dockers were equally solid. On the second day the twenty-nine had been reduced to eighteen; by the third day it was nine. At the Surrey Docks, the lock-gate men continued to turn up, but the docks were effectively closed down by "very strong" mass pickets assembled outside the gates from the first day.

This made the reopening of the docks a most ticklish operation, especially in view of the shortage of volunteer labour for the job, particularly skilled lightermen; but it became a priority for the government by the weekend, when food shortages began to appear in London.[22]

The London Docks (St. Katharine's, etc.) were opened on Saturday, 8 May, by a system of armoured road convoys, both to ensure food supplies and to achieve a psychological impact in both the City and the East End; but it was not until the last day of the strike that the government proposed to open the East and West India and Millwall Docks by the same system. In Deptford and Bermondsey the situation was even more difficult for the government, in view of the mass pickets at the Surrey Docks and in the Tooley Street area. Eighty men taken to the riverside on 7 May to unload foodstuffs refused to move without protection from a large and hostile crowd. The police protection "was so long in arriving that when it had arrived, the eighty men were found to be missing, and the cargo is still awaiting their attention"![23] A party of naval ratings was put into the Surrey Docks, followed by volunteers brought in from Westminster by boat, who spent the weekend unloading foodstuffs to be taken further up-river on lighters.[24] But no arrangements for gaining access to the Surrey Docks by road were even discussed by the government until *after* the General Strike had been called off, when the dockers were still solidly refusing to return to work without satisfactory arrangements being made for reinstatement.[25] Pickets were still on duty at the Port of London docks on Saturday, 15 May, and the naval ratings were finally withdrawn from the Surrey Commercial Docks (by boat) on 17 May.

In Lewisham, well away from the storm-centre of the dockland areas, the main concern of the strike committee was to win over the sympathies of the middle classes and white-collar workers, who formed the majority in the borough, and who had virtually no contact with the labour or trade union movement.[26] It was a problem of getting their own, generally inexperienced, strikers to toe the line—there were those who took the opportunity to take another paid job for a few days; and those who "behaved like schoolboys" and threw bricks through windows; not to mention the free-booters at Catford who were "sending back all vans unless in possession of a permit issued by a local Soviet established at the Standard Public House, Deptford".[27] While dealing with "refractory strikers who resented any effort on the part of the Council of Action to exert its authority", the strike committee directed a lot of energy towards informing those outside the labour movement in Lewisham of the workers' case. Open-air meetings were held every night, attended, according to Leslie Paul, by many middle-class folk as well as workers. The *British Worker* recorded that these crowds of City workers "have shown their sympathy, not only by applauding the speakers, but also by contributing liberally to the collections". Leslie Paul was pleased with the signs of growing support from the Lewisham middle class: now and then "a well-to-do professional or business man stopped his car at our offices and came in shyly and said, 'I think the miners' cause is just—is there anything I can do to help?'" They were put to work as courier drivers, along with the usual cyclists.

In their struggle for public support, the Lewisham activists were most anxious to avoid any violence on the streets. Leslie Paul records that the strike committee became increasingly cautious after the riots in Deptford on Saturday, and bearing in mind the apparently growing trend towards violence throughout south-east London. Lewisham's record was clean up to then, and despite Paul's caustic attitude towards his left-wing comrades, they clearly took the view that the fragile alliance they were beginning to develop with people from outside the labour movement would not have survived the kind of street fighting already seen in Deptford. The strike committee was determined to prevent the Deptford troubles spilling over into Lewisham, and became very suspicious of strangers involving themselves in their organisation, especially after their experience with the local Unemployed Workers' Secretary.

When Harry Lee, the President of the local Painters' Union branch, offered his services as a public speaker, it was with some forebodings that his offer was taken up. He had recently spoken in Deptford Broadway, from which riots had already been reported; and the favourite Lewisham speaking pitch, in Avenue Road near the clock-tower, was within easy access for "that element which had taken part in the Deptford riots". Leslie Paul spoke on the pitch for an hour on Tuesday, 11 May, and then handed over to Lee. No sooner had he got on the rostrum than he began to taunt the police, reminding them that they had had a union once, and he then challenged them to arrest him. "This challenge was very swiftly taken up and within a few moments a squad of mounted men and a posse on foot appeared on the scene and with truncheons drawn charged at the meeting and dispersed it and arrested Lee." Lee, who appeared at Greenwich court next day, was treated "leniently" by the magistrate, and was fined £25.[28] But the Lewisham strike committee was understandably furious at his intervention, and refused to pay his fine; they saw the involvement of "elements" from Deptford as decidedly harmful to their efforts to win over public opinion, and became more suspicious of sabotage after this incident.

Deptford was unlikely to have seen the problem in quite these terms. The middle classes in Lewisham were the people who were travelling to work in the City through Deptford and New Cross in blackleg buses (or driving them); a major point of struggle in Deptford was centred on stopping transport through the borough. The down-river crossings of the Thames were closed down early on, by mass pickets at Blackwall Tunnel,[29] and by the withdrawal of labour by the TGWU on the Woolwich Free Ferry. But the struggle to stop the buses and trains was much more bitter and protracted—a sign of the importance attached by the government to the maintenance of a reasonable public transport service in London. No General buses appeared on the first day, and although many small independent operators kept going, drivers came out on some of the larger independents, such as Tillings, which operated through Lewisham and Catford. The Metropolitan Railway link to New Cross and New Cross Gate closed down throughout the strike.

On 7 May, attempts were made to get trams out of the New Cross LCC Tram Depot—electricity supply having been secured by the drafting of naval ratings into the Greenwich Power Station. Convoys of OMS volunteers and British Fascists, armed with iron bars and with police protection, entered the depot to get the trams out.[30] Jack Waldon recalls that the call went out from the strike committee, and immediately a vast crowd of two or three thousand people mobilised outside the depot. The Transport Union pickets had already taken steps to prevent the trams from moving by jamming objects down into the live pick-up rails. Mounted police tried to clear the way, but the crowd was too big, blocking the wide New Cross Road, and in the end the attempt had to be abandoned. It sparked off a severe and prolonged riot that spread right up Deptford Broadway and lasted well into the evening.

The government pondered its failure in the secrecy of its Supply and Transport Committee, and decided in view of the vulnerability of the trams to concentrate in future on getting the motor buses moving. While easier to man with volunteers, bus operation presented similar problems of fierce picketing, and was restricted to begin with to a few circular routes in safe areas. Lord Ashfield, the Chairman of the London General Omnibus Company, was said to be against subjecting his buses to the hazards of both pickets and volunteer amateur drivers, and to have allowed only the oldest types of vehicles on to the streets.[31] Sir John Anderson reported to the Supply and Transport Committee that on Wednesday, 5 May, forty-seven General buses had been immobilised, and arrangements were being made in future for the buses to be "operated in small groups".

But there was no safety in numbers. The Elephant and Castle—at the other end of the Old Kent Road from Deptford and New Cross—was a continual trouble spot as regards blackleg buses and lorries. A bus was set on fire in St. Georges Road (between the Elephant and Waterloo), and another crashed at the Elephant, killing two people, according to the *Sunday Worker*. Jack Dash remembers one incident at the Elephant:[32] "All eyes were turned in one direction. Coming in from the direction of Westminster were car loads of Special Reserves, all steel-helmeted with truncheons at the ready, the trucks protected with a kind of wire cage over the top to protect them from missiles aimed by the strikers. They were followed by Mounted Police, escorting a General omnibus with passengers, driven by a university student. Stones began to rain down from the tops of the adjacent tenement buildings. . . . The mounted reserves and police were unseated from their horses. Running fights took place with the foot police. The bus was halted, the passengers were dragged out, a great crowd of men overturned the vehicle, which caught fire and began to blaze away. There were casualties everywhere. Eventually reinforcements arrived and the police, Special Constables and Army Reserve men regained control."

Although the government was able to get a slightly augmented service of London buses as the strike went on, using volunteer labour, it was never able to extend the routes much beyond safe areas into the wilds of the working-class regions. No further attempts were made to restart the LCC trams until after the strike was over. On Thursday, 13 May, and again on the 14th, while still refusing full re-instatement for their regular staff, the LCC tried to get trams out of the New Cross Depot with volunteer labour. Once again huge crowds assembled outside the yard. Police battled with pickets to clear a way, but the tram was halted after a journey of just twenty yards; the police ordered the work to stop, to prevent riots.[33] The LCC Tramways Department settled with its employees on Friday, 14 May.

The government had more success in its efforts, to which it also gave great priority, to get a presentable service on London's suburban railways. Most traffic grades of railwaymen on Southern Railways came out and stayed out throughout the strike, but about half the clerical and supervisory staff stayed at work, and these were supplemented by a plentiful supply of volunteers, mostly enthusiastic but unskilled. "Competent signalmen would be useful," commented the Southern Railway on 8 May[34]—especially so on the intricate south suburban network, where the problems of getting amateurs to do the work properly must have been formidable. Ian Hill, an office worker who enrolled as a volunteer on the Southern Railway, finished his week's labours by leaving a dead engine, its fires out, just outside Charing Cross Station.[35] On its Eastern Division—the lines radiating from London Bridge through New Cross and Deptford—the SR could only provide 7 per cent of its normal passenger service on 5 May, but drilled the volunteer labour sufficiently to achieve 17 per cent by 10 May, and more on the following days. The improving train service was undoubtedly influential in pursuading some railway workers to drift back, but the return to work on the SR was strictly limited, and was countered by a drift in the other direction: 20 per cent of the Company's normal staff were available on 5 May, but only 18 per cent on the 10th, and 19 per cent on 11 May. And the value of the trains that did run was dubious. Ian Hill, who piloted a train through Deptford on the North Kent suburban line to Dartford, commented that "as this sort of trip had no connection with the timetable it was very poorly patronised, and apart from carrying a few parcels was really a waste of time". The Deptford railwaymen were sufficiently satisfied with the firmness of the strike locally on the railways to withdraw their pickets in the second week. But some local people were affronted by the passage of blackleg trains through the borough: an obstruction was placed on the lines at Brockley on 9 May, and on Tuesday, 11 May, a bullet struck the cab of a train running between Deptford and Cannon Street.[36]

The calling off of the General Strike cut across all these various developments. In view of the psychological pressures of the opening up of the London docks, and the increasing railway service, it is worth reiterating that the strike in London generally was as solid as ever in the second week, and showed not the slightest sign of weakening. The Ministry of Labour, in its report to the cabinet's Supply and Transport Committee on 11 May (the day before the surrender), pointed to signs of wavering in some regions, but said of London: "There are indications of a growing spirit among the rank-and-file that they will stay out until forced back by hunger." In Lewisham, as elsewhere, the telegram calling off the strike led to chaos on the strike committee, even before the extent of the betrayal became clear. When details of the sell-out were apparent, the struggle for satisfactory terms for resumption began. "The next day was all confusion. Strikers were trying to get from branch secretaries, who were trying to get from district secretaries, who were trying to get from executives the terms on which they should go back. More men than ever were out of work." Some Tillings busmen, hearing the wireless broadcasts, went straight back to work, and found themselves working alongside strike-breakers for a time, before their colleagues marched to the Catford bus depot to call them out again until proper terms were arranged.[37] In south-east London generally, most transport, power and dock workers stayed out until some sort of arrangement had been achieved between the unions and managements. The General Omnibus Company and the LCC trams reached a settlement on 14 May. The ETU members in London power stations had mostly returned by 15 May, but some victimisation took place at the Greenwich power station, and at the Deptford station of the fiercely anti-union London Electric Supply Co.

The dockers and railwaymen held out solidly for complete reinstatement. The Supply and Transport Committee heard on 15 May that the attitude of the London dockers and railmen was "more difficult than it had been since the commencement of the emergency". The Southern Railway, faced with the enormous problems of getting their complex and busy suburban system going again, brought in practically complete reinstatement of its staff,[38] on 15 May, when faced by the solid refusal of the men to return except *en bloc*. The dockers, in Surrey Commercial Docks and elsewhere in the Port of London, held out until Ernest Bevin came to an agreement with the employers, at the weekend.

In other industries there were more cases of victimisation, especially in more weakly organised firms. Jack Waldon, who was employed as a carter by the Mazawattee Tea Company in New Cross, was the only trade unionist in his factory, which was one of the few in Deptford to maintain a strongly anti-union stance. Returning to work, he was faced with a demand to tear up his union card, and on his refusal he was sacked. Some of the worst cases of victimisation took place in government establishments, despite Baldwin's pleas for peace. Of the 600 men employed at the naval victualling yard, 450 came out on strike including 37 established men, the rest being hired workmen. One man, regarded as the "instigator" of the walk-out, was sacked despite twenty-seven years' service. The remaining established men, except four, were taken back on the bottom grade, on the signature of a guarantee of future good conduct, and with a reduction of pension rights. In the Army section of the victualling yard, where 82 men had struck out of 104, eighteen were sacked to make room for volunteers wishing to stay on. At the Woolwich Arsenal, a thousand men were deprived of their wages for the pre-strike week.[39]

Lewisham Borough Council followed the government's example. All the Council employees had stayed at work except for forty permanent road-repair men and twenty casual labourers. The forty permanent men, who reported for work on 14 May, were taken back on a day's notice; the casual labourers were sacked and the Council took on fresh men from the Labour Exchange. By contrast in Deptford, where all Council employees came out except dustmen, road-sweepers and sewage-men, the Labour Council passed a resolution, proposed by Walter Green, reinstating unconditionally all employees on strike: "We congratulate them on their splendid stand in a righteous cause."[40]

With the strike behind it, the Lewisham establishment congratulated itself on its exertions during the emergency.[41] Recruiting for the Organisation for the Maintenance of Supplies had been proceeding apace since January, centred on the Lewisham Town Hall, and with the Mayor of the Borough acting as its Chairman. Lewisham supplied 7–8,000 volunteers out of a total of about 15,000 in the Croydon District—the local unit of the OMS. In addition Lewisham enrolled over a thousand Special Constables; a local jewellery firm had put all its employees on half-pay during the strike and suggested they should enrol. The local Civil Constabulary Reserve began recruiting on 10 May and quickly attained its quota of members, largely drawn from the Blackheath Rugby Club, Goldsmith's College OTC, and local Territorial Army units.

The notables of Deptford had less to congratulate themselves upon. It had a Primrose League, "necessary in Deptford where we live among an overwhelming number of Socialists and Communists". The Deptford and Greenwich British Fascists, commanded by a Brigadier-General from Blackheath, organised "smoking concerts" in the local Conservative Club. The Deptford Conservative Party had met during April and called for a "war spirit without a war". But between them not a single volunteer was enrolled in Deptford during the strike, although a few may have gone to Lewisham to sign on. The government had to draft Scots Guards into the food depot in Deptford and Royal Marines to guard the Victualling Yard. Volunteer workers in these establishments had to be brought in by river. Local firms were in such straits that they put notices in the windows of the Deptford Labour Exchange; "Please Resume Work At Once". The Deptford Tories, in the aftermath of the strike, had to limit themselves to a bitter attack on the Borough Council for its non-co-operation with government, and its refusal to enrol volunteers.

On the Sunday following the strike the local churches entered the fray. At St. Margarets, Lee, the Rev. Gillingham denounced "the deliberate wrecking of the nation's trade and life", and thanked God for the "courage" of Mr. Pugh and Mr. Thomas in calling off the strike.

In both Deptford and Lewisham, the General Strike in May 1926 brought a temporary moment of unity within the organised labour movement, that broke up once the strike was over. In both boroughs the strike committees were almost immediately disbanded, and initiative passed back to the trades councils and individual trade unions. In Lewisham, Leslie Paul recalls: "The right wing, for the most part silent during the struggle, feared the ascendency which the militant days had given to such brutally outspoken left-wing socialists as Frank James, and were relieved to see the strike out of the way." The Lewisham Trades Council and Labour Party, both with Frank James in the chair, continued to refuse to implement the Labour Party's ban on individual Communist Party members; and the East Lewisham Constituency Party was one of seven in London disaffiliated by the national Labour Party in August 1926.[42] A rival "Lewisham Borough Trades Council and Labour Party" was set up, centred around right-wing figures such as John Wilmot, later the MP for Deptford and at that time the East Lewisham parliamentary candidate. In June 1927 the Lewisham Trades Council complained that the new body was "disregarding the existence" of the old trades council, and cutting across its activities.[43] In August 1927 the Lewisham Trades Council was disaffiliated from the London Trades Council, in pursuance of the ban on Communist Party members as delegates, and the new, purged, body substituted.

In Deptford the movement divided on its own traditional lines—Trades Council to the left, Labour Party to the right—leading to a period of bitter feuding within and between the two wings. "After the general strike," writes Herbert Tracey, "great dissatisfaction was manifest among the trade unionists, and delegates who attended the Trades Council meetings formed themselves into a right and left wing. Meetings were very heated and not much business was transacted."[44] Jack Waldon recalls very well one point of division—the allocation of the £45 profit from sales of the strike bulletin, which he handed in to Walter Green at the end of the strike.

"Good God, man," said Green. "Well, what are we going to do with it?"

"Well, I want a say in what's to be done with it," replied Jack Waldon. "£15 to the Labour Party, £15 to the Trades Council, £15 to the Unemployed Organisation. It's the workers of Deptford's money—put it in the organisations, let them carry on the fight."

"Ah, we'll have to have an Executive Meeting of the Labour Party for this."

"You know what after a lot of arguments they finally decided to do?"

says Jack Waldon; "*Give £5 each to nine Councillors*; because they couldn't go down to the Relieving Officer and draw relief, they'd have lost their jobs on the Council; and that's how that £45 went!" The left in the Trades Council and Labour Party, led by Colin Blanchard, fought this decision fiercely and persistently, arguing that it was the trade unions' responsibility to look after their members, but the right wing finally carried the decision through.

The left-wing leadership of the Trades Council and the Unemployed Workers' Movement carried on the fight, throughout the summer, for the cause of the miners—raising money and holding meetings. A leading member of the Women's Section of the Deptford Unemployed Movement wrote to the *Workers' Weekly* on 18 June: "Our committee is organising a weekly collection for the miners at all the picture palaces, and we are also running a social and dance for the same purpose." Both Dick Peek, the Secretary of the Trades Council, and the New Cross Co-op Guild also sent donations to the General Strike Prisoners Fund organised by International Class War Prisoners Aid, acknowledged in the *Workers' Weekly*.

The Deptford Trades Council and NUWCM also worked together to lead the fight against cuts in relief scales imposed on the local Labour-controlled Board of Guardians by the Ministry of Health after the General Strike. The Guardians had run up a large bill due to their generous relief payments during the strike, when nearly five thousand extra claimants had signed on, and had also aroused the ire of the local Tories by insisting on 100 per cent trade unionism among Board employees. Following the strike the majority on the Board were in no mood to resist cuts in the scales, but the left forced the issue. Several Guardians attended the Relief Stations to "incite" recipients against the new scales. "Ask him for it in coppers!" they told the claimants. The unemployed were the victims of "the personal jealousies and bickerings" of the Labour majority, whose "lack of pluck and resolution had resulted in humilitating conditions", pointed out J. Hopkins, chairman of the Deptford NUWCM, at a packed Town's Meeting on 19 May.[45] When a vacancy came up in a Tory seat on the Deptford Borough Council, later in the year, the Labour candidate was Colin Blanchard, the militant chairman of the Trades Council and spokesman for the Deptford Unemployed Movement. The Unemployed Movement mobilised in his support, and Blanchard captured the seat with a handsome majority.

The years following the General Strike saw a growth in support locally for the left, including the NUWCM and the Minority Movement. The Trades Council in Deptford always remained a focus for left unity, but the Labour-controlled Borough Council tended to drift to the right. In 1929 it refused to renew its provision of free office facilities to the National Unemployed Workers' Committee Movement, and free use of the Town Hall for meetings, "particularly having regard to our experience in connection with a previous effort . . . to assist the unemployed by providing a meeting place and office accommodation for them". The Council also refused to open a register of unemployed trade unionists from which to select council labour—instead taking their requirements from the Labour Exchange.[46]

NOTES

1. *South London Press* Centenary publication, 1965, p. 36.
2. *New Survey of London Life and Labour*; P. S. King, London, 1931, a survey undertaken in 1928 by the London School of Economics—especially vol. III, pp. 373–6 (Deptford) and pp. 381–4 (Lewisham). Also Ron Pepper: "The Urban Development of Lewisham—A Geographical Interpretation"; *Lewisham Local History Society Transactions*, 1971, pp. 11–28.
3. Herbert Tracey: "Deptford and Greenwich Trades Council"; *The Industrial Review*, V, no. 5, May 1931, pp. 8–9.
4. *Kentish Mercury*, 12 March 1926: report of Deptford Labour Party AGM, including the secretary's report by Walter Green; also same paper of 11 June 1926.
5. Taped interview with Jack Waldon and Bill Trott, Deptford residents involved in the strike, 8 June 1975. All quotes from Jack Waldon in the present essay are from this interview.
6. Waldon interview; and *Deptford Official Strike Bulletin*, 5 to 12 May 1926, *passim*.
7. *Strike Bull.*, 7 May 1926.
8. *British Worker*, 8 May 1926; and report from Woolwich Trades Council, 10 May 1926 in TUC files.
9. *Workers' Weekly*, 30 April 1926 and 18 June 1926; and Leslie Paul: *Angry Young Man*, Faber & Faber, London, 1951, p. 83. The present account of the General Strike in Lewisham has drawn heavily on Paul's autobiographical account of his activities as publicity organiser.
10. TUC files.
11. Report from Woolwich, 10 May 1926, in TUC files.

12. *Strike Bull.*, 6 May 1926.
13. Waldon interview; and *Who Was Who, 1951–61*. Walter Green's career went from strength to strength—he became MP for Deptford in 1935; was Chairman of the Labour Party in 1941–2; was made a Freeman of Deptford in 1944; and received the CBE in 1949. He died in 1958 at the age of eighty.
14. *Kentish Mercury*, 15 May 1926; *British Gazette*, 11 May 1926. The *Mercury* referred to the Broadway as a "storm-centre". It was "always a haunt of the workless, for whatever reason". Demonstrations often started there and boiled over into other parts of Deptford, but the riots were not as bad as pre-1914. All court cases referred to here are from the *Mercury* of 15 and 21 May.
15. Waldon interview.
16. PRO, Cabinet Papers: progress report by Sir William Joynson-Hicks on the government's emergency arrangements, 22 February 1926.
17. PRO, Cabinet Papers: *Daily Bulletin* of the Supply and Transport Committee (hereafter *STC Bull.*) no. 5, 7 May 1926. Also *Kentish Mercury* 21 May 1926.
18. PRO, Treasury Records: report by the Chief Civil Commissioner to the Supply and Transport Standing Sub-Committee, reviewing the emergency organisation in the light of the General Strike.
19. PRO, Cabinet Papers: STC minutes. The STC, understandably, gave disproportionate attention to the problem of getting London moving, and its deliberations concentrated largely on power supply, the docks, road and rail transport in the capital. Deptford was in the front line on all these questions.
20. PRO, *STC Bull.* Sixty ratings were put into Deptford Power Station, thirty-seven into Greenwich.
21. *British Worker*, 9 May 1926.
22. PRO, *STC Bull., passim.*
23. TUC Intelligence Dept., memo, 8 May 1926, in TUC files.
24. PRO, Admiralty Records: *Daily Situation Reports*, especially no. 5, 9 May 1926, and no. 7, 11 May 1926.
25. PRO, *STC Bull.*, no. 11, 13 May 1926.
26. The following is mainly based on Paul, op. cit., pp. 87–97.
27. PRO, *STC Bull.*, no. 4, 6 May 1926.
28. *Kentish Mercury*, 15 May 1926.
29. *Workers' Bulletin*, 4 May 1926.
30. *Strike Bull.*, 8 May 1926; *Kentish Mercury*, 15 May 1926.
31. Report to TUC Intelligence Committee from Mr. Greenwood, 8 May 1926, in TUC files.
32. Jack Dash: *Good Morning Brothers*, Lawrence & Wishart, London, 1969, pp. 18–19.
33. *Kentish Mercury*, 21 May 1926.

34. PRO, *STC Bull.*, no. 6A, 8 May 1926. The present account of the SR train service is mainly from successive issues of this bulletin.
35. Ian Hill: "Volunteer on the Footplate"; *Railway Magazine*, March 1975, 121.
36. PRO, *STC Bull.*, nos. 8, 10 May 1926, and 11, 13 May 1926.
37. Paul, op. cit., pp. 98–9; *Kentish Mercury*, 21 May 1926.
38. P. S. Bagwell: *The Railwaymen*; G. Allen & Unwin, London, 1963, p. 490.
39. *Kentish Mercury*, 28 May 1926.
40. Lewisham Borough Council minutes, 23 June 1926; Deptford Borough Council minutes, 18 May 1926.
41. The following account is from the *Kentish Mercury* and *Lewisham Borough News*, various issues. These local papers both brought out duplicated bulletins during the strike, of which few survive. Both were Tory papers. The *Borough News* gave a weekly column to the local Labour Party until the strike; the following issue the "Labour Notes" were "held over due to lack of space", and they remain so to this day.
42. L. J. MacFarlane: *The British Communist Party, Its Origin and Development until 1929*; MacGibbon & Kee, London, 1966, p. 189.
43. London Trades Council, Executive Committee minutes, 30 June 1927; and *Annual Report, 1926–7*, in TUC Library.
44. Tracey, loc. cit., 9. Bearing in mind Tracey's normally sedate literary style, the "heated" meetings must have been quite something!
45. *Kentish Mercury*, 21 May 1926.
46. Deptford Borough Council minutes, 24 April 1929.

9 SWINDON

by ANGELA TUCKET

A casual observer visiting Swindon in the spring of 1926 might have supposed that there was little likelihood of major action there in the event of a head-on collision in the mining industry and a confrontation with State power. The town's trade unionists grouped in their many different organisations seemed fully pre-occupied with other questions, many highly divisive, including the effects of five years of mass unemployment which in the railway workshops took the form of continuous short-time working.

Yet when the time came, Swindonians spoke with one voice. Without a moment's hesitation they took on entirely new duties with virtually no outside help and set about solving problems with some unique features. To understand both their remarkable unanimity and the limits of their viewpoint it is enlightening first to see what sort of town this was and what were the formative experiences of the men who had the conduct of the strike thrust upon them.

In 1926 there was scarcely a family amongst Swindon's 57,000 inhabitants whose livelihood was not gained in or around the 310 acre site of the Great Western Railway Company, which employed 14,000 townspeople. Swindon was the headquarters of the Chief Mechanical Engineer together with his personal and design section of the 45,000 total staff in his department. Under the eye of this key Great Western Railway director forty skilled crafts worked on the rolling stock inside the high walls of the huge engineering railshop: of locomotives alone 1,000 were repaired and about 100 were built there each year, some for export. Lord of all he surveyed, C. B. Collett, OBE, MInstCE, MIMechE, was in supreme command of the Great Western Railway's power-house and of those who made it hum. Whenever the wheels stopped turning the whole army of craftsmen and labourers must be directly affected. So too, of course, were the conciliation grades based on this important junction handling a formidable amount of traffic from South Wales and the South-west and between the Midlands and the South Coast. From the South Wales valleys alone fifty million tons of coal—a fifth of Britain's annual output—passed through Swindon, as well as what moved from the then active Somerset coalfield.

The men inside "the Western" and their families knew full well how closely their interests had always been linked with the miners. Whether stoppages started on the railway system, as in 1911 and 1919, or in the coalfields, as in 1910, 1912, 1915, 1920 and 1921, there was no question but they too must be in the thick of it, willy nilly. The Swindon trade unionists holding district and branch office who had to take the day by day decisions during the General Strike were in their 'forties and upwards. Many had taken part fifteen years earlier in the long drawn-out arguments for and against the setting up of the Triple Alliance of miners, railwaymen and transport workers. Retained in the railshop on war work they had all experienced together the great technological, social and ideological changes which took place during the Great War.

But the biggest change for Swindon was that the all-powerful Company had been forced to submit to government wartime control and at last to recognise trade unionism: no longer were proud craftsmen afraid to admit to membership. The right to trade union representation was even at last grudgingly conceded to the clerical grades, who numbered well over a thousand accounting and clerical staff.

On the other hand they had also become deeply preoccupied with facing new problems of technological change introducing the semi-skilled and breaking down craft lines. It was this which gave rise to competition between societies and the fierce inter-union rivalry with the industrial or general unions recruiting the unorganised and less skilled formerly excluded by the craft unions. The Company skilfully played on these divisions which were especially sharp between craft societies and the National Union of Railwaymen. That union was particularly influential in the railshop in Swindon, where fifteen years earlier the young Jimmy Thomas had built a considerable reputation both in the running sheds, the Trades Council and the Town Council, on which he won a seat by defeating the boss of his own department. Reaction to "Black Friday" was to be a foretaste of 1926 and to decide what they did then. Swindon railshop leaders had cause for deep concern watching the first post-war attacks on the miners.

The shopmen in the craft societies of Engineers, Boilermakers, Coachmakers, Foundry Workers, Blacksmiths, Joiners, Bricklayers, Electricians, Patternmakers and Moulders, amongst others, were grouped in the Swindon Railway Federation of Trade Unions. They had been watching with anxiety mounting unemployment and threats to the miners' wages and conditions, the passing of the Emergency Powers Act in 1920 and the formation of "voluntary defence bodies". Now in the spring of 1921 the Lloyd George Government had suddenly brought forward the date for ending public control of the mines and therefore of the nationally determined profits pool which had shielded miners' wages. This precipitated the national miners' strike on 1 April 1921 against the massive district cuts. It was a clear indication of what those in the railway industry might expect when their private companies came to be decontrolled. The miners appealed for support from the Triple Alliance which had been set up to meet exactly this situation. Despite behind-the-scenes manœuvres by J. H. Thomas, the Joint Executives of the NUR and the Transport Workers' Federation declared their support, which was to begin on Friday, 15 April. But that left the vast majority of the Swindon shopmen deeply involved yet without advice from the headquarters of their many societies.

The Engineers' District Committee discussed "the legal position and the miners' strike" and wrote to their Head Office to ask "what action the EC proposed taking with regard to the national crisis" (AEU District Committee minutes, 6 April 1921).

The Railway Federation immediately called a mass meeting at the Swimming Baths on Sunday, 10 April, when "two or three thousand people were crowded into the room". The Chairman, H. Watkins (Boilermakers) opened the meeting by saying that they had to "decide whether we could sit on the fence whilst the miners and others were fighting against an attack on wages which, if successful, would mean ruin to trade union organisation" (Railway Federation minutes, 10 April 1921).

A unanimous resolution declared "wholehearted support to the miners in their struggle for Justice, subject to their respective Headquarters' instructions" and that they should hold another mass meeting on Friday, 15 April to finalise plans locally. They informed the Town Council and the County Chief Constable that "as citizens we demand the respect due to our honourable record and shall claim as an insult any attempt to increase the police force of the town".

Bitter feeling was expressed about the mobilisation of the armed forces and volunteers in the Special Defence Force. A unanimous resolution told the Home Office "that we emphatically protest against the government activities in using Military Reserve Forces for strike-breaking".

The Engineers still had had no instructions from their head office about what they should do when the Triple Alliance went into action; and they had to send their secretary to London on "Black Friday" itself, believing that "the EC did not realise the position of our members on the railway" and to "endeavour to get definite instructions". Meanwhile the Railway Federation had decided, despite the lack of clear instructions from many societies, to "leave work at 11.00 a.m. on Saturday morning and offer this as a lead to our members at the mass meeting".

When the mass meeting met, faced with the news that the Triple Alliance action had been called off, a vote of confidence in the Railway Federation "was carried with great enthusiasm and unanimity". A works collection produced £1,187 for the Miners' Children Fund.

One section of the workforce had been in difficulties. This was the Railway Clerks' Association, with its highly vulnerable membership ranging through the hierarchy from the shop clerk on the works floor to those in the stores, accounts and audit departments, and even to the fringe of the professionals and the CME's personal staff who regarded themselves as "management". The Swindon Railway Clerks had found it hard to make up their minds after holding two mass meetings in the Mechanics Institute with over 600 members present. They had still not reached a firm decision when their head office telephoned to them that the Triple Alliance action was off. Thereafter a number of them withheld their subscriptions or handed in their cards, and branch membership sank from some 1,200 to under 900. A key figure amongst them was Councillor W. R. Robins, their organising secretary when the branch was formed in 1911, later secretary of the Trades Council, Parliamentary candidate and by 1926 on his union's executive committee.

The formative experience of facing "Black Friday" with no advice from their headquarters left them prepared to be fully self-reliant both in civic and industrial action on their home ground. At local level they knew how to fight; here they could see their class duty and rose to the occasion in 1926 with an increase in self-confidence which left many of them amazed at themselves. But when a situation had to be faced in which industrial aims could no longer be achieved without an overall and nationwide political class view, this town of "railway servants" and their families had no answer without a lead from outside their great factory wall.

After 1921 for the next five years trade unionists in Swindon had been deeply concerned with local unemployment, short-time and problems of limitation of overtime; resisting cuts in piece-work prices and threats to wages; above all, with the vexed question of re-grading under Award 728 which caused inevitable demarcation disputes and difficulties about negotiation rights. The fact that the cause of all their troubles was the general crisis of capitalism and the new stage of the decline of British imperialism was far from self-evident to them. Their preoccupation was with the local form of the effects, which was indeed inescapably on their daily agenda. No headway could be made if disunity and trade union weakness were not overcome. Intermittently the Railway Federation found limited common ground with the Joint Committee of the three railway unions, the NUR, ASLEF and RCA. Parallel with these was a third force in the town which provided trade unionists with another meeting ground where united links might be forged. This was the Swindon Trades and Labour Council founded in 1891.

After the war a number of young ex-servicemen who were Independent Labour Party members became delegates and held office in Trades Council and developed strong links with the National Minority Movement. So did the 1926 secretary, J. R. Habgood (Transport and General), together with the chairman from the same union, the highly colourful Harry Hustings; both were also members of the Independent Labour Party. They all met regularly on Sunday evenings at the house of Harry Hustings who had started his working life in the Welsh coalfield. Here they would listen to Marxist lectures on Bergsonian philosophy and Greek History by Ralph Bates from the GWR Spring Testing shop. Bates was also in touch with a younger group of four Communist Party members: Reg Lee (Brass moulder), George Godsell (Footplateman), Morse (Carpenter) and Mills, a railwayman from Newport. These had a visit from W. C. Loeber of Wood Green, the Secretary of the Transport Workers' Minority Movement; a railwayman, he was elected in October 1922 to the National Executive of the Communist Party. He discussed with them the need for preparedness; they bought a typewriter, fixed up a duplicator and ran off and distributed stencilled leaflets. Between them these two groups were responsible for getting Tom Mann and S. Saklatvala, the Communist MP, invited to Swindon for enthusiastic meetings in 1925 and the early months of 1926. Both groups also campaigned strongly for the Industrial Alliance which aimed at bringing engineering unions into a new defensive grouping together with miners, railwaymen and transport workers.

In this they had some success. The Railway Clerks sent three delegates to a conference mandated to support it. The Engineers were less responsive. When AEU No. 5 Branch pressed for a mass meeting to discuss the Industrial Alliance, the DC did not "consider it necessary or the time opportune to hold a mass meeting for this purpose" (AEU DC minutes, 27 January 1926).

The Trades Council activists kept pressing the Engineers to take part in a local Council of Action without success. However, a Council of Action conference was called and gave Trades Council authority to summon two delegates from every union if the Trades Union Congress were unsuccessful in negotiations with the government and decided to impose an embargo. Two days before the historic meeting of Executives in the Memorial Hall in London, which Robins attended, the AEU District Committee had no special advice to give the normal quarterly shop stewards' gathering; their only preparatory step was to send their President Willie Noble to London for explicit guidance from their EC—remembering the pitiful failure of communication in 1921. On the morning of Sunday, 2 May, there were two contrasting events: the Archdeacon, Dr. Talbot, held an industrial service and preached a sermon strongly condemning trade union action; the Trades Council's recall Council of Action conference worked out agreed recommendations for the conduct of the strike in Swindon to be put to mass meetings. Some of the senior district office holders amongst Swindon's trade unionists were convinced that once again government and mine-owners would give way as they had on "red Friday" nine months before. But the moment the call came, these meticulous rule-abiding citizens moved solidly and enthusiastically into action. They welcomed it; it was what they felt should have happened in 1921—necessary action in a just cause.

All divisions amongst them were healed at a stroke. The Railway Federation, the Joint Railway Unions Committee and Clerks and the Trades Council acted in unison. The three railway unions held a membership meeting in the Mechanics Institute early on Monday, 3 May, and selected Billy Robins (RCA), A. J. B. Selwood (ASLEF) and Jack Scrivens, J. B. Bennett and C. Price (NUR) to represent them on the Swindon Central Strike Committee. Usually known as "The General Council" it was set up that evening at a mass meeting in the GWR Park. Selwood was elected chairman with Willie Noble from the Federation as vice-chairman; the secretary was J. R. Habgood from the Trades Council, which also provided a prominent member in Harry Hustings. Amongst the speakers were Robins with Jack Hieatt (T &

GWU) who represented Gloucester Trades Council and Labour Party. Telegrams from head offices of one union after another were read out; and a gathering of 6,000 passed with acclaim a resolution declaring "That this mass meeting of trade unionists pledges itself to carry out the instructions of their executive committees and any duties their local committee may call upon them to do, and to act in no way that would lead to any disturbance" (*Evening Advertiser*, 4 May 1926). This time there was no doubt in their minds.

Amongst those who were fully ready to get going this time were the Railway Clerks, who had had their problems in 1921. Immediately after work on Monday afternoon they hurried out of the factory across the road to crowd into the Mechanics Institute, where their national executive member, Billy Robins, addressed them about the miners' case and what had happened in London. The meeting was minuted as "a splendid one, both from the point of view of numbers and tone". The Company was staggered and angered at the result, to the same degree that fellow unionists in the town were delighted, when no less than 600 clerks stopped work on the Chief Mechanical Engineer's very doorstep.

That morning of Tuesday, 4 May, pickets went to all the gates, but they were not needed. The unions had agreed to allow apprentices to clock in if they wished that first morning and issued instructions to the pickets accordingly. One of these was L. V. Parker, a vehicle builder and one of the young ILP enthusiasts. He describes what happened next. "We let them through, but we took their names and noted which shop they worked in. But there was no work done by them, as the men were out and the machinery stopped. After they had gone inside they organised meetings during the morning, gathering their fellow apprentices together from all over the works. They decided they would go out." When they reached the "Tunnel" entrance in London Street, the manager, W. A. Stanier, was there. To prevent them leaving, he had a hose turned on them. "For a time they held back. Then one tall ginger-haired lad decided he was not going to put up with that. He got in amongst the boys and they decided to rush the exit in a body. And they did. Some got soaked through, but the manager was swept aside, his hat knocked off his head, and the boys swept out, to the cheering of the men outside. It was quite a sight to see the manager treated like that!" By 12.30 p.m. a notice appeared at every entrance signed by C. B. Collett, the Chief Mechanical Engineer: "In view of the large number of men who have failed to report themselves for duty these works are hereby closed until further notice." There was no doubt; the battle was on. The first two groups had already gone into action; the printers at the Swindon Press and the men who worked the municipally-owned trams stopped on Monday night.

All day long on Day One, Tuesday, 4 May, meetings were continuous as the organisational details were worked out. Union members began signing the vacant book each at their own headquarters. Each union provided pickets on the advice of the General Council which was in permanent session. The Co-operative Society put rooms in Harding Street at their disposal; the Railway Clerks provided them with office equipment and staff, including a young accounts clerk with the onerous job of paying out benefit from the Distress Fund to some 10,000 fellow townsfolk. This was W. H. Sargent, who twenty years later was to become the chairman of the Trades Council. "Pleased to report magnificent solidarity", wrote Habgood to the Trades Union Congress, commenting on "a splendid working arrangement" amongst the groups of unions, and that "united action is our watchword".

Ranged against them was the government-backed "Swindon Volunteer Services Committee", the make-up of which was highly predictable. Chairman was Major F. G. Wright, retired Assistant to the Chief Mechanical Engineer. A former mayor and now Wiltshire County Councillor, Borough Magistrate and a leading figure in the Territorials he was also the president of the Swindon branch of the English Church Union. Amongst other members of the committee in his support was Robert Hilton, for twenty-five years Town Clerk, as food officer. The activities, if any, of this body did not come into public view, though it is possible that its influence was at work in the introduction of a number of special constables: indeed, it would seem that central government soon intervened to ride rough-shod over them, as we shall see. Swindon's General Council reacted quickly at the first sign of intervention on Tuesday, 4 May, when the Chief Mechanical Engineer was offered troops and police to protect GWR property. As soon as it became known to them they sent a delegation to see Collett himself. NUR branch secretary A. Wentworth reported back from it to a mass meeting the same afternoon how Collett had replied: 'I don't want them. If you gentleman sitting here are prepared to assist me in protecting the property, I am prepared to do without them.' We at once gave him that guarantee" (*Evening Advertiser*, 5 May 1926). The General Council crossed the road again to the Strike Committee Rooms and proceeded to cope with their many other tasks.

Chief amongst these was the question of the control of the use of alternative fuel supplies for industrial power. It was a difficult question. On 1 May the TUC in its General Strike Order had called on unions concerned with electricity and gas to co-operate in ceasing to provide power and "to meet at once with a view to formulating common policy". But by 5 May these unions had still "not arrived at a well-defined policy", although the Electrical Power Engineers' Association had issued its advice to the government. This was that electricity supply undertakers should be told not to provide any to "an industrial works engaged in work of a non-essential character", and that no volunteers should be introduced. On the eve of the General Strike the government issued instructions that the use of coal, gas or electricity for industrial purposes should be restricted to 50 per cent of the average weekly consumption. Meanwhile the local strike committees were being forced to take their own decisions, such was the lack of guidance and preparedness in Smith Square.

What would happen in Swindon, where both tramways and electricity were municipally owned? A Swindon Corporation Bill was on its way through Parliament to enable the Corporation to build a modern power station at Moredon at the cost of £265,000, capable of supplying the GWR works, which had hitherto generated its own, alongside its own gas-making capacity. Swindon trade unionists were strongly placed. Of the fifteen town councillors making up the Electricity and Tramways Committee, nine were employed by the GWR and one was the Co-operative Society manager; four were small shopkeepers whose livelihood depended on the work force; there remained a solicitor and the Mayor, W. G. Adams, an auctioneer, as *ex officio* member. On the all-important Electricity sub-committee of ten members the preponderance of "insiders" was overwhelming—two fitters, a turner, a boilersmith, a boilermaker, a railway clerk and a foreman, including leading members of the AEU, the RCA and the Boilermakers Society, with Billy Robins, national executive member of the RCA and member of the central strike committee's General Council, as vice-chairman. This left as "outsiders" only the Co-operative manager, a draper and the solicitor, who was in fact absent abroad.

The members of the Electricity sub-committee were called together at once for an emergency meeting on "Strike Tuesday" afternoon, before the full Council held its normal monthly meeting that evening, to discuss what instructions should be given to the managers of the electricity and tramways undertakings. When it was over the mayor took two important actions. He instructed the tramways manager T. Medcalf, not to put trams manned by volunteers on the streets. Then he told the electricity manager, A. Nicklin, to send men at once to the main industrial enterprises and remove their power fuses. By 6 p.m. electricians were already on their way up Victoria Hill to the Swindon Press, which published the *Evening Advertiser* and the two weeklies, the *Swindon Advertiser* and the *North Wilts Herald.* Arguments had been put which convinced the mayor that the power station would close down at once, with disastrous consequences, if he acted otherwise. The strike secretary, J. R. Habgood, forty-five years later made this comment in a letter to the author, dated 9 August 1971: "The Big Stick Brigade had threatened us with troops. So is it surprising that we had to mention that our members were operating the fuses at the power station—and the pumps at the Severn Tunnel?"

Robert Hilton, the Town Clerk, neither minuted the committee nor reported it later that evening to the full Town Council, which dealt only with routine business and made no provision for emergency sittings during the crisis. Asked for an explanation at a subsequent Council meeting, he said that "in his opinion it was not a decision that should be recorded".

Withdrawing the fuses and not putting on the streets public transport manned by volunteers drove the Swindon press into a frenzy and may not have pleased some of the other managers of local industry; but it ensured a peaceful climate throughout Swindon during this first week of unprecedented industrial upheaval. The *Swindon Advertiser* (14 May) itself reported, "the town has been very quiet and orderly. The police have had no trouble whatever." But immediately after the un-minuted Electricity sub-committee meeting, and also without the knowledge of the councillors, behind-the-scenes moves began which were to change the whole peaceful climate when they became known a week later.

The Town Clerk reported the events to Major the Rt. Hon Earl Winterton MP, the Civil Commissioner for the South Midlands District, who called on Sir Arthur Griffith-Boscawen to go as his representative to Swindon, "as the condition of affairs there was serious". His account of what happened next was given in a letter read in the House of Lords when the Swindon Corporation Bill was being debated in July. Griffith-Boscawen hurried to Swindon next day, Thursday, 6 May, and had his first interviews with the Mayor, the Town Clerk and others. We note the smooth phraseology of the practised civil servant in his account of what passed between them: "We discussed the special difficulties in Swindon which arose from the fact that the GWR employed the great majority of the men in the town and they were all on strike. Among the strikers were members of the Corporation and Electricity Committee, including the chairman of the latter. The mayor said that if the power were restored he feared that all the workers at the power station, or the majority of them, would come out and the town would be plunged into darkness; and that volunteers capable of manning the station could not be obtained in Swindon; to which I replied that I might be able to get them from outside."

The next day Hilton wrote to promise that if Griffith-Boscawen could get "competent volunteers from outside, the Mayor and Corporation would at once restore the power, and I accordingly set to work to procure the same". This was not the picture presented by the spokesman for the Swindon Press, who continually attacked "the pusillanimous attitude" of the Corporation.

Swindon trade unionists were quite unaware of what was brewing in the Mayor's Parlour; for it took some days for Griffith-Boscawen to return with fourteen naval pensioners rounded up from Portsmouth to break any strike at the power station.

Billy Robins was always a man of peace outside the sphere of tactics in committees; he returned much relieved from the Town Hall to play his part in Swindon's General Council as the process of planning full programmes began. In the forefront were the daily mass meetings of strikers and their families, numbering several thousand, in the GWR Park. All kinds of social entertainment and educational activities were organised; teams of married versus single men challenged each other at football, cricket, bowls and darts; concerts, socials and literary readings were widely supported. For the leaders, committees seemed always in progress as manifold problems of the hard daily grind of organisation were submitted from the different unions: permit problems, picket allocation, calls for speakers—they were endless.

Rumours were also rife that any railway clerk not reporting for duty would be struck off the GWR's books as having discharged themselves; and an ambiguously worded disavowal by the GWR asserting that clerks would be treated no differently from other employees did not restore confidence. The rumour was only partially successful, however. Although some clerks began to go in, a stronger force of their colleagues turned out to picket them and take names, led by Billy Robins. Few striking clerks broke away.

As the strike continued and the GWR began to get a few trains running from Paddington by using strike-breaking volunteers and

Oxford University students, a very few footplatemen of various grades were induced to go in. There were only a dozen Swindon men at most who worked cleaning, firing or driving. Picket duty on the traffic side was no easy task. Turns might start all round the clock; there was no need to go through an entrance for those ready to sneak into the works over the manager's garden wall or from St. Mark's churchyard or be picked up on the line out of town. The footplatemen were angry that even a handful of their members should lay the union open to criticism, and they decided on a novel form of picketing. Forty-two years later Roy Green, an ASLEF member with a distinguished first world war record, described in an interview with the author how they set about it.

Roy Green was one of the keen young committee men who spent most of his time in the ASLEF branch room making sure they knew the whereabouts of every member. "If they didn't sign the book—and we gave them twenty-four hours to do it—then we began to wonder, if none of the committee had seen them. Mind, there were some who didn't like the idea of going into the Union Hotel to sign the book. There were several who would say: 'Tell them I'm all right'; and we knew when we could take that for granted, you see. I remember one fellow well; a teetotaller, and you couldn't get him into a pub under any conditions. But they were on strike all right."

Of the nine who stood apart, three said bluntly from the start that they would work. One of these was on the branch committee: "Tuckett even arranged a male voice choir concert to raise funds for the strike fund, and yet he went to work. There's no accounting for some people's way of thinking! He lived in Station Road and Jack Neal and I gave him the present of a gallon of tar through his letter-box one day after we had been arguing about how to bring it home to them that they weren't mates of ours any longer. Then Fireman Taylor had the idea of treating them as though they were dead, having a mock funeral procession and cremating them on the Corporation rubbish tip."

The younger fraternity amongst the fireman set to and made coffins, which "the ladies covered with a curtain or a cloth, and made a wreath of dandelions and nettles for each of them."

"We started in the morning with some 500 mourners, mostly our own people. But other grades joined in and by the afternoon at the end of the ceremony there were a thousand following. Of course when we called with a coffin all the neighbours came out. They were delighted! We had no trouble with any of them; almost everyone in those streets had someone on strike themselves. We had the whole population with us in this demonstration."

In the law-abiding spirit of typical Swindonian railwaymen they had first got permission for the procession from the police, who "kept back the traffic for us at one or two of the busy spots at Manchester Road, the Centre and down by The Ship". They called at an ironmonger's shop in Faringdon Road and borrowed his shop sign, a trowel and set square four-foot long which they clashed to represent the passing knell. "You can guess what a row we made going through town. At each house when we knocked we told them we'd come to take them for a ride, and that if they didn't come with us we'd have the pleasure of burying them. The man in Rosebery Street peeped through the window but wouldn't come to the door, he couldn't face us. We had to talk to some with the door half shut."

There came a direct confrontation with an engine driver of some seniority. "We met 'Timber' Higgins and his wife as we went under the Rodbourne bridges. We stopped them and told him that if he'd decided to work against us and wouldn't take the chance now to come out and join us, we'd have no alternative but to go on and bury him. When 'Timber' refused we went on to his street and knocked at his house, although he was out, so that his neighbours could see what was happening."

One of their members called Arthur Moulding "undertook the duties of undertaker. He did it to perfection; top hat, long tail coat, black gloves, striped trousers, and he led the procession on towards the municipal rubbish tip in Morris Street." Here a woman came out of her shop to give them two gallons of paraffin for the cremation. "Then one of our drivers, Joe Baldwin, borrowed a white tablecloth from a lady in the street, and dressed in this as a surplice he said a burial service over the nine coffins. As he set fire to them his last words were 'May the wind blow their remains to the four corners of the earth, and to hell with them all'."

So ended the most remarkable funeral ceremony in Swindon. There were more "mourners" at the rubbish tip than were to follow when J. H. Thomas's remains were brought back to the Radnor Street cemetery twenty-four years later; but there was no press publicity for the earlier event. I asked Roy Green what were his thoughts when he was sent as a representative to "Timber" Higgins second funeral thirty years later. He replied, "Why, I found myself muttering the committal words of his first funeral."

Swindon townsfolk were fast gaining in self-confidence. United in a just cause and learning each day to take new initiatives, they found it a mystery that anyone could stand apart from his neighbours.

For some the fruits were small enough and it was hard to resist pressures. Ten years earlier as a sixteen-year-old apprentice cleaner Harry Avern had a fight with another lad at work and left town. After years of unemployment and wandering he had recently returned with four children to Swindon. Recognising him in the street after the strike had begun, the running shed foreman offered him the lure of a new start and permanent job if he would fire to a blackleg driver. The temptation was too great; but he had a miserable time. Stopped with signals against them outside Reading, he was stoned. Returning from Paddington he was landed with an aristocratic volunteer whose incompetence left them stranded in Box Tunnel without steam. At the end there was no permanent job for Harry; all he got was an illuminated certificate for strike-breaking and a postal order for 21*s*. from a grateful GWR.

If they felt bitterness towards their own people who stooped to blackleg, railwaymen's feelings were fiercely contemptuous against the gentlemanly volunteer strike-breakers, total aliens from another world. It was afterwards said that there were occasions when blacklegging footplatemen were ready to carry strike despatches right down the line under the noses of "the plus-four gentry" at their side.

With the BBC taken over and closely controlled by the government it was important to keep open a strong line of communications. The General Council began at once to produce a single-sheet stencilled bulletin for the union branches. When Habgood sent the first two to the TUC on Wednesday, 5 May, he said that it had been issued to "Plymouth and all intervening strike centres". Connections were also kept up from Oxford and Banbury and southward to Westbury, as well as through Gloucester to Wales, Wolverhampton, Oswestry and Birmingham. Locally young cyclists served as dispatch riders. As soon as the *British Worker* was published Rex Hutchings (coachmakers) drove regularly the eighty miles to London with Percy Fox who fetched it in his motorcycle and sidecar. He found himself involved in the attacks by the Fascists on the *Daily Herald* offices to attempt to stop supplies; he gave an eyewitness account to a mass meeting in the Park on Saturday, 8 May, when he shared the platform on the bandstand with Kyrle Bellew (Mrs. Arthur Bourchier), the actress. In addition, some unions established contact with their own head office by dispatch riders. For the NUR, Charles Knight vividly remembers driving to London in his own car to fetch the members' strike pay. Then aged forty-six, he had started his working life as a motor mechanic when the automobile was a rarity.

By Friday, 7 May, the communications routine was firmly established and Habgood could report to the TUC: "Position at Swindon splendid. Ben Tillett addressed a large mass meeting here this morning. Spirit of all raised to 100 per cent in consequence. Any other national speakers travelling this way we shall be pleased to accommodate. Demand for larger supplies of *British Worker*. Our lines of communication working excellent. We have made certain arrangements for your despatch riders to obtain petrol. The CWS here have fixed us up splendid."

Without electrical fuses the typesetting machines and presses of the local newspapers could not run. But the *Evening Advertiser* did appear as a single sheet with a little news on the front, largely copied from the *British Gazette*; the rest was repeated items and advertisements. Its stable mate, the weekly *North Wilts Herald* for 7 May, was reduced to four pages. In the *North Wilts Herald* of 21 May there was a strong protest about the Corporation's having removed the fuses—a "desperate step to stifle the freedom of the press . . . an amazing action in which Swindon, so far as we have been able to ascertain, stands alone amongst all the civic authorities of the country". It was followed by an interesting description of how the papers were produced during the emergency by the works manager, a veteran poster hand, a machine room labourer, five apprentices, the former proprietor of the *North Wilts Herald* and the retired editor of the *Swindon Advertiser*, Sam Morris. "A Ford motor car engine was purchased and delivered within the hour." Its chassis was mounted on trestles, held firm by timber struts and linked by a belt driven from counter-shafting fitted to the smallest of the three high-speed rotary presses. It made little difference to the dissemination of news at this time, however. The townsfolk got the news from the daily mass meetings of thousands in the Park. As an eyewitness recalls, "It was like a Labour Fête every day." Billy Robins would open up the meeting by trying out the microphone of the loud hailer. He always said: "Can you hear me at the back?"; and they always answered with a roar "NO!" The strike chairman and much respected footplatemen's leader, A. J. B. Selwood, would start each day's announcements with the same opening words, which became his familiar trademark: "As far as we are locally concerned, the situation remains the same." For the first week that was entirely true.

The General Council early posted notices stressing that picketing must be peaceful. But the overwhelming sense of public support made this warning scarcely necessary. The nearest thing to an "incident" never became known outside a very small circle. Half a dozen hotheads amongst the younger footplatemen set off to reverse the points at Dauntsey Bank, where the main line comes off the downs into the vale. The late Roy Green told what happened: "Another lad and I ran after them before they'd gone far. We convinced them that it would be wrong and that it wasn't necessary. Now, greasing the line on an incline really does make heavy going; that was how we made many of these inexperienced firemen sweat." Others have described how people would gather at the Milk Bank when the very few trains crawled slowly through to boo the Oxford University students who manned them. "The women folk were especially to the fore at that. They'd stand there in a line with their aprons full of stones and single out these young fellows, like turmut hoeing."

So big was the turnout every day that the General Council had to appeal to people not to congest the streets. Apart from the meetings and social festivities people would throng the town in the lovely May weather to exchange news and the stories coming in from the country villages and areas outside Swindon. Platelayers at Wroughton passed a unanimous message of "full support to attain the object for which we are called out". Bristol railwaymen sent their thanks for Swindon branches' "inspiring message" to them.

Jokes and jingles were passed on that were current in Bristol or Gloucester, such as the question about the princess who had just been born: "Is the Duke of York claiming 4*d.* per day unemployment benefit for the latest arrival?"

The stories which were perhaps the most appreciated were those about the problems of the gentlemen volunteers. A favourite was the Bristol temporary footplateman who could not stop his train at Temple Meads, and only succeeded in pulling up at last near Bath by emptying the firebox. At Chippenham the stationmaster was single-handed and, according to the Swindon press, had to rely on "a well-known tradesman snipping the tickets, a local landowner acting as porter and a political agent doing duty as a booking clerk". Asked whether the strikers were going to interfere with the stationmaster's arrangements, a union representative kept a straight face as he replied that they would not: "It does not hurt our cause."

Engines were driven by people with little knowledge of proper working. No railwayman, of course, would cause wilful damage to his beloved friend and enemy, the engine; there was no sabotage of rolling stock. But there was no need for sabotage; for the inexperienced volunteers on the footplate themselves did massive damage. Fire-boxes were burnt out. Axle-boxes seized up through lack of oil. Water ran low in the boilers and melted the lead plugs; steam then came on the fire, the engine stopped and had to be towed to workshops. This was common and often happened miles from a station. It was estimated that it took two years to repair all the damage caused during those days by ignorant or inexperienced volunteers. On one occasion the under manager on the locomotive side, J. Dawson, was anxious to get an engine out which was needed at the station for a blackleg team to pull carriages. The engine was steamed up and stood near the closed doors in "A" Shop. To clear a trolley it was necessary first to go forward a few yards. But Dawson put the lever in reverse instead and shot right through the doors. That incident was long remembered and the "A" Shop chargeman never tired of telling it.

When the lower-ranking supervisory staff, under great pressure from the GWR, did decide to go into the empty echoing works they rarely benefited from it in the long run. In the short term they found themselves excluded from the usual social life at Swindon's many working men's clubs and friendly society lodges. The overwhelming mood which people remember of that week is the sense of happiness at being united, with long-standing and difficult divisions healed. "I would rather live in the England today than in the England of a month ago. Spiritual life is higher", wrote veteran Reuben George soon after the strike had ended. In profound contradiction to the *Swindon Advertiser*'s editorial remark that "the men and women on strike whose hearts were in the strike comprised an infinitesimal proportion of the whole", the old Socialist orator of the nineties had this to say: "Wherever the men met, the voice of the politician and sectarian was hushed. There were Liberals, Tories, Labour Socialists; Church, Chapel, Roman Catholic, Unitarian, Salvationists; men of strong political and sectarian bias and men of none whatever. . . . These men and women met as one. They spoke from the various platforms. They joined in the work of organisation; and what is more and greater than all, they forgot all Party bitterness and sectarian strife. They threw themselves wholeheartedly into the question of help for the miners" (*Swindon Advertiser*, 18 June 1926). They had good reason for their united effort which also brought them happiness; as an opponent found on asking many individuals, including the hard-pressed strikers' wives, why they struck, the invariable reply was: "If the miners' wages are reduced, ours will be."

There were bitter hardships; for the financial strain was heavy from the first, and it was felt sharply when the first week's payday passed. During the whole period Swindon banks handled more sovereigns and half sovereigns than for many years, the local paper reported. These were the "little family hoards, curios always redeemable at face value, which people had been compelled to part with". Bill Peacey (Vehicle Builders) remembers coming out of school and finding a shilling on the pavement outside The Empire. He ran home with it to his mother. "Oh, how we can do with that!" she cried, adding: "I only hope whoever lost it doesn't need it as much as we do."

Not only was strike pay low for those entitled to draw it; there were others for whom there was nothing until the TUC called out the second strike wave, which did not happen until the second week. Yet they were not working, either because power fuses had been withdrawn or through shortage of supplies and lack of transport. What, for example, was the position of AEU members at Garrard's engineering factory? The branches pressed the district committee with mounting concern because such members were not getting idle benefit. From the EC no satisfactory answer was forthcoming, even after despatch riders were sent to head office. Their minutes record increasing anger about it. Meanwhile in large families especially there was hunger. The secretary of the National Union of Teachers, A. E. Bullock, proposed that children in need should be fed at the schools; whilst the old Labour stalwart Reuben George was using his good offices to press the Education Committee to authorise it, the teachers themselves supplied milk for the children in school. Teachers tried not to embarrass the children most in need. Edith Stevens was teaching infants at Clarence Street school; she recalled how children were told to put their heads down on their desks and shut their eyes whilst the class was asked, "Hands up those who didn't have any breakfast this morning." The feeding centres were opened Saturdays and Sundays. A Distress Fund was set up under the General Council administered by three members; its food vouchers were honoured by the Co-operative Society, which also provided its own members with a £1 voucher to be spent on goods and paid back at 1*s*. a week. The Society kept a store of 300 gallons of petrol on hand for despatch riders and put its meeting rooms at the disposal of the General Council. The Free Church Council also opened its halls for the strikers' use. There were only about forty members of the Society of Friends, including Willie Noble and Councillor Mrs. Noble; mostly they co-operated. Amongst the clergy of the half a dozen Anglo-Catholic churches associated with St. Mark's there was one shining example. A young curate, Father K. N. Crisford, strode out of St. Mark's Vicarage, crossed the road to the GWR Park and sprang up on the horse-dray which was being used as platform at a mass meeting. A tall figure in his flowing cassock, he spoke in support of the miners and was warmly applauded. He was the only one of the clergy of the established church to take his stand with them openly.

As the first week drew to a close with all in good heart the large chapel and church communities in Swindon learned with a sense of shock that the Baldwin Government had imposed censorship on no less a personage than the Archbishop of Canterbury. But no reference was made to it in the united intercessionary service at the Parish Church that Sunday, attended by the Mayor and members of the Town Council. After lessons were read by the Rev. W. Kelson and the Rev. W. B. Wakefield (Congregationalist), the vicar, the Rev. C. A. Mayell, preached the keynote sermon, urging "his hearers to be tactful and maintain good order in the present time of stress. He urged the people not to be idle but to work and economise in everything. He prayed that justice and truth, good will and mutual understanding would prevail, and peace would soon reign in the country" (*North Wilts Herald*, 14 May). Sir Arthur Griffith-Boscawen's contribution to tact, good order and mutual understanding was already on its way in the form of fourteen naval pensioner strike-beakers to intimidate the workers maintaining the power station in Corporation Street.

He went into action on Monday, 10 May, whilst the naval pensioners stood by, waiting to be lodged by the Corporation. Already that morning there was a new note of anxiety and rising anger in town, because of the latest communication from the GWR which was posted up outside the NUR rooms in Temple Street. Having described the strike in sympathy for the miners as "a deep conspiracy against the State", the GWR circular outlined the conditions under which the works would be re-opened. It was so worded as to be taken to mean that if and when employees were taken back, it would be as new starts, with consequent loss of seniority, pay and privileges. Moreover, they would be subject to claims for damages, having broken their contract; and those in positions of special responsibility would not be taken back nor those taking a leading part in the strike. This brought a very great attendance in the Park that morning at the mass meeting addressed by Selwood, Billy Robins, and the Railway Clerks' branch secretary A. W. Rawlings. Robins was a devout Methodist and Rawlings was said to be an atheist, but they were at one on this, which was specially threatening for their fellow members.

Meanwhile Griffith-Boscawen got his own way with the Swindon Corporation. Mayor Adams gave way to pressure from on high and ordered the fuses to be returned. The naval pensioners were drafted in. Eight councillors put to Mayor Adams a demand, in accordance with Standing Orders, requisitioning a Special Council Meeting. But advised by the Town Clerk, he ignored Standing Orders and refused to call it. He also instructed the Transport Manager to get the municipal trams back on the roads at once, run by volunteers. Griffith-Boscawen went back to London, saying he "regarded the solution as a very satisfactory one".

These developments put an end to the period of "goodwill and mutual understanding" in Swindon. Suddenly all the stops were pulled out and a propaganda chorus against the strikers orchestrated nationally. Lord Astbury delivered a judgment in the High Court restraining seamen's trade union branches from paying strike benefit on the grounds that a sympathetic strike was illegal; the *Daily Mail* called for arrest of the TUC General Council and charged them with treason; Lord Balfour thundered about it not being an industrial action but an attempt at revolution and a plot to overthrow the constitution. The rule-abiding, chapel-going district committee members of Swindon were not talking the same language. To them recent events indicated that it was the employers who were overthrowing the constitution, aided and abetted by local government officials. All the committees became intensely active. The Engineers were meeting all through Monday and Tuesday, with a mass gathering of members at the Mechanics Institute in the afternoon, "one of the finest meetings ever held, the hall being packed to excess and the members very enthusiastic". That evening when the branch officers met and "a telegram was read calling all engineering and shipbuilding members out" in the second wave, it was decided to have another "mass meeting of members as soon as possible, and that the wives of our members be invited". The General Council held a very large mass meeting in the Park, followed by several more on Princess Street Recreation ground, where unanimous protests were recorded about the employment of volunteers. During their morning meeting on Wednesday, 12 May, the Engineers received a deputation from their electricity works members who had got letters from the Corporation stating that if they did not start work next morning "they would consider themselves discharged". The letters were passed on to the General Council who were also taking up the question of the tramwaymen, they being equally under threat. These provocative pinpricks had sharpened the feeling at the same time as the general mood was raised even higher than before with news that the full strength nationally of the Engineers was now to be mobilised; although it did not directly affect the Swindon rail shopmen, who had been on strike from the first, they believed it would quickly settle the vexed question of idle benefit for the others. In fact there were by now 20,000 men and women idle in the town and surrounding villages. Far from there being any sign of a widespread return to work, of the Great Western Railway Company's 27,426 shopmen 92·9 per cent were on strike as against 93 per cent the first day, and in Swindon the proportion was always higher than average.

The Swindon General Council were taking up the case of the electricity and tramways men, with feeling running high at the Mayor's refusal to call a special meeting of the Town Council, when startling news was received on Day Nine. Here is one account of how trade unionists reacted to it. That afternoon Bill Sargent was on picket duty for the Railway Clerks outside the Mechanics Institute. "Someone dashed across from the Park saying that they had heard on the one o'clock news that the strike was over. Of course, we knew that the employers must have given in and that we'd won the victory." They were jubilant.

Full realisation of the facts did not come until late afternoon. Swindon sent Harry Hustings, Billy Robins and J. R. Habgood to London and despatch riders hurried to each organisation with this notice:

Swindon Central Strike Committee
Co-Operative Hall
Harding Street
Swindon

Wednesday 12th May 1925 [*sic*]
There is no satisfactory settlement. Though the strike has been called off nationally, the position so far as Swindon is concerned is in course of negotiation. The leaders are going to London for information. Men must on no account return to work tomorrow in any occupation. A meeting tomorrow in the Park at 12 noon. The

Unions will carry on existing arrangements for maintaining absolute loyalty and solidarity.

H. R. Hustings Chairman
J. R. Habgood Secretary
per AWR

The Strike Picket Committee was once more in action. By next morning all could read at the GWR works a notice signed by Sir Felix J. C. Pole, the General Manager at Paddington, announcing that employees would be accepted for duty "as soon as possible subject to two conditions: 1. Every man who left his work without notice has broken his contract of service and the Companies feel they must reserve any rights they possess in this matter; and 2. A number of men in positions of trust have gone on strike and others have been guilty of acts of violence and intimidation. The Companies propose to examine these cases individually and meanwhile they reserve their decisions in regard to them." From this it was clear that the TUC had got no guarantee against victimisation.

When the leaders came back from London and reported to an immense meeting in the Park that morning, Billy Robins put the TUC's official line, claiming that negotiations could now be resumed on the miners' case; and so, he insisted, "We've won!" At this, Hustings cried out: "That's a lie!" Answering questions from the crowd he said he had put on a red waistcoat when the struggle began and had promised to wear it until they had won. "Look, I'm still wearing it!" For years afterwards Harry Hustings always wore his red waistcoat and a white muffler at Town Council meetings.

The question for Swindon trade unionists that morning, however, was what should they do now? On that there was no division. They were seething with anger at the "intimidation by the railway companies", and passed a resolution expressing it. Whether few or many might be judged "guilty of violence", there was no doubt that all had "broken their contract of service" by leaving "work without notice". Were they to permit the GWR to pick and choose who should return, and when? On this they were unanimous; they voted not to return to work until there was a guarantee that all would be reinstated. They went on to adopt another resolution demanding unconditional release of all prisoners arrested in connection with the General Strike. Pickets then returned to duty to give effect to their resolution with a sharpened sense of vigilance.

As thousands left the Park in determined mood, they found that the first two trams had been put on the streets, one driven by an inspector. In no time at all dense crowds closed round them both at the Tram Centre and at the Town Hall. When police were ordered to stand by the driver's seat to force a passage there were angry scenes. Women fetched stones in their aprons to throw amid loud cheering, booing and cries of "Blackleg!" When the tram from Rodbourne was halted at the Tram Centre they began to rock it. Watching from Lennard's roof where he was working as an electrician, C. Messinger, "honestly thought they'd tip it over. It was fierce!" he recalled forty-two years later. When the Deputy Chief Constable Superintendent Brooks mounted the car and tried to clear the way some jumped on the buffer and clambered all over the trailer. When the tram got away a group of thirty or forty younger men followed after, and each time a crowd stopped it, they shouted up at the driver "Come down you . . . blackleg!" Later a leader amongst them, Harry Grubb, was summonsed under the Emergency Powers Act in a case heard on 10 June and fined £5 for "acts likely to impede or restrict measures taken for maintaining the means of transport". A huge crowd gathered at the Town Hall stopping both trams. Superintendent Brooks appealed for order but could not make himself heard. Then Billy Robins got up and asked the crowd to let the trams go on, but without effect. It was not until he and Selwood hastened to Mayor Adams and persuaded him to order the trams back to the depot that the crowd began to disperse. Later that afternoon there was an incident at the White House bridges between a picket and one of the nine footplatemen who had worked during the strike. First-class driver, Lloyd, with thirty-one years' service to his credit, was fined £4 17*s*. for "intimidation" when the case was heard on 31 May.

That night the Engineers sponsored a concert to raise funds for the Distress Committee. But by Friday, 14 May, the situation was very difficult. In London deeply humiliating Terms of Settlement were signed between the three railway unions and the railway general managers, headed by J. H. Thomas and Sir Felix Pole respectively. The only grain of comfort was that those whom the GWR did not exclude should be taken back by "seniority in each grade" as and when work could be found. But this left it still an entirely open question of what was to happen to the rest of Swindon's trade unionists, constituting the vast majority. In doubt was the position of the rail shopmen within the Railway Federation—all the engineers outside the GWR, the men in the municipally owned tramways and electricity undertakings, and the printers who had been told they would only be taken back on individual contracts. The Engineers' representatives on the Railway Federation reported back that "it was decided by the Federation to carry on, as the Railway Companies were not playing the game. Members were being asked to sign forms and declarations and humiliate themselves" (AEU District Committee minutes, 14 May 1926). By Saturday morning, 15 May, the Engineers received "a telegram from EC instructing members to return to work at firms prepared to agree to start them unconditionally." Garrard's manager had already agreed to do so, stating that "the men would return just as they left; he should not make the slightest difference to them, and would think none the less of them". Their morning meeting stood adjourned whilst they sent their President Willie Noble and other officers to consult directly with the General Council.

It was Swindon's Labour Fête Day. In high spirits despite the pouring rain processions formed up at the Town Hall and marched to the Park to hold May Queen revels and to admire trick cyclists. For the second year in succession the aristocrats of "the Western", the men of AE Shop where the great locomotives were assembled, distinguished themselves in the sports by winning the tug-of-war. The mood was one of high spirits because they believed that their resolute stand had successfully checked intimidation by the GWR and other employers. At their adjourned meeting at 6 p.m. that evening the Engineers' representatives reported back: "The whole position has changed. The Corporation (Electricity and Tramways) had agreed to reinstate all members on the 17th inst. The Printing Offices that had been giving trouble had also agreed the same, and all other outside firms had fell into line. The GWR had agreed to take down the notice re 'Short Time' and to open the factory on the 17th inst, but it was understood that the question of 'Short Time' would have to be definitely considered at an early date."

They had had a telegram direct from their EC that the railway strike was off; they pointedly minuted that they "appreciated the official news from our own organisation". But there was also a first hint that there were serious difficulties to be overcome. Their running shed members had been told to report only as and when they were wanted: but they were all nevertheless going to report for duty on the Monday. Now it was going to be uphill all the way; and they had done well to show determination when the TUC General Council sold out and the railway leaders cracked.

Straightaway they found themselves on a four-day week, with all shops closed "until further notice" on Mondays and Saturdays. In addition they found that the GWR was blocking reinstatement. On Sunday, 23 May, several thousands met in Princess Street Recreation Ground and passed a resolution expressing "disapproval of the spirit in which the GWR has met the settlement of the general and railway strikes". Arthur Selwood gave instances of footplatemen not being put on duty whilst others were working overtime. Robins gave details of national negotiations on it and set himself to defend J. H. Thomas and his Terms of Settlement. Asking the Swindon men for "confidence in your leaders", he went on: "I know you cannot square the present position with the solidarity shown in Swindon during these nine days. Some of you feel that great sacrifices have been made and nothing gained. But I ask you to believe me when I say there is no need for pessimism. I say with a due sense of responsibility that the spirit of the agreement arrived at has been violated again and again in the last few days" (*North Wilts Herald*, 28 May 1926). Railway Clerks had not been reinstated according to traffic and work being found. Referring to his own position, he said: "I don't know what the future holds for me." He was still waiting to answer charges of intimidation of pickets and "watching and besetting" the premises, which the GWR was bringing against him ten days later.

Three days before his case came up for hearing there were lively scenes at the first Town Council meeting following the strike. After a big crowd had packed the public gallery Mayor Adams ruled out a request that the large overflow should be admitted to empty spaces within the Council Chamber. Suspension of standing orders was moved so that the Council could decide, but the Town Clerk intervened on the ground that standing orders could only be suspended to discuss business which was properly before the meeting, and this did not include the admission of strangers to the Council Chamber. As councillor after councillor protested the Mayor ruled each out of order. When the Town Clerk added that no member of the public had any right to attend council meetings, Hustings said: "I challenge that! When the Town Clerk says no ratepayer has the right to attend meetings of the council, I say he is wrong."

The Mayor: "I rule you out of order."

Mr. Hustings: "You rule everything out of order."

Then Robins attempted to move a resolution condemning "the action of the Mayor, who, during the recent strike, deliberately committed acts of provocation and abused the office of Mayor". In particular he had failed to call a Special Meeting "to consider problems arising out of the dispute", and refusing the request for it by eight members. In addition he had varied the policy of the Electricity and Tramways Committee without consulting it or the chairman. Finally, he quoted the order to run the trams, "provoking the townspeople to a breach of the peace, which was prevented by the intervention of prominent citizens whose action caused the order to be cancelled".

Two days after the June Council meeting Robins came before the magistrates, who included Mayor Adams. The GWR lawyer appearing for the prosecution opened by referring to the Astbury Judgment that the "so-called general strike" was illegal, and contended that Robins was not himself involved in a trade dispute which would entitle him under the Trades Disputes Act 1906 to engage in peaceful picketing. He was therefore charged under the penal Conspiracy and Protection of Property Act 1875, with the serious offence of intimidation and "watching and besetting" GWR property. Three prosection witnesses were called; one came very much against his will, but another was no less a figure than the chief personnel clerk to the Chief Mechanical Engineer and appeared more than willing to give hostile evidence. They described going to work on Wednesday, 5 May, past thirty or forty clerks on picket duty outside the Mechanics Institute. As they went in and people they worked with recognised them, their names were called out and noted down. Robins was present. When he himself gave evidence, Robins claimed that he had come to speak to the pickets and insisted that no names were taken whilst he was there. London counsel were engaged on both sides ready to argue the important legal issues; but in the event the defence relied successfully upon the evidence of watching and besetting being "so slender" that there would be no prospect of a jury convicting if Robins were committed for trial. The press account records the end: "After a brief retirement the Mayor said the magistrates had given careful consideration to the case and they had decided to dismiss the charges against the Defendant. The decision was received with applause in the Court." There was good cause for applause.

"We were all terribly concerned about what would happen to him should he be convicted," declares Bill Sargent, who was subpoenaed to give evidence but not in fact called. "But from that time on his future was the same as any of the clerks. In Swindon something like 80 per cent of the clerical staff had been on strike. Throughout the whole period we were under the impression that we had been dismissed by the railway company and that our jobs were at stake, and it seemed a high probability that we would not be re-employed. Other unions returned to work immediately even though on short time; but clerical staff were kept out, their return to duty conditional on their having work to do. Many of our members didn't return for over six months. We felt very let down by the procedure on return. It was impossible that the GWR shouldn't take back the manual workers; the factory depended on their work, whereas it didn't on ours. Because there had been no production carried on there were no figures for us to process. If the accounts hadn't been done for twelve months no one would have been worried; they could have guessed at the figures. Our whole position was more worrying. Railway accountancy was such a specialised affair; it was entirely different from accountancy that you find in a normal business. Built on the basis of abstracts of expenditure, rather than double-entry book-keeping, we were simply posting figures in a one-column ledger. To have tried to enter any of the accountancy jobs 'Outside' would have been impossible. The bitterness against those who had stayed in was keen. When we got back to work eventually some didn't speak to colleagues they sat next to for over a year." Whilst the Railway Clerks branch lost some members they also recruited during the strike, with a net gain to raise their post-strike membership to 703 from 672.

A movement developed in the town sponsored by the Trades Council to start a new local paper, so angered were trade unionists by continued hostility from the Swindon Press; but the money could not be raised. By October "the Western" was reduced to only three-day working and from other railshop centres came enquiries about various methods of work-sharing. Yet despite the continuing hardship, collections for the miners were taken inside the works and strong support was given to a visiting Welsh miners' choir. When it came to the November elections all the Labour councillors defending their seats increased their votes and two new seats were won.

Throughout the aftermath of the betrayal of the General Strike Swindon trade unionists kept up a dogged rearguard action to contain victimisation, not to allow divisions to increase between the unions, and to find their own means of keeping up morale and resisting the enemy onslaught in the battle of ideas. It was needed, not least because the public media shut them out, though always open to the enemy. "A Correspondent" in the *North Wilts Herald* (14 May) thought that the important lesson of the crisis was that trade unions should "put themselves on a more democractic basis if they are to be adequately protected from their own extremists". Concern to save trade unionists from themselves and admiration for the "moderates" was voiced in the same paper the following week by Major Glyn, MP for Abingdon. He much admired trade union leaders whom he had met and was "tremendously struck by their attitude and the frank way in which they acknowledged the complete failure of the General Strike. . . . Many of these men had been consistently opposed to the idea of the General Strike, but owing to the fact that moderate trade unionists had allowed their local executives to get into the hands of extremists, the policy of the trade unions as outlined at the recent annual conferences has shown that the tendency has been to ignore the saner counsels."

The Swindon Tory MP, Mitchell Banks, KC, was ready to come straight out with names. "Reasonable men in the neighbourhood like Mr. J. H. Thomas have said that they thoroughly disapproved of the general strike," he said during the Conservative Fête. The *North Wilts Herald* (8 August) quotes him as adding: "The number of Communists might be few. He did not know how many there were in Swindon, but though they might be few in number they were terribly infectious."

One of the four young Swindon Communists was at the Baths meeting when J. H. Thomas came to explain his part in the General Strike to distrustful and disappointed trade unionists. Knowing his mastery of debating skills, young Reg Lee talked over a plan of campaign beforehand with Harry Hustings and Arthur Selwood. "We decided to separate, because Jimmy was fly and knew them. We left Harry Hustings downstairs and I sat near Selwood in the gallery, having the miners' report and all the official documents ready. At question time we all stood up at the same moment, and of course Thomas took me, rather than his known enemies." By reading out the dated exchange of correspondence with Steel-Maitland, he showed that Thomas had urged the miners to accept an offer which he knew would not be negotiated. "That broke up the meeting in an uproar!"

It was true that there were others who shared Thomas's hatred of strikes. At the Labour Fête the chairman of the Swindon Labour Party, C. R. Palmer, said: "There's no need for strikes. I don't like them. I appeal to all the workers to come along and help us to abolish strikes for ever by the use of the political weapon."

Many from "the Western" were soon obliged to leave Swindon, for the most part never to return. They included younger men like Rex Hutchings, Reg Lee and Ralph Bates. Another to go was the Engineers' leader and President of the Railway Federation. Willie Noble and Mrs. Noble left Swindon in the spring of 1927, to work for the Quakers' community at a camp for the unemployed in Wales.

Amongst the many who had been forced to leave Swindon by 1927 were all but two or three of the ILP members, while George Godsell was the only Communist Party member left in the town. Another enforced emigrant was young Father K. N. Crisford. At a meeting of the English Church Union presided over by no less a figure than Major Wright himself, who bitterly attacked the trade unionists, the courageous young curate from St. Mark's stood up and "dissociated himself from the Chairman's remarks". A courageous working class attracts courageous allies.

Since 1926 the collective experience of the working class, and not least in Swindon, has gained much. To note only three points. Today it would be inconceivable that intrigues would be carried on undetected and uncontrolled in the Civic Offices; no Town Hall lacks trade union organisation today. Secondly, the lesson has been learnt that a "work force" inside is a hundred times more powerful than individuals outside on the stones: of late Swindon too has begun to have its "UCS" actions. Thirdly, the political understanding that comes from democratic unity in action is the beginning of wisdom and the attainment of that collective self-confidence which makes everything possible. To conclude, we may leave the last word to John Habgood, the secretary of the Swindon General Strike's General Council, joyously recalling those days many years afterwards: "The General Strike of 1926 brought us all together: full-time officials, part-time officials, laymen, political and industrial, Co-Ops and religions. What a glorious example of solidarity!"

PART THREE

PERSONAL REMINISCENCES

1 PETER KERRIGAN

FROM GLASGOW

Many happenings and many feelings must always be beyond recapture after fifty years; and after such a half-century as the one since 1926, with all the transformations at home and in the wider world, this sense of remoteness from the event is bound to be even deeper. But some moments still stand out with great clarity for me. One came at the start and the other after the end of the nine days that shook Britain. Those nine days have never since been forgotten by the working class, and have induced on the other side of the social fence a kind of awe, expressed in the spate of writing and rewriting of the history of 1925–6, not diminishing but growing as the momentous event recedes in time.

I think first of the great May Day demonstration on the eve of the strike, when we marched, not as today to Queen's Park but to the Fleshers' Haugh, through the left stronghold of Bridgeton to the wide open spaces behind Glasgow Green, close to the Clyde, where the grass was always worn down to the basic cinder by the hundreds of games of football played there.

Very clearly do I recall the tremendous atmosphere, the enormous feeling of solidarity flowing on that hopeful and exalted day from the huge mass of the workers assembled there. We were on the brink of the showdown with the bosses' government over the miners, and the solidarity with them was a total feeling. The workers were ready, in their minds, for the battle, whatever the shortcomings—easier to see today than in those days—in our practical preparations. Behind us, the militants who had clearly known that the struggle must come even if our notions of the form it would take were much less clear, were memories of the Red Clyde of wartime days, of the historic "Hands off Russia" campaign, of Glasgow's strike for the 40 hours, of the Clyde Group of left Labour MPs which we had sent to Westminster in 1924.

A widely based class consciousness had appeared. One of the greatest forces propagating Marxism and reaching out to thousands of Clyde workers before, during and after the first world war, was John MacLean, who was the greatest leader and mass propagandist of the two decades to his death in November 1923. The Scottish Labour Colleges were his work. The mass lectures he gave and the mass meetings at which he spoke, the demonstrations of the unemployed, all had an effect on the workers. The Clyde Shop Stewards' Movement, in which Willie Gallacher was an outstanding leader, the SDF and the ILP, and its socialist propaganda with a strong pacifist inclination, had all contributed to the strong tide of class consciousness, though this was sometimes very sectarian (I personally was strongly opposed to the Communist Party applying for affiliation to the Labour Party). This was the atmosphere during the elections of 1923 and 1924 when the Clyde group really emerged. Within the group the nearest to today's Tribune Group type of left Labour MPs was John Wheatley, a practising Catholic whose 1924 Housing Act was an outstanding job. The group, however, were not Marxist or even near-Marxists.

All these events taken together formed our mental background in the run-up to the General Strike. They created an atmosphere in which the ardent young socialists, of whom I was one, often said that our city would be the Leningrad of Britain's Socialist revolution. Alas, when the time came we were to have a different kind of leadership and our path was to take another and much longer course.

I was myself a typical product, I suppose, of that movement and hope. On that Sunday I was twenty-six, and since my engineering apprenticeship had ended in 1920 I had been out of work for two and a half years, between April 1921 and October 1923, when I was back in industry again working at "The Forge". For the nine days of the strike I was to be busy, almost to the exclusion of all other activity, with the work of the Central Strike Co-ordinating Committee, of which I was first vice-chairman and then chairman. People ask me today: did I expect the betrayal of the General Strike? I always have to reply that, amid the struggle, I never thought of it, since the confident atmosphere in which day followed day, with the solidarity growing continually stronger, carried us all along, those on the left and the centre and even those on the right to some degree.

The call-off came just after the "second line" in the strike plans had been brought into action, when 100,000 engineering workers—the whole of Clydeside—came out. But they entered the battle, so to speak, just as their power was already being flung away by the TUC leaders. To them as to us the end came as a complete surprise.

The other sharp picture I have is from the days after the strike, when the Glasgow Trades and Labour Council was trying to raise money for the miners, locked in their desperate rearguard fight against the government and the coal-owners. On a brilliant August day, my wife to be Rose and I cycled out from Glasgow to Cowie and Plean in Stirlingshire—the pits there have been shut for many years—where the communists and other militants had been busy building up the Minority Movement, and meetings had been arranged for me to address. We carried in our panniers and haversacks all the food we could collect. The meetings were in green open fields in lovely sunshine and hundreds and hundreds of miners and their wives and children were there. Hundreds, too, signed up on the spot for the Minority Movement. It was a day I have never forgotten. They told me how, during the General Strike, they had blocked the road to Stirling which runs past Plean and Cowie and diverted lorries into a field and got hold of some of the foodstuffs they were carrying. "Privateering" of this sort was rare, however. It was a joyous day, standing out perhaps even more distinctly because of the bitterness of the miners' final defeat which followed those sombre post-strike days.

Recalling this defeat and the grinding down of the miners—which had been the main object of the exercise by the employers and their state machine since 1924—I think of the quite different balance of strength and happier issue of the miners' battle in the seventies. In these days, when a Tory government twice flung down the gauntlet to the miners, it was twice forced to capitulate. The kind of massive solidarity displayed in the Saltley Gate picket in 1972 typified and marked the highest point of support of the same kind happening all over the country. It was a response, like the General Strike, to a power confrontation staged by a Tory government; the quite different result of the battle surely reflects the great political progress made by the movement since those days. For while in 1926 there was this upsurge of solidarity feelings among millions of people, it was not really, in comparison with today, so politically developed, either among the masses of workers or even among the active core. The mass of the working class was not sufficiently prepared politically, and if their response to the call when it came proved so solid this was more a product of the deep class instincts brought into play than of the actual preparations by the militants.

The miners had been at the heart of the working class struggle throughout the early twenties—as they were in the early seventies. We had long known that it was over their wages and conditions that the post-war confrontation between the workers and the employers would come. Looking back over the pre-1926 file of *The Worker* strongly refreshes my recollection today of the insistence with which the Minority Movement's paper warned of the coming showdown and urged the need for practical preparation on the labour side.

Early in 1925 it was calling for Committees of Action of miners, engineers and railwaymen to be formed (21 February). On 25 July it declared: "Each day brings closer the struggle that the employers have been planning for months." Harry Pollitt wrote that the stand of the TUC General Council in its determination to give the fullest support to the miners would be welcomed by all, adding that "the danger to be guarded against in the present mining situation is that of allowing any compromises to take place in order to secure what is termed by the capitalist press a necessary breathing space for the mining industry." (This was after the TUC had decided to put an embargo on the movement of coal.) On 15 August the paper, which was then published in Glasgow under the editorship of Aitken Ferguson, was urging that the postponement of the struggle after the government subsidy to the coal-owners must not lead to the disbanding of the Glasgow Council of Action. It warned that the struggle had only been halted for a brief time and "the workers have now got to face the fact that they must go the whole hog or go under". After the leftward swing at the Scarborough conference of the TUC *The Worker* declared: "The General Council must have power. The Union Executives must give them that power. It will be the task of the Minority Movement to see that no sabotage is permitted behind the scenes." A leader again stressing the need for preparations said the paper's policy was 100 per cent trade unionism, the organisation of the unemployed, and a consistent fight against unemployment. It said that the success at Scarborough had been the result of the untiring efforts of the left wing and a similar result could be achieved at the Labour Party conference.

These hopes were unfortunately not realised. On 10 October the paper was describing the Labour Party conference ruefully as one that "adopted a Liberal policy . . . the left wing of the Labour Party as a political force was never seen at all". Commenting on 24 October on the police raid on the Minority Movement offices in London and the arrests that followed the paper warned: "The storm is about to break on the workers of this country and the arrest of Pollitt and Gallacher is an indication of it."

The flow of warnings continued through the winter and on 17 April the paper declared: "We are sure the Government has made up its mind to fight, that it is preparing with every nerve to get ready, and that it is prepared for the utter breakdown of the negotiations. Are the workers ready? Is the General Council for all its brave words ready? It must stand by the miners in this fight or else trade unionism in Britain receives a shattering blow. Let the General Council co-operate with Trades Councils up and down the country in setting up Workers' Defence Corps. Let there be no mistake about it, they will be needed, and sorely needed at that, in the immediate future."

Such were the warnings that *The Worker*, the communists, the militants, and to a degree the trade unionists influenced by the ILP, kept hammering home. Unhappily the ILP journal, the Glasgow *Forward*, did not ever, as I recall, consistently reflect this feeling. Willie Stewart wrote in the paper on 10 February 1926: "There is a false feeling of security, an anticipation that there will be no crisis." He suggested that, to counter this, Tom Dickson's articles in the *New Leader* should be published as a pamphlet and the 700 ILP branches should distribute them nationally. On 27 February the paper carried an article combating the coal-owners' arguments. An article on 20 March by Ramsay MacDonald used the coal crisis and the unemployment in this industry in support of the Labour candidate in the Bothwell parliamentary by-election. Another by the same author (3 April) averred that whatever the result of the coal negotiations it was "a plain task imposed on the Labour Party to co-ordinate and organise the coal industry so as to secure both the maximum wage and the maximum production". But the Glasgow *Forward* on 1 May, two days before the strike, contained no reference at all to the menacing situation, only an article from the Labour leader under the headline "Wandering from Westminster". No other issues appeared until ten days after the strike. The 22 May number contained an extraordinary article by MacDonald celebrating the "triumph of reason in Eccleston Square". It said that the labour forces had been "kept well in hand" during the strike and "when the substance of victory was gained by a bold and wise stroke, the Mad Mullah and his organ [presumably Stanley Baldwin and Churchill's *British Gazette*] were left to cock-a-doodle to the heavens for nothing".

As the crisis months wore on, I think that a belief that the crunch was coming did take hold of the more active and politically aware, if not of the great mass of the workers. It was in the Glasgow Trades and Labour Council that many of the left-right tussles over the kind of preparation that was necessary took place. The secretary reported on 23 June 1925 that the Council of Action appointed by a conference held a month earlier had met three times and had decided at its last meeting (21 June) to appeal to trade union district committees for financial support. A meeting of trade union officials was to be convened in Central Halls on 3 July to decide on methods of organisation, the provision of speakers and the methods of obtaining support from trade union officials. By a narrow majority (182–175 votes) the Trades and Labour Council meeting on 1 July agreed to affiliate to the Minority Movement. On 14 August its Industrial Committee recommended that the Council draw the attention of the Scottish TUC to the fact that a Council of Action had been set up and request its support. The Trades and Labour Council decided that its secretary attend the Friday meetings of the Council of Action, which were held in the AEU rooms. But in November it was reported that the NUR district committee had decided not to affiliate to the Council of Action.

The same month brought a decision by the Trades and Labour Council executive to hold a protest demonstration on 9 December against the sentences passed on the twelve arrested communist leaders. In January the Trades and Labours Council put forward three motions for the agenda of the Scottish TUC, one to retain the unemployed as members of trade unions, another on international trade union unity, and a third on workers' defence measures.

This last resolution, which was debated at the Scottish TUC on 23 April said: "This Congress, reviewing the capitalists' open and unashamed use of brute force to intimidate and terrorise workers and their organisations, lays it down that the workers must be prepared to defend their own organisations and meetings . . . it endorses the principle of Workers' Defence Corps, and instructs the General Council to actively assist in every way possible in the formation of these corps and take the initiative in co-ordinating their efforts through Scotland, under a unified control." But the motion was decisively voted down at Inverness.

In line with this setback was the failure of the Council of Action to establish itself as the leading body for Glasgow's strike effort. Despite the efforts made, it did not get the necessary support. The consequence was that the leadership in Glasgow when the day came was more narrowly trade unionist in character than in other towns and areas of the West of Scotland. These true Councils of Action, based on the trade unions and on labour movement and community organisations, did emerge, as this record has earlier described.

Especially in the later stages before the strike, the Glasgow Council of Action came to have rather a token existence. The reason for its failure to obtain from the unions the kind of authority and support it required was partly jealousy about the individual unions' own authority. On the eve of the strike the Council of Action was in effect superseded by the Trades and Labour Council. Several of the seventeen area strike committees, however, did acquire much more the character of Councils of Action, many of them having, for instance a Labour councillor as chairman and other widely representative people as well.

In Glasgow it was the Central Strike Co-ordinating Committee of the Trades and Labour Council that took entire charge—and it was set up almost at the last moment. The Industrial Committee, of which I was the convenor, met on the Friday (30 April) and decided to call a meeting of trade union officials on the Monday night to consider and "decide on co-ordinated action in the case of the general stoppage of work", as well as to hold a City Hall meeting on the following Thursday. On the Monday we formed a committee representing the different industrial groups on the Trades and Labour Council. These included Shipbuilding and Engineering as well as the Boilermakers, who were all in the second-line call-out. Harry Hopkins, the AEU district secretary, was also on the committee. A notable absentee, however, was the representative of the Railwaymen, who were in the first line. (There was a technical reason for this, and they were involved later.) A minute of a Trades and Labour Council meeting on 5 May recorded that the committee had held two meetings, that area committees were in process of being formed in each parliamentary division, and that the proposed meeting in the City Hall could not be held. The chairman, Councillor Willie Leonard, then outlined the plans of the Scottish TUC, jointly with the British TUC, for the conduct of the strike, and said that the committee would carry into effect any further instructions that might be issued.

At the 7 May meeting, John McBain, communist organiser of the Foundry Workers, withdrew from the chairmanship because pressure of union work prevented him from attending regularly, and I was appointed to take his place. At this period the position of communists in the Labour Movement, it should be remembered, was in a somewhat transitional state. On the Trades and Labour Council, discussions had taken place after the Liverpool conference of the Labour Party banning communists from holding official positions, and guidance had been sought from the Labour Party executive. We were told in March 1925 that the rule barred communists from official positions on trade and labour councils. However, it had been decided that as convener of the council's important Industrial Committee I could carry on. (As late as

1927 I was myself a delegate to the Labour Party conference at Blackpool, for the Clyde engineers. This was the last conference to which communists were admitted. It was finally decided there that communists could not be admitted even if sent from trades and labour councils. Harry Pollitt and I were admitted as delegates, as were Arthur Horner and other communists. At the Scottish Labour Party conference in the previous year, C. R. Cramp, the chairman, had assured Willie Shaw and me that this was "the last time" communists would be admitted.)

From the outset of the stoppage, the Co-ordinating Committee could report an overwhelming response from all the unions involved in the first call-out (railways, transport, building, chemicals, gas, print, steel, and others). The Caplawhill works, which both manufactured and maintained tramcars, provided one of the two main breaches in the solid front. At our meeting on 4 May George Symington of the Vehicle Builders reported that all his members at the car works had been withdrawn. So had twenty-eight members of the Electrical Trades Union. But the response to an AEU instruction to stop work was only partial. As these were the men who serviced the tramcars this was important. But a series of votes at the Co-ordinating Committee on proposals for mass picketing of the works ended in decisions that meant no effective action. Similar obstacles connected with the number of organisations involved at the Pinkston Power Station, the second breach in the strike front, helped to prevent a stoppage there, and the power that kept some of the tramcars running throughout the strike was never broken off. On 10 May the Co-ordinating Committee chairman reported that a deputation had interviewed the Scottish TUC about Pinkston and a letter giving authority for an immediate withdrawal of labour had been sent to the workers at the power station. It was signed by representatives of the Transport Workers, General and Municipal Workers, Engineers, Electricians, and Building Workers as well as myself as Co-ordinating Committee chairman and William Elger, Scottish TUC secretary. But the instruction was never operated.

Alongside such failures of trade union unity in action we had to contend with a police force which had already during the unemployed demonstrations over many years built up a record of brutal actions, as I well remember. And the OMS specials, of course, were vicious. They had the backing of a rabid Tory majority on the Glasgow City Council and biased courts. The prison system, as John MacLean's life and prison experiences bear out, was the worst in Europe. There was rioting in the East End on the Wednesday, Thursday and Friday. On Thursday a picket of miners from Cambuslang marched to the Ruby Street tram depot. Ruby Street is a dead end, and after the miners had entered it, the depot gates were opened and a large body of police made a baton charge, striking people down right and left. There were 120 arrests in the three days. On the Thursday 64 arrests were also made at Bridgeton Cross. Monday, 10 May, saw 100 people hauled before the Glasgow courts. Twenty-two were given sentences ranging from one to three months' hard labour. There was widespread anger at the conduct of the police and even more at that of the specials, and at the sentences.

The Courts operated as instruments of class hatred and vengeance. In the Thursday hearings a well-dressed young man was charged with stone-throwing in a disturbance on South Side, convicted, and given three months on the evidence of two policemen, in the teeth of testimony by independent witnesses. One woman told the court that the accused was carrying a pair of gloves in his right hand and could not possible have thrown a missile. An Anderston woman, charged with mobbing and rioting, was arrested on Friday, 7 May and refused bail until the hearing a fortnight later, although she was the mother of five young children. The Labour group on the City Council called unanimously on 14 May for a full inquiry into the conduct of the police after it had received several complaints from quite unoffending citizens about unwarranted attacks on them, in particular by the specials.

All this showed how right we had been to press before the strike for defence measures on the workers' side. The question, I recall, kept coming up on the co-ordinating committee, though the discussions were not minuted. The issue *par excellence* was whether to carry walking sticks. I had myself moved the defence corps resolution at the Scottish TUC and I was absolutely for carrying sticks. The argument always employed against even this elementary step to protect ourselves against official ruffianism (especially by some of the specials) was that it would be futile and would flout the general TUC instruction that the strikers must be orderly and scrupulously avoid any breaches of the law. Of course, pickets in several clashes were not entirely defenceless. They used stones and anything that came to hand to protect themselves. Pickets' actions were not always strictly speaking peaceful persuasion, but in the main the attacking party was the police. I have heard many stories of strikers and police playing football together, but it certainly never happened in Glasgow. Our relations with the police were very formal and mainly conducted through the Labour councillors and the magistrates.

The Co-ordinating Committee and its main sub-committees were in more or less permanent session throughout the strike. And most of our time, of course, was taken up, not with the old debates that had been dividing the movement for years before 1926, but with the practical problems. The feeling that it was our job to do all in our power to make the strike solid was an overriding one, that united us—left, right and centre: it was the theme running through the whole conduct of the work. It was over the actual process of carrying out the instruction that the differentiations became clear, and they did so very quickly. Our instructions came to us from the Scottish TUC which was working to the same brief as the British TUC. We had at first the bulletins from the Scottish TUC and then from 10 May onward the *Scottish Worker*, which published the first of its six issues on that date (in 25,000 copies that sold out in about an hour). Earlier we had had discussions on the question of publicity materials, in issuing which we were later and less copious than we could have been. Quite early a number of organisations, including the Communist Party, the Shopworkers and the Clerical Workers, had offered their technical assistance in this field. The Co-ordinating Committee thanked them but never took the offer up. The issuing of the *Scottish Worker* was delayed by the refusal of the Scottish Typographical Association to print it. The Co-ordinating Committee took action to produce a paper locally, and the difficulty with the STA was finally overcome. Nevertheless, valuable time was lost. There were also issued from various places a number of cyclostyled bulletins, as well as the *Workers' Press* incorporating the communist *Workers' Weekly* and *The Worker*.

A good deal has been said about the weakness during the strike of what are today called the information media. I think that it was important. We relied partly on a system of couriers and I remember the encouragement we felt when a courier from the TUC in London arrived and gave us a first-hand description of the spirit in all the main English cities through which he had passed on his way north. Another means of keeping in touch was the reports that the Co-ordinating Committee gave regularly to meetings of the Trades and Labour Council at which there were very large attendances and where separate reports from the unions involved were also given. What published materials we had on the strikers' side were not so well distributed as they could have been, partly because they were in short supply but also because we lacked the forces to do so effectively. For many of the communists and other militants were involved directly in trade union work and in the various local strike committees. On the other hand the enemy publicity, too, was not very effective. The BBC bulletins were openly regarded by the strikers as simple strike-breaking propaganda. So was the Emergency Press got out by the Glasgow newspaper publishers. As to Churchill's notorious *British Gazette*, I do not recall even seeing a single copy during the whole strike. But the General Strike failed, not because of our weaknesses in this field, but because it was betrayed at the top.

After the strike had been called off, we had, I remember, a discussion on this, and decided that the Trades and Labour Council should hold a meeting fairly soon and invite a British TUC representative to be present to explain the settlement.

The call-off not only stunned us but confused many people by the manner in which it came. The main editorial in the *Scottish Worker* on 14 May was headed: "Peace—With a Big Stick". A panel on page 3, headed "The Miners' Position", referred—rather politely—to the "surprise" that had been expressed in the movement that the paper's previous issue had concealed from the readers the fact that the miners had "issued a statement claiming opposition to the terms of Sir Herbert Samuel's Memorandum which had induced the Trades Union Congress to call off the strike". It added: . . . "We desire to make it perfectly clear that the message we received from the TUC General Council was published exactly as we received it." Then, in bold type: "In the message supplied to us there was no hint of any kind that the Miners were not an assenting party." Another "supplied" paragraph in the previous issue said: "The Miners have decided to remain idle pending the Conference of Miners' Delegates which is to be held on Friday. The Miners have expressed to the TUC their 'profound admiration for the wonderful demonstration of loyalty as displayed by the workers who promptly withdrew their labour in support of the Miners' standard of life'." This act of fraud and news suppression increased our bitterness at the sudden call-off.

The weaknesses of our Co-ordinating Committee all proceeded from the dead hand of officialdom, which was probably even stronger in the Scottish than the British TUC leadership. All our strength came from the mass solidarity at grassroots. This flowed powerfully on into the months after the strike, amid the long drawn-out agony of the miners' fight which dominated those days.

Then there was the struggle (especially hard in Glasgow) against victimisation. For the tramwaymen and print workers it had to be conducted for years. Our meeting on 14 May dealt with the Corporation's decision to give 100 car conductors notice, refuse employment to tradesmen and labourers employed by the Parks Department, and not to re-start 200 men on the permanent way. A motion to send a deputation to the Lord Provost to obtain assurances of reinstatement was put. But an amendment moved by John McKenzie and James Richmond, that the secretary's report be accepted and reports be given to the committee from time to time on the progress of reinstatement, was carried. One brighter spot recorded was a report from the Vehicle Builders, who had 149 men involved at Caplawhill, that men in federated and non-federated shops were to start on Monday, 17 May, on pre-strike conditions. There were lengthy discussions on procedures to be followed to obtain the reinstatement of men at Singers Works, Clydebank and at the Clyde Trust.

Pasted down the side of the minutes of this meeting there is a cutting from the *Daily Record*, which was run by Associated Scottish Newspapers Ltd, saying that it would continue to recognise the unions (under certain conditions, including no chapel meetings in working hours without management permission). But the *Glasgow Herald*, the *Evening Times*, *The Bulletin*, and the *Evening Citizen* all refused to negotiate with the unions and indicated their determination not to employ union labour.

The Trades and Labour Council demanded a 5 per cent levy on all workers to help the miners. As late as October we held a march and demonstration in their support followed by a concert, raising the very large sum of £443 15*s*. A resolution was carried asking the TUC to call a special conference that would give effect to the levy, place an embargo on coal, withdraw the safety men and call a one-day strike. Right to the end of the miners' lock-out, the Council majority backed the miners and took the line that the General Strike had been betrayed. At the Galashiels conference of the Scottish TUC on 22 April, Aitken Ferguson moved Motion No. 15 on our behalf, declaring the general strike to be an essential weapon of the trade union movement and stressing the imperative need to learn the correct lessons from the May showdown. It went on: "The lack of preparation prior to the last Strike which characterised the leadership of the Trade Union Movement was equalled by the cowardly and traitorous abandonment of the fight on 12th May, and by their cynical refusal to assist the miners in the most heroic fight in modern British history." It said that "the substitution of a new, militant leadership and of vigorous class-war policies for the present gang of betrayers with their pro-capitalist policies is the main lesson of the General Strike and the driving need of the trade union movement". Opposed by the right-wing NUR leader James Campbell, J. F. Duncan of the Scottish Farm Servants' Union and others, this Motion was supported by myself on behalf of the Glasgow Trades and Labour Council and by James Daly of the Scottish miners, father of today's miners' general secretary Lawrence Daly. The right wing won by a majority of over three to one.

A month earlier *The Worker* (22 May), under the headline "Working Class Betrayed", had declared: "Right from the start of the strike it became evident that the bureaucratic leaders were afraid and nervous about the situation. They tried to confine the General Strike into certain channels which even imposed limitations upon the free development of necessary strike preparations. The officials were not responsible for setting up strike committees in the localities. They opposed the formation of such committees and wanted the men to simply hang about the branch rooms. The men themselves set up strike committees and the officials were simply dragged at their heels. The officials opposed propaganda demonstrations, mass pickets, everything that was vital to the strike. They tried to inculcate pacifism into the workers so as to tie their hands. And they were definitely and signally failing the longer the strike lasted. The General Strike would have been won with ease, provided the leadership was effective. The General Strike was lost because it was betrayed." (I believe that this judgment of ten days after the event has in all its essentials stood the test of time and of every research and analysis since 1926.)

On the Glasgow Trades and Labour Council the left group had to try to cope with plenty of the "heel-dragging" of which Aitken Ferguson wrote. The right wing was in the majority on the committee, though under the impulse from the enthused and combative rank and file the left and progressive side was able sometimes to prevail on immediate questions during the strike. The decision for instance, to set up area strike committees against right-wing opposition with Scottish TUC backing, was taken by seven votes to five on 4 May.

On the Co-ordinating Committee's small executive body, where I was in the chair, the chief right-wing spokesman was John McKenzie, a full-time official of the General and Municipal Workers. A strong opponent of all the militants, this quiet-spoken and pleasant Highlander was, I recall, very well disposed toward me personally. Later, during the second world war, we even became friendly. He was rigid for the line of his union and the general directives of the Scottish TUC. Another stickler for the rights and interests—as he conceived them—of his own union was James Richmond, full-time official of the Patternmakers, who was especially shocked by any proposals that might bring the strikers into conflict with the police. Willie Shaw, who was an ASW member and Glasgow Trades and Labour Council's full-time secretary, was a most meticulous type of trade union administrator. He liked me personally, maybe because he saw me as a young man who might one day be saved from my own militant past and politics. One day he held forth to me at length about how I had been spoiled by my association with Aitken Ferguson and could become an MP easily if I left the Communist Party.

On the left, apart from Jock McBain, who was not usually at our meetings after the first two days, there was Frank Stephenson, another communist, from the Vehicle Builders, J. Scanlan of the Construction Workers, and one or two more who veered sometimes to militant positions.

The calling off of the strike came as a big shock to all of us on the Co-ordinating Committee, as I have said. Today one can see how much greater and more long lasting was the shock given to the bourgeoisie by the solid effectiveness of the strike itself. It must have become clear to many of the ruling class that unless the strike could be called off it was bound, out of the steadily mounting solidarity which was its chief feature, to develop into at least some effort to take over the running of the country. If it had gone on, a stage must have come at which these people would have had to decide about how to hold on to their position. It would have been necessary to have, if not a capitulation, some sort of compromise. This would have made it much more difficult for the Baldwin Government to grind down the miners; it would have meant them going back with some kind of arrangement. It is not easy to make parallels. But the main thing in 1926 was this enormous class solidarity of millions of people. They were not, so to speak, politically developed, and even the active core was not so politically developed as it is today. But the strength shown was tremendous.

How significant it was, too, that the unemployed in their great mass did not blackleg, despite all their sufferings in the recession which had started. I put this to the credit of the National Unemployed Workers' Movement—which had shown its strength in many struggles, particularly during the three-month lockout of the Engineers in 1922—and of course of the Minority Movement's work from its setting up in 1924.

It was claimed that 300–400 students joined the OMS. Some were certainly very aggressive indeed, expressing the eagerness of the upper and lower middle class sections of society—from which the students mostly came in those days—to take a crack at the workers and trade unions. But even so they were a small, if virulent, minority. There was no real mass-appeal force on the capitalists' side that could not have been neutralised and overcome if the preparations on the workers' side had been more effectively made and led. Anger in the Glasgow movement over the students' part in the strike continued for years. In December 1926 the Trades and Labour Council voted to boycott Students' Day, 15 January, as a protest against their strike-breaking on the trams and in the docks under police and naval protection. What a happy contrast between this sorry rift and today's friendly relations between the students and the trade union movement!

Today, however, my strongest remembrance remains, as it has been ever since 1926, not of such discords but of the impressive strength and endurance displayed by the General Strike camp as a whole, both during and after the strike, in spite of the small failures at our local level and the big betrayal by the strike's general staff.

Glasgow was then inside Scotland's biggest coalfield of Lanarkshire, with pits coming almost up to the city. When the Scottish miners voted in November on the government's humiliating terms for the return to work, after all the suffering and near-starvation and inevitable bitterness, five of the seven districts still voted against return on such terms. The five, with a total of 57,700 miners voting, were Lanarkshire, Fife, East Lothian, Stirlingshire and Kirkintilloch. The two districts which voted for acceptance, West Lothian and Ayrshire, had only 12,000 miners voting between them.

Behind these figures lies a story of incredible human dignity and courage. It provided an example of the permanent capacity of the working class to win, provided that in addition to being united it is boldly and honestly led. That is still for me the chief conviction stemming from those days.

2 BOB DAVIES

FROM ST. HELENS

In St. Helens the trade unions had made some preparations early for the possibility of a general strike despite the inactivity of the TUC General Council. In the Trades and Labour Council there were five or six members of the Communist Party, who were delegates for their trade union branches, and along with other left-wingers we pressed for the formation of a Council of Action to take control in the event of a general stoppage. After Red Friday we all thought a general strike was a possibility in May 1926. We got the Trades and Labour Council to agree to a Council of Action, with delegates drawn from union branches, and we pressed for it to meet before 1 May. We also got the Trades Council officials to meet the St. Helens Co-operative Society to arrange for the Co-op to help in food distribution during a general strike, and a preliminary understanding was arrived at. We had not much idea how this was to work, but we thought our pickets could direct any transport coming into the town into the Co-op warehouses and shops. We even discussed forming a Workers' Defence Force to guard the food once we had got control of it, but no steps were taken towards this. In previous miners' disputes, in 1912 and 1921, the St. Helens Co-op had shown its sympathy for the miners in very practical ways, giving extended credit, or selling very cheap any goods that were starting to go stale.

When the Council of Action met for the first time, at 10.30 a.m. on Tuesday, 4 May, many of the local union branches had already met that morning to elect delegates. My own branch, the Passenger Branch TGWU, met at 9.30 a.m. I had been very lucky to drop almost immediately into a job as tram-conductor at the end of 1925, after being made redundant from the coal-pits where I had worked for nearly two years. At the age of eighteen in 1920, while working for Pilkington's, I had joined the St. Helens Socialist Society, which in August 1920 became the St. Helens Branch of the Communist Party.

The union branch met in the Tram-men's Social Club, at Sefton Place in the Town Centre. The rules stipulated that all members on strike must answer a roll-call to qualify for strike pay, so this ensured a near 100 per cent attendance on this occasion. The Club was on the third floor, and consisted of a large room with a billiard table, bar-counter, etc., a smaller room with tables and forms used as a canteen, and another small room. The meeting was held in the club-room, and about three hundred men crowded into it and the smaller rooms. The roll-call answering was very lively and good-humoured, but showed its teeth when a particularly unpopular inspector was slow in answering his name; a voice said, "he's hiding behind a pole", causing a general laugh. The inspectors were members of our TGWU branch because we had a Labour Town Council who insisted on all their employees being in the union, but to my knowledge they had never previously attended a union meeting. They had tried to join NALGO, but at this time NALGO had no provisions in its rules for strike action, and our local Trades and Labour Council had ruled it was not a *bona fide* trade union and had refused its application to affiliate.

After the roll-call, Jim Thornton, Branch Chairman and a tram-driver, called for the election of a delegate to the Council of Action and suggested that I should be the delegate. The suggestion was moved and seconded and I was elected unanimously. It was by then after 10 a.m. and I left the meeting to go to the Council of Action in the Railway Institute, Salisbury Street. There was nothing very remarkable in my election, as I was a member of the Branch Committee and the chief delegate to the St. Helens Trades and Labour Council. I had been a Trades Council delegate then for six years, first for the AEU and later for the TGWU, and I was an enthusiast, always taking a lot of trouble to prepare my reports and make them interesting. In addition, in the last few years I had done a lot of public speaking at meetings of various sorts, open-air Communist Party and National Unemployed Workers' Movement meetings, reporting back at trade union branch meetings, and giving indoor lectures on history and economics.

About sixty or seventy delegates had assembled in the Railway Institute, and the meeting was opened by Councillor T. H. Boscow, President of the Trades and Labour Council and the local Branch Secretary of the Foundary Workers' Union, although I could never see him working in a foundry. He kept a newsagent and tobacconist shop in Sutton, St. Helens. First business was the election of officials. Boscow was elected chairman; I was the vice-chairman; Councillor R. Waring, the full-time Secretary-Agent of the Labour party, was elected secretary; Percy Lowe, the part-time AEU District Secretary, was elected assistant secretary. The meeting then went on to take reports on the strike position. The most important and largest in numbers were the miners, who had been locked out since Friday night. There were about 12,000 of them in the St. Helens District, divided into about twelve branches or lodges, and they had an unofficial district committee, not part of the organisation of the Miners' Federation.

Then there were the railways—they reported all stopped. There was a small loco-shed at Sutton in addition to the usual railway yards and workshops; there were four NUR branches and one loco-men's branch. All the trams, and what busmen there were, were out. In road transport, over half of which was still horse-drawn, practically all the men in the transport depots of the glass and chemical works were out. But the railways were the major transport. The engineering workers had not been called out, but a lot came out all the same. Most tradesmen in the St. Helens area were maintenance men working in the glassworks, of which there were three sheet and plate glass works (Pilkington's) and three glass-bottle works (two UGB and one John Foster & Sons, now Rockware). These men were not called out. This did not worry us unduly—the glassworks would soon stop as coal supplies ran out. They were heavy coal users, to make gas to heat their furnaces.

As I walked the two miles into town that morning from Thatto Heath where I lived, what struck me most forcibly was the quietness in the streets. It was like early Sunday morning, but even more silent. It was not even the absence of the noise of the trams and buses, but the more distant sounds of railway trains, railway engines shunting wagons, etc., and works noises from the foundries. There was a lot of this in St. Helens—all the six glassworks, collieries and other works had their own branch lines, and some had their own shunting engines. These were everyday noises that one had never noticed normally, but now they were not there it was very noticeable.

At the first meeting of the Council of Action there was some discussion on whether all transport should be stopped by our pickets. The Council of Action was intent on getting control of food supplies, which we thought would begin to run short after the first week or so. The Co-op had been approached with a view to their being the main controller and distributor of the town's food supplies. Although all rail traffic was stopped, there was still some road transport, running mainly to Liverpool, twelve miles away. After discussion it was decided to issue permits to lorry owners and drivers to carry food only, but these had to be applied for personally to the Council of Action, which would then consider each application. From the first meeting the NUR delegates opposed the issuing of permits, arguing that if permits were issued to carry food the railways should also have permits. The difficulty, we explained to them, was that the railways were run by large national companies whom we could not control, while road transport was owned locally. There were two railway companies with lines into St. Helens: the principal one was the LNWR, while the other, the Great Central, had a small branch line into the town. The NUR men continued to raise this issue, until I and others began to regard the NUR delegates as Jimmy Thomas's men, out to sabotage the strike and taking part in the strike but not by any wish of theirs. This view was strengthened by the past local record of the NUR branches. Although affiliated to the Trades and Labour Council their delegates seldom attended the monthly meetings and generally took no part in local political and union activities.

Most of the people applying for permits owned one or two, or up to half a dozen lorries. The larger firms with vehicles were mainly glassworks, six of them, with road transport depots using half-dozen to twenty motor-lorries. But their drivers were out on strike. The glass workers had not been called out by the TUC, but a lot of their maintenance tradesmen, fitters, blacksmiths, electricians, etc., had come out. The TUC had also called out the building trades, but told those men engaged in building houses and hospitals to stay at work. This calling out of some and not others caused some confusion, but the workers locally for the most part settled it by all coming out. All picketing was organised by the union branches, but the miners in our area had a lot of surplus pickets which the Council of Action could call on. There were then about ten or twelve thousand miners in the St. Helens District—about as many as in the whole North-Western Area today.

After the Council of Action meeting had ended at about 2.00 p.m. on this first day, I returned to the tram-men's headquarters in the Social Club to find it a hive of activity. Pickets on push-bikes were coming in and reporting that Crosville buses were still running on the Liverpool–Warrington road through Prescot and Rainhill. They had pulled up a number of these buses, only to be told by the crews, "We have nothing to do with the strike, we are not in a union." Arrangements were being made to send out much stronger pickets the following morning. This was in the capable hands of Bill Terry, an ex-navy man who had been taking lessons in ju-jitsu from a teacher in Liverpool. He said that he could easily break a man's arm or leg and that this was the best thing to do with a stubborn blackleg. I told him the time was not yet ripe for such tactics, to which he agreed, but added "It may come to that yet."

The men had organised a continuous sub-committee to sit from 8 a.m. to 8 p.m. This committee was of three men, one acting as secretary and taking everything down that was reported to them. The committee would sit for two hours and then be relieved by another three men. The whole day's reports were to be handed to the Branch Secretary, who would then report to the Branch Committee that met every night at 8 p.m. I thought, this is just first-day enthusiasm, it will peter out. To my surprise this committee carried on for every day of the strike. Tram-men, of course, were accustomed to changing shifts—or duties, as they called them—with each other, and they were accustomed to writing reports. The methods used in their jobs were transferred to their own use during the strike. Other men were busy painting posters to advertise open-air meetings in the Market Square. Perhaps the greatest marvel was to see those tram-men going out to walk the main streets with a double-board hanging back and front from their shoulders, acting as what we called sandwich-board-men, a job only done as a rule by down-and-outs. Other, smaller boards were made to carry a poster on the handle-bars of a bike, which would then be pushed by hand along the streets. Small groups would go out chalking messages and slogans on the tarmac side-streets where they ran into the main streets. Messages included one urging everyone to ignore the lies and half-truths broadcast by the wireless.

Meetings were held every day on the Market Square in Bridge Street, and from Wednesday preparations were made for a great meeting-demonstration to be held on Sunday in the variety theatre, the Hippodrome. The meeting was arranged by the Council of Action, but the advertising was done by the union branches, in which a big part was played by the tram-men with their sandwich-boards and chalking. Another activity of the tram-men was their courier service: six of them had motor-bikes, and they volunteered as dispatch riders. They took messages and bulletins to all the surrounding towns and cities, and brought other messages and bulletins back with them. With no newspapers being printed, almost every workers' organisation got out a duplicated news bulletin in the various localities. The Liverpool District of the Communist Party got one out, and it was a very good production. The Communist Party had considerable experience in bulletins, issuing many pit and factory newspapers. They used a block for the title and often printed in double columns to give the appearance of a newspaper. In St. Helens there were two bi-weekly newspapers, one of which got out a very small printed edition, not unlike our own bulletins, at the weekend.

Each morning, groups of two or three tram-men with pedal-bikes went out four or five miles on the Liverpool–Warrington road to picket the Crosville buses. On the second day they reported very few running, and on the third day they reported all had stopped on this route. Crosville were based at Chester and ran mainly in Cheshire, only spilling over the Mersey into Lancashire at Liverpool, Widnes and Warrington. We sent word to the tram and busmen in these places to be on the look-out for blackleg Crosville buses. After the first day our pickets began stopping motor-lorries and asking to see their permits. Tram-men were very good at this picketing of roads. They knew many of the local policemen, and when the police objected to them pulling up lorries they would laugh and joke with the police and then ride off on their bikes to another bus-stop and continue the picketing. The policemen were usually on foot, so they could not follow.

The pickets caused a spate of applications for permits from the Council of Action. Once when I was chairman in the absence of Councillor Boscow, a man came before us for a permit. One of the delegates said he had seen the man driving a lorry with a load of red oxide on. What sort of foodstuff is red oxide, he wanted to know. The applicant admitted the fact, but said he was carrying foodstuffs on the return journey—it did not pay to ride empty one way. He promised to carry only foodstuffs in future, but the Council of Action would take no excuses and by a large majority refused to grant a permit. Most of these haulage-carriers were known to one or other of the delegates, so it was very difficult for them to pull wool over the eyes of the Council.

The Council of Action never formally discussed the idea of forming a Workers' Defence Force, but many of the delegates, mostly from the left, did. We all felt this should be a later development, but the General Strike only lasted nine days and this was far too short a time. The known left-wingers on the Council numbered about ten, including about four members of the Communist Party. Neither the Communist Party members among the delegates, nor the left wing as a whole, ever met on their own, although of course there was plenty of informal discussion. Right and left wings did not seem to matter in this struggle. I was always aware that Boscow and Waring and others were on the right of the

Labour Party, but we all seemed to be united in this great struggle. Perhaps if the TUC General Council members had come to some of these Council of Action meetings they would have been inspired with the determination to carry the struggle to a successful conclusion. I fear, however, that the principal leaders of the TUC were more afraid of the workers than they were of the government and employers.

On Sunday the great meetings were held. Boscow was to chair the inside meeting, and I, as vice-chairman, was to take the outside overflow meeting if necessary. There was a fairly large piece of vacant land at the side of the Hippodrome, and arrangements had been made for a flat-topped lorry to act as a platform. To my great surprise, James Sexton, our local MP, had turned up to speak, and so had Joe Tinker, the miner's MP for Leigh—which was not a surprise. The Hippodrome was packed full: not only the seats were occupied but all the passageways and gangways, and there were a couple of thousand outside. At the outside meeting I was in something of a quandary. As chairman I did not know if either or both of the principal speakers would come outside to speak. I thought Joe Tinker would, but I did not expect Sexton—he never spoke outside if he could help it. Jack Byrne, another Communist Party member and the delegate of the Woodworkers' Union, started the meeting off. I opened for about ten minutes and then called on Jack Byrne. There was great enthusiasm, and the crowd clapped every reference to the General Strike.

Jack Byrne had been speaking for over half an hour and I had no one else to call on. However, just as I was getting desperate, Joe Tinker came from the inside meeting, and in less than another half-hour out came Sexton. From the speeches these two made one would have thought they were the reddest revolutionaries: this was the effect the situation and a large and enthusiastic crowd had on them. Normally neither of them was at all revolutionary, although Sexton was much more right-wing than Tinker. Large numbers of workers had shed their usual caution or reserve. This was especially noticeable among the tram-men, who were usually very cautious of expressing controversial opinions in public. The same applied to many others. There was always the fear of being reported to the people in control of their livelihood, especially in the 1920s, when there were never less than a million unemployed.

On the Monday, at the Council of Action, the NUR delegates raised more strongly than ever the argument that permits to carry food should be issued to rail as well as road transport, but the Council voted them down again. On this day too, the TUC General Council called out on strike the so-called second line of light industries. But this was scarcely noticed in St. Helens, where the glass production workers were not called out. Whether this was the fault of the TUC or of the union, the General and Municipal Workers, I do not know. In any case, the glass works were beginning to run short of coal.

Tuesday, the beginning of the second week of the strike, was the same as other days. I began it by giving my report to the assembled tram-men, which ended with a warning not to be influenced by any rumours they heard, from either the BBC radio or the next-door neighbour—the Council of Action would tell them the truth. When I got to the Railway Institute for the Council of Action meeting the NUR men were saying that they had heard the General Strike was being settled, but the Council went on with its business as usual. During the afternoon the rumour of a settlement grew stronger, and when I got back to the Tram-men's Club I had a talk with Jim Thornton and some other committee-men, and we agreed to get out some posters and parade the streets of the town. We were convinced that someone strongly opposed to the strike was circulating rumours in order to break the morale of the workers. We had half expected this to happen. Our posters said, "Take no notice of rumours, the Council of Action will tell you the truth." These posters were paraded around the streets for a few hours by the tram-men.

However, on Wednesday morning at the Council of Action meeting the NUR men were openly saying that the General Strike was settled: they had received a telegram from their union to this effect. No one else had any information, and as I did not want to believe it, I did not—until I got back to the Tram-men's Club where Jim Thornton told me that the Secretary had received a telegram saying the strike was settled. This telegram had arrived while I was still at the Council of Action meeting, and they had had a meeting with the Tramways Manager, who wanted them to take the trams out immediately, that afternoon. They had refused, saying tomorrow would be soon enough.

I think we were all in a state of confused shock, and hoping to hear more about this so-called settlement. There was much discussion in low tones, as though some calamity had occurred—which, indeed, it had. Some said we might have won, but not many could believe that, although we hoped that a decent settlement had been arrived at. Some suggested we continue on strike until we knew what had happened, but this was opposed on the grounds that having come out united we should return united. Also, to remain on strike would mean unofficial action.

The trouble was, we did not know what the settlement terms were. I had vaguely expected that the workers would be consulted before any settlement. It is highly probable that if they had known the truth the workers would have remained on strike. I should have realised that democracy only works when it is favourable to the right-wing union leaders. The whole feeling was one of gloom and shock—could it be true that we were having Black Friday all over again?

On Thursday morning the newspapers were on the streets again. The *Daily Herald* came out with the story that the settlement was a workers' victory. Many of the workers returning to work were to find out what sort of victory they were supposed to have got. Many thousands were thrown out of work, particularly railwaymen, while many others were faced with the scrapping of their agreements, wage reductions, changed working conditions, or the imposition of a document undertaking not to take part in a strike again. Some workers came out again, and in the end the government sent out warnings to the employers to take things easy.

When we learned that the miners had not been consulted and had refused to accept the wage reductions accepted by the TUC for them, we became convinced that it was another sell-out of the workers, even worse than Black Friday. It was many days before we got much idea of the terms, and even then there was much dispute among the leaders as to their exact nature. It became increasingly obvious that the General Strike settlement had been an unconditional surrender. J. H. Thomas insisted that the government had agreed there should be no victimisation. But Baldwin said he could not undertake any such thing, and could not speak for employers, who were free agents.

We communists and left-wingers quickly picked ourselves up after the strike ended, and set to work to help the miners. On the trams we had our guaranteed week, of forty-eight hours, or thirty-two hours for spare-men, set aside temporarily because of abnormal conditions. Apparently the Tramway Manager had the right to do this under the National Agreement. I was still a spare-man, which meant three or four days work a week, and I used my time off to help the miners.

The St. Helens Branch of the Communist Party was holding meetings and lectures every day, covering all the outlying areas of the town as well as the central area. I remember one day, being off work, I rode on my bike to Sutton Manor, about four miles from my home, where I had heard that Charlie Hoyle, the Liverpool Communist Party District Organiser, was conducting a course of political education. He was not at the Sutton Manor Labour Club, so I rode on to Clock Face

British Legion Club, about a mile away. They told me they thought he was out across the fields somewhere, and pointed the direction. I pushed my bike across grassy fields, but could see nothing, until I heard the sound of someone speaking. Quite suddenly I came upon a large hollow in the field, and there was Charlie addressing more than a hundred men seated on the sloping banks of the hollow. He was shouting his wisdom at them, or I would probably never have found them. This shouting in the open air was a habit got from addressing many open-air meetings, and was not usual in a class. I believe his subject was capitalist exploitation.

During the General Strike our Communist Party Branch had already doubled in size, from thirty to sixty members. We had never encouraged a mass membership, but this is what we got. For by the middle of the miners' lockout the one St. Helens Branch had become eight branches with over a thousand members. New branches were set up in Haydock, 250 members; Sutton Manor, 200 members; Thatto Heath, 150; Sutton, 150; Peasley Cross, 100; Parr, 200; Cronton, 100, and Billenge, 70—all card-carrying members. This was one of the outstanding experiences of 1926. At Thatto Heath we had fairly regular meetings of fifty to sixty people in a wooden hut in our backyard. It was packed to suffocation, but we had no money to hire a better place.

Similar developments took place further towards Wigan, where new branches were established at Garswood and Ashton-in-Makerfield. Maurice Ferguson, the Wigan Area Organiser, told me he had addressed a meeting in Garswood Labour Club on the outskirts of Ashton. Towards the end of the meeting he had made the usual appeal for new members, only for every one of three hundred people at the meeting to produce Party membership cards. Sad to say, most of these recruits drifted away in 1927, but we did retain some very valuable members. The only other time we got a comparable flood of new membership was during the second world war, when Bolton Branch grew from between twenty and thirty at the beginning of the war to over four hundred in 1942–4.

3 BILL CARR

From the Yorkshire Coalfield

I was eighteen at the time of the General Strike. I lived at Millfield, near Newcastle-on-Tyne, and worked at the Maria pit. Seven months later, when the miners lockout ended, the pit was manned by blacklegs drawn from other parts of Britain, and none of my family were accepted when they presented themselves for work. Yet the family—my grandfather, father and I—had worked in the industry for a total of 110 years (grandfather first went down the pit at the age of eleven). Throughout that age of time the coal-owners got coal at knockdown prices. Never was there a commodity which yielded such huge fortunes, and in times of recession the owner usually found ways to pass the burden on to the man in the darkness down below.

For the five years before 1926, owners and government had been continuously engaged in attempts to deal with a post-war crisis of falling demand for coal. The war itself had brought vast prosperity to coal-owners, a measure of full employment to the miners, and even a semblance of prosperity in comparison with their previous condition. After the wartime controls ended, however, the miner and his family had to pay for any sweet crumbs that might have fallen their way. And on 1 May 1926 came the owners' decree that all the pits must close, after the miners' union had rejected their demands that the working day be increased from $7\frac{1}{2}$ to 8 hours a day and that the workers in the industry should accept a 10 per cent wage cut, with more reductions to follow.

Every miner knew what this meant, in extreme poverty in the home and greater back-breaking effort in the pit. The existing minimum wage was in most cases, the maximum, since productivity achievement had been set barely above the minimum wage level. A very high level of productivity was required for the miner to obtain any reasonable reward and only in parts of a pit did conditions prevail for this to be possible. For most of the workers who worked away from the coal-face on a day wage, a further reduction in his already devalued wage packet was to ask him to participate in ultimate suicide for his family.

The miner had no choice but to reject the terms and prepare himself for struggle. He was to prove equal to the task he had to face, and was not dishonoured by the final result. A notice was put up at the pit-heads informing the men that they would be required to sign a new contract if they desired to stay in employment.

My two uncles and my grandad, with whom I lived, had already determined that they would not sign. Their good judgement decided my action. It was good to hear them debating the issue. Rough, tough, proud, honest, uncompromising, bull-dog types, limited in expression, fierce in denunciation of the coal-owners, they formed part of the backbone of resistance to the tyranny of what was being demanded. With no political aspirations or education, they were Labour in affiliation. Above all they had a loyalty to their class—but not a shred of understanding of the underlying causes of capitalist crisis, which they were now chosen to meet.

The miners were greatly heartened by the support of the TUC. On 4 May, jubilation in the mining villages was at its height, though all knew the going would be tough. The Government had already indicated that it had plans in preparation to oppose the TUC's efforts in their support of the miners.

Glowing speeches of support for the miners from TUC leaders, from Bevin, Ramsay MacDonald (the traitor), Thomas (another one) and other eminent Labour figures were good for sustaining morale. It was good to know that the day had arrived when miners were not to be pulverised by the enemy in our isolation, especially since the government had now declared a State of Emergency. My family deduced correctly that troops would be used to break the strike.

Councils of Action were set up in our area. The plans outlined at these TUC-organised groups in the villages, which I attended, were in effect to set up at strategic points barriers to be manned by pickets to control the movement of any vehicle in and out of the village. Any article delivered would be scrutinised, and only those needed for the sustenance of the community would be allowed. The vehicle driver would need a chit to grant him free passage. It was the start of a fortnight in which masses of workers learned their tremendous political power.

Inevitably, VIPs of many shades of honesty were driven to the conclusion that their whole future depended on the goodwill of the local Council of Action. Though they supported the government, they had no scruples in applying to the council for preferential treatment in the issuing of chits. To my delight they were rebuffed. Picketing at the pit was intensive, though I cannot recollect any person at that time who would have dreamt of blacklegging in the face of the complete solidarity of the miners and their families.

The news media were already blazing out unprincipled lies about breakaways from the strike, and denunciations against the strikers coupled with veiled threats. At odd times, I saw militant revolutionary sheets urging the lads on to victory, and giving clear lines for progress in the struggle. Tremendous forces had been unleashed in the struggle. I felt this on the picket line. They were daily reinforced by the loud promptings of TUC leaders urging greater efforts to consolidate the strike.

There was total paralysis of the mines, railways, and factories, teaching a plain lesson for all to see of the glorious fruits of unity in action for victory. But at this vital stage, grave doubts, given great publicity by the TUC leaders, began to appear. Meetings behind the scenes of the union leaders supporting the miners became common. It was no secret that the way was being prepared for retreat. Warrants issued for the arrest of several trade union leaders in the North aroused fierce opposition. The Council of Action in Newcastle were dealing quite effectively with the Government's Commissioner who was trying desperately but without success to hold back the tide.

But after nine days, despite the high level of discipline and resolve of the men in dispute, came the tragic call to surrender. We could know of no other reason for this outrageous act than the repeated "conciliation" pleas of TUC leaders toward the end of this time. These pleas were in line with government attitudes. But the TUC decision did not cause the miners to flinch from their struggle. In fact, in our village, it produced a further closing of our ranks, meeting blow with blow, whatever was inflicted on us. It was the same elsewhere. Boards of Guardians, long hated for their means-test manner of doling out food to the sick, injured, and miners' families, were the target of many demonstrations. Their function was to try to undermine the spirit of the miners for struggle by keeping the bellies of women and children empty. We can find echoes today in the demands of reaction to refuse public aid to striking families.

We had our share too of the Specials, and Volunteers—those "steady, loyal, patriots, heroes in support of our freedom, and constitutional rights" as Baldwin called them. Even the children of our village, fed in the main by our manned soup kitchens, had a whale of a time watching these contingents form fours, about turn, quick march in sometimes mindless confusion. They were in the main composed of boneheaded "Rule Britannia" zealots, sprinkled with lower-rank realists hankering after the softer life. I never had any doubts about their abilities when it came to lashing out at a striker with a baton, or even a gun. The press played its usual role. Through it I learned first about unheard-of creatures—"Moscow reds" and "alien workshy agitators"—who were supposed to have infiltrated our British way of life and had to be rooted out.

What all this crap had to do with the fact that we as miners, all known to each other, solidly rejected the abject poverty of the coal-owners' terms, was beyond us. But I learned over the years how important a weapon for the Establishment was this water-on-stone treatment by the press. I think that lesson I learned was responsible later for my tireless agitation and work, long before I joined the Communist Party, to promote the sales of the *Daily Worker*.

This was a most exciting period of my life. The collapse of the General Strike, while disheartening to the miners, did not lead to any weakening of resolve. My family expressed the reactions of everyone around us when they vilified the traitors who left us to struggle alone, though care was taken not to denounce the workers who had responded to the call. Miners' leaders throughout Britain redoubled their efforts to rally the miners for struggle. Arrests of miners' leaders were denounced, and at the several mass meetings I attended on Newcastle Town Moor, the anger of the miners was clearly shown by calls for more retaliation in reply to the attacks by the government.

It seemed that nothing but death could silence this great roar, this demand for justice. Great fighters without a doubt! Each day in the villages was marked by some new event. The women organised all kinds of supper evenings. The supper my aunt provided was from a wash boiler and consisted of chips fried in fat provided free by the local butcher. Others produced boiled peas, and there was always plenty of home-baked loaves standing on window ledges to cool off for consumption later in the day. Herrings were ten a penny. At our village on the fringe of the Northumbrian moors, netting rabbits was a nightly pursuit. Wild birds' eggs we could obtain easily. We even helped farmers in their fields for the reward of a bag of potatoes. Pinching went on too, but it was mostly from public or private property which had little or no relevance for the owners.

Fuel was needed for cooking too—mining families had no such luxuries as electric cookers. There were plenty of trees in the area, but wood was not much use on solid fuel cooking ranges. So the miners made their own coal-mine in a nearby wood, Walbottle Dene, where thin seams of poor brown coal existed.

My two brawny uncles and I set out our "claim" in the Dene, breaking into the three-foot seam on the sides of a steep ravine. Roof supports for the tunnel were obtained from the trees around us. Driving in a pilot heading, fanning out further tunnelling to left and right, and providing the essential ventilation, offered few problems to my uncles, who were experts. My role in the venture was haulage; I had a large tin bath which I pushed in ahead of me empty into the heading. With a clothes line attached to the handle, my uncle, hewing the coal, then filled the tin bath with coal. I dragged the bath back out of the heading. My other uncle at the heading entrance emptied the coal into a sack. When we had obtained sufficient coal for our use, we discontinued our mining until more coal was needed. We did, of course, provide coal for the less fortunate where we could. The coal was carted away from the heading to the village by cycles—at night time. This was a tricky operation through the Dene in the dark. The Specials, too, were very active in stopping and searching anyone carrying anything suspicious. Later in the strike, they clamped down on the Dene coal-digging operations; presumably these were far too successful for authorities directing the crushing of the strike. But stealthily it still went on. I must say also, that a "black market", unwholesome in many respects for the strikers, did develop. But people were often short of necessities and selling coal could buy food.

From the first days of the strike, the local Council of Action had organised morale-boosting social events and these were carried on long after the strike ended. On special days children participated in concerts on waste land; buns and cocoa were distributed. The women excelled in soup kitchen work, and various charitable organisations helped.

We had many sports days, too. Football and cricket matches for men and women as well as walking and running competitions and swimming races in the nearby Tyne were skilfully planned and executed. No effort was spared to solidify the unity of the people, a necessity for victory.

My sister, who was nineteen, and is still a beautiful woman at sixty-seven, was quite an expert at track and long distance running. Her trophies were, fortunately, parcels of groceries donated by a local grocer. Such local characters as these made splendid contributions of credit to miners during the strike, with really little hope of ever recovering their losses. They never had much themselves to tide them over difficult times. No others were employed in the shops but themselves. Most miners remembered them and gave loyal customer support to the end of their lives.

The means test applied by the Board of Guardians was always the subject of bitterness. Then, as now, the miner was on the receiving end of heavy attacks from both the press and the authorities. Shiftlessness was the main charge laid against him. True, I had myself no incentive to want to resume the backbreaking toil underground, but then I remember it was fantastically lovely summer weather, and also I had no dependants. It was degrading for any family to apply for "Guardian" relief. Many did not bother to undergo the humiliating experience and refused to join the queue. Union hand-outs to the strikers was small and became less week by week. The miners' leaders worked incessantly to obtain financial support for us, internationally as well as nationally, but whatever they obtained had to be shared out among many. Baldwin parried the appeal of our leaders to the USA for financial aid by publishing a message to them that there was no hardship or destitution among the miners. The miners regarded this as Government help to the coal-owners to starve the men back to work.

Evan Williams, the coal-owners' representative, said at a meeting with miners' leaders in August 1926, when they were still searching for an honourable settlement: "I do not know whether, with your recent ecclesiastical associations, you have developed the habit of starting proceedings with a prayer and a hymn, and I hope you will not find it strange if we do away with it this afternoon, and get straight down to business." This was a reference to meetings that bishops had with union leaders in attempts to find a formula for ending the strike. The attitude was typical of the contempt and ridicule of the tyrant class, arrogant in their might, merciless in what they felt was to be their victory. My gentle though rough family, slow to react to cruelty, were enraged. I think they knew the nature of the beast from past experience, but this clinched it. I think also that despite the great hardship experienced, these well-publicised arrogant expressions of overwhelming power against the more helpless, helped greatly to decide the miners, come what may, not to submit. As their resources grew less, the miners' firmness grew stronger. Robin Page Arnot, historian of the mineworkers, correctly stated the position in his reference to this period when he quoted a few lines from the *Song of the Fight at Malden*:

Mind shall be harder
Heart the keener
Mood shall be greater
As our might lessens.

I recall that in our village A. J. Cook, the miners' leader was regarded as a heroic figure of great stature. His ceaseless campaigning to stem any breach in the wall had a remarkable impact. Some say he gave his life for the miners. I can date my own entry into active radical politics from this period. The example of a naked class confrontation with all the forces of the Establishment, there for all to see, trying to crush a section of the community down to semi-starvation level was the final confirmation of what I needed to know of class society. And I had not even read a Marxist sheet! Strike pay amounted to four shillings a head—half for juniors—and even this meagre sum came under violent attack from the government and the press. The patient courage shown by the miners was answered by a torrent of hatred and abuse. Lying about supposed stealing and cheating by the miners was commonplace. With the Specials strutting around in their scores, watching, searching, overlooking any ordinary action, we experienced the embryo of a Fascist state. And as the strike went on, contributions to the miners grew less, and even the tiny strike pay dried up. It was sorely missed. These small sums had been used almost always to buy food.

Opposite where we lived was a steelworks. For the first three months of the lockout, coal had been poured into the smelting yard. Picketing had not succeeded in preventing this; there was a Special for every yard of ground. Harassment of the people by these "supermen" could, and did, provoke counter-action. Night after night, raids on the coal-stocks took place within 100 yards of where the Specials were stationed. Coal wagons were raided on their way to the yard; many arrived empty, the drop floor of the wagon expertly released. Some of the men were caught and fined, but most were not. This was entirely unorganised, in some ways counter-productive, but who can say that it was any more criminal than the never-ending attempts by authority to starve the miners' families into submission?

A colliery nearby, the newly constructed Coronation pit, re-opened, and some of the first blacklegs appeared. In the beginning none of these came from our village. Coal was transported from the pit for some two miles by a rope-drawn tubway. The blacklegs at this pit were the scum of Newcastle. Without mining experience or training, they were guided and coerced by pit officials to produce coal by direction. It needed an army of Specials to guard them night and day from the pickets. To reach its destination at the rail terminals at Lemington, the coal had to pass through many open fields, woodlands and culverts. Along with several young mates, I decided that we would, like the old Red Indians, raid these wagon trains without impeding their two-mile-an-hour progress, fill up our bags with coal and proceed home with the booty. This had been done many times before successfully. The Specials found it difficult to guard a two-mile area. Well, there we were, one midday, contemptuous of any intervention, eight of us marching in single file, each carrying a sack of coal on our shoulders. Suddenly police and Specials surged through the bushes, pouncing on the nearest. I was at the rear of the file, and dropped my bag and ran like a hare across the ploughed fields. Looking back, I saw two uniforms travelling faster, and in a short time I was hooked, taken to the police station and put in a cell with another lad. Done to frighten us! The gruff sergeant had invited us to promise to go back to work. Idleness, he claimed, was the breeder of crime. After a few hours we were released, but the village was agog with excitement over our confinement. Our appropriated coal, stored in the police station yard, later disappeared in the night. And we did not go back to work.

I remember, too, the excitement caused by our first blackleg in the village. An ex-sergeant-major, he always walked about with the arrogance of a ruler. He had little credit as a miner, nor did his loud voice gain him respect. What makes a blackleg? They vary in type. What they have in common is a shrinking away from any social responsibility. They are often expert at fawning on the boss, and almost serf-like in their appreciation of authority.

When ours returned from his first day's blacklegging, the whole village seemed to have turned out for the occasion. Marching at the head of an army of Specials, they provided a spectacle indeed of state might. The blackleg even appeared to be enjoying his glory. He chose his way. He certainly could not expect the manly joy of being recognised as a man of principle. Rather he was treated as one would treat a snake.

The younger element, having agreed that he should not enjoy any of the spoils of his treachery, decided to extract the concessionary coal delivered to him. This was done in the middle of the night by the simple act of taking his coal-house door off its hinges, and removing the coal in bags. The cat-calls as he returned from his daily work must have made his life wretched. Or is a blackleg's brain specially insulated against such deprecation?

The morale seemed to be similar wherever I went. At Ashington, where my aunt and uncle lived, the miners were a potent force in the strike. A close-knit community of thousands of miners and their families (there were eight pits around the town) they irradiated messages of sturdy resistance to the outside isolated villages in Northumberland. On my visit to Yorkshire on a pitiful boneshaker of a bike, it was great to see the unified process of a village playing its part to the full in the struggle.

I met my first wife on this Yorkshire visit, when I often watched her performance in women's cricket matches for the soup kitchen funds. For our Yorkshire friends the only needed credential was to be a striking miner. My relatives, who had lived and worked at the local pit for some time before the strike, had already become part of the miners' struggle in the village.

Back at home, however, the continuous pressure of trying to provide an adequate meal brought strains and stresses. Where the family spirit of togetherness was deeply rooted, great hardship could be borne. There were other cases, though, where ill-health had already existed before any strike had started; where existence had depended for a long time on pittances. Here the cruelest blows fell. A neighbours, in such a plight, cut her throat, but her life was saved by neighbours. One chap hanged himself in the yard of the steelworks. These tragedies to people not connected with the mining industry were linked to the strike, I believe, by the venomous action of local Boards of Guardians. With hindsight I can see that any unfortunate family could be denied the financial help needed to sustain them—if only to try to show the harm the wicked miners were causing to the community.

The House of Commons was also used by the Government as a propaganda platform against the miners. Though they professed impartiality, for most of the time the issue of why the miners were resisting was buried by vile abuse in debate, endless wailing about our "way of life" being endangered, mixed with threats against the culprits. An honest presentation of the miners' case was howled down as anti-British. Financial aid from any country, particularly the Soviet Union's £1 million donation to the miners, was regarded as a hostile act against our country.

Contrast this with the selfless sacrifices of Communists who in their small numbers were working under great strain to obtain solidarity backing for the miners, as well as being deeply involved in obtaining bread from nowhere. Across the river, militants among the miners like Will Lawther, who led demonstrations of support for the miners, ended up in prison. And in Newcastle a great movement of trade unionists, in existence from the first days of the General Strike, carried on its work in support of the miners.

Meeting after meeting of the Government simply brought new variations of the original demand that the miners accept a reduction of wages and an increase in hours. As well as passing a law to make an increase in miners' hours of work compulsory, the government allowed the importation of foreign coal and this was a grave blow. An approach to the TUC General Council by the miners' leaders failed to get a response. And these were people who three months before had been swearing with both hands on their hearts that they would not for a moment agree to a betrayal of their brothers. The miners, however, never did at any time identify these people with the rank-and-file workers.

The strain of the lockout was beginning to tell on the whole community. The organised churches tried to intervene for a settlement. The Government adamantly rejected all such moves. Differences appeared over the proposals the Miners' Federation should make to the Government, showing clearly the changing character of the struggle. The inferiority of resources of the miners was beginning to tell. And yet in the worst hours it was astonishing to see miners' union branches registering almost unanimous decisions to carry on the struggle. How pitifully, in contrast, both the Tory Government and the General Council came out of it all!

By September, the Soviet Union and its trade unions had agreed to one per cent of their members' wages going as a contribution to our lads. What jubilation in our ranks this caused? I have often found it difficult to understand why miners ever allowed themselves to be used in anti-Soviet diatribes during and before the cold-war period. Here was a powerful friend, with little to give, but actually prepared to give of that little to help their class brothers far away. The action was heart-warming. My family described it in glowing terms. Everyone called it fondly "Russian money", as distinct from any other aid from other quarters.

The last seven weeks of the struggle presented more problems. The hard core of the men still battled on daily to maintain a high level of conscious activity, picketing, food kitchens, keeping open lines of communication from leading levels of the union to branch and village level. But despite these valiant efforts, cracks were appearing in the unity previously maintained. By the end of September 81,000 had gone back to work, led by bosses' stooges like Spencer of Derbyshire. Yet the miners could still vote 737,000 to 42,000 on 6 October against acceptance of the Government's variegated proposals for ending the strike. The strike-breaking activities of G. A. Spencer, Labour MP in Nottingham, came as a terrible blow. I believe the sowing of the seeds of impending disaster for the miners if the strike continued was a deliberate attempt to split the ranks and leave the hard-core remnants to suffer further brutal government assault.

As strike funds dried up, a growing number of men did return to work. It was not serious in our village, but not all the village worked in the pits. One of my own firm friends, young, vital, and naturally loving the bright lights went back to work. He was not a rat; it was the sheer boredom of life without the pit work that at least gave him, as a single man, a reasonable social life, coupled with family pressures, that caused him finally to make the break. It was a deep, sad blow to me. He was blacklisted from our home for ever. Many more young people were driven back by the apparent hopelessness. Our family stuck to its guns. But many others were influenced by these cases of workers trickling back. By November, the majority of miners were still standing firm, though a quarter of the work force, nearly a quarter of a million workers, had returned to work. The Government now offered what they thought were reasonable terms as conquerors: (*a*) Immediate resumption of work. (*b*) Longer hours to be discussed at district level. (*c*) Rates of pay "*temporarily*" at pre-strike level (but conditional on acceptance of longer hours). (*d*) No guarantee against victimisation, etc.

It was not surprising, after these humiliating terms were referred by the miners' executive to the districts, that they were rejected. We knew, though, that the end was near. On November 29, it was all over. The lockout had lasted seven months, and things would never be the same again. The bitter hatred of the miners against the Tories was deep indeed, and has continued until today. This is reflected in the almost obsessional desire in every miner's family to vote Labour in every mining village. Our lads know of the tortures inflicted on their innocent families and it will never be forgotten.

The blacklist at our pit was operated ruthlessly. No mercy was shown, by the coal-owner—or even expected by the miner. Yet the locked-out men were rated among the most highly qualified, conscientious pitmen in Britain. The men who had returned to work during the lockout formed the basis of the new man-power in the industry. They were mostly raw, and had little idea how to cope with geological conditions in the primitive mining of those days. Their productive results were not outstanding. Over a period of a few months after the end of the lockout, managements were coming to see the necessity of little by little re-employing the old hands, but not at the pits where they had worked before the strike.

I finally got a job at a pit near Blaydon across the river from where we lived—called Stargate. Conditions were appalling, with the water coming through the roof in cascades. Earning power in the circumstances was poor. My uncles had similar problems where they had finally got jobs, and in 1928 we left the North for the new Yorkshire coalfields, where we joined, at a new Thorne Colliery, hundreds of colliers from other areas of Britain, who were also victims of the blacklist.

This pit (now closed) proved to be one of the most militant in Britain—an expression of the dauntless spirit of men driven from their homeland, but never forgetting the lessons of struggle against the class enemy.

4 D. A. WILSON

FROM BRADFORD

I was born in 1897, and was therefore twenty-eight years old at the time of the General Strike. I came of a semi-rural family near Leeds: my mother's family were small farmers declining towards unskilled labourers; my father was a dealer in agricultural goods travelling the Yorkshire farms. It was with my mother's family I was brought up. Father walked out on her, and so we lived for a time with her parents on the farm, until she got together a small home of her own, living by taking in lodgers. Her family was Conservative and Church, since all the "best" people were naturally so, just as grass is green.

As soon as I could leave school, at thirteen, I became an odd-job boy at a quarry for 6*s*. or 7*s*. a week. But after six months or so, trade fell slack and I was put off. I was unemployed for two or three months, and then got a job as office boy in a foundry at 5*s*. a week. It was then that a friend of my mother's got me on the railway at Bradford as a messenger, and later as junior clerk. This was considered a great triumph, because it meant a job for life with no more unemployment. The wage, to start with, was 8*s*. a week.

When I was eighteen my mother died suddenly, and my brother and I, just able to keep ourselves in kindly lodgings, found ourselves on our own. The war was on, and six months later, early in 1916, I volunteered for the navy. When I was demobilised I went back to my old job on the railway—glad to have a job, because a slump soon came on. My old patriotism and family conservatism had quite gone, and I joined the ILP/Labour Party (there was little differentiation in East Bradford then, though it quickly developed). The leading lights then were people like F. W. Jowett and Willie Leach, and their propaganda mainly centred upon poor relief, housing, child feeding, education and municipal socialism. I sympathised, but paid more attention to the trade union branch (then of the Railway Clerks' Association). I was much influenced by what we should now call a "leftish" group in the railway unions, among whom the most prominent was Rowland Hill, slightly my senior, a declared socialist who I think had been a foundation member of the Communist

Party from the BSP. I did not find his ideology convincing, but liked his militantly active line in pressing for more vigorous trade union organisation. He leaned towards syndicalism.

There were about 430 railway clerks in Bradford District, and perhaps 2,500 other railwaymen. Our branch had nearly 400 members out of the 430. The work of the left group was directed towards the policy of one union for all railwaymen, and on this policy we won the support of a majority, but not a large majority, in our branch. The prevailing attitude in the union was the separateness of "white-collar" workers, conscious of their minor privileges over the generality. We, the younger and more militant, were acutely aware of our powerlessness to exercise real economic pressure separate from the rest of the railway workers.

I think my wages at this time were about £4 a week. I had a wife with one small child and another on the way, and we rented a council house of four rooms after being three or four years on the waiting list. We had no savings except the "holiday club"—what we contributed each week, to draw out when we went on holiday.

Bradford at this time had a strong Labour Party (for those days), largely developed from ILP roots with only hazy border lines between the two. There was a "Plebs" Labour College group, centred around the Trades Council, and there was a very small Communist Party somewhere in the background, whose roots seemed to be in Shipley, because some of the most important Yorkshire members lived there.

For me the class-war propaganda of the communists and near-communists cut little ice. Class solidarity was a mirage when one had such difficulty bridging the gulf between one group of workers and another. Communist propagandists, whom one heard of when they got themselves arrested, seemed like Don Quixote tilting at windmills. For the most part I took the *Daily Herald* and the weekly *New Leader*, and sometimes *The Clarion*; but for long periods I knocked off papers altogether for economy's sake. The only marxist journals I saw were the *Labour Monthly*, and occasionally some paper—perhaps the *Workers' Weekly*—from someone around a street orator on the stump at weekends. I read these with quite sharp curiosity and interest, but much scepticism.

In the lead-up to the General Strike we were aware of the consequences of Red Friday, and that the big and militant unions wanted to make a stand. Baldwin's statement that "the wages of all workers will have to come down" was a big factor, as I recall, in preparing the ground for the strike. But so far as I was aware few actual preparations were made locally. The only discussions I heard, of conflicts in other countries, took place in the Trades Council, to which I was a branch delegate. The Trades Council was a quite considerable educational influence, and there was a vigorous "left" in it, to which I listened with interest but no strong conviction. The activists in our particular branch felt that, while we tended towards a more militant general line, if any radical action did develop we would have a difficult job to bring our very unmilitant colleagues into line. Ours was a union that had never had a strike, and our members had never known what it meant to place the welfare of their wives and children at risk in actual struggle. But somehow we never really thought it would come to the point.

When it became clear, that weekend, that it was going to, our Committee got together for an emergency meeting to discuss our attitude and tactics. There was some surprise that our National Executive Committee had sided with the other railwaymen and the TUC General Council; we had rather thought they would find some plausible pretext to shuffle out of it, and we believed it would be extremely difficult to get anything like a solid strike of railway clerks. We were well aware of remarks already being heard around the offices: "What, me? Strike for the miners? Not bloody likely! Why, we'll be striking next for the bricklayers and dustmen and God knows who—we'll never be working!"

We agreed there should be a meeting, a general meeting, the night before the strike, at which we should give a recital of events and a vigorous lead from the branch officers in favour of an effective strike organisation. A large part of the membership attended, including a number who had already expressed themselves against the strike. I prepared myself, as chairman, for an unruly meeting, and braced myself to squash any attempt to force a vote against the strike by insisting that our Executive had already taken the decision on our behalf, and our concern was simply to ensure that our action was united and effective. But the opposition crumbled away with a feebleness which surprised me. We got busy drawing up the rota for picketing the various stations, and for liaison with other unions. Next morning our efforts were rewarded, with 360 out of 400 on strike, and the job effectively stopped in every department.

The strike committee used part of the Labour Party rooms in Forster Square; this was thronged with people for the next ten days, and a furore of committees to organise this and that began to grow up. There was picketing, registering of strikers and blacklegs, circulation of the circulars and bulletins that began to emerge. Delegates were sent to the Transport Workers' Joint Committee, and to the railway Joint Committee; also to the Council of Action the Trades Council had set up. There were arrangements for paying strike pay; and lobbying and moral persuasion of blacklegs.

As the week went on various problems arose on which decisions had to be taken which only the Joint Committees and Council of Action could take. For humanitarian reasons a permit system had to be set up, to enable essential supplies for hospitals, etc., to get through. No separate branch could arrange this, only the joint committees. All manner of incidental minor clashes and conflicts began to arise. A joint committee might initiate some action, or perhaps define some doubtful borderline case, and some fresh workers not yet involved had to be called out. From that point the joint committee, and not the London Executive, was responsible; we found ourselves looking steadily more towards local leads than national ones.

In this atmosphere, and with the strike in Bradford becoming more firmly organised and stabilised, its calling off came as a surprise. Our committee was taken aback, but set about carrying out the decision, feeling sure that the leaders who had appeared to give such a vigorous lead only a few days before could not have retreated without at least the achievement of some part of our objectives, and safeguards about resumption of work. But when our members began to present themselves for work they found themselves faced with conditions. There were lists of who could resume and who could not; there were demands for undertakings as to future conduct. We were to be taken back as people who had been giving a whipping, whilst all the while we were conscious that this was in no wise the case. When the first reports began to come in, the railway strike was immediately called on again, and angry telegrams and phone calls sent to Head Office and our representatives on the Executive.

A chaos of argument, consternation and growing anger followed. We re-established the strike organisation and tried to revive the spirit of a few days before. But while the strike went on, the old unity and conviction was shaken. There came a lengthy telegram from Walkden, our General Secretary, saying that a new agreement had been negotiated and points of misunderstanding removed, and that an unconditional resumption had been secured for everybody. It was a lying message, however, plausibly worded to conceal a complete capitulation. But it did what it was intended to do; it broke the unity, broke the strike, and we began to resume work, visited by all the consequences of defeat. We were taken back "as work offered" or words to that effect, and we were taken back in order of seniority. We set about organising a levy on those taken back, and drew up a scale of supplements to the national strike pay for those who were not, according to their family responsibilities.

The fury among those who had borne the main burden of the strike was intense. But there was complete mystification and incredulity. Of the national leaders we thought: "*You* called us out on strike. We backed you up to the hilt, and did everything you asked us to do; and then you sold out, turned round, and helped the bosses to give us a hiding! Where does the sense lie? You, Walkden—we thought you a man of principle and character; you have a fine record in founding our union; you have a history of personal sacrifice for it in its early days. Why should you trick us and lie to us in this manner?" It was incredible.

In consequence of the General Strike I joined the Communist Party, and I know others who did the same; but not there and then—it was some three or four years later that I took the decision. Experiences such as the strike create a turmoil of mind; they require a re-orientation of one's attitude to life, of one's judgments of one's fellow men. Such changes take time to develop. They involve readjustment of relationships with every one you know: family, fellow-workers, friends, acquaintances. Only a less stable person could make such a change quickly, and would be very liable to reverse action on short-term pretexts.

The atmosphere of the nine days—not to be on holiday but not going to work, to be on strike—was a novel experience, and large numbers of strikers spent all their time at the rooms. This was useful, of course, in that volunteers were always on hand for the multifarious tasks that cropped up. But only a part could be fully occupied, and the rooms became a day-long venue. Visitors from elsewhere were seized upon and required to give an account of what was happening *there*. Bulletins of news began to be got out and circulated. A service of cyclists and motor-cycle despatch-riders seemed to spring almost spontaneously into existence. The government announcements on the radio had to be answered, and so had the leaflets and posters and botched-up newspapers that the other side was circulating. There was a continuous, feverish, keeping-up-morale operation in being, and one was conscious that the committee-room atmosphere was one thing, and that of the home, where the women were, another. *She* had to face feeding the family with the prospect of no wage at the weekend. We began to devise ways of involving the women, such as organising some sort of scratch meals collectively at the rooms.

The minds of some of us were turning to this problem. The government and employers had taken the gloves off: they meant business. It may prove an extended struggle; we would have to settle down from this feverishness to a routine that we could maintain for some time. I remember, one day, venturing to suggest that it would do some of us good to take time off from sitting about in town, not always very usefully, and to go home and plant some potatoes in the garden if you had one (as I had). I don't think it was the right psychological note to strike at that moment, but it was a groping for a longer-term perspective. And it is an indication that the idea of capitulation was not in our minds at all, but rather, how to stabilise the situation.

The point was that some of us had not thought the strike was really likely to be called, and had been somewhat surprised by the vigour and competence of the General Council, through Ernie Bevin, in the calling of it. This was a challenge to the very government itself, and when such solid and level-headed men took such a decision, they *must* mean business. So we responded in that spirit. I remember quoting Shakespeare: "Beware of entrance to a quarrel, but being in, bear't that the opposed may beware of thee!"

I don't recall the OMS counting for much in the Bradford area. We knew of the railway's attempts to get trains going by volunteers: university students and middle-class people and officials who got an engine running for fun perhaps, earning nothing but our ridicule for their futility in not then knowing anything useful to do with it. The small handful of blacklegs who succeeded in getting in to stations by devious means (goods agents, cashiers sometimes, and a few toadies), just didn't know what to do when they *were* in. I remember we permitted the necessary number of horsekeepers to work, so as to feed the large number of heavy shire-horses the railways then employed. There was a request, after a few days, for additional carters to be let in, to *exercise* the horses, which were beginning to damage their feet, kicking and stamping because they had no work. We suggested that the blacklegs could serve a useful purpose by walking the horses round and round the yards. We got some pleasure in imagining it.

Our branch membership, as I have said, was about four hundred. The branch committee would number, as far as I recall, about twelve. In normal, quiet times the monthly members' meeting would be attended by about twenty-four people, except when we staged and advertised a special speaker. During the General Strike almost *all* available members except the few blacklegs came down to the committee rooms, off and on. (Those I speak of as less available were the many who lived away from the Bradford district; many lived in Leeds.)

While the miners' strike went on, the heightened emotions generated amongst the other workers continued to boil and bubble. There was a steady process of stifling these, which took perhaps six months or more, before it was eventually accomplished, until the union branch rooms were forced back to the desirable normality of relative apathy. As branch chairman I was acutely aware of this: in our particular area I had to "hold the baby".

The monthly meetings in June, July and August, and so on into the autumn and winter, were quite abnormally well attended—something over a hundred perhaps, but dwindling steadily as the months went on. They came, of course, in concern about their prospects of resumption, and the resumption of comrades still not offered work; they came about the business of the special levy supplementing strike pay. But they came, above all, seeking answers to the burning questions—"Why, having called the strike, did you then betray it? If, as was hinted, *our* strike was all right but somebody else's was collapsing, who was it? Where was it? If there *were* these mysterious influences working against it—as was hinted—then why did you call the strike in the first place?" And there was the desire to face Walkden up to his "lying subterfuge of a telegram", which were the words I myself used as branch chairman in a letter to the union journal.

No answers were forthcoming, only pleas of injured innocence—the injustice done to other people because *we* did not know all the facts. These were facts that could not yet be disclosed because they involved other unions, and might endanger the miners' continued heroic struggle. But, all in good time, there would be the TUC inquest into the whole matter, and then we would be fully informed. This "inquest" took place the following spring, and the record of it is probably the most illuminating document of the strike (not the official statement of the outcome, but the report of the discussions of its participants).

But none of this was relevant for those who had attended our abnormally numerous branch meetings. By the spring our meetings were back, as I have said, to "normality", and to an apathy which had a mood of depression added to it. The only force fighting this stifling process was the Minority Movement; but it *was* a minority, and a small one. Rowland Hill had been associated with it for some time and had some following in a small way; my own attitude to him and it had been a sort of friendly neutrality. I now became an active supporter and we developed our connection with the national organisation in the years immediately ahead. This led eventually to my removal from branch office by Executive Committee decree, and to my living for some years under the embargo of being ineligible for election to *any* office in the union, or to serve in *any* form in a representative capacity.

Were the workers properly class conscious in 1926? They were class conscious enough to strike with an unexpected vigour which transcended very strong vocational consciousness. I would think that this level of class consciousness had been created in the broader sense by the war, supplemented in a narrower sense by the trade union activities of the early 1920s. But in its broader sense it was not accompanied by a real understanding of its potential power. "Yes, we're the working class and they're the bosses, and there have always been bosses, and no doubt always will be." After the General Strike there was a much wider consciousness of the *potential power* of the workers. People were only pushed back slowly into apathy and pessimism. But there were insufficient numbers among them with the conviction and understanding ever to put a line of action that seemed plausible and practical in exercising that power.

Did the strike mark an end of a period of real mass militancy? It marked an end of any possibility for many years of concerted action between official trade union movements. Working-class militancy was forced into other channels: into Labour Party activity towards the time of the 1929 Labour Government; into the rank-and-file movements of the Minority Movement kind in the 1930s; into the unemployed workers' movement; and generally, I think it existed within the trade unions. But the "establishment" had learned much, and did its best to further institutionalise the established right-wing control in the unions.

The ruling class has shown a great capacity to learn by its experience in the General Strike how to direct the social forces to its own advantage. And it has been very flexible in developing its own economic theorising and propaganda.

I feel very strongly that there are not, permeating the working class, a sufficient number of people with an adequate social philosophy and understanding to give a vision and perspective to our actions. Yet we need unceasingly to seek to acquire this understanding, so that we may know, within the continuous pattern of change, where we need to go, and why.

5 JULIE JACOBS

FROM HACKNEY

I was only nineteen at the time of the General Strike, and the never-to-be-forgotten experience of it started for me with the May Day Sunday demonstration to Hyde Park on 2 May 1926.

We assembled outside the old Hackney Town Hall (on the site of the present one) with trades unions, Labour Party, CP, YCL, ILP, unemployed organisation and other banners and posters, plus a couple of gaily decorated horse-drawn cars for the children. A short meeting and a cheer for socialism and off we marched along Mare Street into the neighbouring borough of Bethnal Green to the "Salmon and Ball", a great and traditional place for public meetings where we picked up, amidst cheers, the demonstrators from Bethnal Green who were waiting. On again into Stepney, and another halt to pick up the rest of the East London contingent converging from Stepney, Poplar, West Ham and East Ham. A slightly longer stop, with a further meeting addressed by several local leaders, and we were off again, gathering reinforcements of demonstrators—police, and a second demonstration marching all the way with us on the pavement—past Aldgate, the City—with further reinforcements of City police—St. Paul's Cathedral, Fleet Street and the Strand and into Kingsway. Here we got the biggest boost of the day, for on the pavement outside the Kingsway Hall were standing members of the General Council of the Trades Union Congress, and as we came abreast of them they shouted: "All out from Monday midnight!", and "The General Strike is on!" Cheers broke out and were echoed all along the marching columns. Marchers rushed to shake the General Council members' hands—if we could have looked nine days forward would it have been hands we rushed to shake?

As we marched along, backs straightened up, the column smartened, the band—yes, we had one—struck up a workers' tune and everyone sang with a new and great heart, because the miners were not going to be left in the lurch, the great trade union brotherhood was coming into the struggle and the slogans on the trade union banners reading: "An injury to one is an injury to all"—"Unity is strength—strength united is all powerful"—"United we stand", were coming to life. And so along Oxford Street into Hyde Park, greeted at the Marble Arch and the entrance to the Park by thousands of cheering Londoners who had been waiting to welcome us and who had already heard the news.

In the park were six platforms and around each of them great crowds of expectant and excited people waiting for, and listening to, the speeches. Every reference to the miners and the coming solidarity strike action brought renewed volumes of cheers.

A special Conference of Executives of unions affiliated to the TUC had been meeting at the Memorial Hall, Farringdon Road (near Ludgate Circus), over the weekend and after considerable discussion had enthusiastically carried by 3,653,529 votes to 49,911 the General Council's recommendation for the General Strike to begin at midnight on Monday, 3 May.

The Agreed Document declared, in part:

> The following trades and undertakings shall cease work as and when required by the General Council:
>
> All Transport, i.e. Railways, sea transport, docks, wharves, harbours, canals, road transport, railway repair shops, and contractors for railways and all unions connected with the maintenance of, or equipment, manufacturing, repairs and groundsmen employed in connection with air transport;
>
> Printing trades, including the Press;
>
> Productive industries, iron and steel, metal, and heavy chemicals group, including all metal workers and other workers who are engaged or may be engaged in installing alternative Plants to take the place of coal;
>
> Building Trades—all workers engaged on building, except such as are engaged definitely on housing and hospital work, together with all workers engaged in the supply of equipment to the building industry;
>
> Electricity and Gas—the trade unions . . . shall co-operate with the object of ceasing to supply power;
>
> Sanitary Services . . . shall be continued;
>
> Health and Food Services . . . there should be no interference in regard to these, and the trade unions concerned should do everything in their power to organise the distribution of milk and food to the whole population;
>
> With regard to hospitals, clinics, convalescent homes, sanatoria,

infant welfare centres, maternity homes, nursing homes, schools, the General Council direct that affiliated unions take every opportunity to ensure that food, milk, medical and surgical supplies shall be efficiently provided.

The document also outlined the functions of local trades councils:

They shall together with the local officers of the trades unions actually participating in the dispute assist in carrying out the foregoing provisions, and they shall be charged with the responsibility of organising the trades unionists in dispute in the most effective manner for the preservation of peace and order.

Hackney Trades Council, like many other trades councils, interpreted this broadly as making them the official local Agent of the TUC, and their function as being to organise the General Strike locally as efficiently as possible.

Harry Lee, the local Trades Council secretary and the assistant secretary, Lucy Hyde, got busy gathering the Trades Council executive committee members, plus some local trade union officials to form a Council of Action.

The Manor Hall in Kenmore Road (a boxing hall no longer existent) was hired for the duration as the strike headquarters and was manned 24 hours a day by members of the Committee, and there were always groups of trades unionists and pickets in attendance.

We whiled the hours away with dominoes—East London is famous for its domino players—draughts, cards, and discussions. The latter ranged over politics, trade unions, socialism, Baldwin, Churchill —including the troops in Sidney Street and South Wales—MacDonald, Thomas. You name it and we discussed it. I was not, at that time, a delegate to the trades Council. But I was already active in the trade union movement and in the Young Communist League, and was the local organising secretary of the National Unemployed Workers' Committee Movement. I was brought in by the Trades Council Secretary as a messenger and general dog's body to assist particularly with meeting and general propaganda activities, such as chalking the streets and walls with slogans, dates of meetings, etc.

The work at the Manor Hall headquarters was very exciting. Reports from all over the Borough and even from neighbouring Bethnal Green, Stepney, Poplar and West Ham were constantly coming in. There were reports of factories joining the strike. For example, a clothing factory, not called out, held a meeting and under the leadership of a young (then) Morry Blaston (later a communist Councillor in Hackney) decided to join the strike. Incidentally, Morry, too, was made a messenger to the Strike Committee. Our main form of locomotion were two feet and, if lucky, a bicycle. There were also cases reported where the responses to the strike call was not immediately 100 per cent but where as a result of efficient picketing, discussion and persuasion it soon became 100 per cent.

Hackney's response to the strike call was good, and in fact on the day the strike was called off more workers were out than on the first few days, with still further sections asking to be brought out. Mention must be made of the part played by the Hackney Branch of the National Unemployed Workers' Committee Movement (later the word "Committee" was dropped from the title). Their motto was "Blackleg Proof", and from the beginning of the General Strike they proved it. They offered every assistance to the Strike Committee and gave very good service indeed in helping on the picket lines, organising meetings and demonstrations and in doing whatever was asked of them.

Many times a day local employers and tradesmen came to the Strike Committee for permission to continue working, generally pleading that under the terms of the TUC strike decision their work was exempted from the strike call. They always declared that they supported the miners and the trade union movement's decision to support them—BUT, it was essential for the welfare of the ordinary people that they be allowed to go on working. How pleased they were when, and if, the Strike Committee agreed and gave them a permit and stickers for their vehicles which read: "By permission of the TUC"!

An amusing, but very satisfying, incident took place at the Hackney tram depot, which was situated in what is known as the narrow Mare Street, where Amhurst Road runs into it.

There were, of course, no trams running. For the tram men, cleaners, mechanics, etc., and all public transport, was at a standstill and maintaining a strong picket line. But the local police and some would-be blacklegs from the Organisation for Maintenance of Supplies or, as the local trades unionists always called it, the "Organisation of Mugs and Scabs", decided they would break the picket line and run the trams. Some of them did break through, and they got into the depot. The picket reported the breakthrough to the Council of Action and, within a couple of minutes, hundreds of trade unionists were manning the picket line and the blacklegs were really faced with a problem. How to get out?

They very quickly gave up any idea of running the trams. Now their only concern was to get out and get away. Also, they were beginning to feel hungry. The canteen staff was on strike, and the would-be blacklegs had omitted to take food in with them. Despite all the efforts by the police, the picket line remained solid and could not be broken, and the blacklegs could not get out.

Further hours passed, and it was near to midnight when into the strike headquarters came the local Police Chief. All jolly and friendly he was, and the following conversation, or something like it, took place:

Police Superintendent: "Well, gentlemen, we want your help. You know there are some people in the Tram Depot who want to come out, they are worried that their families will be worrying, but they are being prevented by some of your people. Will you help?"

A free translation of Harry Lee's reply: "You —— took them in, now you —— get them out!" Exit the Superintendent.

Some hours later, in the wee small hours, they managed to get out—I think by climbing over a wall into the churchyard. But they were spotted and a chase ensued along Mare Street. By Westgate Street there stood, and I think still stands, a horse-trough full of water. And here the blacklegs were caught and dumped into the trough. There were no further attempts to get the trams out. And, I understand, no horses were, as had been feared, poisoned or suffered any ill effects.

In Hackney, unlike some other parts of the East End—Poplar and West Ham—there were no major clashes with either the police, the military or the Organisation for Maintenance of Supplies, although there were a number of minor incidents of police provocation and baton-drawing accompanied by pushing and shoving, with a few arrests—the charge usually being "obstructing the police in the execution of their duty", which included selling or distributing news sheets and bulletins.

Propaganda was one of the main activities throughout the whole strike period. Marches and demonstrations to various factories, discussions in the open air and public meetings at all times of the day and particularly at night from about 7 p.m. to 10 or 11 p.m. And then groups would continue discussion.

Meetings at the corners of most streets leading off both sides of Mare Street, from Hackney Station to King Edward Road, Ridley Road, Clapton Square, Urswick Road, etc., took place. Here I had my baptism as a public speaker and was thrown in at the deep end. I was supposed to have chaired a meeting at the side of the Town Hall, but when I arrived Harry Lee said: "Sorry, Julie, the speaker has been delayed, you will have to carry on until he gets here." With all the confidence of nineteen years plus, I got on to the platform and, castastrophe, my mind went a complete blank and I stood there unable to remember a single word of my speech. I could not even see the audience, except as a blur. But after a few seconds—which seemed like hours—salvation came from the crowd. A voice shouted: "Tell them about those B——s in Parliament." Thoughts and speech flooded back, my crisis was past and we had a good meeting. I have spoken at thousands of meetings since then and never again blacked out. I often suffered badly beforehand from a tightening of my stomach muscles, but never again a blackout.

In the situation of the General Strike we learned quickly, and in a few days I was a confident "old hand"—so much so, that by Sunday the 9th I was to be one of the speakers at Victoria Park.

Victoria Park is a large open lung that serves Hackney, Bethnal Green, Stepney and Poplar. It was a traditional and very popular spot for meetings on Sundays from morning to dusk. All kinds of organisations held regular meetings there—Christian Evidence Society, Catholic Evidence Guild, Freethinkers, Socialist Party of Great Britain, Social Democratic Federation, British Socialist Party, ILP—and from the early 1920s the Communist Party, as well as many other bodies and individuals.

On this first Sunday of the General Strike mass meetings were being organised in all parts of Greater London and, I believe, throughout the United Kingdom. In London a shuttle service of speakers would do two or perhaps three meetings during the day. The speaker who was to follow me was coming from Clapham Common or Battersea Park, anyhow he never turned up and I spoke that day for more than five hours. But, let me hurriedly add, not making one speech all the time but answering questions and taking collections for the miners' solidarity fund whenever I was in danger of drying up. Incidentally, collection taking in London Parks was at that time legal and many fine sums were collected. On this Sunday we shared Victoria Park with the First Battalion of the Guards; although they were kept segregated from us, they had been drafted into the area to protect blacklegs, to act as convoys for good from the Docks and, above all, to intimidate the ordinary people of East London. But, just as Hitler could not do it in the early 1940s, so Baldwin, Churchill and their gang could not do it during the General Strike.

Here is a true but typical story of the use of troops to intimidate and overwhelm the people. "A convoy of 140 flour and other food lorries was taken yesterday from the London Docks to Hyde Park." Quite an ordinary normal picture, particularly as the TUC's instructions were absolutely clear and unambiguous; "Health and food services . . . there should be no interference in regard to these, and the trade unions concerned should do everything in their power to organise the distribution of milk and food to the whole of the population." Also, permits to carry and transport food were always given by the trade unions. So what did the government do? It provided "an escort of sixteen armoured cars, cavalry and mounted police" (*British Worker*, 9 May). We were not told whether Churchill was there in person directing operations.

The stretch of Commercial Road from Aldgate to the Docks was the scene of many provocations by the military and the civil police alike, and the stationing of troops in the Docks, Woolwich Arsenal, utility undertakings, etc., caused great anger, because this action was completely unnecessary. A further cause of anger were the invariably exaggerated reports by the wireless of extremely minor incidents. Often such reports were manufactured from a broadcloth of lies and fantasy, without even a vestige of substance.

Money-raising activities on behalf of the miners, their wives and dependants were an important function of the Strike Committee and, indeed, of every trade unionist. And Hackney responded very well.

Street and job (where working) collections were made regularly, and a miners' choir from South Wales came to us and stayed for several weeks, being put up and cared for by local residents. Their hospitality was overwhelming and, indeed, in the early days created physical difficulties for the miners—but our friendly doctors soon put that right.

Every day the choir would go around the main streets singing and explaining, with the help of members of the Strike Committee, the reasons for the miners' lockout and the solidarity of the General Strike.

Several of us would walk from Hackney to Clerkenwell where we hired a barrel organ which we pushed—and sweated—all the way back to Hackney, playing all the latest [*sic*] tunes, collecting money all the while. Arrived back in Hackney we toured the streets playing the barrel organ and with very short meetings of explanation—and then pushed the barrel organ back to Clerkenwell. Finally walking back home, tired but enthusiastic.

Miners' solidarity badges, in the form of a miner's lamp, were sold throughout the Borough and proudly worn by men, women and children. A few years ago an old lady gave me one which she had saved for more than forty-five years. She had been sorry for the miners and felt they were being given a raw deal, then she began to get interested in politics and became an active member of the Labour Party and the Unemployed Workers' Movement. A grand old socialist stalwart. This miner's lamp now occupies a place of honour in the Communist Party's Library at 16 King Street.

6 AN INCIDENT ON THE RIVER THAMES

by HARRY WATSON

From the first hour of the strike work stopped on the river. There were a couple of destroyers in the Pool—but we did not let them worry us. And the strike had already entered its second week without our having had any cause for concern about work of any sort being done. So far as we knew, every lighterman, waterman and tugman was solidly on strike in support of the miners, and nothing whatever could move in the shape of a barge, boat or tug. The question of picketing did not even arise.

But then a couple of the lads came along—I was an apprentice lighterman at that time—and told us they had seen two tugs under way in Woolwich Reach, towing craft up river. At first we thought they were having us on, and asked them who the crew were—but they said the tugs and craft had been too far away for them to tell. After questioning them a bit more, however, we came to the conclusion that there might be something in it. And there was no better way to find out for sure than to get hold of a skiff and go afloat to see for ourselves.

So Frank Ling and myself set off for Ratcliffe Causeway, where we knew a waterman called Gus Fitzgerald who owned a skiff. He was a very good-natured bloke and we were sure he would loan it for a while.

It was about ten o'clock in the morning when we first heard of the tugs. And as we had to walk from Canning Town to Ratcliffe Cross, it was getting on for eleven-thirty when we fetched up at "The Vine"—which was the pub that Gus frequented. As I remember, high water was between one and two, or thereabouts. It was about mid-day when Gus showed up. So we explained the situation to him, and he told us that the Navy had been manning a tug or two and towing a few barges. He agreed to our using his skiff—but was very anxious about getting it back safely. He warned us not to get into any trouble which could result in damage. And we assured him we had no intention of allowing anything like that to happen.

Frank and I rowed out to mid-stream, and there was not a sign of any tugs or barges under way. So we just let the boat drop up river and kept our eyes open for anything that might be coming along.

We had got abreast of London Dock, Shadwell entrance, when three police launches came down full pelt—presumably from Wapping Thames Police Station. Instead of the usual sergeant and one constable to each launch there were four police in each, and among them two inspectors. They circled round us—and then one kept above us, one below, and the third edged alongside.

The inspector wanted to know who we were and what we were doing. So we told him we were pickets and just having a look round. Then he wanted to see our waterman and lighterman licences, and we produced them for him to read and identify us. After that he said there was nothing happening on the river of any interest to us and that we had better get ashore. But we couldn't agree with him on that, and told him we had heard that navy men were manning tugs and barges and that if that was the case then we were very much interested.

He said, "If I see you interfering in any way with tugs or craft, you're for it."

We replied that we had no intention of jeopardising either the boat or our lives. But he warned us again, and threatened to put a line into the skiff and tow us to Wapping if we did not agree to get ashore. After that, we had to tell him that as licensed men we had every right to be on the river and that our purpose was quite legal.

By then it was high water, and we had dropped up to abreast of Wapping entrance to London Dock. We began to paddle back down along. And before he left, the inspector told a sergeant in one launch to keep up with us and tow us to the Police Station if we gave any trouble.

We continued to paddle gently down river. There was still no sign of any tugs, however—so I suggested to Frank Ling that we should row down as far as Limehouse and, if there were still no signs of activity, we should go back to Ratcliffe and tie the boat up. He agreed.

The tide was beginning to race down a bit by then, and we kept the skiff well over to the south side in order to make the job of rowing back easier in the slack water. With our police-boat escort we continued down, and when we got abreast of Limehouse Cut we eased up altogether. There was no sign of any tugs or barges moving. So we rowed into the south shore and then turned up river.

Up river we went, trying to keep a fair distance between the skiff and the police launch outside of us. We had been rowing for about ten minutes when Frank, who was bowman, looked over his shoulder to take note of our course. I heard him say, "Oh yeah! Look at this lot." I stopped rowing and looked round. And there, coming down river, was the tug *Vigilant*, owned by Vokins—a lighterage company.

As I worked for Vokins, I was of course very much interested. Yes, it was her all right—and she was towing two barges, one astern of the other. It was a cockeyed way to tow. And to make it worse, the barge astern was towing on a long lead of rope and sheering about like a sailing barge on a tacking course. There were eight sailors on the deck of the tug and two in the wheel box. I suppose there must have been at least two or three more below in the stoke-hold and engine room—which all together made roughly three times the normal scale of manning.

As we lay there, looking, the sternmost barge took a sheer—and she was going like the clappers. Suddenly she brought up, and the way of her took the tow rope barge almost athwart the river, while the head of the tug turned towards the north shore just below Limehouse Cut. The inevitable happened. The fellow at the wheel turned it hard over to starboard, the tug went athwart the tide, and by then the sternmost barge had completed its first sheer and was coming round in an enormous sweep into its next run.

We had never seen anything like it. And neither had the police. They left us and went after the tug, shouting to the sailors to stop the tug and shorten up the tow. If they heard, they paid no attention—and the next thing was, crash, bang, wallop, the craft had sheered right round and gone athwart the barge roads, where naturally there were many more barges lying than normal.

The sudden weight and impact of the crash caused mooring ropes to tauten and break as if made of cotton instead of two-inch manilla. And immediately, there was a tug out of control, eight barges adrift, and everything going down river at a fine rate of knots headfirst to another roads—this time, a tug roads.

There were ten tugs lying there, moored—and soon the shambles of craft had to be seen to be believed.

The sailors had no idea and neither had the bloke at the wheel. The *Vigilant* was hemmed in with drifting barges, and he had stopped the engines too, which made matters worse. He had no control over her at all. Meanwhile, the police were shouting to the sailors to keep the craft clear of the tug roads. They knew very well what the result would be if the craft did the same thing again—this time it would not be thousands of pounds' damage, but tens of thousands, and money was money in those days. They were shouting "Pull them clear!", "Pull them clear!" But the sailors on deck only waved their arms in despair.

Some more ropes broke with the strain of craft being girted, and then barges began to drift away singly and in pairs—and only two of them fell athwart the leads of the moored tugs and did little or no damage.

The last we saw of that lot was a Thames policeman trying to get aboard the *Vigilant*—presumably to explain to the chap at the wheel that to work in restricted areas like Limehouse Reach of the River Thames called for vastly different techniques than those required for destroyers on an open sea. The last thing we saw was great barges chasing down river out of control, several single, one a pair, and three still tied together. We both shut our eyes at the thought of the damage they were going to do to whatever they hit—jetties, wharfs, tugs and barges, and even coppers' craft on their course down the river. Thousands and thousands of pounds' worth of damage was in prospect—and we felt sure there would be plenty of work for the barge-builders later on.

On our way back to Ratcliffe the police launch which had earlier carried the inspector came down at full speed. She eased down and stopped just abreast of us, and again told us to get ashore. We called out, "What are you going to do about those blokes? You were going to tow us to your Police Station if we caused trouble. What are you going to do with those sailors?" The only reply we got was a dirty look. So Frank and I were having a good laugh when we finally tied up the skiff.

There was a sequel to all that. After the strike was called off—we thought at first it was off because the government had given way, not because it was betrayed—we had orders to board a tug at Blackwall Pier at six o'clock on the Monday morning. And the tug was, of course, the *Vigilant*. The crew arrived, and there were four lightermen including myself with orders to tow with some craft. We went down into the after cabin to wait until we were required—and what a sight! There were twenty-four crates of beer bottles (that is, 288 pints), and only six bottles among them that had not been opened. We took all the empties on deck and slung them overboard. There were canned goods in plenty too, and they went overboard as well. Those sailors were certainly able to fodder and refresh themselves—but they were not so good at navigating tugs and barges.

PART FOUR

AFTERMATH

CONSEQUENCES OF THE GENERAL STRIKE

by MARTIN JACQUES

The General Strike remains the most dramatic expression of working class solidarity so far this century. It directly involved almost two million workers and indirectly a million or so more. It led to unprecedented and countless examples of local initiative and activity. It provoked a massive display of power by the various arms of the state apparatus. On all these counts, the General Strike deserves our closest attention.

But there is another important reason why the General Strike is significant for us today. 1926 proved to be a turning-point in the development of the working-class movement: it marked the end of the last great period of working-class militancy and it saw a massive shift in the outlook and orientation of the trade union movement. The present-day practice of the TUC, for example, was originally evolved in the aftermath of the General Strike. The General Strike is, thus, not simply an interesting historical problem: in a real sense, it still poses us with important political questions today.

BACKGROUND

Gramsci has suggested three moments of class consciousness.[1] Firstly, there is limited sectional consciousness between members of a particular craft, trade or profession. Secondly, there is the moment when members of a social class become aware of a common interest but where that interest remains economic. Thus, while political perspectives are advanced, they lie within the existing fundamental structures of society. This might be described as corporate consciousness. Thirdly, there is the moment when a class becomes aware of its overall role in society and begins to acquire a hegemonic outlook in relation to other subordinate groups and society as a whole. While consciousness is an extremely complex question which defies neat categorisation, these stages provide us with a useful framework with which to examine the development of the British working class since the late nineteenth century.

Prior to around 1900, the consciousness of the working class can largely be described in terms of the sectional-economic moment, although elements of a corporate consciousness were also evident amongst some sections. Between around 1900 and 1920, however, a fundamental transformation took place in the consciousness of important segments of the working class: firstly, key sections came to acquire a corporate consciousness and, secondly, a very small minority began to move hesitatingly in the direction of a hegemonic outlook.

Of this period 1906–20, the years 1918–20 probably saw the most rapid change. There was the transformation of the Labour Party and its emergence as a major electoral force, the establishment of the TUC General Council and the formation of the Communist Party. Moreover, it was during this period that the working-class movement posed the most serious challenge to the ruling class. After 1920, however, the situation began to change. Mass employment appeared for the first time. And the ruling class rapidly succeeded in regrouping its forces and re-establishing its hegemonic apparatus. Thus, by 1923, the problem presented by the rise of the Labour Party had, in large measure, been defused. The threat posed by the trade union movement, however, proved more intractable and was, in the event, not resolved until 1926. This latter problem will form the central theme of this essay.

THE IDEOLOGY AND POLITICS OF TRADE UNIONISM, 1918–26

The trade union movement emerged from the first world war and immediate post-war boom of 1918–20 in a greatly-strengthened position. Trade union membership rose from 4·15 millions in 1914 to 6·53 millions in 1918, reaching a peak of 8·35 millions in 1920.[2] A series of trade union amalgamations resulted in the creation of a number of relatively large unions including the AEU in 1920 and the TGWU in 1921. At the same time, unions sought new forms of co-operation and joint action. The Triple Alliance, embracing the Transport Workers, Miners' Federation and NUR, had been formed in 1915 and this was followed in 1920–1 by the transformation of the Parliamentary Committee of the TUC into a greatly-strengthened General Council.[3]

The economic downturn of late 1920–early 1921 brought about a rapid change in the situation. During the post-war boom, the trade union movement had been on the offensive in a situation of full employment. The appearance of mass unemployment, however, forced the trade unions on to the defensive and, beginning with Black Friday, they suffered a series of major defeats. In the longer-run, mass unemployment was to have a number of crucial consequences: it gradually undermined the combativity of industrial workers, weakened the feeling and possibility of solidarity which had developed prior to 1921 and strengthened the power of trade union leaderships *vis-à-vis* the rank and file.

These tendencies did not, however, really become decisive until after the General Strike. Thus between 1921 and 1926 the mood of key sections of industrial workers remained militant, combative and cohesive. At the same time, the trade union movement was, within limits, willing and prepared to fight. Thus, while the appearance of mass unemployment had an important impact on the trade union movement, it did not in itself mark a decisive turning-point.

With this background, I want to look at the ideology of the trade union movement between 1918–26. The main problem I want to focus upon, in this context, concerns the relationship between the industrial and political spheres. The traditional Labourist conception of this relationship sees the two spheres as essentially separate and independent; it thus accepts a fairly total form of parliamentary sovereignty while recognising the legitimacy of collective bargaining. In this light, the trade unions are seen as engaging solely in industrial activity, while the Labour Party is seen as exclusively responsible for political activity, which is essentially defined in electoral and parliamentary terms. The syndicalist conception, on the other hand, in effect blurs the distinction between the two spheres: it maintains the legitimacy of trade unions engaging in industrial action for political ends of the most far-reaching kind while rejecting the need for a working-class political party.

During the period between 1918 and 1926, the dominant ideology within the trade union movement was neither syndicalist nor conventionally Labourist. Rather, it contained elements of both. Thus, while most trade union leaders accepted the principle of parliamentary sovereignty, they also maintained that it was legitimate to use industrial action in order to influence political decisions. As a consequence, whilst recognising the role of the Labour Party, they also believed in the right of the unions to use industrial action of a political character.

Some distinction must be made here, however, between 1918–20 and 1921–6. During the former period, when the working-class movement was on the offensive, there occurred the two clearest examples of a semi-syndicalist conception of the relationship between the industrial and political spheres. Firstly, there was the decision of the trade union movement to use industrial action to prevent military intervention by the British Government against the new Soviet Republic and, secondly, there were the TUC discussions in 1919–20 on the use of industrial action to secure the nationalisation of the mines.[4]

From 1921, however, with the trade union movement forced on to the defensive, such action for explicity political ends became relatively impractical. And this, together with the development of the Labour Party, particularly prior to the first Labour government,[5] led sections of the centre within the trade union movement to look upon such action as of secondary importance and even of dubious political validity. Here, however, we must think in terms of a drift rather than a decisive break: it was a product of pragmatism rather than theory.

This is borne out by the nature of industrial action during the period 1921–6. Thus, although there were no examples of industrial action for explicitly political ends, there were three instances of actual or attempted industrial action which had important political implications. We are concerned here with the abortive threat of industrial action by the Triple Alliance leading to Black Friday in 1921, the successful threat of action by the General Council in 1925 resulting in Red Friday and, finally, the General Strike of 1926. Each of these, in contrast to the two earlier examples, was an attempt to secure collective industrial action to prevent a cut in living standards being forced on the miners: each was thus explicitly industrial in objective.

Nevertheless, all had important political implications. Let us take the General Strike as an example.[6] Firstly, a trade union victory would have inevitably forced a major shift in government policy involving drastic intervention in the coal industry. Secondly, a victory for the miners achieved on the basis of mass sympathetic action would have had important consequences for the economic struggles of other workers. Indeed, it could even have threatened the government's gold standard policy. Thirdly, the very involvement of the state on such a scale as took place in the General Strike meant that, if the strike had succeeded, a new political situation must have followed. Finally, a victory would have acted as confirmation of the effectiveness of industrial action for political ends and ensured its implicit legitimation.

Collective mass industrial action for industrial objectives, therefore, carried with it many of the same implications as industrial action for explicitly political ends. Thus, while there was an implicit shift amongst sections of trade union leaders towards a more Labourist conception of the role of the trade union movement over the period 1918–26, the majority still held a largely Labourist but also partially syndicalist conception of the relationship between the industrial and political spheres.

Earlier I mentioned that while mass unemployment left its mark on the combativity of industrial workers, this impact was not crucial until after 1926. Indeed, allied to the continuity in the ideology of the trade union movement over the period 1918–26, there was also an important continuity in its industrial politics. The most militant and politically conscious section of the working class throughout the period, as measured in terms of their attitude towards the Labour Party and the nationalisation of the mines, remained the miners. They were also by far and away its most powerful, cohesive and numerous element.[7] The engineers, especially in certain areas such as Sheffield and Clydeside, were also militant and well organised but, as a national force, they tended to be less cohesive and less political than the miners. The transport workers (including rail workers) were the third main organised force. Nevertheless, compared with the miners and engineers, they were relatively disparate and lacking in cohesion, being more difficult to organise and, at least on the railways, markedly affected by sectional and craft divisions.[8]

In this context, it should be noted that four out of the five examples of industrial action cited earlier, namely the 1919 nationalisation question, Black Friday, Red Friday and the General Strike, involved the miners. This was a crucial feature of the 1918–26 period. The miners were seen by many trade unionists as the key section of workers and it is this which explains their ability, from time to time, to unite around them in their struggles other sections of industrial workers. Their capacity to do this, however, varied according to the economic situation and the consciousness of different groups of workers.

I have argued that a majority in the trade union movement between 1918 and 1926 believed in the legitimacy of industrial action of an objectively or subjectively political character. What constituted this majority? It is always difficult to categorise trade union opinion into neat political compartments, partly because of the importance of industrial variations: nevertheless, we can broadly identify three main tendencies which comprised the majority amongst trade union leaderships on this question.

Firstly, there was the centre, such as Bevin (General Secretary of the TGWU) and Citrine (General Secretary of the TUC), who gave what might be described as rather pragmatic support to the notion of large-scale industrial action for industrial ends.[9] However, although the issue was never actually put, it is likely that by this time they would have opposed industrial action for explicitly political objectives.[10]

Secondly, there was what I shall loosely describe as the trade union left, embracing such figures as Swales (AEU), Hicks (Building Workers), Purcell (Furnishing Trades) and, in a somewhat different sense, Smith (Miners). They similarly accepted the validity of large-scale industrial action for industrial ends, but they also acknowledged the legitimacy of industrial action for explicitly political objectives. Indeed, there was a strong element of syndicalism in their rhetoric: Purcell, in his presidential address at the 1924 TUC Congress, for example, argued that the trade union movement should be transformed into "an instrument of solidarity capable of changing the existing structure of capitalism and bringing into being a Workers' State".[11] Nevertheless, at its core, their position did embody a division between the industrial and political spheres.

Finally, there was the revolutionary and syndicalist element. The most important centre of this group was the Minority Movement which was largely Leninist in inspiration but which also contained strong syndicalist influences.[12] Its most prominent associate was A. J. Cook, who was secretary of the Miners' Federation. Throughout this period, however, the influence of this tendency remained limited.

Of these three elements, the most powerful, by 1926, was undoubtedly the centre, although both the trade union left and the marxist left (through the Minority Movement) made important advances between 1923–6.[13] When united, however, given the strength of the various unions, these three accounted for a comfortable majority both in the TUC Congress and on the General Council. It is this alignment of forces, in fact, which explains the overwhelming vote in favour of a General Strike at the TUC Conference of Executives in April 1926. In this context, the only force opposed in principle to the use of collective industrial action and operating with a more or less traditional Labourist conception of the relationship between the political and industrial spheres, was the right comprising figures like Thomas[14] and Cramp of the NUR. And yet, such was the feeling at the

Conference of Trade Union Executives in April 1926, that they too felt forced, for tactical reasons, to acquiesce in the decision to call a General Strike.

Once the strike was underway, however, the eclectic character of the centre and trade-union left's conception of the role of the trade union movement was thrown into sharp relief for the first time. For while the General Council, on which these two tendencies were in the majority, insisted on the essentially industrial character of the strike, in reality the political meaning became daily more evident. As a consequence, the centre and trade-union left's conception of the relationship between the political and industrial spheres entered a state of acute crisis.[15] For while they both accepted the specificity of the political sphere and notably the sovereignty of Parliament and its processes, they also believed in the use of collective industrial action which, though having industrial objectives, was of such a scale that it inevitably had enormous political implications. How were these to be reconciled?

The answer, of course, was by calling off the strike. The centre and trade-union left thus joined forces with the right to be opposed only by the marxist left. It is this which explains why the General Council voted unanimously and unconditionally to end the strike.

THE RESULTS OF THE GENERAL STRIKE

The most obvious consequence of the General Strike was the defeat of the miners. They fought on alone for almost seven months but were finally forced to surrender in November 1926. The miners, however, had hitherto occupied a crucial position in the trade union movement. It was, therefore, inevitable that their defeat should leave its mark on the rest of the trade union movement. The nature of the strike, moreover, served to emphasise this effect. For it had taken the form of an open struggle between leading sections of the working class on the one hand and the state and the employers on the other. A defeat for the miners, thus, also meant a setback for the entire trade union movement.

The latter took a number of forms. In some trades, such as railways and printing, there was widespread victimisation after the strike.[16] Amongst large sections of workers, following an initial feeling of disbelief and bewilderment at the General Council's decision, a mood of defensiveness and demoralisation set in.[17] Trade union membership fell from $5\frac{1}{2}$ millions before the strike to well under 5 millions in 1927, while the accumulated funds of the unions dropped from £12½ millions at the beginning of 1926 to under £8½ millions by the end.

The government also moved to exploit the TUC's defeat. During the strike it had pursued a two-pronged strategy. Firstly, at an ideological level, it had sought to emphasise the political nature of the strike. Secondly, it had attempted to minimise its effectiveness through strike-breaking activities. Together, these had served to reinforce the General Council's doubts about both its legitimacy and its viability. At the same time, moreover, the government had avoided the use of excessive coercion or drastic legislation which might have pushed the TUC into a corner. Once the strike was over, however, the government began to consider the question of punitive legislation against the unions and, in 1927, finally introduced the Trade Disputes and Trade Unions Act.

The government's victory must also be seen on a more general plane. Between 1918 and 1920 the economic strategy of the ruling class had come under persistent threat from the militancy of the working class. After 1920, this pressure eased as the unions were forced on to the defensive. Nevertheless, even during this period, the unions still posed a threat to aspects of the ruling class's strategy. This was most obviously the case in relation to the miners. Throughout this period they pressed for the nationalisation of the mines and threatened, at a minimum, to force drastic state intervention in the industry. After the General Strike, however, neither the miners, nor any other section of workers, nor indeed the working class as a whole, succeeded in making any major impact on the general direction of government economic policy during the rest of the inter-war period.

I now want to consider the impact of the General Strike on the politics and ideology of the trade union movement. The General Strike had confronted the General Council with a fundamental contradiction in its ideology: in the event, it had resolved that contradiction by calling off the strike. Following this, it faced two main tasks; firstly, to defend its handling of the strike and, secondly, as we shall see later, to elaborate an alternative strategy for the trade union movement. This first task was largely accomplished at the Conference of Trade Union Executives called to discuss the General Council's report on the strike and held in January 1927. Here the General Council's report was endorsed by the fairly comfortable margin of 2·8 million votes to 1·1 million.[18]

It is not immediately apparent, however, why the General Council should have carried the day in this fashion. Its ideological paralysis in the General Strike had, after all, stood in marked contrast to the enthusiastic response to the strike call displayed by the several million workers involved.[19] The mood of enthusiasm and combativity, moreover, continued in the fight against victimisation afterwards: thus, on the day after the strike ended, there were actually 100,000 more people out on strike than there had been the previous day.[20]

How, then, do we explain the General Council's success in defending its role during the General Strike? I want to consider three factors here. Firstly, as we saw earlier, the General Strike had resulted in a realignment of political forces within the trade union movement. The centre and trade-union left joined forces with the right to end the strike, leaving only the marxist left and a handful of other leaders in opposition. As a consequence, the obvious source of opposition to the General Council's policy, namely the left, found itself split, with left leaders such as Hicks, Bromley and Swales, who had been sympathetic to the Minority Movement, now supporting the right. The left was thus divided at a national level and thrown into a state of some confusion lower down. And, without the support of the left leaders, the marxist left remained small and vulnerable. Between 1924 and 1926, the Minority Movement had made important progress amongst some sections of workers, notably the miners and engineers, but also the transport workers.[21] These advances, however, remained very limited. In particular, the Minority Movement gained only a relatively tenuous foothold in the official machinery of the trade union movement. We can cite two examples to illustrate this point. Firstly, only one key leader of a major union could be counted as a reasonably consistent supporter of the Minority Movement, namely A. J. Cook, the secretary of the Miners' Federation. Secondly, only nine Communist Party members were present as delegates at the 1927 TUC Congress.[22] This weakness of the Minority Movement made its relationship with the trade-union left leaders, which it had pursued with some success, even more important. The General Strike, however, undermined this relationship and left the Minority Movement in a position of vulnerable isolation.

The second factor concerns the miners. As we saw earlier, the miners occupied a crucial position in the trade union movement prior to the General Strike. They were the largest, most powerful, most cohesive and most political section of workers. During the years 1918–26, they had been at the centre of virtually every major national industrial struggle involving more than one section of workers. The termination of the General Strike, however, saw their sudden and dramatic isolation. They were left to fight on alone. This they did, but after seven months they were forced to surrender, impoverished, demoralised and divided.[23] From this point onwards the miners became a relatively insignificant force. Never again, indeed, during the inter-war period, were they to assume a central position in the trade union movement.

The third factor concerns the effect of mass unemployment. Already, in 1921, the appearance of mass unemployment had led to important changes in the perspectives and struggles of the trade union movement. It was not until after the General Strike, however, that the effects of unemployment were, along with other factors, to play a critical role in determining the politics and ideology of the trade union movement. In this context, the General Strike must be seen as the last straw rather than as a great climax. From 1921, beginning with Black Friday, the trade union movement had been forced onto the defensive and had suffered a series of defeats. The General Strike débâcle thus came after $5\frac{1}{2}$ years of mass unemployment and largely defensive struggle. It is, therefore, hardly suprising that the mood of disbelief and astonishment which first greeted the General Council's decision rapidly gave way to a growing feeling of disillusionment, bitterness and apathy.

THE TUC'S NEW DIRECTION

What was the General Council's response to the problems posed by the General Strike?

The first and most obvious reaction was the rejection of the General Strike weapon by the great majority of trade union leaders. The centre and, in large measure, the trade-union left now joined the right in regarding industrial action for political ends, whether explicit or implicit, as unacceptable. By and large, for tactical reasons, this rejection was not publicly articulated by figures like Citrine and Bevin: nevertheless, it became a basic assumption behind TUC policy. Ben Turner summed up their attitude succinctly when, writing about the General Strike, he declared: "and I never want to see another".[24]

The rejection of industrial action of a political character, however, implied the rejection not only of the General Strike weapon but also of large-scale industrial action involving more limited forms of solidarity. The General Council's attitude towards the miners' strike, in which it gave tacit support to the transport unions' leaders refusal to entertain the idea of an embargo on coal, was the first indication of this. In a situation of mass unemployment, however, unions like the Miner's Federation were largely dependent on forms of solidarity action. Thus, in practice, the General Council's attitude involved not only a rejection of industrial action of a political character but also a move away from the use of large-scale industrial action in general. As Citrine wrote in 1929: "A Trade Union body cannot bring out two million men with the same light heart as it might bring out fifty men."[25]

This scepticism about the use of large-scale industrial action, however, in practice also meant a generally reduced emphasis on the efficacy of militancy and strikes in general: for, in a situation of mass unemployment, the feasibility of more localised strike action inevitably remained rather limited. Indeed, while Citrine, for example, defended the right to strike, he also emphasised that it "should only be used as a last resort".[26] And, elsewhere, he argued: "We shall not get rid of strikes and lockouts completely, but I believe that they will be fewer, that reason will play a greater part, and that the community itself will develop a keener interest and a greater sense of social justice."[27]

If not strikes then what? The rejection of militancy inevitably meant a complete reappraisal of the strategy of the trade union movement. Its starting-point was a recognition of the seriousness of the economic crisis. Thus, the Mond–Turner Interim Joint Report, which was adopted by the General Council in 1928, stated: "It is true that during the last century there were occasionally long periods of poor trade but it was something quite outside the experience of pre-war years to have approximately one-tenth to one-eighth of the insured industrial population out-of-work for eight years."[28] This recognition of the gravity of the economic crisis, however, was no longer accompanied by a belief in the imminent collapse of capitalism. Indeed, in response to Brownlie, one of the AEU leaders, who had argued, "I am one of those who recognise that the present social and industrial system is rapidly coming to an end",[29] Bevin replied at the 1929 TUC Congress: "I do not see this demise of the capitalist system coming so quickly as my friend Brownlie does."[30] Similarly, Citrine wrote in 1928: "The system which we call capitalism has changed in its form in the last 100 years tremendously and has adapted itself with remarkable flexibility to changing conditions. That it will change even more in the next few generations cannot be doubted."[31]

On this basis, the General Council sought to emphasise that in all probability a solution to the crisis would be found within the existing system. At the 1928 TUC Congress, for example, Citrine argued that: "The position of the workers in the post-war period, the effect of that period, the long continued depression, particularly in the basic industries, have created something which in the view of eminent economists may be compared with the industrial revolution in the last part of the 18th century."[32] And it is clear that Bevin's experiences in the United States during an official visit at the end of 1926 helped him to reach the same conclusion.[33]

What did this mean for the trade union movement? Citrine argued: "the unions should actively participate in a concerted effort to raise industry to its highest efficiency by developing the most scientific methods of production, eliminating waste and harmful restrictions, removing causes of friction and unavoidable conflict . . .".[34] The General Council's Report to the 1928 TUC Congress suggested that the trade union movement should "say boldly that not only is it concerned with the prosperity of industry, but that it is going to have a voice as to the way industry is carried on, so that it can influence the new developments that are taking place. The ultimate policy of the movement can find more use for an efficient industry than a derelict one, and the unions can use their power to promote and guide the scientific re-organisation of industry as well as to obtain material advantages from that reorganisation."[35] In other words, the trade union movement should co-operate in the rationalisation of private industry. And, it was argued, this policy would help the movement in two ways: firstly, it would boost living standards and, secondly, it would enhance the status of the unions.

The General Council, however, saw industrial recovery not only as a problem for employers and the unions but also as a matter requiring government encouragement. In this context, the General Council increasingly came round to the view that government policy was geared to the needs of finance rather than industry and, as such, acted as an impediment on the development of industry. At the 1929 TUC Congress, for example, in his presidential address, Tillett argued, with regard to Bank Rate changes: "That such a step should be taken without consultation with those responsible for the maintenance of industry is, to my mind, an outrage. . . . In my opinion industry should control finance, and not finance industry."[36] The issue around which this concern had crystallised was the return to the gold standard in 1925. And here Keynes, whom Citrine "regarded as Britain's foremost economist",[37] was to exercise a considerable influence both on himself and Bevin. Citrine, for example, wrote that Kenes' pamphlet, *The Economic Consequences of Mr Churchill*, "made a deep impression on me, and it was simply uncanny to see how Keynes' prophecies worked out".[38] Bevin expressed their position very clearly at the 1931 TUC Congress: "You return to the gold standard in 1925 and you gave the miner and mine-owner the job of adjusting industry. They do not know what has hit them . . . I think that is where our trouble starts."[39]

It was not, however, until 1929 that the need to develop an alternative economic policy really began to acquire central importance in the TUC's thinking: prior to this it remained somewhat overshadowed by the emphasis on rationalisation.

A COMPARISON BETWEEN THE NEW DIRECTION AND THE 1918–26 IDEOLOGY

The General Strike thus provoked a complete transformation in the strategy and outlook of the General Council and, indeed, of most trade union leaders. In this context, it is worth comparing the new post-1926 direction with the 1918–26 approach considered earlier. There are four main differences.

The first concerns the economic crisis and the future of capitalism. Both, of course, recognised the seriousness of the crisis. But, while the new direction saw it as solvable within the existing system, the pre-1926 position tended to see it as symptomatic of capitalism's decline and even as capitalism's last crisis. These different analyses of the crisis led to different conceptions of union strategy. The pre-1926 approach tended to lay stress on the inevitability of conflict and therefore the importance of both defensive and, where possible, offensive militancy. The new direction, on the other hand, while recognising the need to protect living standards, preferred to place its stress on the need for the unions to collaborate in achieving economic recovery. Bevin, for example, wrote: "Our movement has its two sides—its fighting side and its constructive sides."[40] While Citrine argued: "Trade Unionism has reached the end of a defensive stage in its evolution."[41]

The second major difference concerns the conception of class. The pre-1926 position was infected by a strong belief in the idea that wage-labour as a whole shared common interests and that these were in direct contradiction with those of capital. This belief, indeed, had played an important role in the formation of the General Council (in 1920–1), the Triple Alliance (in 1915) and the Industrial Alliance (in 1925), and in the various examples of mass industrial action cited earlier. It remains, of course, that the conception of class involved was essentially economic rather than politico-ideological, and was heavily sectionalised. These, however, are general characteristics of trade-union consciousness. Rather, the important point to stress here is the extent to which the pre-1926 position was infused with the concept of wage-labour as a class with common and distinct economic interests.

The new direction also recognised that wage-labour enjoyed certain common economic interests. But this was now accompanied by the notion that wage-labour and employers had common interests with respect to rationalisation and government economic policy. And the effect of this notion was to narrow the extent to which wage-labour was seen as having distinct economic interests and thereby to weaken the concept of wage-labour as an economic class.

The new direction also adopted the idea of a changing industrial structure consequent upon the divorce of control and ownership: and the effect of this process was seen as the growing irrelevence of owners coupled with the rise of "employers" or "managers" who, as paid labour, were regarded as having much in common with wage-labour. As Bevin argued at the 1927 TUC Congress: "We are willing to meet our employers across the table and face them with our problems, but I agree with many of our leading industrialists, not on the capitalist side but on the management side of industry, which is somewhat distinct from the owning side, the management side has a good deal in common with ourselves. They are exploited by capital just as we are exploited . . .".[42] This process, of course, while well-advanced, was seen as still lying largely in the future. Nevertheless, implicit in this approach was the idea that socio-industrial developments were gradually changing industry from a situation where it was dominated by the struggle between labour and capital to a position where it was characterised by the co-operation of workers and management.

Thus, while the new direction maintained the notion of wage-labour as an economic class with common and distinct interests, this concept was in practice weakened, firstly by the idea of an "industrial interest" and secondly, by the suggestion that a new kind of relationship was emerging in industry between managers and workers as a consequence of the growing irrelevance of ownership.

The third main difference concerns perspectives. The pre-1926 position was committed to the replacement of capitalism by socialism with the latter being defined essentially in terms of the public ownership of the means of production, distribution and exchange. The new direction still held to this aim but the time-perspective was now lengthened and its content importantly changed.

The starting-point was the conception of a changing industrial structure as mentioned above. It was argued that planning was replacing competition—through concentration and centralisation—and control replacing ownership—through the divorce of control and ownership. But ownership and competition were regarded by many trade union leaders as essential features of capitalism and planning and disappearance of competition as characteristic of socialism. In other words, it was suggested that, by a process of natural technical evolution, capitalism was gradually transforming itself into socialism or some intermediate system. As Citrine tentatively suggested in a speech in 1927: "There are people who are forming the opinion that the last word in development between private ownership and national ownership has not been said, that there may lie in between the two systems the possibilities of modifications inside the capitalist structure itself which will make a higher standard of life possible."[43] A new perspective thus emerged which emphasised the evolutionary nature of change, blurred the nature of the socialist objective and tended to identify the latter with the characteristics of monopoly and especially state monopoly capitalism.

The fourth major difference concerns the relationship between the political and industrial spheres. As I suggested earlier, in holding to the legitimacy of industrial action of a political character, the pre-1926 position had maintained a part-syndicalist, part-Labourist conception of the relationship between the political and industrial spheres. In rejecting the use of industrial action of a political character, however, the new direction adopted a Labourist conception of this relationship where the two spheres were seen as strictly separate.

THE MOND–TURNER TALKS

After the General Strike, a number of "feelers" were put out by individual trade union leaders and employers about the possibility of national talks between the employers' organisations and the TUC. In the event, nothing came of them.[44] However, in November 1928, Mond, the chairman of ICI, together with twenty-one other employers, sent a letter to the TUC General Council suggesting: "the prosperity of industry can, in our view, be fully attained only by full and frank recognition of the facts as they exist and an equally full and frank determination to increase the competitive power of British industries in the world's markets, coupled with free discussion of the essentials upon which that can be based. That can be achieved most usefully by direct negotiation with the twin objects of restoration of industrial prosperity and the corresponding improvement in the standard of living of the population."[45] The General Council accepted the invitation for joint discussions and so began the Mond–Turner talks.[46]

In all, three conferences were held between January 1928 and March 1929. The decisions reached were contained in three reports and covered the following areas: trade union recognition, victimisation, industrial relations machinery, rationalisation, unemployment and the gold standard.[47]

What did the respective parties hope to achieve by the talks? There can be little doubt that the two most important topics for the General Council were trade union recognition and victimisation. Why? Firstly it was crucial to prevent victimisation and secure trade union recognition at a time when the trade union movement was under attack from many quarters. And, secondly, without including these topics the talks could hardly have proceeded very far.

They were, however, what might be described as the TUC's minimum expectations in relation to the talks. More optimistically, it anticipated progress in two main areas: the status of unions and industrial recovery. As far as the status of unions was concerned, the General Council hoped that a closer relationship between the trade unions and employers would, on the one hand, give the unions some say in the reorganisation and management of industry and, on the other hand, lead to the formation of, in effect, an industrial bloc or pressure group which would influence the determination of government economic policy. As for industrial recovery, the shift away from militancy and what was regarded as a previous defensive posture was accompanied by a new emphasis on the seriousness of the economic crisis and the culpability of government policy for that situation. The Mond–Turner talks, in presenting the possibility of wholesale industrial reorganisation through rationalisation, together with an economic policy geared to the needs of "industry" (i.e. employers and workers), thus also offered, in the eyes of the General Council, the prospect of a solution to the economic crisis.

We now come to the employers' side. Without question, the most important consideration for the employers was rationalisation. However, they regarded the co-operation of labour as critical to the success of rationalisation: without it, such measures were seen as being very much more difficult, perhaps even impossible, to achieve. The Mondist conception of the talks was thus, in essence, the rationalisation of industry through the co-operation of labour. Indeed it is in this light that we should understand the Mond employers' attitude towards such questions as recognition and victimisation. That is, labour's co-operation in rationalisation schemes was regarded as conditional upon the recognition of the unions by employers; similarly, the assurances on victimisation and the provisions with regard to the prevention of disputes were clearly efforts to generate goodwill and the right atmosphere respectively.

In July 1928, the Interim Joint Report of the Mond–Turner Conference was sent to the two main national employers' organisations, the National Confederation of Employers' Organisations (NCEO) and the Federation of British Industries (FBI), for their comments. The Report embraced the following propositions; trade union recognition, opposition to victimisation, the establishment of joint conciliation boards (for dealing with industrial disputes) and the formation of a National Industrial Council (to consist of equal numbers of employers and trade union representatives nominated by the NCEO, FBI and TUC respectively, and to engage in "general consultation on the widest questions concerning industry and industrial progress").[48] In the event, however, both the FBI and the NCEO decided, by overwhelming majorities, to oppose the recommendations contained in the report.[49] Moreover, they both remained deeply suspicious of the new turn in TUC policy. Rather than recognising it as a significant shift to the right, indeed, they tended to see it as merely a continuation of previous policies or even as a subtle new tactic of conquest by stealth.

How do we explain these differing attitudes of the NCEO and the FBI on the one hand and the Mond employers on the other? There are several factors which must be taken into consideration, but by far the most important concerns the nature of the capital which each represented. Of the 33 Mond employers,[50] 9 came from large-scale international "science-based" industries like chemicals, artificial silk, rubber and oil (type one); 15 came from a range of newer industries such as electrical engineering, cars and gas, which were expanding and largely, though not exclusively, based on the domestic market (type two); and 13 came from the older export-orientated trades like coal, textiles and iron and steel (type three).[51] This meant that, given the structure of British capital at the time and, in particular, the relative importance of the staple industries like coal and textiles, the type one and two employers were in effect over-represented in the Mond group. Moreover, it is clear that the type one employers wielded the main influence within the group: for, of the seven full members of the Mond employers' sub-committee, four were directors of ICI.[52]

The composition of the FBI and the NCEO was very different. For, in representing the employers of approximately seven million workers in each case,[53] they inevitably embraced a much broader cross-section of industrial capital than did the Mond group. And, to the extent that "small" and "medium" rather than "large" and "old" rather than "new" capital were predominant in British industry, so these organisations tended to give rather greater weight to these elements than did the Mond group. Indeed, by far and away the most influential voices within the FBI and NCEO were those of the basic industries. Thus, for example, 10 out of the 16 members of the NCEO General Purposes Committee came from these trades.

The influence of employers from the staple industries goes a long way towards explaining the hostility of the NCEO, FBI and most of their constituent organisations to the Mond–Turner proposals and, indeed, trade unionism more generally. For firms in these trades were generally faced with low profits and a labour-intensive production process. As a consequence, employers in these trades tended to see reductions in labour costs as the obvious solution to their difficulties. In contrast, firms in the newer industries tended to be larger, more profitable and more capital-intensive. Consequently, employers from these industries were in a better position to take a more strategic view of their industry and, indeed, the economy.

In this light, the Mond approach can reasonably be described as the response of sections of big industrial capital but, even more, the response of what were relatively representative sections of very big industrial capital to the problems of the British economy. Thus, the Mond–Turner talks can be seen as a deal or even an alliance between sections of big industrial capital on the one hand and the TUC General Council on the other.

In fact, the formal alliance remained short-lived. The future of Mond–Turner depended on a positive response to the Interim Joint Report from the employers' organisations which, in the event, did not materialise. Indeed, the only concrete result proved to be limited talks on specific subjects between the NCEO and TUC on the one hand and the FBI and TUC on the other.[54]

In a sense, therefore, judged by their own criteria, the Mond–Turner talks failed. However, coming in the period after the General Strike when the determination of new policies and relationships was still in the melting-pot, it is evident that they had an important impact on the evolution of the attitudes of the TUC, the employers and also the Conservative Government. In particular, the talks performed a very significant role in moulding the TUC's new policy-orientation. Indeed, while the formal alliance between big industrial capital and the TUC ended with the conclusion of the Mond–Turner talks in 1929, the example and interests of that capital were to remain a central feature of the economic policy which the TUC began to elaborate between 1929 and 1935.

THE POLITICS OF THE TRADE UNION MOVEMENT

Having emerged successfully from the National Conference of Trade Union Executives on the General Strike (or National Strike, as it was called) in January 1927, the General Council proceeded to elaborate its new direction. Between 1927 and 1929, this meant primarily the Mond–Turner talks. Although the latter marked a sharp rightward shift by the General Council, they never came under serious threat from within the trade union movement. Thus, the initial vote to embark on the talks was carried by 24 votes to 3[55] in the General Council and at no subsequent stage was the margin ever closer than 15–6.[56] A similar situation prevailed at Congress with the closest vote being 2,921,000 for and 768,000 against in 1928.[57] This pattern, moreover, continued after the end of the talks in 1929, with the right steadily consolidating its position and the left becoming increasingly isolated. Indeed, it is difficult to find a major issue on which the General Council was defeated or even threatened in the entire period 1926–35.

How do we explain the declining influence of the left over this period?

Between 1924 and 1926, the left had begun to emerge as a significant and identifiable force within the trade union movement. At a political level, it came to embrace various left leaders together with the marxist left around the Minority Movement, while industrially its main areas of support were to be found amongst sections of miners and engineers on the one hand and various smaller unions such as the Furnishing Trades on the other.

Following the General Strike, the left found itself confronted with two major problems. Firstly, with the defeat of the miners, the centre of gravity within the trade union movement rapidly shifted away from the Miners' Federation and, to a lesser extent, the AEU and towards the TGWU and NUGMW,[58] in which the left enjoyed relatively little support. At the same time, with the demoralisation and divisions produced by unemployment and defeat, both the Miners' Federation and the AEU tended to move rightwards.[59]

Secondly, the left was subject to growing fragmentation. I want to consider three aspects of this problem: the right shift by the trade-union left leaders after the General Strike, the General Council's offensive against communists and the policy of the Communist Party itself.

The General Strike exposed a fundamental contradiction in the position of both the centre and trade-union left leaders. On the one hand they accepted the legitimacy of industrial action of a political character and yet on the other hand they both ultimately held a highly parliamentarian concept of the nature of politics. This contradiction was posed in dramatic fashion by the General Strike. The centre and trade-union left's response was to adopt a traditional Labourist conception of the relationship between the industrial and political spheres and therefore also between the unions and the Labour Party.

We need, however, to consider the nature of the trade-union left's position more closely. In some respects, their ideological crisis was of an even more acute nature than that of the centre: for these leaders had hitherto supported not only mass industrial action for industrial ends but also industrial action for explicitly political objectives. In other words, their position was an eclectic mixture of both parliamentarianism and syndicalism. Their conception of capitalist society and class struggle was thus essentially economistic. The left leaders must therefore be seen as an industrial or trade-union left rather than as a political left. Indeed, they enjoyed relatively little contact with the Labour left (such as the ILP) and had no political programme. Consequently, when presented with the dichotomy between their industrial and political views during the strike, they ultimately accepted the political hegemony of the right. Similarly, after the strike, when unemployment and defeats had undermined the effectiveness of trade union action, they were unable, in the absence of any serious analysis of the nature of the crisis, to present a coherent political alternative to that of the right.

We now come to the General Council's attack on the Communist Party. The only political tendency which consistently opposed the new direction after the General Strike was the Minority Movement. Moreover, in the new situation created by the failure of the strike, the gulf between right and left became very much wider than it had been previously. The General Council's response to this was a major offensive against the Communist Party. The first move came in late 1927 when Citrine, acting on his own initiative, wrote a series of articles in the TUC's *Labour Magazine* attacking the Minority Movement, the Communist Party and associated organisations.[60] These were followed, in 1929, by a long General Council report entitled "Inquiry into Disruption" which sought to demonstrate the essentially "undemocratic" and "disruptive" nature of communist activity in the unions and to show that its inspiration came ultimately from Moscow.[61] These political and ideological attacks eventually culminated in various forms of administrative action with, for example, the TUC Congress in 1935, on the advice of the General Council, recommending that affiliated trades councils ban delegates who were communists or who had any associations with communists.[62] The effect of these attacks was undoubtedly to weaken the influence of the Communist Party within the trade union movement and to make unity between communists and other left elements more difficult.

This brings us to the question of the Communist Party. Prior to, during and immediately following the strike, the Communist Party had pursued a policy of co-operation with other left forces, primarily through the Minority Movement. On the basis of this approach, the party had played a significant role, despite its very limited size, in influencing the course of events between 1924 and 1926.[63] From 1928, however, the party began to move leftwards. This involved, firstly, an emphasis on the inadequacy and futility of the trade union left leaders, stemming from their not opposing the decision to call off the General Strike, and, secondly, a new assessment of the mood of the working class. It was argued that millions had learned the lessons of the betrayal, seen through the General Council, and had consequently moved sharply to the left. The reality was different. The shift in approach was completed at the 11th Congress in 1929 when, following decisions of the 6th Comintern Congress, the party endorsed the "class against class" position and adopted a sectarian policy towards the Labour Party and the Labour left.[64] The effect, however, given the incorrect assessment of the mood of the working class, was further to isolate the party, reduce its size and fragment the left. Indeed, only in the 'thirties did the party again begin to gain ground.

SOCIO-ECONOMIC FACTORS IN THE INTER-WAR PERIOD

So far I have discussed the shift to the right in the trade union movement after 1926 largely in terms of the politics and ideology of the various tendencies within the movement. We must also, however, consider the effect of a number of socio-economic factors which were operating during this period.

Firstly, mass unemployment. I earlier characterised the period 1906–20 as the phase in which the core of the working class, above all the miners and engineers, began to acquire a corporate consciousness and 1921–6 as the period in which in a sense the expression and direction of that consciousness was determined. The crucial dividing-line between these two phases was the economic downturn in late 1920 and the appearance of what was to be a permanent feature of the inter-war period, namely mass unemployment. Unemployment affected all sections of the working class, but, as it was concentrated in the staple industries, its most serious effects were reserved for such sections as the miners, engineers, textile workers and shipbuilders. In other words, the workers most seriously affected were what might be described as the more advanced sections of the working class. Indeed, as the trade union movement was forced on to the defensive after 1920, the two most serious defeats sustained by the trade union movement in 1921–2 were those of the miners on Black Friday and the engineers in their lockout.

The effect of unemployment on the consciousness of workers was threefold: it forced them on to the defensive, it weakened sectional solidarity and it undermined multi-sectional consciousness. Unemployment did not, however, lead to an immediate and decisive shift in the politics and ideology of the trade union movement. Rather, the decisive break, as we have seen, came with the General Strike in 1926. After this, on the one hand the sectional solidarity of groups like the miners and engineers, as well as less militant and well-organised groups, was considerably weakened while, on the other hand, the corporate consciousness of the working class, as expressed in such collective industrial action as that threatened on Red Friday in 1925 and that which happened in the General Strike, was undermined. In other words, the working class, as a group, was weakened, made less cohesive and more fragmented. This, indeed, was reflected in the strike figures for this period as indicated in Table 1 opposite.

The second problem concerns the changing industrial structure of the British economy and the changing composition of the working class. Amongst economic historians there has been much debate on the relative importance of the rise of the "new" inustries such as vehicle manufacturing, chemicals, electrical engineering, rayon, non-ferrous metals, and paper, printing and publishing during the inter-war period.[65]

TABLE 1 STRIKE FIGURES[66]

	No. of stoppages beginning in year	*Aggregate duration in working days of stoppages in progress in year*
1924	710	8,420,000
1925	603	7,950,000
1926	323	162,230,000
1927	308	1,170,000
1928	302	1,390,000
1929	431	8,290,000
1930	422	4,400,000
1931	420	6,980,000
1932	389	6,490,000
1933	357	1,070,000
1934	471	960,000
1935	553	1,960,000

That some shift took place is fairly certain, though there is considerable disagreement on how much. What is clear, however, is that this was accompanied by a major change in employment patterns.

TABLE 2 ANNUAL RATE OF GROWTH OF EMPLOYMENT IN SELECTED INDUSTRIES, 1920–38[67]

Industry	*Rate*
Vehicles	3·0
Electricity, gas, water	2·5
Electrical engineering	3·6
Paper and printing	1·3
Non-ferrous metal manufacture	1·2
Mechanical engineering	−2·0
Iron and steel	−2·4
Textiles	−1·4
Mining and quarrying	−2·3
Shipbuilding	−4·6

What were the implications of this occupational shift?

Firstly, it meant the declining relative (and sometimes absolute) quantitative importance within the working class of those sections employed in the older industries and especially the miners, but also the textile workers. The sections involved, moreover, were also in many cases the best-organised and most militant groups within the working class, part of its historically-evolved core. Secondly, it meant the increasing relative importance of newer sections like the car workers, printers, chemical workers, distribution workers and also white-collar strata.

What can we say about these latter groups? Firstly, they were, by and large, employed in industries which were relatively prosperous compared with the staple industries and which were therefore often in a position to pay somewhat higher wages. Secondly, as these industries were relatively new, these sections of workers did not in most cases possess the same experience or tradition of organisation and solidarity as groups like the miners and sections of engineers. It was not until 1929, for example, that Austin's at Longbridge was unionised.[68] These industries, moreover, tended to be concentrated in newer industrial areas like the south-east and the Midlands, unlike the older industries. Consequently, the communities from which these workers were drawn were less cohesive and more fragmented. Indeed, the newer industrial areas were to nurture a rather different set of political, social and economic experiences to those of the older areas during the thirties. Thus, while a strong socialist tradition lived on amongst the miners and unemployed in areas like South Wales and Fife, cities like Coventry and Oxford presented a rather different picture.[69]

Throughout the inter-war period, thus, an important structural shift was taking place in the composition of the industrial working class which tended to reduce the significance of its traditional core and increase the importance of various newer sections which were less organised, less militant and less cohesive. This had important political consequences for the working-class movement as a whole. To take one example: in the trade union movement, the general unions, namely the TGWU (which merged with the Workers' Union in 1929) and the NUGMW, became increasingly important in the politics of the TUC over the inter-war period and, after the General Strike, tended to overshadow the industrial-based unions, such as the AEU, Miners' Federation and NUR, which had been influential prior to 1926. Moreover, while the influence of the left was considerable in both the Miners' Federation and the AEU, even after the General Strike, the two general unions were dominated by the right. It remains to add that this whole question of a changing industrial structure is closely related to Gramsci's discussion of "Americanism and Fordism".[70]

The third question I want to discuss concerns the movement of real wages. Despite the depression and mass unemployment, real wages increased during most years in the inter-war period and particularly during the world economic crisis of 1929–33.

TABLE 3 WAGE MOVEMENTS[71]

	Money wages	*Cost of living*	*Real wage*	*Net terms of trade*
1924	194	175	111	116
1925	196	175	112	120
1926	195	172	113	117
1927	196	167	117	118
1928	194	166	117	121
1929	193	164	118	120
1930	191	157	122	111
1931	189	147	129	100
1932	185	143	129	100
1933	183	140	131	97
1934	183	141	130	100
1935	185	143	130	101

The primary cause, as can be seen from the above table, was a fall in prices. Thus, while money wages declined, the cost of living fell even more rapidly. The main reason for the fall in prices was a favourable movement in the terms of trade consequent upon the collapse of primary product prices during the world economic crisis. This was a feature common to most advanced capitalist countries, but Britain benefited more than most because of her Empire. Thus, in effect, the fall in money wages was cushioned by the collapse in primary product prices and this obviously had important implications for the mood of the working class.

Mass unemployment, structural change and the rise in real wages do not in themselves explain the politics and ideology of the working-class movement during the inter-war period. Nevertheless, they provide an essential part of the explanation. For they help to reveal what might be described as the objective basis of the shift to the right in the trade union movement after 1926.

POSTSCRIPT

In analysing the General Strike and the militancy of the early twenties, it is obviously tempting to draw various parallels with the present period of industrial unrest. Such comparisons, of course, must be treated with extreme caution but, in concluding this essay, it might be useful to indicate four important differences between the militancy of the twenties and that of the late sixties and early seventies.

Firstly, the working-class movement was forced on to the defensive from 1920 by the appearance of mass unemployment which was to persist throughout the inter-war period. In contrast, the sixties and early seventies (at least until early 1975) have been characterised by a situation of relative full employment. What is more, the nature of the unemployment is somewhat different. Apart from the period 1929–33, much of that in the inter-war period was of a structural character. By comparison, most of the present unemployment is of a cyclical nature.

Secondly, while important structural changes are taking place in the economy, these are of a rather different nature to those of the inter-war period. In particular, they are not such as to undermine the position of the more advanced sections of the working class as happened in the inter-war period.

Thirdly, despite the existence of mass unemployment for most of the inter-war years, real wages continued to rise over virtually the whole period. The chief cause of this increase, as we saw earlier, was the favourable movement in the terms of trade consequent upon the fall in primary product prices. In other words, Britain's imperialist position acted so as to ameliorate the effects of the depression. The picture, of course, is very different today. Firstly, Britain has lost most of her empire and secondly, the primary producing countries have, by and large, succeeded in preventing any major unfavourable movement in the terms of trade. As a consequence, the British ruling class's room to manœuvre has been considerably reduced.

Finally, we come to the politics of the situation. On the surface, it might appear that relatively little has changed. The working class retains an essentially corporatist outlook while both the Labour Party and the TUC are still under right-wing leadership. At the same time, the Communist Party remains relatively small. Nevertheless, important changes have indeed taken place. Here I will briefly mention two.

Firstly, the left is now more powerful and coherent. Thus, within both the Labour Party and the trade union movement, for example, the left enjoys a much greater influence than it did in the mid-twenties, while the Communist Party is significantly larger and more influential. At the same time, there is a much closer relationship between the trade union left and the Labour left. The left, moreover, has begun to emerge as a credible political alternative to the right, based on the concept of a

Labour Government committed to left policies which begins to alter the balance of class forces in favour of the working-class and progressive sections. As a consequence, the trade union left (and the trade union movement in general) now has a far more political perspective than it did in 1926: the General Strike, indeed, can only be understood in terms of the influence of syndicalist ideas within the trade union movement.

Secondly, although the working class remains essentially reformist in outlook, important changes have nevertheless taken place in its consciousness. In particular, it no longer accepts the hegemony of bourgeois ideology in such a complete form. The development of sit-ins and occupations, for example, has involved an assertion of a new concept of property and the rights of labour. Perhaps the best example of this changed mood, however, concerns the miners' strike in 1974. Here, in important respects, was a close parallel with 1926: the same section of workers, the development of solidarity action and the attempt by the Conservative Government to turn an industrial dispute into a wider political question. In contrast to 1926, however, the miners, this time backed by the trade union movement, refused to be diverted. In the process the Conservative Government fell, a minority Labour Government was elected and the miners' demands were met.

NOTES

1. A. Gramsci, *Selections from the Prison Notebooks* (London, 1971), p. 181.
2. H. Pelling, *A History of British Trade Unionism* (London, 1963), p. 262.
3. V. L. Allen, *The Sociology of Industrial Relations* (London, 1971), ch. 13.
4. Though in neither case was anything actually done; E. Eldon Barry, *Nationalisation in British Politics* (London, 1965), pp. 228, 239–40.
5. A. Bullock, *The Life and Times of Ernest Bevin*, Vol. 1 (London, 1960), ch. 9 and pp. 236–43.
6. See also R. Miliband, *Parliamentary Socialism* (London, 1973), pp. 126, 144–5.
7. For background, P. Renshaw, *The General Strike* (London, 1975), chs. 1–2.
8. Ibid., p. 72.
9. Bullock, op. cit., pp. 270–6 and chs. 11, 12.
10. Ibid., p. 271; Citrine, *Men and Work* (London, 1964), pp. 143–53.
11. TUC Annual Congress Report, 1924, p. 68.

12. R. Martin, *Communism and the British Trade Unions, 1924–1933* (London, 1969), pp. 37–9; H. Pollitt, "Statement of Aims", quoted by A. Hutt, *British Trade Unionism; A Short History* (London, 1962), p. 99.
13. Martin, op. cit., pp. 59–76.
14. Citrine, op. cit., p. 157; Renshaw, op. cit., pp. 220–1.
15. Citrine, op. cit.: "The fact is that the theory of the General Strike had never been thought out" (p. 216) and: "However illogical it may seem for me to say so, it was never aimed against the State as a challenge to the Constitution" (p. 217). Bullock, op. cit., p. 346.
16. For example, C. Farman, *The General Strike* (London, 1974), pp. 295, 297–300.
17. Ibid., pp. 291–2; Bullock, op. cit., pp. 353, 373, 376; J. B. Jeffreys, *The Story of the Engineers, 1800–1945* (London, 1946), p. 236.
18. "National Strike: Special Conference", p. 64, in TUC, *The Mining Crisis*. The miners were responsible for 800,000 of the 1·1 million votes against.
19. For example, Farman, op. cit., pp. 155, 335; Citrine, op. cit., p. 205; Renshaw, op. cit., p. 175.
20. Farman, op. cit., p. 294.
21. For example, Martin, op. cit., pp. 57–76.
22. The Communist International, "Between the 5th and 6th World Congresses, 1924–8", July 1928, p. 129.
23. R. Page Arnot, *The Miners: Years of Struggle* (London, 1953), pp. 457–63.
24. Ben Turner, *About Myself* (Bristol, 1930), p. 290.
25. Citrine, *The Future of Trade Unionism*, TUC Summer School Pamphlet II (1929), p. 7.
26. Citrine, *Industrial Review*, April 1928, p. 3.
27. Citrine, "The Future of Trade Unionism", in *The Listener*, 11/7/34, p. 60.
28. TUC Annual Congress Report, 1929, p. 189; E. J. Hobsbawm, *Labouring Men* (London, 1968), p. 320.
29. TUC Annual Congress Report, 1929, p. 381.
30. Ibid., p. 385.
31. Citrine, "Tendencies in Industry Today" in *The Labour Magazine*, December 1928, p. 347.
32. TUC Annual Congress Report, 1928, p. 409.
33. Bullock, op. cit., pp. 357–63.
34. Citrine, *Manchester Guardian Industrial Relations Supplement*, 30/11/27, p. 8.
35. TUC Annual Congress Report, 1928, p. 209.
36. TUC Annual Congress Report, 1929, p. 64.
37. Citrine, *Men and Work*, p. 240.
38. Ibid., p. 137.
39. Quoted by S. Pollard in "Trade Union Reactions to the Economic Crisis", in *Journal of Contemporary History*, Vol. 4, No. 4, 1969, p. 107.

40. Bevin, *Manchester Guardian Industrial Relations Supplement*, 30/11/27, p. 11.
41. Citrine, *Manchester Guardian Industrial Relations Supplement*, 30/11/27, p. 8.
42. TUC Annual Congress Report, 1927, pp. 315–16.
43. Citrine, "Industrial Relations and the Social System", in *Towards Industrial Peace*, Report of Proceedings of a Conference organised by the League of Nations, 1927, p. 267. Also, W. Milne-Bailey, *Trade Unions and the State* (London, 1934), pp. 353–4.
44. For example, G. W. McDonald and H. F. Gospel, "The Mond–Turner Talks, 1927–33: A Study in Industrial Co-operation", in *The Historical Journal*, XVI, 4, 1973, pp. 810–16.
45. TUC Annual Congress Report, 1928, p. 220.
46. Further details of the Mond–Turner talks can be found in McDonald and Gospel, op. cit., and R. Charles, *The Development of Industrial Relations in Britain, 1911–1939* (London, 1973), pp. 261–94.
47. TUC Annual Congress Reports, 1928, pp. 209–30, and 1929, pp. 186–209.
48. TUC Annual Congress Report, 1928, p. 227.
49. NCEO GPC Sub-Committee's Report to GPC, pp. 3–4 (Ref. NC 2578) in NCEO File "Industrial Peace" C 66 Pt. 7.
50. Four employers have been "double-counted" because their interests lay more or less equally in two different spheres. Hence the total comes to 37 rather than 33.
51. This analysis is based on information derived from: *Stock Exchange Year Book* (1928 and 1929) (London); *Who's Who* (1928, 1929 and 1930) (London); miscellaneous papers in TUC; 3 memoranda on "Industrial Influence of Employers-Members" in NCEO File "Industrial Peace" C. 66 Pt. 1.
52. TUC Annual Congress Report, 1928, p. 221
53. NCEO Annual Report for Administrative Year 1927–8 (Ref. NC 2412), p. 1.
54. Charles, op. cit., pp. 290–4.
55. GC 7 (1927–8), 20/12/27, pp. 35–6.
56. GC 11 (1927–8), 24/1/28, pp. 51–2.
57. TUC Annual Congress Report, 1928, p. 451.
58. Hobsbawm, op. cit., pp. 327–8.
59. For details of Miners' Federation and AEU in this period, see Page Arnot, op. cit. and Jefferys, op. cit., respectively.
60. Citrine, "Democracy or Disruption", in *The Labour Magazine*, December 1927–June 1928. These were reproduced as a TUC pamphlet with the same title. Also, Citrine, *Men and Work*, p. 255.
61. TUC Annual Congress Report, 1929, pp. 168–78.
62. TUC Annual Congress Report, 1935, pp. 110–12, 260–330.

63. See J. Klugmann, *History of the Communist Party of Great Britain*, Vols. 1 and 2 (London, 1968 and 1969 respectively). Also, L. J. MacFarlane, *The British Communist Party* (London 1966), chs. 4–7; Martin, op. cit., chs. 3–4. M. Johnstone, "The Communist Party in the 1920s", *New Left Review* 41.
64. MacFarlane, op. cit., chs. 8–11
65. For review of debate, see B. W. E. Alford, *Depression and Recovery? British Economic Growth, 1918–1939* (London, 1972), ch. 2.
66. H. Pelling, *A History of British Trade Unionism* (London, 1963), pp. 262–3.
67. This table is based on D. H. Aldcroft, *The Inter-War Economy: Britain 1919–39* (London, 1970), p. 121. But also see J. A. Dowie, "Growth in the Inter-war Period: Some More Arithmetic" in *The Economic History Review*, 2nd series, Vol. XXI, No. 1, 1968, pp. 108–11.
68. *Industrial Review*, May 1929, p. 14.
69. For example, N. Branson and M. Heinemann, *Britain in the Nineteen Thirties* (London, 1971), chs. 3–5.
70. Gramsci, op. cit., pp. 279–318.
71. B. R. Mitchell and P. Deane, *Abstract of British Historical Statistics* (Cambridge, 1962), pp. 332, 345.

CHRONOLOGY

EVENTS OF 1925–7 AND DIARY OF THE GENERAL STRIKE

1925

April — Churchill's budget speech (20 April) announces return to the gold standard. (J. M. Keynes comments, in *Economic Consequences of Mr Churchill*, that this must produce an atmosphere favourable to reductions in wages.)

June — The coalowners give notice (30 June) to terminate the National Agreement with the miners in force since 1924, and of reductions in wages and the end of the guaranteed minimum wage. The MFGB Executive at once recommends rejection of the owners' proposals—which is endorsed in early July by National Conference.

July — The miners put their case to the TUC General Council on the 10th. The General Council pledges that the miners "will not be left to fight alone". The transport unions undertake to impose an embargo on all movement of coal in case of a lockout. On the 29th Baldwin states that the government "will not grant any subsidy" to maintain the level of wages in the mining industry.

30th. Baldwin tells the miners that "all workers of this country have got to take reductions in wages to help put industry on its feet". A TUC Special Conference replies by empowering the General Council to issue strike notices.

31st ("Red Friday"). The government climbs down and offers a 9-month subsidy to the coal industry, in return for which the coalowners will withdraw notices of wage reductions. It is announced that a full inquiry into the coal industry will be made by a Royal Commission.

Aug. — A National Conference is convened by the Minority Movement, on the 29th–30th.

Sept. — 5th. The Royal Warrant is issued for the Commission on the Coal Industry under the chairmanship of Sir Herbert Samuel.

7th–12th. At the Scarborough TUC a militant atmosphere prevails and a resolution empowering the TUC to call a general strike is remitted to the General Council.

25th. The formation of the Organisation for Maintenance of Supplies is announced. Meantime the government is starting preparations to defeat a general strike, for which purpose England and Wales will be divided (as earlier secretly planned) into ten "Divisions" each under a Civil Commissioner and with a network of local committees.

29th. The Labour Party Annual Conference at Liverpool resolves to expel communists from the Labour Party.

Oct. Police raid CPGB headquarters at King Street, Covent Garden, followed by the arrest of twelve communist leaders who are subsequently put on trial and sentenced to from 6 to 12 months' imprisonment.

Nov. 167 anthracite miners are put on trial at Carmarthen, on charges arising from a local strike in July–August: fifty are sentenced to from 14 days' to 12 months' imprisonment.

20th. The government sends a circular to Local Authorities on organisation for the coming emergency.

Dec. Continuing the preparations to defeat a General Strike, the government organises special local conferences on transport and police. A comprehensive Plan of Action is laid down.

1926

March The Samuel Commission on the Coal Industry reports, recommending reorganisation of the industry but rejection of nationalisation, no continuation of the subsidy and reductions in wages. The coalowners further demand longer hours and reversion from a National Agreement to District Agreements.

The Minority Movement convenes a Conference of Action.

April There are fruitless conferences between the government, coalowners and miners and the TUC Industrial Committee. The coalowners post lockout notices to expire on 30 April, when the subsidy ends.

May *1st.* A Special Conference of Trade Union Executives, meeting at Memorial Hall, Farringdon Road, approves the General

Council"s proposals for a General Strike in defence of the miners' wages and hours to begin at midnight on Monday, 3 May—instructions to call out sections of workers to be issued by their respective unions. The General Council directs that if any "trade union agreements are placed in jeopardy . . . it be definitely agreed that there will be no general resumption of work until those agreements are fully recognised".

The government proclaims a State of Emergency. Baldwin broadcasts a message to the nation, "Keep steady". Unions begin to issue strike orders.

At 9 p.m. the TUC and Baldwin resume negotiations.

2nd. The TUC and Premier are in negotiation, adjourning during the day for separate meetings of the TUC General Council and of the cabinet. At 11.45 p.m. members of the Miners' Executive join discussion with the TUC.

3rd. At 1.5 a.m. it is announced from Downing Street that negotiations have finally broken down. Overnight the *Daily Mail* printers had refused to print a leading article denouncing the General Strike. The government considers this a challenge to constitutional rights and demands "immediate and unconditional withdrawal of the instruction for the General Strike". During the afternoon, the government refuses appeals in the House of Commons for a resumption of negotiations.

The General Strike begins as day shifts end and night shifts fail to turn up for work.

4th. First day of the stoppage. The response from those sections called out exceeds expectations. Many non-unionists join the strike. There are no passenger trains, hardly any buses or trams, and docks are at a standstill. No national newspapers appear. The BBC issues news bulletins at three-hourly intervals. Various strike sheets are got out by local Trades Councils, etc.

5th. The government appeals for "volunteers" to act as blacklegs and as special constables, and issues the *British Gazette* from the *Morning Post* premises under the editorship of Winston Churchill. The TUC begins printing the *British Worker* at the *Daily Herald* premises—but a police raid holds it up for 5 hours. Local strike organisations (Councils of

Action, Joint Strike Committees, etc.) go into action. London taxi-drivers, who have not been called out, insist on joining the strike.

6th. The government assures blacklegs that measures will be taken to prevent their victimisation by trade unions and that they will lose no trade union benefits. Sir John Simon declares in the House of Commons that the General Strike is illegal.

7th. The Archbishop of Canterbury, on behalf of Christian Churches, puts forward proposals for a settlement: these are printed in the *British Worker* but suppressed by the *British Gazette* and BBC.

Sir Herbert Samuel, chairman of the Royal Commission on the Coal Industry, makes approaches to the TUC General Council with offers of mediation. The TUC Negotiating Committee meets him—but conceals this fact from the miners.

8th. Food supplies are convoyed to Hyde Park, as distributing camp, under the protection of armoured cars. The government decides to recruit a Civil Reserve Constabulary, equipped with steel helmets, truncheons and armlets, and notifies the Armed Forces that any action they may find necessary to take "in an honest endeavour to aid the Civil Power" will receive "the full support of H.M. Government".

9th. Sunday. Gigantic local meetings of strikers and their supporters take place in many areas.

At High Mass, Cardinal Bourne declares that the General Strike is a sin against God. A military cordon is drawn round the London docks.

The TUC leaders, having met Samuel without informing the miners, place the draft of the Samuel recommendations, which include reductions in miners' wages, before the miners' leaders. These recommendations have no authority from the government. At a joint meeting of the General Council and the full MFGB Executive the miners insist that no settlement is possible which includes wage cuts.

10th. Sir Herbert Samuel meets the TUC Negotiating Committee, together with the miners' representatives. The miners make clear that they cannot accept wage cuts.

The BBC announces many arrests. The TUC General

Council issues a call to strikers: "Stand firm. Be loyal to instructions and trust your leaders."

11th. All the engineering and shipbuilding workers not yet called out are instructed to down tools at midnight. Bevin and Gosling, on behalf of the T&GWU, publish a message: "Hold fast. We must see the miners through".

Justice Astbury lays it down that the General Strike is illegal and that trade union funds may not legally be used for strike pay to strikers obeying illegal orders.

The TUC Negotiating Committee puts the final draft of the Samuel Memorandum before the General Council, which accepts it. The MFGB Executive rejects it, however, because it involves wage cuts.

12th. The TUC General Council visits Downing Street at noon and informs Baldwin that the General Strike is to be unconditionally called off. The news is broadcast at 1 p.m. and the King issues a message urging co-operation and amity.

13th. It becomes known that the settlement does not include withdrawal of miners' lockout notices and that the MFGB has refused to agree to it. Employers in various industries demand unacceptable conditions of reinstatement. Workers resume the strike, and there are more on strike than on any previous day.

14th. Baldwin sends proposals to the miners and coalowners even less favourable to the miners than those of the Samuel Memorandum.

The Railway unions accept terms proposed by the Railway Companies and "admit that in calling a strike they comitted a wrongful act".

15th–18th. Various agreements made for resumption of work by dockers, printworkers, and others. There is widespread victimisation, particularly on the railways.

20th. The miners' Delegate Conference rejects Baldwin's proposals of the 14th.

21st. The coalowners also reject Baldwin's proposals.

25th. The government is reported to be arranging for import of foreign coal.

June 8th. A Conference between the miners and coalowners ends in deadlock. On the 21st, a Bill to suspend the miners' Seven Hours Act for five years and to permit return to an 8-hour day for miners is introduced into the House of Commons with the support of the coalowners. On the 23rd, the TUC General Council and the MFGB agree to postponement of a conference of trade union executives which was called for 24 June.

29th. The National Society for the Prevention of Cruelty to Children denies that miners' families are in need of assistance.

July On the 5th, the coalowners post notices of new terms of employment, based on an 8-hour day. On the 15th, the MFGB requests the TUC General Council to impose an embargo on movements of coal: the General Council refuses, but undertakes to urge financial support for the locked-out miners. On the 15th–19th, Church leaders make conciliation proposals to end the miners' lockout: the MFGB Executive is prepared to accept, but the proposals are rejected by Baldwin.

Aug. 7th. Baldwin informs Americans who are considering aid for British miners that the miners are in fact suffering no hardship or destitution.

On the 17th, a MFGB Delegate Conference empowers the Executive to re-open negotiations with the coalowners and government without prior conditions. A meeting of miners and coalowners on the 19th ends in deadlock, since the owners make clear that they will accept nothing short of total surrender. On the 26th the miners interview Churchill and other representatives of the government, and are informed that there will be no further subsidy for the coal industry. No steps are taken towards a settlement.

Sept. On the 13th the coalowners reject a government request to enter into national negotiations with the miners on wages and conditions, and state that they will agree only to enter into district negotiations. On the 17th Baldwin urges that district agreements on miners' wages and hours be negotiated.

Oct. It is reported to a miners' Delegate Conference on the 7th that all MFGB Districts, except Leicester, have rejected Baldwin's proposal for district negotiations. Voting was 737,000 against, 42,000 for.

On the 9th the Leicestershire Miners' Council instructs workers in the Leicester coalfield to return to work.

On the 18th the Nottingham miners vote against a return to work under a district settlement. A section of the Notts. Miners' Council which wants a district settlement is subsequently suspended.

A drift back to work by miners becomes noticeable, particularly in the Notts. and Derby coalfields.

Nov. Suspended members of the Notts. Miners' Council, led by G. A. Spencer, decide on 1 November to meet the coalowners to negotiate a district settlement.

On the 3rd, a Conference of Trade Union Executives calls for a penny-a-day levy of trade union members to aid the miners.

13th–19th. The miners' Delegate Conference decides to refer the government's proposals for district agreements to a ballot. When the ballot is held, a majority of 147,000 rejects the proposals. The Delegate Conference nevertheless recommends all Districts to open district negotiations with the coalowners.

23rd. A breakaway miners' union is set up in Notts., headed by G. A. Spencer.

26th. The miners' Delegate Conference instructs Districts to make their own district agreements with the coalowners on their own responsibility.

27th–30th. Miners report back for work in the various coalfields. Many are victimised and left unemployed or on short-time.

1927

Jan. On the 20th–21st a Conference of Trade Union Executives is convened to review the experience and lessons of the General Strike. The TUC General Council's report blames the miners for not accepting the Samuel Memorandum. A resolution approving the General Council's report is adopted by 2,840,000 votes for, 1,095,000 against.

April The government introduces the Trades Disputes and Trade Unions Bill in the House of Commons. Fairly rapidly passed into law as the Trades Disputes and Trades Union Act, this makes all sympathetic strikes illegal, illegalises mass picketing and "intimidation" by pickets, forbids the "political levy" in trade unions (which must become voluntary "contracting in"), forbids Civil Service unions to affiliate to the TUC, and prohibits Local Authority workers on pain of imprisonment to break their contracts of employment.

May 12th. The government organises the Arcos Raid on the Soviet Trade Delegation in London. On the 24th the government breaks off trade relations with the Soviet Union.

Sept. The Edinburgh TUC endorses the General Council's refusal to recognise trades councils affiliated to the Minority Movement, and terminates the Anglo-Russian Trade Union Committee.

Nov. A march of 250 unemployed miners sets off on the 8th from Rhondda to London.

On the 23rd a group of industrialists, headed by Sir Alfred Mond, writes to the TUC proposing joint discussions on ways and means "to restore industrial prosperity and the corresponding improvement in the standard of living of the population".

Dec. The TUC General Council, on 20 December, accepts the Mond proposals for discussions.

After this, the first Joint Conference between the TUC General Council and the group of industrialists headed by Sir Alfred Mond met at Burlington House on 12 January 1928. Mond and Ben Turner for the TUC occupied the chair at alternate sessions. Mond proposed that the discussions should include the rationalisation of industry, methods for avoiding trade disputes, and the creation of a permanent committee of consultation.

The first Joint Report from the discussions was issued on 4 July 1928. It welcomed measures for rationalisation of industry, and proposed the setting up of a National Industrial Council of the TUC and FBI, with compulsory arbitration through a Joint Standing Committee.

1926 Disturbances & Agitations.

SUBJECT

Miners Fedn & General Council – Recommendations – Memorand
"Lansbury's Weekly" Cuttings
Altrincham Express Strike Sheet Nos 3 & 4. Copies
Birmingham T.U. " Bulletin : for Order E.R. 33 (2a).
Communist " " "
" Party meetings Reports
" " for Order to prohibit
"Sheffield Forward" Copy
Situation in Birmingham Report
Brit. Gas Light Co. Sculcoates Copy lr from Ld. Mayor.
Severn Tunnel Protection arrangements
Outbreaks of Hooliganism Reports
Cleveland Miners Assoc Applicn for dole. Recommends dole be granted.
~~Broadcast~~ message from Holland on behalf of strikers ~~Refer~~ Reports
" "
Emergency Regulations 1926. Ask whether they still in force.
Railways. Guarding against sabotage. Reports.
Sheffield. Special Strike Bulletins. Report of raid on house of Simon Abraham
Emergency Overseas telegrams. Report of telegrams.
Visit of Mr A.A. Purcell M.P. to Paris. Ido reports
W. Fearnhead JP. Suggests removal from Commission
Ipswich Rose Bowl 10.5.26. Reports
" " " "
E.R. 22 meeting & procession (Streatham) 13/5/26.
" 22 (1) " (Battersea) "
" 22 (1) " " (Greenwich) "
J.H. Infield JP: Proprietor "Sussex Daily News" Reports
Holding of Strike meeting "
Glamorganshire Progress of enrolment
"British Worker" at J.J. Collins Shop. ~~Question~~ Reports
"Derby Worker" 6th May 1926: Copy posted outside "Unity Hall" "
E.R. 22 (1) : Woolwich Labour Party : meetings for authority to prohibit
" : Leyton " : Procession "
Bolton Jr: Chairman of Blaydon U.D.C. Wm Lawther. (member of Durham Co. C. Report